VANISHING PRIMITIVE MAN

THE HORIZON BOOK OF

VANISHING PRIMITIVE MAN

by
TIMOTHY SEVERIN

Foreword by Colin M. Turnbull

EDITOR
Alvin M. Josephy, Jr.

PICTURE EDITOR
Douglas Tunstell

Published by
AMERICAN HERITAGE PUBLISHING CO., INC., NEW YORK
Book Trade Distribution by
McGRAW-HILL BOOK COMPANY

Staff for this Book

EDITOR
Alvın M. Josephy, Jr.

PICTURE EDITOR
Douglas Tunstell

ART DIRECTOR
Mervyn Edward Clay

ASSISTANT EDITOR
Mary Elizabeth Wise

COPY EDITOR
Helen C. Dunn

RESEARCHERS
Alfred Baman
Diane Kaiser-Cooper
Laura Lane Masters
Sarah Waters

EUROPEAN BUREAU
Gertrudis Feliu, *Chief*
Christine Sutherland

CONSULTANT
Colin M. Turnbull

AMERICAN HERITAGE
PUBLISHING CO., INC.

PRESIDENT AND PUBLISHER
Paul Gottlieb

EDITOR-IN-CHIEF
Joseph J. Thorndike

SENIOR EDITOR, BOOK DIVISION
Alvin M. Josephy, Jr.

EDITORIAL ART DIRECTOR
Murray Belsky

GENERAL MANAGER, BOOK DIVISION
Kenneth W. Leish

Library of Congress Cataloging in Publication Data
Severin, Timothy.
  The Horizon book of vanishing primitive man.

  1. Society, Primitive. 2. Civilization—History.
I. Horizon (New York, 1958–   ). II. Title.
GN400.S48 1973 301.2 73–7781
ISBN 0-07-056348-9
ISBN 0-07-056349-7 (de luxe)

Material in Chapter 10 based on AKWE-
SHAVANTE SOCIETY by David Maybury-
Lewis, © 1967 by Oxford University Press. Used
by permission of the publisher.

Photographs by Laurence K. Marshall on pages
155, 164, 177, 178–79, 181, 249 © 1973 by
Laurence K. Marshall.

Hawaiian dancer, by an artist with Captain Cook, 1778
LIBRARY OF CONGRESS

HALF-TITLE PAGE: *Tukuna Indian charm necklace, Brazil*
BROOKLYN MUSEUM

TITLE PAGE: *a Txikão Indian of the Mato Grosso is a
member of one of Brazil's fast-vanishing tribes. Contacted
for the first time by whites only a few years ago, his people
now number approximately only fifty.*
ROYAL SOCIETY/ROYAL GEOGRAPHICAL SOCIETY, 1971

Contents

Foreword

by Colin M. Turnbull

One of the greatest sources of mankind's success in the game of survival has been our ability, and willingness, to ask questions. For us, as opposed to felines, it would be the lack of curiosity that would prove lethal. But it is equally true that curiosity, if too limited or selective, or if inadequately fulfilled, can lead to an even greater and more dangerous ignorance in which we mistake a superficial acquaintance with limited facts for knowledge, equating mere observation with wisdom. It is eminently right that man should be curious, and be especially curious about man, but it is essential that this vital curiosity should be satisfied not only with facts, but with understanding; and that, I believe, is what anthropology tries to do.

With the world opening up around us it is important that all of us, not just a few, should have the ability to look at other peoples, other ways of life and thought, with such understanding. Newspaper reports and even television documentaries are all too fleeting. Although they illuminate new horizons, they are most often compiled by people who may be on the spot but who are unable to spend the time necessary for a profound study. That, after all, is not their job. The result is that the reports and documentaries and our own consequent opinions are framed in terms of our own experience, our own values. True understanding then becomes impossible, and the door is opened to that comfortable sense of superiority that can lead, all too subtly, to bigotry.

Anthropology, by its very nature, makes no initial judgments. It observes what people do but also asks itself *why* they do it. Frequently, in this way, we come to realize that however odd something that other people do may seem to be, in effect it may be directed toward a goal that is not odd at all. It is, surprisingly, often embarrassing to find that despite the apparent oddity of his customs, "primitive" man may not only share many goals with "civilized" man, but seems able to achieve them more readily and surely. We begin to question just what we mean by such terms as "primitive" and "civilized." Above all, anthropology and the anthropological approach tell us to look below and beyond the superficial exotica, the mere descriptive facts, and learn something about the process, about what is really going on, avoiding the pitfalls of those initial, hasty judgments. That strange and often disturbing world beyond our own familiar realm of experience then becomes far less strange and disturbing. To read about another people becomes one of the most exciting intellectual adventures, carrying us far beyond the empty half-truths of glossy photograph magazines. And the most exciting thing of all is when, instead of seeing some exotic native resplendent in robes of feathers and cowrie shells, or stark staring naked, we begin to recognize a dim reflection of ourselves.

This I believe to be the true significance of anthropology, that it informs us about ourselves more than about others. It does this in terms of our biology, our history and evolution, our social and cultural forms. Social anthropology in particular, dealing with the many ways in which men band together in societies, voluntarily cooperating in the joint effort toward survival, has its origins firmly rooted in those moral philosophers who, like Montesquieu in France and Hume in Scotland, were primarily concerned with their *own* societies and with the dangers so evidently facing them. It was in the effort to establish a technique for better understanding one's own society that social anthropology had its first beginnings, yet we have grown sadly away from that very legitimate goal and have become more engrossed with the technique itself. Indeed the technique and the body of theory have become goals in themselves, and the people we live among while conducting our field research are sometimes treated as though they were mere experimental guinea pigs.

This is not to say that there is not still plenty of room for more morally oriented field research, and for the further sharpening of our tools and elaboration of our body of theory, but there is both room and need for anthropology also to return to a consideration of our own society. We do not have all the answers, by any means, nor are we yet in a position to manipulate our social structure to achieve any desired goal. But we *have* arrived at a general understanding of the social process in small-scale societies (a better term than "primitive"), and this is of profound significance for our understanding of our own society. Just as we learn not to be dismayed or elated by what we see on the surface in exotic society, so should we not be too readily delighted or disgusted by what we see in our own. In the field situation we ask ourselves what is being achieved by a given custom for society as a whole; and by the application of the same technique to our own society and its frequently bizarre customs we should be less ready to rush into judgments that really are founded only on the superficial appearance of what things seem to be.

There is no doubt that the vast majority of anthropologists, whatever branch of the discipline they pursue, would agree that despite man's immense and glorious superficial diversity, the basic unity of man is even more striking. Anthropological findings have been and probably will be used, for some time to come, by a few to support self-centered theories of racial, social, or intellectual supremacy, just as earlier findings were used to support and justify colonial rule, even to show colonial powers how to rule more "effectively." But this is plainly the fault of current philosophical attitudes, not of anthropology itself. The main controversy today is perhaps whether or not anthropology should concern itself with contemporary Western society, or whether it should retreat still further into its intellectual ivory tower, abnegating all social responsibility in the name of "pure science."

Be that as it may, this book, perhaps just because it is *not* written by an anthropologist, makes free use of the findings of anthropologists for the very real benefit of the public, and of society at large. The cold scientific facts are presented by the author, tempered and brought to life by his personal reflections, in an attempt to stimulate the reader to interpret the facts for himself, in terms of his own experience.

Reading some of the accounts, even the one drawn from my own field work, I found myself led forward not as an anthropologist but as a person whose experience of the world, however wide, was still infinitesimal. In reading about my own material, for instance, I saw things I had not seen before because the author uses the facts differently and asks different questions. Even more, when reading about areas I have never visited, I experienced that old excitement that still makes me feel slightly sick and weak at the knees every time I go into the field. I wonder how on earth I will make the first contact; what the language will be like; whether we will have *any* language in common or whether I will have to be treated like a baby all over again — taught to talk, what and how to eat, where to go, and what to do and not do. The exotic context still appeals to me as much as ever, but not just for itself, not by any means. It appeals to me because by now I know, beyond any doubt, that however strange a people may seem, however much I may even detest what they do, I will find, in them, a new part of myself that I have never known before. Any reader who reads with his eyes open, asking himself *why* people do this or that, trying to see what it is they are achieving for their society as a whole, can share this sensation of self-discovery.

But apart from learning about ourselves as individuals, we should also learn a great deal about our own society, its goals and its values, and the direction in which it is going. The parallels are by no means exact, and even the comparisons are not simple to make, and the result is sometimes discouraging because we seem to have advanced so little, except in terms of technology. Some of the accounts given in this book illustrate the damage that can be done to humanity from the unthinking application of other standards and values, presumed to be superior simply because they are our own. Even in our own society the gap between the preaching and the practice seems to be almost irreconcilable. That, however, far from discouraging us, should move us to ask pertinent questions about our chosen life style and the direction in which it is leading us. Here, perhaps more than anywhere, each reader will have to make up his own mind for himself.

Even scientists get their facts wrong sometimes, and scientists are notable for their interminable controversies over interpretation of data. One of their perpetual problems, of course, is that one can never be quite sure what is going to be discovered tomorrow that might upset all the interpretations of today. In some areas the danger is greater than in others. In anthropology, for instance, a single new skeletal find could easily upset all the current beliefs about man's origins, though the likelihood grows less and less. Historical and social data are less ambiguous, though different scholars working in exactly the same field at exactly the same time will almost certainly see different things. This I know from personal experience. It does not mean that one is right and the other is wrong; it means that any single observer, necessarily, is partial, and selective. Such a caution would be as true of any scientific monograph as it would be of this book, and this book has the advantage, for the general public, of being infinitely more readable than most monographs.

Read with this awareness, in recognition of the fact that the word "primitive" (which some would prefer to avoid) is not used in any derogatory way, the accounts given here should lead any reader well down that life-giving path of self-discovery where he will find that "primitive man" is not so unlike ourselves at all, and has as much to teach us about our own present and future as about the past.

Genesis:
An Introduction

It was a butterfly hunter who discovered Olduvai Gorge. In 1911 a German entomologist with the resounding name of Professor Kattwinkel was hot in pursuit of a butterfly in the scrub-covered countryside of what is now Tanzania in East Africa, when he was led to the lip of an uncharted chasm. Before him opened a sharp gash in the earth's surface, an ancient river canyon some three hundred feet deep and about twenty-five miles long, whose eroded walls exposed layer upon layer of the rock strata. Even to the untutored eye of the butterfly hunter it was obvious that the site was immensely rich in fossils. Climbing down into the gorge, Kattwinkel picked up some of the bones and took them back to Germany, where they caused a sensation when they were found to be the relics of several long-extinct animals. A German expedition promptly set out to explore the new discovery, but its work was cut short by the outbreak of World War I. Not until 1931 did the first major expedition of trained archeologists finally examine Olduvai in detail. Its members realized at once that they stood in possibly the world's richest known fossil site — the ancient stamping ground, for generation upon generation, of an extraordinary menagerie of prehistoric fauna, and as it turned out, one of the homes of an apelike creature who could have been ancestral to man.

In some respects Olduvai is an archeologist's dream site. The rock strata so conveniently exposed along the sides of the canyon offer a steady and remarkably comprehensive progression of local geological history. Handily too, the time span of this geology begins almost exactly with the early Pleistocene epoch, about 1.9 million years ago, and continues right through the crucial periods of the Ice Age, when so many vital changes took place in the animal life of the world. Olduvai is also something of a geological freak. Sandwiched between the layers of sedimentary rocks, mostly laid down by an ancient lake, are layers of lava flows. These lava bands can be dated with some accuracy by a potassium-argon technique; and so Olduvai has become one of the best dated archeological sites in existence, and most of its fossil bones can be placed very precisely in their correct time zones. It is as though Nature — having first marked her lines of dates by the rocks — then considerately left behind the fossil bones to show exactly what

A stone tool used by Java man, a Far Eastern type of Homo erectus

Olduvai Gorge and Dr. Louis Leakey, who began work there in 1931

animals existed in the region during each period. Most important of all, however, is Olduvai's brief glimpse into man's early history. Scattered among the bones of more than 150 different species of animals are a few—pitifully few—human and near-human fragments, the remains of apelike or manlike creatures that once inhabited this region of East Africa, and that in the opinion of some experts evolved into modern man.

The oldest ape-man fossils found at Olduvai belong to a group usually known as the australopithecines. Strong contenders for the title of "the earliest men," they make up a loose grouping of hominid (manlike) creatures whose remains have been found in South Africa as well as East Africa and also in Asia. Characterized by their upright posture, near-human teeth structure, and a brain size equal to or greater than that of the gorilla, the australopithecines hover somewhere on the borderline between apes and men as far as the anatomists are concerned. The picture is complicated by the fact that at least two types of australopithecines existed, and both types are represented at Olduvai. One was a well-built animal weighing some 140 pounds and standing about 5 feet tall. Because his teeth were fairly massive and well adapted for chewing, it appears that he was probably a vegetarian. The other form of australopithecine was smaller and more delicate, perhaps 12 inches shorter and about 80 pounds lighter. But his appearance was deceptive, for this smaller version was the more deadly. The broken scraps of small and weak animals near his occupation sites indicate that the smaller australopithecine was carnivorous, and it has been suggested by some authorities that he might even have caught and killed the babies and infirm dotards among his more robust cousins if he could get his hands on them.

The differences between the large and small australopithecines illustrate very well the sort of dilemmas that plague the paleoanthropologists as they try to establish just where and how mankind arose. When all is said and done, the fossil evidence of man's ancestry is still embarrassingly scanty. It is often the result of chance discoveries like Kattwinkel's, followed by painstaking years of toil on hands and knees with dental picks and camel's-hair brushes to clear away the rubble and produce half a drawerful of bone fragments. In Olduvai, for example, nearly twenty-eight years of labor were required before the first human skull was found, and the wealthy sponsors who then arrived got seven thousand tons of rubble among the rewards for their first year's cash grants. It is not surprising that challenged by this paucity of evidence and the enormous implications of any new discovery, few archeologists can agree on a precise scenario for the rise of man from ape to *sapiens*. For instance, with the two types of australopithecines, there is still no consensus of opinion on whether they were members of the same species or whether either type is a direct ancestor to man. All that can be said is that the lighter, smaller, and carnivorous australopithecine could have evolved into an intermediate form of the genus *Homo,* while the burly vegetarian strain apparently became extinct.

The truth of the matter—and its fascination—is that Charles Darwin in the mid-nineteenth century only set in motion the theory of human evolution. Since then its precise course has been remarkably erratic. In the days before Darwin there was a clear-cut and comforting simplicity to the notion that man had appeared full-fledged at a biblical Creation—on the morning

In his On the Origin of Species *in 1859, Charles Darwin proposed the then-shocking idea that man and apes evolved from a common ancestor.*

This hypothetical drawing depicts australopithecines, early ape-men who lived at least two million years ago, carried themselves erect, and had legs nearly as well adapted for walking as those of modern man.

of the 23rd of October, 4004 B.C., according to a tidy-minded church mathematician. But after Darwin it has become increasingly apparent that human evolution was considerably more complex and widespread than even the great evolutionist had supposed. Indeed, if Darwin shook the comfortable notions of the creationists, much the same sort of shock was registered in 1924 at a lower notch on the academic Richter scale when the first australopithecine was found by Raymond Dart, a young professor of anatomy in South Africa. Dart boldly announced that he had identified a member of "an extinct race of apes intermediate between living anthropoids and man." His claim for what was in some respects a missing link was based on his examination of the fossilized skull of a juvenile apelike creature found in a South African limestone quarry at Taung. That skull and more recent discoveries at half a dozen other sites, particularly at Olduvai, established beyond doubt that man is far more ancient than had previously been supposed and has been on earth for more than two million years,

13

instead of the five hundred thousand years or less of earlier estimates.

When the Taung find abruptly pushed the archeologists' base line back by at least 1.5 million years, the scholarly reflex was simply to look at all the existing fossil material and reclassify it accordingly. Such famous relics as Peking man, excavated from the caves at Choukoutien in North China during the 1920's and 1930's, or the bones of Java man found at the end of the nineteenth century were reallocated to a new intermediate group collectively labeled *Homo erectus*. It seemed a reasonable hypothesis that these creatures of the *Homo erectus* type must have evolved out of the australopithecines during the 1.5-million-year gap between them. Unfortunately the last thirty years have seen even this neat theory fall into disrepute. Fresh discoveries of fossil ape-men have cast doubt on the idea of direct ancestral links between australopithecine and *erectus*, since several of the earliest *erectus* fossils are actually older than the later australopithecines, overlapping them somewhere about a million years ago.

Even more disconcerting is the discovery that the later australopithecine skeletons, instead of being more physically evolved, are actually more primitive and regressive than their ancestors. This has led to some speculation that the australopithecines died out entirely as an independent line,

Archeologists excavate at the site in Choukoutien, China, where the fossilized remains of the so-called Peking man, a localized type of Homo erectus *that lived approximately 400,000 years ago, were discovered.*

and that man's earliest known ancestors should now be sought among a puzzling series of hominid fossils recently retrieved from Olduvai Gorge and the shores of Lake Rudolf, some five hundred miles to the north. These fossils, in one case apparently coexistent with the earliest australopithecines, belonged to upright, manlike creatures with a brain almost twice the size of the average australopithecine's. Much work still has to be done on these maverick and in many ways precocious East African fossils, including a close study to see if the Olduvai and Lake Rudolf specimens are in fact related. But their enthusiasts would claim that it was these creatures, alternatively named *Homo habilis* (handy man) from Olduvai and "1470 man" (after the catalogue number) from Lake Rudolf, who stood closest to that essential fork in the evolutionary tree when man branched off from a common ancestor with the apes.

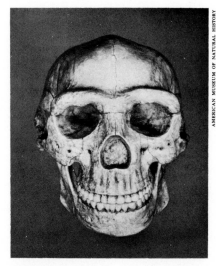

The skull of Peking man reveals a small forehead, protruding brow ridges, and a broad, low-bridged nose.

A good part of the confusion has undoubtedly been contributed by the paleoanthropologists themselves. As each fresh archeological site reveals a new treasure, the happy discoverer is tempted to claim a unique characteristic for his find, christen it with a grandiose Latin name, and then defend the importance of his trophy against all comers. The kind of uproar that greeted Raymond Dart still reverberates on other battlefields. One school of South African fossil hunters, faced with exceptionally tough rock strata, resorted to breaking them up with dynamite and rock drills, a blockbuster technique that appalled the brush-and-trowel men. The unfortunate pioneer archeologist Eugène Dubois, who first discovered Java man, felt so persecuted by his critics that he locked up his priceless specimens in strongboxes, deposited them with his local museum at Haarlem, the Netherlands, and for thirty years refused to let anyone examine his evidence. Other human fossils fared even worse. Overeager researchers in Southeast Asia rashly promised a small reward to any native who brought in a piece of fossil, only to learn that the more wily natives were using hammers on perfectly good skulls and smashing them up to improve their market value, fragment by fragment. The evidence for Peking man—sixteen skulls, assorted jaws, teeth, and all—was lost to posterity soon after Pearl Harbor when the high-security train carrying the fossils and other priority material out of China was captured by Japanese troops. The relics were never seen again (though plaster casts luckily survived).

The anthropologists, at least, generally agree on what they are looking for in an evolving man: a creature who walks upright; has human physical characteristics, such as a large brain, a human teeth pattern, or an evolved skull shape; and who shows some evidence of learned behavior. Clearly several of the criteria are affected by the type of fossils available. Teeth, for example, are a particularly common fossil because they are preserved by their hard coat of enamel, and so a whole school of archeological dentistry has developed, able to glean as much information as possible from a single molar. Such detective work can be quite spectacular. In one Olduvai example it has been possible to interpolate considerable information about an australopithecine specimen from the only piece of evidence available—the last bone in the big toe.

Certainly by anatomical standards *Homo erectus*, who lived between one million and four hundred thousand years ago, was considerably closer to modern man than the australopithecines. As far as his physique was

Neanderthal man, a form of Homo sapiens *that developed about 110,000 years ago, is reconstructed here as a robust, muscular being who hunted animals for sustenance and clothing.*

concerned, *Homo erectus*'s most spectacular advance was the dramatic increase in his brain size. It expanded to an average of 974 cubic centimeters from the australopithecine norm of 508 cubic centimeters. This compares with 498 cubic centimeters for the gorilla and 1,300 cubic centimeters for modern *Homo sapiens*. Also, as *erectus*'s name implies, he was much more accustomed to walking upright and was more nimble on his feet. In fact, his body and limbs were very similar in structure to modern man's, though *erectus*'s less developed brain centers did not allow him the same degree of manual dexterity. Despite this disadvantage, however, *erectus* achieved a notable cultural innovation: he made regular use of fire. The squads of Chinese workers who cleaned out the Choukoutien caves under the careful eyes of the archeologists came across layers of ash, charred animal bones, and telltale pockmarks of ancient hearths, evidence that Peking man not only warmed himself by fire but probably cooked with it as well. If, as Darwin proposed, early man first evolved within the tropics, then it is striking that he should have been able to move to the cold regions, and because of fire and perhaps because of clothing, been able to survive there. It was this ability to exist in difficult environments and adapt to them successfully that marked man as an evolutionary winner, rather than an evolutionary loser. Indeed, by the end of the main phase of *Homo erectus,* there were *erectus* populations living in places as far apart as Hungary, Southeast Asia, China, and the whole African continent.

At this point, according to some anthropologists, the differences between the main races of the world began to emerge. Over the next 200,000 years local *Homo erectus* populations slowly evolved into early *Homo sapiens,* retaining existing local differentiations such as cranial shape, stature, skin color, and so forth, and establishing these characteristics as racial features. This view has been hotly contested by other experts, not least because the evidence from this crucial period of change is exceedingly sparse. Over a frustrating gap from 300,000 to 150,000 years ago, the fossil record offers only six or seven human specimens, some of them no more than a few scraps of bone. Like a changing landscape lit by an occasional flash of lightning, there are only random glimpses of man slowly making his way toward his modern condition. Moreover, just as happened with the replacement of the australopithecines by *Homo erectus,* there is too much overlap and too much contradiction for anyone to define precisely the boundary between the two phases. *Homo erectus* did not alter uniformly into the early versions of *Homo sapiens*. Rather, certain pockets seem to have regressed into more primitive forms; others, in Java for example, showed considerable precocity in displaying advanced *sapiens* features at a very early date. In the case of skeletons found in Rhodesia, it actually seems that a primitive form of man may have lingered there far longer than elsewhere, surviving in isolation when other populations had long since become fully modern.

Nevertheless, as the light fades on *Homo erectus,* leaving him an extremely widespread creature, so it dawns again about 200,000 years ago to illuminate early *Homo sapiens* scattered all over the Old World and differing markedly from one region to the next. By careful analysis of the thirty or forty major archeological sites where human skeletons of the era 200,000–35,000 years ago have been found, it is possible to identify several distinct types that gradually evolved, including the Neanderthal men—whose traces from 110,000 to 35,000 years ago have turned up in Europe, the Middle East, and North Africa—and a later group, the Cro-Magnons, who were among the direct precursors of modern man (or *Homo sapiens sapiens,* as the anthropologists rather boastfully dub us).

Until quite recently Neanderthal man suffered an almost universally bad image. This was partly because the most complete Neanderthal skeleton to have been studied in detail was that of a cave man stricken with arthritis. The symptoms of his disease, instead of being recognized as such, were mistaken for typical Neanderthal characteristics, with the result that the "classic Neanderthal" was stigmatized as a low-browed, hunch-shouldered lout, awkwardly shambling about on bowed legs and, with a thick rug of body hair, resembling an ape as much as a man. More balanced judgment now shows that the typical Neanderthal man was a rather stocky, powerfully built specimen with exceptionally strong arms and legs. Certainly he could not have been as ungainly as his critics made him out to be; otherwise it is difficult to imagine how he could have hunted down the wild animals whose flesh formed a good part of his diet. Only in the shape of his head did the Neanderthal man conform to the popular image. Compared with modern man, the average Neanderthal had a retreating forehead, a heavy bar of bone running in a ridge over his eyes and presumably giving him a permanently scowling expression, a weak chin accentuated by a long upper lip, and a skull that projected noticeably toward the rear. The misconception was to presume that this long, low cranial package contained a brutish mind. In straightforward cubic capacity, Neanderthal man possessed a brain at least as large as, and sometimes larger than, the brain of *Homo sapiens sapiens.*

A second unlucky accident for Neanderthal man was that he was disastrously overshadowed by his flamboyant successors of about 40,000 to 35,000 years ago, the Cro-Magnons, who drew the eye-catching cave paintings so well known in France and Spain. The Neanderthals by contrast were self-effacing and rather shadowy creatures, whose way of life is still being reconstructed with much stolid labor among the humdrum rubbish of their middens and the buried debris in the earth floors of their rock shelters. The comparison is like trying to judge a culture from its art galleries or from its refuse. But fortunately one category of detritus, namely, the stone tools he left behind, does allow some reconstruction of the achievements of Neanderthal man. On this evidence alone, Neanderthal was by no means as oafish as he was once thought to be.

Like his teeth, man's artifacts are a durable and revealing index of his development. As his advance may be measured by the changes in his anatomy, so his evolution can be recorded in terms of the tools he learned to make and use. The beginning, of course, was when man discovered that he could fabricate his implements, rather than simply pick them up readymade. In the South African caves where the australopithecine fossils were found, there were also present large fossilized animal bones that the ape-men may have used as clubs to crack the skulls of their prey (and rivals). But it is from Olduvai Gorge, again, that one of the oldest major assemblages of deliberately manufactured stone tools has been identified and named. They are the Oldowan tool culture, and though they appear

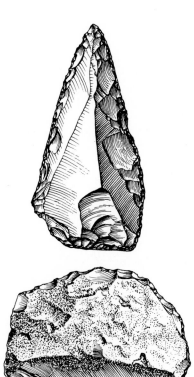

Carefully fashioned stone tools like the Mousterian point, above, and the flint knife, below, enabled Neanderthal man to master his environment.
BOTH: PIERRE LAURENT

scarcely more than large pebbles with one end knocked off, a careful inspection of the broken facets shows that the stones were deliberately shaped. They have an artificially formed striking edge, which turns each stone into a crude bludgeon fit to chop or batter, hammer or smash. From such raw beginnings began the long slow climb to the technological plateau where man had the imagination and experience to manufacture stone implements that would give him a fine edge to trim, a saw tooth to rip across a fiber, or a chisel point to gouge wood and bone. The Oldowan tool culture was to last almost 1½ million years before mankind eventually acquired the refined techniques necessary for such craftwork, learning to shape tools with a delicate touch instead of knocking them into rough-and-ready form with a few mighty blows against another chunk of rock.

Surprisingly, perhaps, even such brittle stones as flint and chert take kindly to crisp but precise handling. The archeologists now recognize as key steps in the rise of man such discoveries as the use of a soft hammer of wood or bone to shape stone implements more precisely, or the technique whereby the toolmaker works up a special cone-shaped mother stone and then rapidly punches off from it a whole series of useful fragments, like peeling leaves from an artichoke. By the time Neanderthal man appeared on the scene several such techniques were available to him, and he not only used them all but considerably improved the quality of the product. Neanderthal

This depiction of life as it may have been for Swanscombe man, a type that lived in England some 250,000 years ago and may have bridged the time gap between Homo erectus *and* Homo sapiens, *shows nimble hunters pursuing wild game with spears.*

sites are littered with hundreds and sometimes thousands of stone tools of different shapes and sizes, from Oldowan-style choppers to pointed awls to several weird-looking tools whose precise functions remain a mystery. By quantitive analysis it now seems likely that Neanderthal populations concentrated on certain occupations such as preparing skins, butchering meat, or working on wood with their stone implements. Why these specializations arose is not clear, though their development may have had something to do with climatic changes, which in Neanderthal times were great.

But Neanderthal man is important, and just as puzzling, to prehistory for another reason. With the Neanderthals appear the first consistent signs of a metaphysical awareness. Of course, such ideas may have existed earlier, but no traces survive. From the Neanderthal sites, on the other hand, there are tantalizing and not wholly understood clues to the existence of spiritual beliefs. For instance, some Neanderthals formally buried their dead. In the Crimea, Israel, and Uzbekistan in central Asia, graves that date back to Neanderthal times have been found. Some were scooped out to fit the corpse; others contain the carefully arranged bones of the dead, usually placed in a cramped fetal position with the legs doubled up against the body. At one Neanderthal burial in Iran the dead man was apparently laid to rest on a bed of wildflowers, whose fragments remained for modern analysis. Another grave, in France this time, contained a stone axe and the charred bones of wild cattle, perhaps the earliest evidence of the custom of sending a dead man to the next world with food for the journey and weapons to use when he got there. Similar speculation is even more tempting with Neanderthal sites that hint at age-old cult worship and ritual cannibalism. A cave at Monte Circeo in Italy yielded up the forty-thousand-year-old skull of a man who was bludgeoned to death with several terrific blows to the right temple. Not only had the skull been cut open, presumably to remove and eat the brain, but it was found in a specially selected spot, a shallow depression scraped in the floor of the cave at a point near the center of the rear wall. There, carefully arranged around the skull, was an oval ring of small stones, and beneath the skull someone had placed the deliberately broken foot bones of an ox and a fallow deer. To some scholars this was evidence of ancestor worship; to others the Monte Circeo skull seemed to be a relic of a cannibalistic ceremony. In either event, it is clear that the corpse of Circeo man was not simply cast away as meaningless dross.

Less macabre are signs that some Neanderthal men may also have practiced a cult having some connection with the cave bear *Ursus Spelaeus*. A ferocious-looking animal as big as the largest grizzly (though probably a harmless enough berry-eater), the cave bear seems to have been singled out as a target for deliberate attack, followed by some form of ceremony that treated the dead animal with special veneration. At Petershöhle, near Nuremberg, bear skulls were found poised in stone niches in a prehistoric cave wall like ancient hunting trophies. At Drackenloch in the Alps, fifty-four thigh bones of bears were laid out, all pointing in one direction, while most curious of all, the thigh bone of one cave bear was deliberately rammed through the skull of another, quite different bear, leaving the two bones locked together in a prehistoric puzzle.

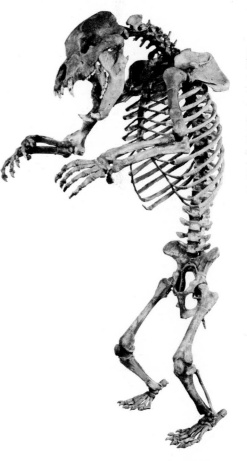

The giant cave bear, closely associated with some Neanderthal groups, served as food and as a cult object.

Barbed harpoons of reindeer antler, fashioned by Magdalenian artisans about 15,000 years ago, made effective missiles, whether attached to javelins or hurled by spear-throwers.

<small>MUSÉE DES ANTIQUITÉS NATIONALES</small>

True to form in the story of man's evolution, the Neanderthals vanish from archeological history as mysteriously and dramatically as do their more ancient predecessors. With the Neanderthals the exit is even more frustrating because it occurred so much more recently in time, namely, some 40,000 to 30,000 years ago. Nonetheless, it is difficult to see just why or how they vanished. There is the old problem that the later Neanderthal populations were not necessarily more physically evolved than their ancestors. Indeed, some of the very last Neanderthals showed strongly regressive tendencies. Then, too, it seems that the Neanderthals did not vanish all at once from their occupation sites, but sank quietly out of view, band by band, across the whole of their inhabited world, which extended from Northern Europe to Africa and across part of Asia. One somewhat romantic theory even has a few Neanderthal survivors living today as "yetis" in the remote fastnesses of the Himalayas. But whatever the fate of Neanderthal, the creature who replaced him was unmistakable: he was *Homo sapiens sapiens,* with his high vaulted skull, and his advent can be set at approximately 40,000 to 35,000 years ago.

It was once thought that *Homo sapiens sapiens* was some sort of invader, a foreign race of men who had evolved separately from the Neanderthals and simply killed or dispossessed their predecessors. A whole group of Neanderthal skeletons found in a Yugoslavian cave was put forward as evidence of one such massacre. Now, however, the Yugoslavian skeletons are explained as the remains of a Neanderthal cannibal ceremony, and the usurping race of *Homo sapiens sapiens* is considered closely related to the Neanderthals. This new theory is based very largely upon evidence dug up in the Middle East. Here, instead of the "pure" Neanderthal skeletons found in Europe, the sites have provided mixed populations that include individuals with the high cranial shape and physical characteristics of modern *Homo sapiens sapiens,* as well as more normal Neanderthal men. Quite possibly, therefore, the "moderns" were simply another offshoot from the common genetic pool of man, a people who showed themselves more suited to the environment or who were more aggressive. It has been suggested that these "moderns" evolved somewhere in the Middle East and then spread out to take over the existing or abandoned Neanderthal sites. Perhaps more important is that the appearance of the "moderns" means that the major physical evolution of mankind had come to fruition. In most features the skeleton of a *Homo sapiens sapiens* who lived thirty-five thousand years ago would be indistinguishable from that of a man alive now.

It is with something close to a sense of relief that many prehistorians turn to the Cro-Magnons (*Homo sapiens sapiens*) after the murkier byways of *Homo erectus* and the Neanderthals. Compared to his lesser-known predecessors, Cro-Magnon looms in much greater detail, and thanks to the intensity of the archeological investigations, considerably more is known about his way of life. Yet even here caution is needed, because the vast majority of research has been undertaken at European sites, giving a distinctly European bias to the subject. Furthermore, there is the irony that Cro-Magnon man has fallen foul of his own artistic flamboyance. The splendors of his cave paintings often obscure his other, equally significant achievements. The Cro-Magnons also bring a major shift of emphasis to paleoanthropology. Broadly speaking, the stabilization of the human species as a physical type some 35,000 to 40,000 years ago diverts attention from man as a physically evolving animal to man as a culturally evolving creature. The decline in new anatomical data is matched by a great surge in cultural evidence. The number, variety, and distribution of human artifacts increase, and the pace of change begins to accelerate. Steps of evolution that the anatomists measured in scores or hundreds of thousands of years are now replaced by cultural strides that take place every 10,000 years or less. The only satisfactory way to monitor this program is to identify and count off the milestones of man's cultural advance.

The grand cultural era of the Cro-Magnons was the Upper Paleolithic or late Old Stone Age. Just as each stage of man's physical development owed much to its predecessors, so the Upper Paleolithic culture enjoyed a considerable heritage from earlier cultures. The men of the late Old Stone Age used ancient Oldowan-phase tools and techniques as well as the recent scallop-edged scrapers of the Neanderthals. To this basic stock the men of the Upper Paleolithic added their own inventory of technology. In stonework the most significant advances were the perfection of a stone tool shaped very much like the blade of a penknife—and in its own way almost as effective—and the introduction of an implement known as a burin. Often no more than a spur on the corner of a hand-held pebble, occasionally a long, slender stone like a carpenter's flat pencil, the burin was similarly sharpened by removing chips from the working, or pointed, end, and it served as a combination gouge and chisel. The burin's great virtue was that it made possible the much more controlled working of wood and bone; Upper Paleolithic man could now manufacture better tools from these materials and also add artistic expression by carving and engraving the surfaces with patterns and designs that had previously been impossible.

While sharpened stone still provided the cutting edge in most Upper

This diorama, created by Frederick Blaschke, represents a painter of the Aurignacian culture in France—about 30,000 B.C.—outlining impressions of his hand on a cave wall. Such art may have been created for pleasure or for its magical associations.

Paleolithic implements, the body and design of tools usually depended on other materials. Wood was used for spear shafts, staves, and spear-throwers; bone or ivory for fishhooks, harpoon heads, awls, and needles. Stone, in modern parlance, remained the basic or heavy industry. But the secondary products from other materials produced the most dramatic differences in living conditions. Awls and needles could be used to stitch fitted clothing from animal skins, and wood and ivory fishing tridents expanded the main food-catchment area to include rivers, lakes, and the seashore. Like all men before them, the late Paleolithic peoples lived by hunting and gathering wild food. Yet their new implements undoubtedly gave them a far greater mastery of their environment than any of their predecessors had possessed. The Neanderthals had known how to mire herds of mammoths by chasing them into bogs, or how to drive wild horses and ibexes over cliffs to their death and feast on the shattered remains. But such methods were wasteful and haphazard when compared to the devices of the men who displaced them. Upper Paleolithic hunters used sharper and more deadly spears to strike their prey from ambush, dug sophisticated pitfalls for larger game, and butchered their kills much more efficiently with the stone knives. In some respects, they were the last true big-game hunters that many areas of the world would ever see. The Upper Paleolithic peoples lived—and thrived—during the fourth and last of the great Ice Ages, when, paradoxically, hunting was extraordinarily rich and rewarding. All along the fringes of the ice sheet moved immense herds of grazing animals, particularly reindeer, whose migratory habits were so fixed that it was virtually impossible either to scare them away or to overkill them with the limited weapons at hand. Out of caves, rock shelters, and open campsites of late Paleolithic hunters come the bones of thousands upon thousands of large cold-weather animals. In some French sites the bones are predominantly those of reindeer killed at about the same age in life, presumably in a great seasonal slaughter. Some Russian tribes of the Late Stone Age slew so many woolly mammoths that they were able to build their huts from the bones of the enormous beasts.

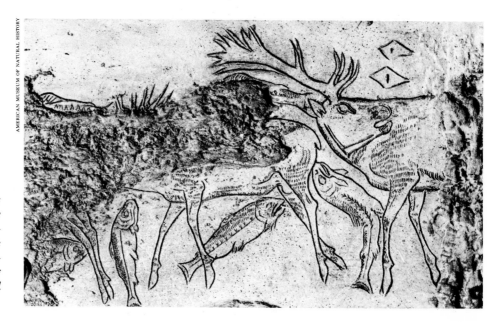

This etching of deer and salmon was made in France toward the end of the Ice Age, when the climate was warming, forests were spreading across southern Europe, and tundra-dwelling reindeer were retreating to the north, being replaced as food by fish, boar, and red deer.

A second clue to man's increased mastery of his surroundings was the time he was now able to devote to aesthetic activities. The Upper Paleolithic Age witnessed an explosion of artistic consciousness that began with the fashioning of crude little figurines of naked pear-shaped women optimistically known as Venuses, and eventually burst forth into the astonishing wall paintings of animals and mythical beasts that glow from the walls of French and Spanish caves. The men of the Magdalenian, the coldest, phase of the Upper Paleolithic did the vast majority of this work. Its significance is unfathomable, though there is no lack of theories connecting Stone Age paintings with hunting magic, cult rituals, or fertility symbols. But no one, for example, has yet been able to explain satisfactorily why some animals were painted high on cave roofs like cathedral backdrops and others were drawn in the darkest and least accessible corners, where the Stone Age artist had to work lying on his back. Color and shape were two of the great fascinations of the age. Reds, browns, and black seem to have been the most popular and easily available colors. Traces of various ochers have been found daubed on pebbles, on inexplicable bone artifacts that look like magicians' wands, and on the corpses of Upper Paleolithic men buried with honors and a full complement of weapons. Shapes and motifs mingle and vary from simple hand silhouettes outlined in black powder on cave walls like a child's school mementoes, to beautiful "leaf point" spear points made of translucent stone as delicate as any jewelry. Magdalenian man, it appears, could not resist an artistic challenge. Presented with a bone harpoon head, he crosshatched its surface in geometric designs that picked up and enhanced the natural strike line of the barbs. Faced by a rough wall of rock, he sought its natural contours and turned them to the shapes and shadows of the bison, deer, horses, and mammoths that were his favorite subjects.

Trade and travel were also hallmarks of late Paleolithic times. Outcrops of rock suitable for high-grade tools were scarce, and so fragments of the raw stone or rough-finished stone tool blanks were traded over considerable distances. Bones of sea fish dug from the floors of caves far inland indicate that coast-dwelling peoples probably traded their catch to the settlements of the interior. Nothing is known of human journeys on a local scale, for these trade articles could easily have been passed from hand to hand to reach their eventual destination. But large-scale population movements were certainly taking place. On several fronts there was a slow drift of peoples—northward to follow the retreating fringe of the ice cap and its attendant animal herds; eastward out of Asia and across the Bering land bridge into the Americas; and southeast toward Australia. This dispersal was to bequeath entirely new problems to the archeologists. The tangled routeways of the great migrations that ebbed and flowed for centuries have still not been unraveled satisfactorily, and once the diaspora was accomplished, mankind was left so widely spread that it is difficult to identify just where and when any subsequent cultural innovations took place. By comparison the final concentrated climax of the late Paleolithic Age stands foursquare and familiar, a Gothic high-water mark of Stone Age culture—vigorous, ornate, and distinctive.

In Europe the climate forced the change. Some ten to eleven thousand years ago the intensely cold conditions that had encouraged man to remain

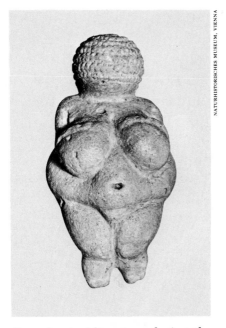

Carved out of limestone during the Aurignacian period in Austria, this four-inch-high "Venus," with its emphasized sexual characteristics, may have been a fertility symbol.

a cave dweller gave way to a much more temperate climate. Forests grew where once had been tundra, and the balance between hunting and gathering as the means of obtaining food changed in favor of the latter. In Europe, at any rate, man was encouraged to leave the shelter of his caves and move out in small groups to occupy woodland glades, riverbanks, and other open sites. There, despite its apparent lushness, the woodland was a challenging environment. Forest animals would have been more timid than the tundra dwellers, and they did not move in large herds. Hunting had to be done more cunningly—trapping such animals as rabbit or fox, or patiently stalking the woodland red deer, whose venison now replaced reindeer meat as the main source of protein. The cold-weather regime of feast or famine was eased, but it was replaced by a life pattern that made its own demands, a regular day-to-day foraging that in all likelihood was just as exacting. The artifacts of this time, the Mesolithic, or Middle Stone Age, mirror this trend toward a more local, small-scale culture. The characteristic artifact is the microlith, a tiny stone point that either served as an arrowhead or was imbedded as a stone tooth in spear shafts and harpoons. Competently made and effective, it lacks the refinement and high-quality workmanship that was so characteristic of its precursors.

Utilitarian though it was, the Mesolithic culture demonstrated a flexibility that made it astonishingly successful. While a Paleolithic way of life presumably lingered among the climatic refugees who moved north with the reindeer, the new Mesolithic culture multiplied, flourished, and spread into an assortment of habitats ranging from open savannah country to dense forest. Hunting technology was dramatically improved by the invention of the bow and arrow and by the domestication of the dog, whose ancestors were probably wolves that had come to live near campfires and beg scraps of waste food. Less impressive but equally useful was a new technique of putting a fine edge on stone tools by grinding and polishing instead of chipping them. This allowed the toolmaker greater freedom in the design of his product and at the same time made the stone tool more robust and less likely to shatter. A well-balanced blade of polished stone set in a wooden haft made an effective axe capable of clearing brushwood and cutting through branches several inches in diameter. Yet the most impressive feature of Mesolithic culture was its durability. With very little modification a Mesolithic way of life was to survive among the hunter-gatherers of the world right up to modern times—and in fact a Mesolithic culture still exists in a few isolated pockets of the world: among the Aborigines of Australia; in the deserts of South West Africa; in the forests of the Congo, Southeast Asia, and South America; and on the fringes of the polar wastelands.

Fortunately, enough is known about the original Mesolithic peoples for a useful comparison to be made with these modern-day survivors. It was typical of the early Mesolithic peoples that while they did not create the sensuous, full-color art of Magdalenian times, they left behind a more modest and in its own way much more complete pictorial record of their activities. Impressionistic and stylized, there are Mesolithic rock paintings in Sicily, North Africa, and Spain, which show the sticklike figures of men and women engaged in a whole range of activities from fishing with harpoons from canoes to chasing wild boar and aiming arrows at deer and

Dating from the Aurignacian period in France, this beautiful ivory figurine, only 1½ inches high, vividly portrays a woman of the Ice Age.
MUSÉE DES ANTIQUITÉS NATIONALES

25

A stag hunt, painted on rock in Spain at least 5,000 years ago
AMERICAN MUSEUM OF NATURAL HISTORY

The finely rippled edges of this flaked flint dagger reflect the high degree of workmanship that went into implements produced at the end of the Late Stone Age, about 4000 B.C.

COPENHAGEN NATIONAL MUSEUM

mountain goats. One figure—man or woman, it is difficult to tell—is drawn robbing honey from a wild bees' nest in a cliff; a woman is depicted collecting fruit in a pannier. There are scenes of war and battle, of animals like the hippopotamuses that once flourished in a then well-watered and greener Sahara, and—finally—there is the appearance of the first agriculturists, who are drawn with sickles in hand and with what look like wheatstalks in their hair.

Just where and when agriculture first appeared is still a moot point, but an important one, for traditionally agriculture and the domestication of animals divide the Mesolithic from the Neolithic, or New Stone Age. Once again in a strictly European context, the clues all indicate a Middle Eastern origin for agriculture about ten thousand years ago, because the first signs of an agricultural regime in Europe appear coming via the Balkans on a path leading out of Asia. On the other hand, agriculture seems also to have started quite independently in Southeast Asia and in Middle America, though in the latter area it may have taken place some two thousand years later. In the opinion of several authorities, any community that possessed the polished stone axe was capable of clearing the land, breaking the soil, and so beginning its own plantations. The evident truth is that the dividing line between Mesolithic and Neolithic cultures is very hazy indeed. Agricultural communities and wandering hunter groups could, and still do, live side by side without severely disrupting one another, and one of them could merge insensibly into the next. By the end of the Ice Age some ten thousand years ago, mankind was so widely spread that there was every opportunity for a community to find its own regional niche and there preserve or alter its way of life. It was precisely the most isolated of these niches that preserved their unique and often anachronistic culture patterns well into historical times.

The importance of such niches has not been overlooked by the anthropologists. The Mesolithic peoples who survive today are primitive in the sense that they represent an early stage in human technical development. Furthermore, their way of life enshrines many of the cultural features that are so mystifying to prehistorians, and of which no original record remains. By studying the music, religion, dance, and social customs of the surviving primitive peoples, we can bring some notion of man's intangible past into focus. Naturally the analogy is not exact, for the way of life of surviving primitive peoples has been modified by external influences and internal development. Moreover the survivors, without exception, live in areas with very demanding environments, whether in deserts of ice or aridity or in the depths of tropical forests. The difficulties of life in these places are far more severe than those in the pleasanter lands where the Mesolithic hunters of ten thousand years ago once flourished.

The primitive peoples of today also provide an irreplaceable pool of biological data. Their long period of isolation has often meant that they preserve physical characteristics which died out or were submerged by population movements elsewhere. Genetically, for example, they are probably closer to prehistoric peoples than any other populations living today. Equally important is the fact that they are firsthand examples of environmental adaptation, which is in itself a field of biology imperfectly understood and of the most vital significance in trying to unravel man's physical

26

evolution. In the words of J. S. Weiner, professor of Environmental Physiology at the University of London, the "last remnants of the pre-agricultural world provide us with the only direct information we can hope to obtain of the biology of the hunter-gatherer populations exposed to the multiple hazards of the natural environment. The mesolithic state of culture was basically the continuation of the age old hunting, fishing, and gathering economy into post-Pleistocene times." Thus when each new technique is discovered as a fresh probe into the investigation of man's evolutionary past, it is then rushed into the field to be tested among the last few Mesolithic peoples of the world, many of whom are themselves threatened by modern technological culture. In recent years gene analysis, tests on sweat-producing mechanisms and metabolic adaptations (which have revealed the mysterious fact that Australian Aborigines are less liable to shivering than any other peoples), and studies of skin pigmentation have all been conducted most usefully among Mesolithic peoples as the "purest" human stock available.

It has now been realized, belatedly perhaps, that quantitive analysis of modern Stone Age peoples can help to establish the basic rules for earlier hunter-gatherer populations. For example, rough calculations show that prehistoric hunter-gatherer groups were unlikely to exceed a density of one person every 1.5 square miles, as this figure represents the effective range of movement for the amount of energy expended by a hunter-gatherer

The cave-dwelling Tasadays of the Philippines, only recently contacted by the outside world, exemplify societies that have lived in isolated niches of the world, maintaining Mesolithic-stage cultural traits.

27

going about his daily tasks. Similarly, an examination of the campsites of modern Stone Age hunters gives some idea of the size, construction, and distribution of prehistoric Mesolithic settlements. Not all research is necessarily done in the field. A technique lately in favor combines microscope observations in the laboratory with analogy tests under working conditions. Modern replicas of old Stone Age tools are placed in the hands of hunter-gatherers, and after they have been used for specified tasks, the edges are examined for signs of wear. The scratch marks shown by the microscope are often sufficiently distinctive for the same patterns to be recognized on genuine fossil tools and the original use of these tools identified.

But the surviving Mesolithic peoples are much more than a living relic of man's past. To sociologists in particular, the surviving primitive peoples are remarkable examples of social behavior, that least understood side of the human condition. A Stone Age society still functioning in Australia or in the Brazilian jungle, for instance, is just as modern in its own context as any other culture that exists today. What is different is that these peoples obviously achieved a cultural stability at a far earlier stage in the evolutionary process and remained in equilibrium at that level. They are, in essence, alternative facets to human society in general, and they are all the more intriguing because their comparatively few numbers make them convenient subjects for study. Many of their more notable beliefs and customs pose startling questions. It is strange, for instance, that among the Mesolithic survivors there is seldom any deep-rooted notion of property rights or of aggression. Far from being the violent creature "red in tooth and claw" that some behavioral evolutionists postulate, primitive man as he survives today proves, more often than not, to be an easygoing person whose culture puts much greater value upon cooperation than upon competition. Among the Tasadays, a Stone Age culture group recently discovered living in the Philippine jungle, anthropologists were amazed to find that there was not even any animosity toward harmful insects, which were permitted to share the same rock shelter as the Tasadays without any attempt by the people to destroy or evict these potentially harmful co-residents.

Above all, it is true to say that those primitive peoples who have survived into historical times managed to achieve unique and self-sustaining cultures. When mankind was straddling the boundary of the Mesolithic and Neolithic eras, the human race could have been compared to a vast living network laid across the surface of the world from Eurasia and the tropics to the polar wastes and the islands of the Pacific. Along the strands of the net ran lines of communication, and at each intersection existed a local culture. Changes were liable to take place at several intersections, and from these focii radiated the influences that were to alter almost the entire network. Occasionally, however, there were remote places that were unaffected. Here the cultures neither perished for want of outside assistance nor expanded to disrupt their neighbors. They were admirably suited to their environments and they struck deep roots, replenishing themselves and achieving considerable stature. This is how they existed when, along the strands of the human network, came observers from other, more mobile cultures, and in the first blush of contact were amazed.

The Life of Primitive Man

At One with Nature

"If we shall not be ashamed to confess the truth," wrote the sixteenth-century historian Peter Martyr about the Indians of America, "they seem to live in that golden world of which old writers speak so much: wherein men lived simply and innocently . . . content only to satisfy nature." Martyr wrote in ignorance of the actual richness and complexities of primitive societies. But from his day to this, primitive peoples like the Melanesian archer hunting fish in New Guinea (above) have frequently seemed to be a reflection of mankind's own youth. Living close to nature, keenly aware of its everyday demands and habits, and attuning themselves to everything in creation of which they consider themselves a spiritual part, they have learned the ultimate art of existing in harmony with their universe.

Inheriting the legacies of cultures thousands
of years old, primitive societies still live in
balance with environments usually judged too
severe for civilized man (unless he destroys and
remakes them). In the Arctic, left, Eskimos and
their ancestral cultures adapted ingeniously
with dog sleds, icehouses, snow goggles, and
other inventions that permitted survival. The
Tasadays of Mindanao in the Philippines, right,
with an economy of the Stone Age, have been at
home in a jungle penetrated by outsiders only
in 1966. In the rocks and stern desert of South
Africa's Kalahari, still shunned by more complex
societies, Bushmen, seen ambushing a stream
of game below, continue to exist in isolation.

As only one element of an intimately linked spiritual world, primitive societies have integrated their economic, social, and religious lives with the forces and creatures of nature with which they must cope and, for their well-being, attain harmony. The *Mandan Indian Bull Society Dance*, right, propitiated the buffalo, the basis of the tribe's economy, seeking to draw big herds close enough to be hunted. New Guinea men, on the opposite page, attain social and economic prestige through the wearing of feathers, tusks, and other attributes of the wildlife of their country. Below, Australian Aborigines perform a ritual dance, accompanied by songs, to become fused with their totemic ancestor, a kangaroo.

Iconographic Encyclopaedia, J. HECK AFTER BODMER, NEW YORK, 185

In the ingenuity of his efforts to contend with
and master his environment, primitive man has
been called mankind's greatest inventor. More
than civilized man realizes, he has inherited from
the simpler societies all the elemental material discoveries and innovations, from fire and clothing
to cutting tools and navigable craft, on which his
more complex cultures rest. In their widely differing environments, primitive men poured forth
a stream of unique inventions, each one a distinctive response to a local necessity. The blowgun,
developed in Asia and used there as well as by
South American Indians (left), is a handy weapon
in the thick undergrowth of a rain forest. It is
also a forerunner of compressed-air devices. The
Lapps, right, devised skis perhaps more than
3,000 years ago for travel over the snow. Below,
a navigation chart of rattan and fiber helped
Micronesians of the Marshall Islands make
long-distance sea voyages in the Pacific Ocean.

OLAUS MAGNUS, 1567

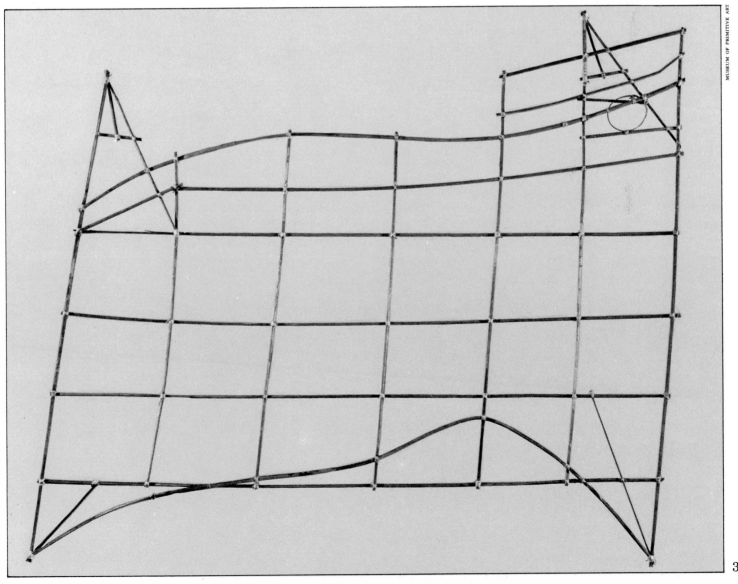

MUSEUM OF PRIMITIVE ART

35

Sharpening a long arrow, a Tapirapé Indian on Brazil's Araguaia River sits in a hammock, one of the many contributions made by primitive societies in America.

The organization of economic pursuits and the inventions and knowledge applied to them often reflected a rudimentary science. New Guinea natives of the Wahgi River devised a complex salt-making process that began with filling a battery of bamboo tubes with sulfurous water, below.

Though the pygmies of the equatorial forest apparently learned the skill from other African peoples, they became adept at making suspension bridges in the form of huge nets woven of giant liana vines, sometimes 300 feet long, stringing them across rivers from trees on the banks, right.

1

A Living Stone Age

To stumble upon the Middle Stone Age in reality must be among the more astonishing moments in any man's life. Yet this is precisely what happened on Monday, July 23, 1770, to an ordinary English seaman when he accidentally intruded upon a group of Stone Age hunters and effectively sidestepped some seven or eight thousand years of history. The sailor was from the British exploring ship *Endeavour,* beached on the east coast of Australia to undergo repairs after colliding with the Great Barrier Reef. A shore party had been ordered to search inland for green plants that the crew might eat as a protection against scurvy. But the sailor, straggling behind his companions in the dense undergrowth, lost his way and stepped suddenly into a clearing where four naked men were grouped around a campfire.

The men were like no people the sailor had seen elsewhere on his voyages. Slender in build, they had long, thin limbs, chocolate-brown skin, and delicately formed hands and feet. Their faces bore a vaguely familiar, faintly European cast, though their eyes were rather more sunken and they had pronounced bulbous tips to their noses. Their hair and beards grew long and matted, and they talked a strange language in shrill voices. Clearly, they were as surprised to see the sailor in his European clothes as he was to see them in their nakedness, and for a moment there was a mutual shock. Then the sailor made a courageous decision. Realizing that it was too late to duck back into the bushes and that, having no weapons, he could be hunted down in a trice, he walked calmly forward and sat down beside the fire. He saw that on the embers the hunters were broiling the half-plucked carcass of a wild bird and the hind leg of one of the strange leaping animals that his ship's naturalist could only describe as a cross between a deer and a hare. After an interval, the nearest of the naked men reached out and touched the visitor. Soon he was joined by the other hunters, and curiously but gently they felt the sailor's hands and the rest of his body, as if to make sure that he too was human. Then they allowed him to leave, and when he started out in the wrong direction for his ship, they courteously redirected him so that he arrived safely at the *Endeavour.*

To this day the sailor's name remains unknown, though the incidents of

AUSTRALIAN INFORMATION SERVICE

Hunting a kangaroo

Aborigine children in the northern part of South Australia

BLACK STAR, DAVID MOORE

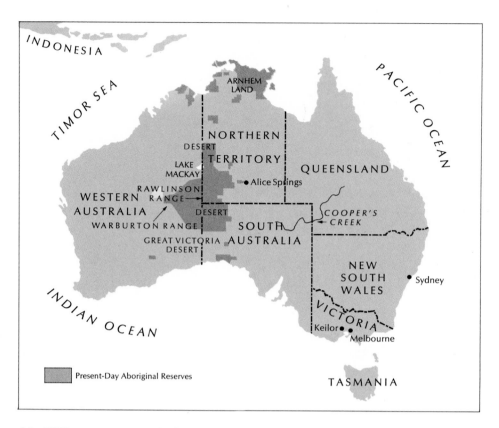

Present-Day Aboriginal Reserves

his 1770 encounter with the Aborigines of Australia were carefully recorded in the journal of his soon-to-be renowned captain, James Cook. That the confrontation should have gone off so smoothly speaks well for the mutual tolerance, albeit temporary, of the participants at such a humble level. In a sense, the meeting underscored the basic similarity between the two sides, regardless of their large cultural gap. Possessing neither metal nor pottery, nor domesticated animals other than the half-wild dingo, the Aborigines grew no crops and did not live in permanent habitations. They were, in effect, members of a living Mesolithic culture. Yet their reaction differed scarcely at all from that of the most cultured man aboard the *Endeavour,* the plutocrat and gentleman traveler Joseph Banks, who in a few years would be elected president of the Royal Society, the most august scientific body of that age. When Banks himself soon afterward came within touching distance of an Australian Aborigine, his first act was to take out his handkerchief, spit on it, and try rubbing the man's skin to see if the color was indelible.

There had been vague reports of the Australian natives ever since Terra Australis, the southern land, had been sighted by Dutch navigators at the end of the seventeenth century. But few of the descriptions were very flattering. Being on their way to the Spice Islands, the Dutch were understandably disappointed that there were no trade prospects with these naked inhabitants of an apparently barren country. Shipwrecked Dutch crews reported gloomily on "wild, cruel black savages," and even the tough-minded ex-buccaneer William Dampier, who twice touched on the north coast of Australia, wrote caustically that "the Inhabitants of this country are the miserablest People in the World." Fortunately Dampier had been

Three Expeditions . . . , T. L. MITCHELL, LONDON, 1839

A nineteenth-century illustration, left, depicts a meeting between an explorer and Aborigines, including a chief (wearing large feather) and a youth garbed in foliage of trees. Body paint, like that on the warrior below, was ridiculed by whites who did not understand that it had a personal meaning for its wearer.

Reconnoitering Voyages . . . , W. H. LEIGH, LONDON, 1839

a ship's surgeon and at least had an accurate eye for anatomy. "They have great Heads, round Foreheads and great Brows. Their Eyelids are always half closed to keep the Flies out of their Eyes . . ." he wrote. "They have great Bottle-Noses, pretty full Lips and wide Mouths. The two Fore-teeth of their Upper-jaw are wanting in all of them, Men and Women, old and young; whether they draw them out, I know not . . . They are long-visaged, and of very unpleasing Aspect, having no one graceful Feature in their Faces."

Modern anthropologists would shun Dampier's aesthetic judgments, though his physical description of the people he met is accurate enough to apply to Aborigine groups still occupying the inhospitable northern coast where he landed. Certainly it is easy to see why the early observers quickly began to puzzle how these beetle-browed men with their Stone Age implements came to be living in the isolation of the Australian continent. Were they a marooned branch of the family of man? Had they developed there in isolation, or were they immigrants from outside? If the last were true, where had they come from? Some hopefuls wondered if the Aborigines were not throwbacks, relics of an earlier civilization. Pessimists maintained that they must be creatures of low intelligence, since they had obviously been incapable of advancing past the Stone Age. The Victorian novelist Anthony Trollope had no doubt about the Aborigines' station in life. "They were and are savages of the lowest kind," he announced after a year's tour of Australia; and though he admired many of their skills, he could see no future for them in a land that was being settled by the white man. "Of the Australian black man we may certainly say that he has to go," he concluded damningly. "That he should perish without unnecessary suffering should

43

The kangaroo was important in the economy of many Aborigines. It provided them with food, and its skin was used for shelter and clothing.

be the aim of all those who are concerned in the matter."

When the white man first arrived in Australia, an estimated 300,000 Aborigines lived there. In 1962 the census listed only 44,000 full-blooded and 85,000 part Aborigines (a slight increase from the low point in their population, recorded in 1930). By 1960 most of them were to be found in marginal territory where the white man had little economic interest. Like water through a man's fingers, the Aboriginal population of the country had been seeping away. Today none survive where Cook's sailor once met them by the campfire on the New South Wales coast, and the last full-blooded Aborigine on the island of Tasmania was dead by 1876.

Yet it was not always like this. The exploration of inland Australia by the white man could not have been accomplished so smoothly without the active help of the Australian Aborigine to show him the safe routes and the water holes in the parched interior of the continent. "Without their [the Aborigines'] guidance," wrote Edward Eyre, one of Australia's most successful explorers and the first man to cross the southern part of the continent, "we could never have removed from one encampment without previously ascertaining where the next water could be procured; and to have done this would have caused us great delay, much additional toil. By having them with us we were enabled to move with confidence and celerity; and in following their guidance we knew that we were taking that line of route which was the shortest, and best practicable under the circumstances."

Eyre and men like him—Charles Sturt, who trusted his life to Nadbuck, his Aborigine guide, and Ernest Giles, a flamboyant traveler who had the septum of his nose pierced so that he too could wear a nose ornament—preached the doctrine that the Aborigines should be respected as a free and proud people. It was the Aborigine, they said, who was the prior occupant of the land, and the white man who was the intruder. But despite the best intentions, including the appointment of a government protector of the Aborigines, the native race of Australia dwindled with appalling rapidity.

The process began on the fertile coastal fringes where the Aborigines had lived in the greatest numbers. The newcomers—European sheep and cattle farmers—shot or drove away the wildlife on which the Aborigines depended for existence. When the Aborigines started to kill sheep for food, they too were intimidated or dispossessed. This abuse was seldom vicious or coordinated. The Aborigine's culture and that of the white man simply could not exist side by side. "The smell of the white man is killing us," was how the Aborigines put it; and even in the far desert country, visited only by an occasional white prospector or misguided cattleman, the decay was rapid and near-total. The Aborigines contracted white men's diseases like measles that proved fatal to them, or they simply pined away when the fragile structure of their culture was bruised by the ignorant stranger. The decline was so swift, and the white man so concerned with other problems, that when the first major anthropological expeditions were undertaken toward the end of the nineteenth century, they had to be focused on the desert Aborigines, who already represented the last fragments of unchanged Aboriginal culture. In fact, it was F. J. Gillen, the postmaster of Alice Springs, a town on the fringe of the desert, who led William Baldwin Spencer, Professor of Zoology at Melbourne University, to make his pioneer study of the great Aranda "nation" of central Australia, for it was Gillen in his travels who had first gotten to know members of the Aranda. Since that day, the anthropological investigation of the Australian Aborigine has been a competition against time, a hurried dash to contact the surviving Aborigine groups while their culture remains relatively pure. The only alternative is to winnow through the stories of the explorers and pioneers who first encountered the Aborigines.

The sheer size of the area once occupied by the natives is significant. The Australian Aborigines lived in every part of a continent that was as broad as Europe from London to the Urals. Within this vast area the terrain ranged from flat, stony desert to coastal mangrove swamps and high scrub country just below the snow line. The climatic environment included some of the most ferocious desert heat in the world, where wise men lie motionless in the noonday shade to avoid heat stroke, as well as soggy monsoon country where huts are built on stilts to avoid flood water. Within this immensity the countryside supported a variety of exotic plants and creatures, many of them unique to the southern continent. There were the kangaroos and wallabies, the strange leaping creatures that so puzzled the *Endeavour*'s naturalists and formed an important source of meat for the Aborigines. Like treasures from an evolutionist's reliquary, Australia also had the platypus and the echidna, the world's only egg-laying mammals. There was a lungfish that breathed air, and a water-holding frog that bloated itself up to the size of a tennis ball and survived droughts by immuring itself in clay for months on end. Of 119 marsupial species, some, like the startled-looking

Journal of an Expedition . . . . T. L. MITCHELL, LONDON, 1848

As white immigration to Australia increased, the Aborigines fell victim to disease and poverty. Many dispossessed and helpless people, like the wanderer above, hobbled dispiritedly from place to place. Below, an Aborigine family cling to their ancestral homesite as the European intruders' future city of Sydney begins to rise around them

koala, crawled slowly through the trees; others, like the wombat, burrowed underground. Huge areas of the countryside had a dusty gray-green aspect where it supported acreages of eucalyptus trees shielding their trunks behind a thickened cortex of bark. Acacias and thornbushes grew in profusion at the fringes of the continent, gradually petering out as one approached the arid heart of the country. But even there, in the dry lands, after a cloudburst a thick carpet of flowering annuals would flourish briefly before the searing heat of summer drove them back to their dormant state.

Across this surrealist landscape stalked the Australian Aborigine with the angular grace of the spindle-legged emus whose gait he so often imitated in his dances. Biologically, he and his dingo were newcomers, as much immigrants as the only other mammalian species, the bats and rodents that he sometimes caught and ate. But in his Aboriginal culture, which varied surprisingly little from one side of the continent to the other, he was uniquely Australian, the supreme inhabitant of a huge living laboratory of evolution.

The Aborigine came to Australia, it now seems fairly certain, from the north, where the arcing Indonesian islands hang down like easy stepping-stones from mainland Asia. But the time and manner of his arrival are far from settled. It was once thought that the Aborigine came when there was a land bridge joining Australia with the north, but this theory has been discarded on the grounds that other placental mammals would have used the same route. The placental bats, it is postulated, could have crossed by flying or, like the rodents, by riding on drifting logs. Similarly, the Aborigines could have crossed the 400-mile straits in canoes, just as windblown

In harmony with his environment: an Aborigine makes his way in the stern desert of Western Australia.

RICHARD A. GOULD

castaways still arrive by accident from the north. But whether this happened 100,000 or 10,000 years ago is in doubt. The archeological evidence of man's antiquity in Australia is too slight to be of much help. An age of 150,000 years has been claimed for a fossil human skull found at Keilor, ten miles northwest of Melbourne, but this is exceptional. Most authorities would favor a date for man's arrival in Australia of not less than 8,000 and probably nearer 18,000 years ago. In any event, the paleologists must tread carefully because the problem is complicated by the fact that their yardsticks are based on Northern Hemisphere experience and may not apply to the special conditions of Australia. Equally, Australia's living Stone Age may have confused some of the available data. It is difficult to identify, for instance, the difference between a genuinely prehistoric stone implement and one that was made quickly and casually as a throwaway implement by an Aborigine a few centuries ago.

The physiological evidence of the Aborigines' ancestry is equally intriguing and perplexing. It was Darwin's champion, Thomas H. Huxley, who first pointed out a similarity between Aboriginal skulls and the skulls of Neanderthal men. Later scholars enthusiastically took up further comparisons between the craniology of Javanese fossils, such as the pithecanthropus, and the modern Australian Aborigine, claiming a direct line of descent. In truth, such evidence was far too slim. Some modern European skull shapes are even more "Neanderthal" than those of the Aborigines, and the available number of fossil skulls in southeast Asia is insufficient for a true statistical comparison. The modern inclination is to point up the similarities between the Aborigines and the Veddas of Ceylon or the Dravidian

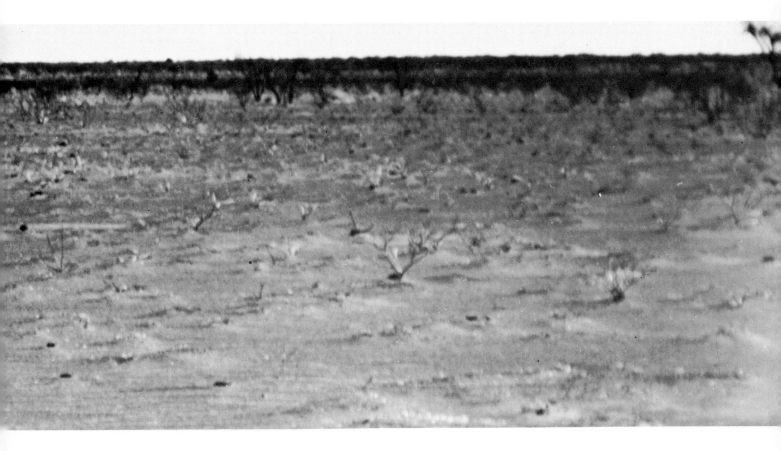

Members of Aborigine groups still unknown to whites are sometimes forced from the desert by drought or famine to seek help at settlements. This man turned up at one of them in 1959 — his first contact with modern-day civilization.

tribes of south India. They share certain physiological features, such as hand prints and a hairy pinna (the broad upper part of the external ear), and there are cultural affinities both in language structure and in the use of the boomerang. This theory has been extended — on the basis of blood-type similarities and other physiological indexes — to include the Aborigines with the Europeans and the Ainu of northern Japan as descendants of the "proto-Caucasoids." These proto-Caucasoids, it is suggested, lived in central Asia perhaps about 70,000 B.C. and spread outward to inhabit the periphery of their world. But until such time as this notion is proved, or replaced by another, anthropologists are content to classify the Aborigines as a special group of their own: the Australoids, physically dissimilar either to the Negroes or to the Mongoloids, and therefore, by default, distant cousins of the Caucasians.

One argument for suggesting a recent immigration of the Aborigines into Australia is that they show a remarkable physical homogeneity. Whether living in mountain or desert, they do not appear to have adapted to specific environments. In stature they are little different from Europeans. Men average 5 feet 6 to 8 inches, and women 5 feet 3 to 4 inches. On Cooper's Creek, near the present Queensland border, the explorer Charles Sturt came across a band of some seventy natives, not one of whom stood less than his own 5 feet 10 inches, while several were more than 6 feet tall. The Aborigines are, moreover, slender people. Long, thin arms and legs, slim, straight backs, and narrow heads give them an elegant vertical aspect, an impression that is accentuated by their short necks, almost as if they are deliberately hunching their shoulders. The anthropometric gauge of "the relative sitting height," i.e., the ratio of total height occupied by head and trunk, shows that the Aborigines have much longer legs in proportion to their bodies than is common with Europeans. Above all, they are a lean and fit people, and their leanness emphasizes their narrow build. Few races are as wiry and in such good physical condition as the Australian Aborigines, living as they do in conditions of constant exercise. Men and women carry very little subcutaneous fat and are capable of considerable stamina. Moreover, medical tests have shown that they are subject to few diseases, partly because weakly Aborigines seldom survive for long and partly, it is suspected, because of the sterilizing effect of the strong sunlight. Nevertheless, the rigors of their existence result in comparatively early signs of aging, frequent mutilations, and in the women the rapid onset of such features as slack abdomens and flat, pendulous breasts.

Pigmentation is one of the few variables of Aborigine physiology, and a most intriguing one. Probably no other race shows such a range of skin color, extending from very dark brown to a coppery tint, depending on the melanin content in the skin. Furthermore, it has been noticed that when an Aborigine wears clothes, the protected areas of skin begin to turn a lighter shade, and if then re-exposed to intense sunlight, become badly sunburned. This chameleon quality of the skin has led some physical anthropologists to suggest that the Australian Aborigine may show a modern instance of some very early trait of man to adapt his skin to environmental conditions, and that this is how black-, yellow-, and white-skinned races may have evolved.

Even more spectacular is the existence of flaxen-haired Aborigines, the so-called blond Aborigines who are found quite widely throughout western Australia. It was Daisy Bates, perhaps the most famous of all the experts on the Aborigines, who did most to publicize the anomaly of these blonds. Daisy Bates went out to Australia toward the end of Victoria's reign to report for the London *Times* on the Aborigines. But she became so concerned with their plight that she disposed of her private fortune in order to go and live among them, a prim little figure dressed in black Victorian costume who spent thirty-five years with the natives, much of the time in a tent near the trans-Australia railway line where the Aborigines could come for succor from their "Kabbarli" (grandmother). Finally retiring at the age of seventy-six, as a Commander of the Order of the British Empire, Daisy Bates subscribed to the notion that the blond Aborigines were the descendants of long-lost Dutch castaways who had wandered off into the desert and interbred with the tribes. More recent observation has shown that this blondness is usually a temporary condition and somehow related to the subject's age. As many as 80 per cent of the children in some Aborigine groups are born with blond- or honey-colored hair, but this color changes as the children grow up. The boys' hair normally goes dark just before their teens, and the girls' hair during puberty. The precise reason for this change remains a mystery, though it may once again have something to do with the variable pigmentation of the Aborigines. Still, it is startling to encounter an adult desert Aborigine who has retained his fair hair or an Aborigine woman with bold streaks of blonde running through her coiffure.

The facial features of the Aborigines, about which William Dampier was so scathing, also vary considerably. Deep-set eyes, "long visages," and a broadened tip to the nose are characteristic, but the alleged "Neanderthal" features—sloping foreheads and heavy brow ridges that give a scowling expression—are not, in fact, very common, especially in combination. Structurally the face is long and narrow, with high cheekbones and a wide mouth that has strong, large teeth and lips that may be thin or fairly thick but are rarely everted in the manner of Negroes' lips. The irises of the eyes are almost invariably brown, with the sclera, or "white" of the eyeball, having a yellowish background often mottled by darker blotches due to irregular concentrations of melanin. Eyelashes are long and fine, and the hair of scalp and beard varies from lank to deeply wavy but is rarely spiral. Scalp hair usually grows luxuriantly, a feature of considerable advantage to the Aborigines, for they use their own hair to weave belts and small purse nets, and may even carry light articles of special value bound up in their hair. Facial hair is often considered a mark of masculinity, an attitude which led the Aborigines to think that the clean-shaven European explorers were all women—a misconception which in one case at least had to be disproved by physical exhibition.

The material possessions of the Aborigine are few and extremely simple, being suited to his wandering life, which militates against any item that cannot either be easily carried or cached against his return to the same spot. The most prized possession of the Aborigine hunter is his stock of spears. From six to more than twelve feet long, the spear shafts are made of wood, either single branches carefully straightened or various lengths of wood built up in the manner of a sectional fishing pole and joined together with wrappings of string and resin. The tips are either fire-hardened or

Primly veiled and gloved, the dedicated Daisy Bates clothes an Aborigine in pants and shirt "for his entry into civilization." For 35 years she labored as a friend of the Australian natives, helping to focus attention on their problems.

One test of a man's coming of age was his prowess with the boomerang and throwing sticks, which were mastered only after long practice.

armed with any of a variety of suitable materials—a stingray's spine, a sharp bone, or a jagged row of stone microliths set in a groove. In more recent times, the Aborigines have taken to adapting odd scraps of iron, broken steel tools, and lengths of telegraph wire for their spear points. Although the spear can be used as a hand-to-hand weapon, it is more often thrown as a javelin. In this case it is frequently hurled with the aid of another Mesolithic device—the spear launcher. Often called a "woomera" (and hence the name for modern-day Australia's main rocket-launching site), the spear launcher is similar to the atlatl that the Aztecs employed in their war against Cortés and the Stone Age hunters used in Europe. Essentially, the Aborigine version is a stick or board some three feet long that serves as an extension of the thrower's arm, exerting greater leverage and giving increased impetus to the thrown spear. The user holds one end of the spear launcher in his throwing hand, fits the notched butt of his spear against a peg in the opposite end of the spear launcher, gives the spear and its launcher a characteristic "waggle" to ensure a snug fit and true balance, and then slings the spear in a low, flat trajectory. "It flew," wrote Joseph Banks after watching a demonstration of spear-throwing, "with a degree of swiftness and steadyness that realy surprized me, never being above 4 feet from the ground and stuck deep in at the distance of 50 paces."

Reflecting the need for portable equipment, many Aborigine spear launchers are multipurpose items. The board-shaped woomeras, which are characteristic of arid areas, frequently take on a concave shape and serve also as carrying bowls. Sometimes they are fitted with a stone fang near the handle so that they are combination chisels-adzes-spear-throwers. Naturally these modifications reduce the woomera's efficiency as a spear launcher, but after years of practice in childhood the Aborigine hunter can still achieve a high degree of accuracy.

The other long-range weapon of the Aborigine is the throwing stick, made famous as the returning boomerang of Australian publicity. The boomerang, however, is essentially a toy, a carefully shaped and delicately made device that takes its aerodynamic properties from the two curved and slightly twisted blades. Correctly thrown, the boomerang spins high in the air, travels forward, then begins to curve around in a circle, and finally falls back at the feet of the thrower. Experts can launch a boomerang into several different flight patterns, and, in fact, the boomerang was originally intended as a test of throwing skill by the Aborigines of the east and west coasts, who alone used it in the days before the white man. Now, of course, boomerangs are made and sold to tourists by enterprising members of tribes across the entire width of Australia. By contrast, the true throwing stick is a much more ugly and deadly weapon. Shaped like a foreshortened hockey stick, it is usually some three feet long and is held at the end of its longer arm. It is then hurled as a bruising, damaging projectile at birds or animals, or in warfare at men, with the intention of disabling the victim by breaking a bone. Very often it is aimed so that it hits the ground first, then rebounds onto the target on the ricochet, striking an upward blow.

For hand-to-hand combat there are simpler clubs, perhaps doubling as throwing sticks or as spear-throwers; shields, usually of bark or wood; and in the northeast a long, curved, wooden slashing weapon, shaped like a Japanese kendo sword, which Dampier described as a "cutlass." The

Aborigines are sufficiently skilled in the use of these weapons for two groups to stand opposite one another in a ritual fight, hurling spears alternately at each other and deflecting the missiles in midair with a tap from a thin woomera.

The simplicity of the Aborigines' weapons of war and hunting is carried over into the material objects of their civil existence. Fire is made either with a fire drill or a fire saw, the principle being the same of ignition through friction by rubbing hard wood against soft, either by being twirled in the drill or dragged back and forth with a sawing motion. A near-complete Mesolithic inventory of stone tools is also kept, ranging from hafted stone axes to small cutters mounted like graving tools in stubby handles. In every case the Aborigines employ the identical stoneworking techniques that were practiced in the archaic Stone Ages, whether in their use of hammerstones to shape workable material or delicate pressure-flaking to produce a serrated edge. Supplies of flint are traded over considerable distances to provide raw material, and as with Mesolithic sites, there are "quarries" and "workshops" littered with the debris of Aboriginal stoneworking. It is perhaps significant for the paleontologists that the Aborigines show little regard for technical consistency. Though capable of skilled and sophisticated stone dressing, an Aborigine is quite content to rough out a crude hand ax, for example, if it serves his immediate purpose, and then throw it away. Greater care is taken with more permanent tools, and these are generally mounted in wooden handles with bindings of string and sinew reinforced by gum adhesives. Conveniently, the tendons of kangaroos make an excellent thread, so strong that until recently it was used in modern hospital surgery. A gluelike resin can be obtained from the gum of yacca

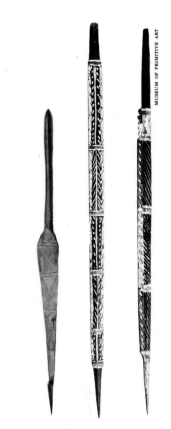

Wherever he goes, the Aborigine carries his spear-thrower (left). These spears (right) are purely ceremonial, not intended for hunting

A hunter poises to hurl his spear with the help of a spear-thrower. The launcher increases velocity but limits accuracy to about 100 feet.

trees or by burning common spinifex grass. An even easier way of collecting this resin is to raid the nests of desert ants that garner and hoard the gum for their own purposes.

It is also a convenient feature of most Australian marsupials that the skeleton of their lower jaws falls into two parts on death. If the large lower incisor remains in place, the Aborigine is provided with a ready-made cutting or boring tool. Alternatively, he can use the serrated row of cheek teeth as a powerful rasp, finishing off his work with a polish from the abrasive leaf of ficus plants. Other uses for bone include the manufacture of fishhooks, scrapers, and the carefully shaped prongs of fishing tridents.

The equipment of the women is even sparer. As gatherers of vegetable products and small edible insects, they need little more than a simple digging stick to turn up underground roots and burrowing grubs and the characteristic shallow bowl in which to carry back their harvest. These saucer-shaped containers of bark or wood, variously known as "coolamons," "pitchis," or "wirras," have a number of functions. They are used as scoops when winnowing the chaff from wild-grass grains, as mixing bowls when

A family scene in northern Queensland about 1920 shows a shelter fashioned from nearby shrubs and trees. The group is about to prepare a meal of roasted kangaroo.

preparing food, as water carriers when moving from one water hole to the next. To establish camp is simplicity itself. Most Aborigines are content with no more than a windbreak to provide shelter, and a small fire, constantly replenished, on each side of the body to provide warmth during the cold nights. The "wurley" or "gunyah," as the windbreak is most commonly called, is quite effective in practice since the wind-chill temperatures on the lee side are consistently higher and only in rainy weather are living conditions really miserable. In areas where frequent rainfall is to be expected, the Aborigines prefer to build huts out of local materials: bark lean-tos, small grass shelters, or in the monsoon season of northern Arnhem Land bark-strip sheds propped up out of the flood water.

Much of an Aborigine's daily life is inevitably spent in the hunt for food. Tribes on the coast can live relatively comfortably on a fish and shellfish diet, and undoubtedly the Aborigines of the well-watered uplands had easy hunting of large marsupials and bird life in the days before the white men. For the desert Aborigines, however, the quest for food has always been a much more serious matter. Virtually every living creature, except man himself, is considered edible; and the Aborigines' senses are extraordinarily finely honed to identify, track, and kill their prey. The most trifling signs are instantly observed and interpreted in relation to a possible quarry. Kangaroos and wallabies leave characteristic tracks when dragging their heavy tails, but far more common are the minute traces of rats, mice, bandicoots (an insectivorous mammal about the size of a large rat), and possums, which are caught in the open and stunned with a quick blow from a stick, chased up trees, or plucked or laboriously unearthed from their burrows. In one place Charles Sturt watched three Aborigines consume between 150 and 200 jerboas, a small type of rodent, among them in a single evening, "furs, skins, entrails, and all, only breaking away the under jaw and nipping off the tail with their teeth." Snakes are dispatched with a quick bite behind the head. Emus are lured within range by the hunter imitating the birds' own movements and arousing their curiosity, or by drugging their water holes with the pituri plant. The stalking hunter may plaster his armpits with mud to stifle any warning odor, or shuffle quietly up to his prey with empty hands and a concealed spear held between his toes. On ponds the unsuspecting waterfowl are snatched down and drowned by an underwater swimmer, and in the air a bird is disabled by a well-flung throwing stick. Driven hunts, or battues, are occasionally organized with a line of beaters or a grass fire to start the animals toward the waiting hunters, and in the tracking and capture of large game the dingo is claimed to be of help. Like his master, the precise date of the dingo's arrival in Australia is in dispute, but undoubtedly the animal is an import, useful in hunting and as a scavenger around the campsite, a role identical with the domesticated dog of the Middle Stone Age.

Less spectacular but probably more reliable is the steady humdrum gathering of food by the women. As a Scottish sea captain's wife, Mrs. Eliza Fraser, found in 1836, when she was shipwrecked on the Queensland coast and fell into the hands of an Aborigine tribe, an Aboriginal woman has a harsh life by European standards. Roots and tubers must be collected; firewood gathered on the march (twigs are picked up between the toes and transferred to the hand without break of step); and wild grass seed plucked,

An Aborigine's teeth are among his most important and frequently used tools. Here a man debarks an acacia branch for use as a digging stick.

A man's basket from Arnhem Land is ornamented with a totemic design.

winnowed in pitchis, and ground between two stones into a coarse flour before being mixed with water and baked into dampers. Otherwise, Aborigine cooking is simple in the extreme. Nearly all animals are simply broiled on the embers, with or without being gutted. Many delicacies are eaten raw, in particular the honey ant, whose swollen abdomen is placed in the mouth and nipped off with the teeth like a liqueur-filled sweet. Another highly prized insect, eaten lightly toasted, is the fat white witchetty grub (the cossus moth larva), which burrows inside the bark of trees and provides a nutritive source of fat in the Aborigines' diet. To trace the burrowing grub, the Aborigine listens intently near a likely looking branch until he hears the characteristic rustle, and then rips away the bark to expose the larva in its gallery. Mrs. Fraser was grateful to be rescued before she, like most Aborigine wives, was handed on from husband to husband. Aborigine girls are betrothed at an early age to men much older than themselves, and can be exchanged, lent, or inherited by their husbands, who will usually keep two or three other women. Excluded on pain of death from much Aborigine ritual life, they play—most authorities agree—a decidedly secondary role in Aborigine society.

The search for water is the starkest challenge that the desert Aborigine must meet. Traveling many miles with his senses alert for a chance to catch an edible reptile or find plant food, he leads a life that is a constant cycle of journeys from one water hole to the next, staying only as long as the water supply itself, available foodstuffs in the area, or the Aborigine's own caution allows. The knowledge of where to find water, and at what seasons of the year, is the Aborigine's most vital heritage. In some tribes, before being admitted to full adult status, he must be able to recite from memory the entire list of possible watering places available to him over an immense tract of territory. Nothing is overlooked: silted-up soaks where the sand can be scraped away to open a small well; a rock pool where last year's rains have collected; a fissure that leads to an artesian supply when the water table rises high enough. If a sequence of water supplies fails, the Aborigine is faced with disaster. As a precaution, he may carry water for a long journey in a pitchi with twigs floating in it to prevent splashing, or chew the succulent leaves of the purple-flowered parakeelia. He finds emergency supplies of water in the cavities of water-bearing trees like the baobab, by digging up and eating the bloated bodies of water frogs, and in the last extremity by opening a vein and drinking his own blood. But in the end even the most desert-canny Aborigines have been known to die of thirst at the height of a major Australian drought.

This life-and-death relationship between the seminomadic Aborigine and the territory he occupies is a fundamental concept of his life. On a grand scale it produces across the continent a vast, gently coruscating mosaic that is the Aboriginal occupation of Australia. Each fragment in the mosaic is the defined territory of its inhabitants, and within its boundaries they move and live according to season or inclination. From the harsh desert, where the only practicable occupation unit is the "myall," or family of one man, his wives, and his children, with a population density of one person to two hundred square miles of land, the mosaic fragments vary in size and density of population up to the lush coastal region, where a single river can support three or four small tribes on its banks. But in every case

The use of every weapon, including fire — an episode in the Aborigines' vain attempt to repel white invaders of their homeland — is pictured in this 1835 water color.

the territorial concept is paramount, the Aborigine's only notion of home and the basis of most of his material and spiritual existence.

Time and again the white explorers encountered this acute sense of territorial ownership. "The natives," wrote Charles Sturt, "certainly do not allow strangers to pass through their territory without permission first obtained, and their passions and fears are both excited when intruded upon. To my early observation of this fact, and to my forbearing any forced interview, but giving them time to recover from the surprise into which my presence had thrown them, I attribute my success in avoiding any hostile collision." Nevertheless, Sturt described how at one water hole a brave native "painted in all the colours of the rainbow, and armed to the teeth with spear and shield" came running up to threaten the entire expedition if they did not leave the place at once. When Sturt only smiled, the astonished warrior "sat down and sulked." On other occasions explorers who only wanted to ask directions of an Aborigine caused hysterics by trespassing on his land. The Aborigine would shout and scream, frantically wave them away, or — in several instances — burst into tears.

For the anthropologist it is perhaps fortunate that the Aborigines have such a highly developed sense of territory. It provides the research worker with a reassuring reference point while he is threading his way through the extraordinarily tangled maze of Aborigine beliefs, customs, and ceremonies. The complexity of Aboriginal culture can be gauged from a glance at the vagaries of their language. It is estimated that when Captain Cook first came to Australia in 1770, at least five hundred different Aborigine languages were being spoken in the continent. Though all sprang from a single root, most of them were mutually unintelligible. Even today philologists working in the field are recovering languages believed to have been

An Aborigine drinks from a desert water hole in Western Australia after a brief rain. Such sites, which permit life, are often held sacred.

extinct, but which have been preserved within one Aborigine family or in the memory of a single person. Because many Aborigine languages are such local affairs, the Aborigines have to learn to understand, if not to speak, the languages of at least one or two neighboring groups. In west-central Australia the Aranda tribes have evolved a sign language akin to the sign talk of the North American Plains Indians, which is useful in inter-tribal communication and for passing silent messages when hunting easily scared game (a secretive purpose it shares with the third known sign language—other than that of the deaf and dumb—which was used among Armenian women). But the linguistic position in Aboriginal Australia is greatly complicated, even in quite small areas, by the fact that many languages are subdivided into regional dialects, and speakers of one dialect do not necessarily understand speakers of another dialect within the same language. Superimposed upon these differences is a thick crust of secret words and special vocabularies—to be used, for instance, when talking about one's mother-in-law, when referring to sacred objects, or while standing as a candidate for certain initiation ceremonies. To the outsider the Aborigines' languages may seem sterile and overcomplicated. Instead of adding adjectives to qualify a noun—as in most Indo-European languages—the Aborigines prefer to add extra syllables to the end of the word (with the exception of the north Australian prefixing group of languages) and assist the meaning through an elaborate system of inflections. It is scarcely surprising, therefore, that Aborigines cannot even converse with a neighbor at more than one remove in the linguistic geography of the continent.

Yet to the Aborigine his language is a sophisticated sensor to guide him through the tortuous material and metaphysical world around him. It is a language so precise that in describing a distant acquaintance a single word will define not only his identity but his exact relationship by blood, clan, and totem to every other member of the same tribe. Similarly, when the white explorers disdainfully noted that Aborigines were unable to count beyond three because they had no words for the higher numerals, they failed to appreciate that the Aborigines prefer to convey the idea of numbers according to the specific situation, and do so by building compound, extremely precise words to suit the occasion.

Even the notion of the "tribe" must be handled with caution in the terminology of the Aborigines. The anthropological definition is applied to a group of people who are bound together by common beliefs, speech, ceremonies, territorial ownership, and a common name; and the Australian tribes answer very well to this description. Nearly all Aborigines, moreover, blithely announce that they are members of a tribe, though the position is sometimes obscured by the fact that the tribe does not actually give itself a name—a further quirk of the language. But an Aborigine's tribe does not necessarily exert the same influence on his life as is normally the case in tribal societies. The reason for this is the division and subdivision of the tribe into a number of special subsections that play a more important role in the Aborigine's daily existence than does the overall tribal structure.

The primary division of the tribe is the moiety, which is simply the splitting of the tribe into halves with the rule that any tribesman must marry a woman from the opposite half. The moiety, in turn, is divided into a number

An 1830 drawing for Tasmanian natives depicts English policy (interracial friendship and equal punishment).

of clans, and each clan has a spiritual link with its own totem, or sacred object—for instance, an emu totem or a wallaby totem. Next, the clans are themselves divided into subsections known as kinship groups, which may total between two or sixteen per moiety, though four- and eight-group totals are most frequent. It is this kinship group that is the dominating factor in an Aborigine's life.

In the first place, it dictates the choice of his wife or wives, as they must be selected not only from the opposite moiety, as we have seen, but from a specific kinship group within that moiety. Usually the wife's kinship group stands in relation to the husband's group as distant cousins of some degree. Secondly, any children born to the union become members of a third kinship group related in a particular manner either to the mother's kinship group (if the system reckons descent by the female side and is therefore matrilineal) or to the father's kinship group (in a father-descent, or patrilineal, group). In turn, the child, when he or she grows up, will find a spouse in a particular kinship group of the opposite moiety, and thus continue an endless cat's cradle of cross-marriages and child placements within the internal subdivisions of the tribe. Within a few generations these marital proscriptions can become so complex that anthropologists must resort to a form of shorthand simply to identify the potential relationship of, for example, FZS–MBD, or father's sister's son–mother's brother's daughter. Ironically, this has become much more clumsy than the Aborigine words for the same situations.

It is only inevitable within such a complicated system—and the one outlined is a reasonably straightforward version—that knotty problems arise which would have puzzled even the grandees of Spain with their insistence on thirty-two armorial quarterings of nobility. As in Spain, there are courts to decide such matters, and the elders of an Aborigine tribe will meet to describe what is to be done when, say, a girl has eloped with a man of another tribe or one from an unsuitable kinship group. Occasionally the punishment is death, or the edict of thigh-spearing, but more frequently the official rules are bent to allow the liaison, though this in turn creates obscure problems of precedent and future complications for the correct placement of children in their right kinship groups. It is little wonder that tribal problems of this type can only be solved by the older men who have vast experience with the system and minds like those of case lawyers. In consequence, the Australian tribes are often said to be ruled by gerontocracies, cabals of the aged.

The third, and perhaps the most important, way in which the kinship group affects every Aborigine is that it decides his status vis-à-vis every other member of the tribe. His closest ties will be with the other members of the same kinship group. They all share the same totem, attend the same ceremonies, render one another assistance, and carry the same second, or "skin," name. They assume, in effect, overlapping identities and are regarded in this way by other members of the tribe. Thus, an Aborigine boy will not merely regard his real father as being his parent but will look upon all the males in his father's kinship group—who were, of course, in the correct kinship status to have married his mother—as proxy, or "classifactory," fathers and treat them like his real father. The obvious extension of this classifactory system is that all members of a tribe immediately

Bark paintings, made mostly in Arnhem Land, are commonly divided into sections. Their sacred meanings are revealed by the artist only to the initiated. This one is Fan Palm Dance of the Sacred Wallabies.

fall into certain social groupings. The Aborigine boy has not only a number of classifactory fathers but groups of classifactory mothers, mothers-in-law, uncles, and so forth. He will also know precisely from which group of girls he will be permitted to marry, and exactly how to treat even a casual acquaintance within the tribe. Thus all fathers, real or classifactory, will be accorded certain duties, and in many tribes all mothers-in-law, even potential ones, will be treated according to a strict set of rules. This may take the form of being totally shunned, of being addressed only via a third person or while looking fixedly at an inanimate object, or of being referred to by the pseudonym of "rubbish."

The totems of kinship groups, clans, and moieties are by no means exclusive to them, and when totem objects are shared, this also superimposes a new set of loyalties. Thus the Aborigine may have the bandicoot as the totem object of his kinship group and also as his clan totem. He will then have a double loyalty and a double set of ceremonies. But he may find a kinship group in a neighboring tribe who also has the bandicoot as its totem and uses the same ceremonies. In such a case he may feel stronger ties with this group than with many members of his own tribe. Perhaps the only Western analogy to this system of links and cross-links is to be found in the army. There, a soldier in a regiment (tribe) has battalion (moiety), company (clan), and platoon (kinship) loyalties. But he may also be airborne-trained (his totem) and feel a kindred link with airborne troops of other units. Add to this his regional ties, the kinship of holding equivalent rank, plus, perhaps, a group of comrades who graduated from officer-training school in the same class, and one approaches the multiplicity of links within the Aborigine's experience. Yet by being educated in the system, the soldier, like the Aborigine, can instantly locate his position within it and his correct behavior toward all other members of the system.

If his relation to other Aborigines is the two-dimensional outlook of the Australian Aborigine, his concept of the spirit world adds a third dimension of great significance. Basically, the Aborigine is animistic; that is, he attributes a living soul to inanimate objects and natural phenomena. All around him — in rocks and trees, animals and places — he sees the dwelling places of peculiar and powerful spirits who must be respected if they are not to harm him. He himself is the abode of a spirit that is related to his own totem and that entered into his mother at his conception and caused her to give birth. It is this belief which has given rise to the impression that the Aborigines do not understand the idea of physical paternity. But this is not strictly true. The Aborigine sees physical paternity simply as one factor, one dimension so to speak, in his three-dimensional world. He believes that spirit paternity is equally necessary. Thus he attaches great importance to the actual locality where a woman becomes pregnant, because this may indicate the identity of the paternal spirit. Equally, he may hold specific notions of physical paternity. Several tribes believe that sexual relations "prepare" the woman for conception, and this belief may be so precise as to stipulate, as among the western Arnhem Landers, that a man must have five ejaculations on successive days before his woman will be impregnated through the connivance of the spirits. The position for sexual relations is unusual. The Aborigine man squats on the ground and rests back on his heels. The woman lies on her back on the ground and

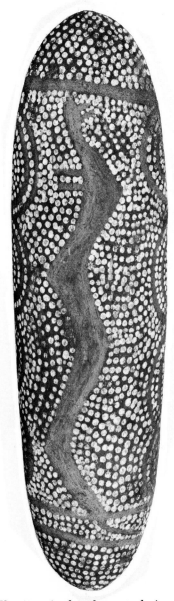

The seemingly abstract design on this Aborigine tray from Australia's Northern Territory is composed of the traditional symbols of totemic ancestors, conveying to the native viewer the abode of their spirits.
MUSEUM OF PRIMITIVE ART

59

This bark painting shows stages of a corroboree, a part-sacred, part-secular ceremony. Many of them are based on legends and have been compared to Christian miracle plays.

spreads her outstretched legs over the man's thighs. As in most primitive societies, sexual activity is frequent and considered a normal and natural factor in human life.

To pinpoint their own existence within the vast three-dimensional world of spirits and material culture, the Aborigines refer back to their origins in the "dreamtime." As in Greek mythology, this was when the great spirits walked the earth. They came out of the sky and sea and land, and in their journeys over the face of the country—sometimes in spirit form, sometimes disguised as plants or animals—they brought life to all its features, including the Aborigines themselves. Whenever a great spirit passed through an object, be it rock, cave, or tree, that object was left infused with a minor spirit of its own. These minor spirits in their turn remained to send forth spirit forces, perhaps to impregnate an Aboriginal woman, perhaps to bring good or ill luck to anything they encountered. The Aborigine believes that survival among these strange and mystic hazards depends upon the protection of his own totem. He must know its powers, its lore, the occasions of its own dreamtime, and the correct ceremonial treatment by which he reaffirms his vital link with it. Without such knowledge, he is as ill-prepared to pass through his three-dimensional world as if he did not know the water supplies in his desert.

The Aborigine's spiritual education is, therefore, long and grueling. It is a process that the doyen of Australian anthropologists, Professor A. P. Elkin, has compared to the elevation of candidates through the various degrees of Freemasonry. Instruction, examination, and induction through the various grades take many forms, according to local totemic customs and rules. Often there are painful physical ordeals: at an early age there may be "tooth-rapping," which is the knocking out of one or more front

Aboriginal dances often imitate the movements of birds and animals. This one mimics an Australian bird, the brolga. Note the blond youths.

teeth; puberty may bring circumcision for boys and introcision for girls (thereafter the girls drop out of the mainstream of totemic ritual); and finally there are a number of tribes that practice subincision, the cutting of a slit in the rear of the penis, when the young men join the fully initiated adults (a custom that Sturt, one of the first people to report this practice, described in decorous Latin). In nearly every case, these ceremonies are attended by indoctrination into the mysteries of the new status. In the Great Victoria Desert the whole process takes from three to four years, with circumcision, subincision, and ritual scarring done in stages and interspersed with long periods of education. In most totem cults the postulant is shown the totemic "churingas," the sacred objects associated with the cult, and receives his instruction in the secret chants and ceremonies with which his fellow totemites commemorate the cult history and reaffirm their membership.

The form and content of the cult ceremonies vary considerably. Members of the emu totem wear tall feather-and-wood plumes and imitate the stalking gait of their spirit forebears when they first traveled the country. Initiates of the rainbow serpent totem produce the sacred opals that symbolize his joining of the water and sky, and in their dances shake bird's down into the air to imitate rain-bearing clouds. Immense care is taken in the preparation of the sacred emblems for Aborigine ceremonies. Mystic prayer boards and various wicker structures are constructed and painted. The holy "bora ground" where the ceremony actually takes place is often laid out with intricate colored patterns. Participants spend hours daubing ritual designs on their skins with paints of red and yellow ocher and streaks of white clay, charcoal, and oxide of manganese, which gives a pearl-gray color. Bird's down or plant fuzz is appliquéd to the dancers' skins, with the use of their own blood as an adhesive. All this is done, as often as not, to the accompaniment of sacred chants. Paints and appliqué are "sung on" to make them sacred. Then follow ritual maneuvers—the high athletic leaps of the kangaroo totemites, the chain dance of the snake cult members, or the mimicry of the sacred goanna lizard. Perhaps the most moving description of any Aborigine ceremony was written by Daisy Bates, describing how she herself became the "guardian" of the totem boards for the Aborigine clans who visited her tent:

"On a shrill, high note, with the branches beating the ground, began the song of the totems, native cat, curlew, eagle hawk, kangaroo, wallaby, emu, mallee-hen, and so on through the whole gamut of those assembled.

"'Yudu!' came a shout from one of the elders. ('Shut your eyes!') With bowed heads, in a tense silence and with closed eyes, the great crowd of squatting natives bent to the ground. I ventured to watch.

"At the other end of the road, in the cleared ground that was, as it were, the altar, or sanctuary, appeared an ancient tribal father, an extremely tall and imposing figure with a long black beard, Wardunda. He was holding before him a totem board at least fifteen feet high, a *koondain,* the father of all totem boards, deeply-grooved and painted in red ochre and white pipe-clay with the sacred markings of the maalu, the kangaroo. Arriving at the centre of the cleared ground, he turned to face the prostrate circle, and lifted the *koondain* in the same manner and to the same hushed reverence as the elevation of the Host in the Roman Catholic church or as

An old man sits at the edge of a decorated sacred "bora ground," awaiting the start of a corroboree.

Aborigines in Arnhem Land prepare to lift four young men whose bodies have been painted with clan designs before the beginning of ceremonial dances. The painting, accompanied by chants, took three hours.

Moses lifting the serpent in the Wilderness.

"At a whispered word the natives raised their eyes. Immediately a frenzied chanting arose, the song of the kangaroo, ringing and echoing from men's throats in that lonely place to the rhythm of beating branches, while man and board remained absolutely motionless. The board was then slowly lowered and as it lay flat on the ground, Wardunda prostrated himself upon it, then rose and reverently carried it out as the singing died away. A smaller kangaroo board, about four feet long, was silently placed in my lap from behind.

"Again 'Yudu!' was the cry, and a second long totem was exhibited. Again a smaller board, with its special markings, was given to me in the same way, until I held twenty or thirty boards of groups living and dead, identical with the large ones, long seasoned with age and weather, bearing the concentric circles, diamonds, squares, and transverse markings and crude drawings signifying birds and animals. These totems have their sacred significance back in the dream time, and hold the mystery of life. No native knows more than that.

"We now rose to our feet. The natives, still in single file, twice made the circuit of the ground, then all stood with their spears in fighting position while Jilburnda came towards me. Taking the boards, which I held in my arms, he touched me with every one of them, upon breast, back, shoulders and knees, finally laying them at my feet."

Aborigine ceremonial is not always so solemn. Tribes meet simply to hold "corroborees," as the entertainment gatherings are called, or perhaps to re-enact some episode in their secular history. On the southwest coast of Australia, for instance, it is said that they commemorate the landing of the marines from Matthew Flinders' ship H.M.S. *Investigator*. The natives paint white belts and crossbelts on their skin with clay and then stamp up and down in military fashion. At corroborees there is great demand for the outstanding songmen and musicians of the day. Like the medieval

Corroboree dancers in their body paint, the colors and designs of which are dictated by tribal traditions

AUSTRALIAN INFORMATION SERVICE

Like most corroborees, the one pictured here consists of singing and dancing. The long musical instrument at right is a "didjeridu," which produces two basic sounds, one like an organ, and the other like a drum.

jongleur, the songman is respected for his style and for the breadth of his repertoire. His subject matter is mostly mythical in content, but he has the freedom to invent new stanzas of his own and to add new events in the song cycles. Above all, his audience will appreciate the subtlety of his composition, the internal metaphors, the use of archaic words, and the invention of new-sung vocabulary. In a sense, the songman exercises a copyright over his authorship, for any song he composes can remain his property unless he wishes to dispose of it. Curiously enough, this same copyright notion applies to cult ceremonies, which are "owned" by one group and may be loaned or actually sold to a neighboring group. In this way certain characteristic ceremonies actually travel across the country, passed on from tribe to tribe.

The musician, like the songman, is a role to be envied in Aborigine society. Most Aboriginal music is highly rhythmical, with the audience beating time by stamping their feet, clapping their hands, or hitting the ground with spear-throwers and clubs. Drums are little more than open-ended logs, and though a membrane drum exists, it was probably a cultural

import from New Guinea. More typical of Aborigine music are the special beating sticks, which, when struck together, produce a sound like a wooden clappered bell, and the unmistakable drone pipe known as a "didjeridu." The latter is a straightforward, unstopped hollow tube, usually of bamboo, between two-and-a-half and eight feet long, and played by blowing down one end into a mouthpiece. Essentially it provides a low-pitched background note that is punctuated by the sharper sounds of the beating sticks. But skilled didjeridu players use tremendous lung control and a positioning of the muscles around the mouth to produce overtones pitched a major tenth apart and, in combination with beating sticks, various contrapuntal combinations.

A geometric appreciation also infuses much of Aboriginal artwork. Whorls, concentric circles, zigzags (often representing snakes), spirals, and meanders are furrowed in the sand, scratched on rocks and tree bark, or painted on rock faces with chewed twigs for brushes. "One device," wrote Ernest Giles of some rock pictures in north Australia, "represents a snake going into a hole: the hole is actually in the rock, while the snake

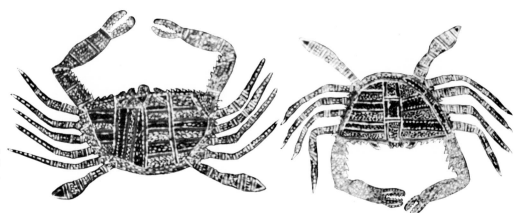

The "x-ray" style of bark paintings, showing inner structure like that of these crabs, reflects the Aborigines' familiarity with nature.

is painted on the wall, and a spectator is to suppose that the head is just inside the hole; the body of the reptile is curled round and round the hole, though its breadth is out of all proportion to its length being seven or eight inches thick, and only two or three feet long. It is painted with charcoal ashes which had been mixed up with some animal's or reptile's fat." Many of these patterns have a mystical rather than decorative intent. Sacred churingas and "bull roarers," specially shaped wooden pendulums that are whirled through the air to produce a warning roar at ceremonies, often bear parallel striations, rows of dots, and painted designs. Less stylized — and remarkably evocative of European Stone Age art — are so-called x-ray paintings of animals with their skeletons showing through the skin, and "calling card" hand prints left in silhouette on cave walls.

Death, in the Aborigine's notion, seldom arises from natural causes. Because he lives under such continual stress from malignant spirits, he feels that a man dies only when he has been cursed by an enemy or has crossed an ill-natured spirit. In the north of the continent the dead body is usually exposed in a tree until the skeleton is clean and can then be buried or the bones put into a hollow log. Sometimes, as in Upper Paleolithic burials, the body is first smeared with red ocher. In the south the corpse is buried either sitting or lying down, and facing its totem ground. But in both cases, after the initial signs of grief, such as thigh-gashing and finger-chopping, the medicine man is called in to identify the cause of death. As the most skilled member of the community in reading psychic signs, the medicine man identifies the "murderer" and a ritual revenge is instigated. Nowadays the culprit seldom suffers more than a token punishment, though in earlier times it was not unknown for special revenge parties to set out to hunt down and kill the offender. Among the Aranda the killers even wore special emu-feather "kurdaitcha" shoes so that when the culprit saw the tracks around his camp, he knew he was doomed and simply died without any physical violence being necessary. Similarly, it is within the power of a medicine man to use black magic and kill an Aborigine from a distance by "boning" him to death. The "boning" is done with two pieces of bone, preferably from a human leg, which are pointed in the general direction of the victim while curses are sung against him. When the victim hears that he has been "boned," modern doctors find it difficult to save his life because he loses the will to live and is shunned, as if he were already dead, by his tribesmen.

The many Paleolithic and Mesolithic traits of Aborigine culture — tools, art, burial customs, and so forth—make it tempting to draw comparisons between the archaic Stone Ages and Australia's own Stone Age. In part, these comparisons are useful. Aboriginal Australia is, after all, the single largest existing model of a Stone Age habitat. The Australian Aborigines show many facets of how early man could have lived in relationship to his environment, using only wood and stone tools. Yet many anthropologists have been fearful that Australian Aborigines should be stigmatized as being "Stone Age" in the sense of being retarded or inadequate. Rather, the example of the Aborigine with his extraordinarily diverse and complex spiritual beliefs and social order can be projected back onto the possibilities of archaic Stone Age culture. Because so many tangible relics overlap, it is reasonable to imagine that archaic Stone Age peoples were able to display a similar, if not identical, sophistication in the realms of metaphysics and social relations.

But even in Australia, apart from a handful of clans, this rich vein of culture is on the point of vanishing. In the entire continent today there is scarcely an Aboriginal family that has not been contacted and in some way influenced by the white man. If there are tiny, as yet unknown groups of Aborigines, they will very likely be found wandering in the Great Western Desert or perhaps around Lake Mackay on the borders of the Northern Territory. Of those Aborigines who still retain their traditional way of life, the majority now live on government-established Aborigines' reserves and clustered around missions. In western Australia there are about three thousand Aborigines, mostly in the Warburton Range and around the Rawlinsons. Another four thousand live in the Northern Territory, and in South Australia, where Edward Eyre once found so many, there are scarcely five hundred survivors. This remains the total of the tradition-oriented Aborigines of Australia, and ironically, even the future of the reservation Aborigines is in doubt. The Australian government has blocked the direct ownership of any land by the Aborigines, and with the quickening search for minerals in the Australian backlands, it is questionable whether the last enduring blooms of Australian Aboriginal culture will survive much longer.

The flowing rhythm of four running women is caught in this outstanding cave painting discovered in 1948 in Australia's Northern Territory.

Children of
the Forest

A drum used by pygmies

To the Victorian explorers the Ituri forest was the most baleful place in Equatorial Africa. Lying almost exactly in the geographic center of the continent, it presented the dark and lowering image of the forest primeval, a region where huge trees rose a hundred feet above the secondary vegetation, their straight trunks often more than twelve feet in circumference and buttressed by tangled roots thrusting powerfully through the crust of the earth. Lianas and tendrils dripped down toward the undergrowth; prickly bushes and shrubs plucked at the canvas trousers and Norfolk tweeds of the perspiring explorers. It was a place of unexpected silence — not the familiar, noisy jungle with its insect buzzings and bird screechings, but a forest where for hours on end there was no sound. The immensity of the woodland seemed to muffle noise. The mold of dead leaves covering the ground absorbed footfalls; and the general gloom where sunlight failed to penetrate the dense foliage had a somber, sepulchral quality. Near water one heard the evening chorus of frogs or, at dawn, the occasional screaming of a troupe of chimpanzees. But for most of the day there was nothing but the sudden harsh croak of the hornbill to punctuate the stillness.

The forest, almost 50,000 square miles in extent, takes its name from the Ituri River, whose waters flow some 800 miles before joining the Congo in the vicinity of present-day Kisangani. The forest fills the Ituri's drainage basin. To the north, where the Zaire-Sudan border is now, it edges against the watershed of the Nile. To the east the trees of the forest march with the open plateau savanna that gives onto Lakes Albert and Edward, named by the Victorians in honor of their royalties. On the other two sides the Ituri merges gradually into the more widespread rain forests of the Congo basin.

In the beginning the river itself was the only highway through the region. The most successful African explorer of his day, Henry Morton Stanley, American newspaperman, adventurer, and the man who had found Livingstone, came up it in 1877 with a hand-picked force of native riflemen, porters, and volunteer white officers to attempt the first complete traverse of the Ituri. By the time he abandoned the river to strike directly for Lake Edward, fifty-two of his men were so crippled by leg ulcers and malnutri-

A pygmy home of mongongo leaves in the African Equatorial forest

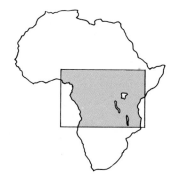

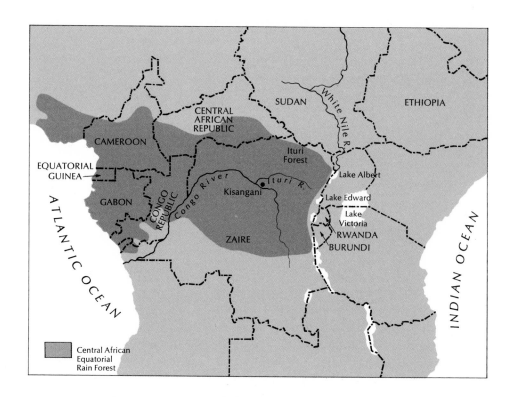

Central African
Equatorial
Rain Forest

tion that he had to leave them on the riverbank at a place he named Starvation Camp. His description of that scene was High Victoriana, the epitome of the Ituri wilderness: "No more gloomy spot," he wrote, "could have been selected for a camp than that sandy terrace, encompassed as it was by rocks and by those dark woods, which rose in tier upon tier from the river's edge to the height of 600 feet, and the never-ceasing uproar of the writhing and tortured stream and the twin cataracts eternally thundering in the ear. The imagination shudders at the hapless position of those crippled men, doomed to remain inactive, listening every moment to the monotonous roar of plunging rivers, with eyes fixed on leaping waves, coiling and twisting waters, or dark, relentless woods spread upward and around them. The night, with its palpable blackness, dead black shadows of wooded hills, ceaseless boom of cataracts, indefinite forms born of fearfulness, misery engendered by loneliness, and the creeping sense of abandonment, would be still worse."

It was almost inconceivable to men like Stanley that anyone should dwell in this silent wilderness. Yet the Ituri forest was, and is, the home of the Mbuti pygmies, the largest single concentration of pygmy hunter-gatherers in Africa. Today an estimated 32,000 to 42,000 Mbuti live scattered throughout the forest. No accurate census has ever been possible because they are a shy and elusive people. Moreover, it has been realized only recently that the Mbuti dwell in the forest largely by choice. Biologically and culturally, they have adapted to the forest, and live in a close and cheerful symbiotic relationship to it. They regard it as their ally, provider, and refuge. If taken away from it, they catch fevers and suffer from sunstroke; a curious lassitude sets in; and very often they pine away and die. In the words of the anthropologist Colin Turnbull, perhaps the world's leading authority on the Mbuti: "The pygmies see the forest as their friend; they talk to it and sing to it; they believe that it will always look after them and they have complete trust in it. In their own language they refer to themselves as 'children of the forest,' and they talk of the forest and address it as 'Mother' and 'Father.' It is the source of their life, and it *is* their life. It is their God."

Thus the Victorian image of the menacing Ituri forest was utterly wrong. As a habitat for man, it has many advantages. Movement between the immense tree trunks is easy enough for a small and nimble person, far easier than in the adjacent reed-choked river marshes. Edible fruits and plants, as well as a few wild animals, can sustain a skilled and active community of hunter-gatherers. Water is easily obtained from the many small streams, and an equatorial climate assures moist, mild weather. Temperatures, daily or annual, never drop below 70 degrees or rise above 90 degrees, and there is no need either for warm clothing or for a shelter more substantial than a leaf hut. Above all, the forest offers sanctuary. The same fearsome image that so discouraged the white explorers of the nineteenth century also discourages the black native village dwellers. One theory for the present distribution of the pygmies postulates that formerly they were spread over an immense tropical belt, from Liberia to Rwanda, but retreated into the forests before the advancing and more powerful villagers. Today, pygmy people still live in areas as far apart as Cameroon and Burundi, and almost everywhere they are to be found in a forest environ-

In adventure books of the nineteenth century, pygmies were usually pictured as elusive, terrified dwarfs. Here, an American explorer with his African guides tries to lure pygmies from their huts. Several are already running away in fright.

A Journey to Ashango-Land . . ., PAUL B. DU CHAILLU, LONDON, 1867

Until knowledge supplied the truth, Europeans often peopled unexplored lands with fancifully conceived inhabitants. A staple was pygmies, who were even pictured as dwelling in North America, along with flamingos (which were actually in Florida) and a unicorn, as in this 1550 French map of part of Canada.

ment. The exception is Rwanda, where they live among the villagers in open country. But even in Rwanda, it seems, pygmies were once the inhabitants of dense forests that have now been cut back, exposing them to cultural and physical intermingling with the larger village peoples. The Mbuti, on the other hand, continue to live in the inviolate fastness of the Ituri much as the explorers found them a century ago.

The entire history of contacts with pygmies has been a bizarre succession of misapprehensions right down to the present day. Over the centuries educated opinion grew so jaded with rumors of dwarf people that the whole notion was often rejected out of hand. The topic smacked of fantasy. It had a traveler's-tale quality, a comic preposterousness associated with stunted court jesters, dwarf buffoons, and the occasional unhappy freak. It was as easy to believe in the pygmies as in the Mountains of the Moon. Both were said to lie in central Africa, and as it turned out, both were found exactly where rumor said they would be.

The earliest reference to an African pygmy had its cap-and-bells gloss. Pharaoh Pepi II of the Sixth Dynasty wrote an excited letter to one of his generals returning from the land of Punt. The general had reported he had a pygmy dancer in his baggage train, and with royal anticipation the Pharaoh strictly enjoined that this strange little man was to receive special attention. Ten strong men were to escort him on each side, in particular during the Red Sea voyage, lest he fall overboard. In a European context Herodotus, the "Prince of Liars," spread a wild tale that miniature men — he actually called them *Pygmaioi* — lived a harassed life fending off the attacks of fierce birds like cranes. This yarn, told in one form or another, was taken up, repeated, embroidered, and reintroduced so often that the whole topic became grievously suspect. In 1699 one Edward Tyson, an English savant and Fellow of the Royal Society, sought to scuttle the rumor by writing a long and learned paper to the effect that the African pygmy was no more than an ape, probably a chimpanzee. Curiously enough, Stanley

72

heard this same story from Congo natives. They told him of chance encounters in the forest with fierce, tailless monkeys who shot poisoned arrows and fought viciously, and for proof the village-dwelling natives produced chimpanzee skulls.

It was not until the German botanist-explorer Georg Schweinfurth approached the Ituri forest from Lake Edward in the late 1860's that the outside world had its first unquestionable account of an Mbuti pygmy. Schweinfurth had heard of pygmies at the Negro court of King Munza of the Monbuttoo, where they were kept as professional hunters and soldiers. But not until he visited Monbuttoo and actually saw a pygmy for himself was Schweinfurth prepared to believe in their existence. One morning, he wrote, "my attention was arrested by a shouting in the camp, and I learned that Mohammed [his servant] had surprised one of the Pygmies in attendance upon the king, and was conveying him, in spite of a strenuous resistance, straight to my tent. I looked up, and *there,* sure enough, was the strange little creature, perched upon Mohammed's right shoulder, nervously hugging his head, and casting glances of alarm in every direction. Mohammed soon deposited him in the seat of honour. A royal interpreter was stationed at his side. Thus, at last, was I able veritably to feast my eyes upon a living embodiment of the myths of some thousand years!"

The pygmy, named Adimokoo, was a man of the Akka subdivision of the Mbuti, and though Schweinfurth was later to see several other pygmies—in fact, he managed to trade King Munza a dog for a young pygmy and kept the lad as a companion until the pygmy died of dysentery in Berber—it was Adimokoo who left the most vivid impression. After measuring, feasting, and questioning him, Schweinfurth persuaded Adimokoo to put on a display of dancing. "I confess that my amazement was greater than ever," he recalled, "when I looked upon the exhibition which the Pygmy afforded. In spite of his large, bloated belly, and short bandy legs—in spite of his age, which by the way was considerable—Adimokoo's agility was perfectly marvellous, and I could not help wondering whether cranes would ever be likely to contend with such creatures. The little man's leaps and attitudes were accompanied by such lively and grotesque varieties of expression that the spectators shook again and held their sides with laughter. The interpreter to the Niam-niam said that the Akka jump about in the grass like grasshoppers, and that they are so nimble that they shoot their arrows into an elephant's eye and drive their lances into their bellies."

As it happened, the true-to-life size of the pygmies was something of a disappointment. Literally, the Greek word *pygmaioi* means "people as tall as the distance from a man's elbows to his knuckles," but this was a palpable exaggeration. Adimokoo was less than 4 feet 10 inches tall, and a series of recent anthropometric measurements among 510 male and 382 female Mbuti gives an average stature of 4 feet 8½ inches and 4 feet 6 inches respectively. Moreover, the Mbuti are ranked as the smallest of the African pygmy groups. In the 1920's the favorite device to demonstrate their comparative height was to line up a pygmy family beneath the horizontally outstretched arm of a white explorer. The pygmies just fitted, looking slightly bemused, while the posed explorer tried hard not to resemble a benign semaphore. More significant is the light weight of the Mbuti. Weight for size, they weigh less than the African villager or the European, seldom averaging more than

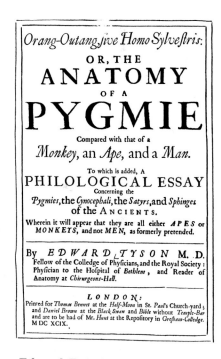

Edward Tyson's influential book of 1699 announced quite clearly on the title page that pygmies were not humans. Tyson's studies, however, were done with skeletons that were later proved to be those of chimpanzees.

70 pounds. This light weight, coupled with the pygmies' extreme agility, quickly led some observers to surmise that the pygmies had adapted biologically to forest conditions. Certainly the Mbuti appreciate the distinction. Whereas the native villagers often find a white man to be clumsy in the forest, the Mbuti consider the villager to be a blundering, noisy fumbler in comparison to themselves.

A new crop of misconceptions quickly sprang up as early theorists nurtured an exotic variety of reasons to explain the small size of the pygmies. Stanley can be excused for thinking that they were "Ishmaels," a tribe of manikin freaks cast out the day the Ark unloaded and condemned to wander eternally in the woodland gloom. But as late as 1920, Dr. Leonard John Vanden Bergh, the leader of an expedition sent by the American Museum of Natural History and several American universities, opined that "lack of sunlight and prowling about in a stooping position are the most forceful argument for their size, in my estimation." The same authority, however, was at a loss to explain why pygmies had dark skins though they lived constantly in the shade; and why, if the North American Iroquois Indians lived also in the forest, they were not similarly stunted but among the tallest native peoples in the New World. Georg Schweinfurth, commenting on the pygmies' characteristic lordity (sway-backed condition), put forward the ingenious theory of natural equilibrium. Pygmies, he stated, were small in stature but large in appetite. After eating a hearty meal, it was necessary for them to stick their bottoms out in order to keep their balance.

Despite considerable research, it is still not settled exactly why pygmies are so small, though physical anthropologists have shown that pygmies represent a high standard of genetic purity. A few pygmy women go to the native villages to marry, and in most instances they and their children stay on there. But the village men almost never marry into the forest-dwelling pygmy groups. The result is that the genetic pool of pygmies remains relatively unaffected by outside influences. Thus pygmy skin color differs from that of the black villagers, ranging from yellowish and yellow with brown overtones to the characteristic mahogany shade of the Mbuti. Henry M. Stanley, who could write with splendidly inverted pomp at times, said that " 'partial roast coffee,' 'chocolate,' 'cocoa' and 'cafe au lait,' are terms that do not describe the colour correctly, but half-baked red-clay brick would best correspond in colour to that of the complexion of these little people." The pygmy's extreme loose-jointed suppleness has been ascribed to certain differences in the make-up and workings of growth hormones in the anterior lobe of the pituitary and to an abundance of female sex hormones. These conditions, taken together, produce a general flexibility, a reduced amount of joint cartilage, bony crests throughout the skeleton, and—due to the exercising of particular muscles in daily life—the appearance in some men of femalelike breasts. Considering the pygmy's extraordinary suppleness, it is not surprising that nearly every traveler in the forest has commented on their superb ability to perform their dances with quite remarkable dexterity, and that their ancient name to the Egyptians was "The Dancers of God."

Early travelers also complimented the pygmies on having the well-muscled torsos of small wrestlers, albeit on stumpy legs. Modern anthropometric terminology reduces this description to "achondroplastic," the

This grotesque and wholly imaginary version of what a pygmy looked like was passed off to his readers by Tyson in his 1699 book. The author's reputation established the caricature as truth for many generations.

Orang-Outang, or the Anatomy of a Pygmie, LONDON, 1699

In Darkest Africa, HENRY M. STANLEY, LONDON, 1890

A 19th-century photograph, typical of those depicting the wonders of Africa, shows a group of pygmies posing with British officers and their Sudanese and Zanzibari guides.

bulldog syndrome of large head, powerful body, short face, and short lower legs and forearms. Technically, the pygmy, with a cephalic mean between 75 and 77, is classified as submesocephalic. Visually, the face is dominated by a pronounced upper jaw, a forehead which slants back, a somewhat receding chin, and a nose that is both broad and low and terminates in wide, flaring nostrils. The eyes are usually brown and slightly bulging, hair is of the tightly curled peppercorn variety, and on the men wiry beards are common. The other terminal hair—in the crotch and armpits—is profuse, and some pygmies are born with a good deal of fetal body hair, which is sometimes retained, changing from blondish-red to dark brown. This body hair may well have had something to do with the villagers' traditions of furry man-monkeys in the forest. The other complaint, that pygmies give off a strong smell, has been tentatively explained as the function of powerful apocrine glands exuding a natural insect repellent for forest conditions.

Still to be explained, if not confirmed, are indications that pygmies have a high thyroid level, a slow heartbeat, and possibly the lowest basal metabolism in the world. The presence of the special "sickle cell" in the blood is one of the few traits shared with the black natives and provides a genetic shield against malaria. With so little research completed, and so many unusual physical characteristics yet to be defined, it is not surprising that the questions of pygmy stature and evolution remain unanswered. While one theory promotes the achondroplastic doctrine, another postulates infantilism. Most theorists at least agree that the pygmies represent an independently developed stock, probably descended from an early type of man who may have been full-sized, flat-nosed, with a mahogany-colored skin, and showing great prognathism. The intriguing possibility thus arises that the nearest early man of this type in Africa was Rhodesian man, who

75

The Reverend Paul Schebesta helps a pygmy to a bowl of soup. Schebesta's studies examined the racial differences between the Mbuti pygmies and the tall village dwellers.

existed about 50,000 years ago. But this conjecture must remain purely speculative until more evidence, probably archeological, is available.

The serious anthropological investigation of the Mbuti began as late as 1929. In January of that year a Viennese anthropologist, Rev. Paul Schebesta, took advantage of a new road-building program in the Ituri region to visit the Mbuti and make a general survey of the pygmy camps. Schebesta was interested in comparing the Mbuti with the pygmy peoples of Southeast Asia, where he had already done field work, and his first encounter with an Mbuti bore a striking resemblance to Schweinfurth's experience. Once again it was a full-sized villager who, in answer to Schebesta's requests to see a pygmy, forcibly produced a male Mbuti for his inspection. The little man was dragged up, kicking and protesting and scowling so angrily that, in Schebesta's words, "he looked exactly like a hobgoblin on the cover of a book of fairy tales." Despite this unpromising start, Schebesta soon became sufficiently popular with the Mbuti to acquire the nickname "Baba wa Bambuti" ("the father of the pygmies") as they came to his mobile camp to receive presents and answer his questions. The work of Schebesta, who made a number of field trips to the Ituri forest, was followed by that of an American anthropologist, Patrick Putnam, who was later joined by his wife, Anne. Together they operated a field hospital-cum-guesthouse at Camp Putnam on the main trans-Ituri road. It was here, in the early 1950's, that the third of the well-known authorities on the Mbuti, Colin Turnbull, came into contact with the pygmies. By a curious set of circumstances, Turnbull, who had only recently graduated from Oxford University, was mistaken by the Mbuti for a relative of their friend Patrick Putnam, an error that was further enhanced by the close physical likeness between the two men. By this lucky accident Turnbull was able to live in the forest with a pygmy hunter-band, learning to hunt and travel with them and—significantly, as it turned out—eliminating the intermediary role of native villagers at the more permanent camps, with the result that he saw the pygmies in their forest habitat. It is on the foundation of these three studies, those of Schebesta, the Putnams, and particularly Turnbull, that the whole social anthropological study of the Mbuti rests.

Occupationally, the forest pygmies and particularly the Mbuti are classified as true hunter-gatherers. Under normal conditions they live in small bands, varying in size from three to forty families, and build temporary camps in their own hunting zones. They do not raise crops; they do not possess domestic animals, except a mute dog that must have a wooden bell hung around its neck while hunting; and they do not know how to make fire. When they change camp, the Mbuti simply carry a burning ember with them to the site and kindle a new flame. The pygmies' life is therefore dominated by their hunting and gathering, and among the Mbuti of the Ituri forest a primary distinction must be made between those bands who hunt with bow and arrow and those groups who hunt with nets. The difference in their hunting methods is reflected in their social organization, in their relationship with their village neighbors, and to a certain extent in their geographic distribution throughout the Ituri region. Generally speaking, although both groups live intermingled in the forest, the net-hunting bands live in greater isolation than the archer bands and are held to represent a purer form of pygmy culture.

Net hunting is a skilled but uncomplicated technique. Every hunting day, usually four or five times each week, most of the members of a pygmy band leave their encampment and walk to the area selected for the hunt. There the owners of the nets, usually the married men, set up their equipment in a large semicircle. Each net is like an elongated tennis net, about 4 feet in height and 100 to 300 feet in length, so that the complete semicircle, depending on the number of hunters, extends between several hundred feet and almost a mile in diameter. The size of the hunting circle helps determine the size of a net-hunting pygmy band, which averages between ten and fifteen families. A hunting circle under 200 feet in diameter cannot be erected without scaring away the animals within its radius; anything over a mile is too unwieldy and becomes dangerous. The men conceal themselves near the nets while the women and children form a crescent on the open side of the circle and, acting as beaters, drive the forest game toward the trap. When an animal is entangled in the net or threatens to double back and break through the line of beaters, the hunters dispatch it with a spear or dagger thrust or shoot it with a poisoned arrow.

Anne Putnam, who must be one of the very few white women ever to have guarded a pygmy hunting net, has described the tension of waiting for a

Mbuti pygmies and one of their hunting nets (hung on a pole) are shown in this quiet scene of a village in the Ituri forest, photographed by the anthropologist Colin Turnbull.

beaters' drive to close in: "There was nothing to do but wait, not knowing whether the din would send harmless antelope or maddened leopards or buffalo towards the nets. Before the place where Faizi [her pygmy companion] and I stood guard there was a fairly open area, brown carpeted with fallen leaves, in which the trees grew high towards the sunlight without any low branches. It was a little like a well tended park or picnic grove. It afforded us a view, not a good one, but one where running game would not be upon us before we could spot it.

"By now the sun was high in the sky, sending its hot rays through the lacework of the trees. Faizi was sweating, probably more from excitement than heat, and my clothing grew steadily more moist. In the distance the beaters were making an unholy racket that grew closer and closer by the minute.

"Faizi saw the antelope first. A second later, between the great tracks of the trees, I saw the small grey deer bounding towards us, nose straight out, short antlers laid back upon its neck, and its little hooves barely touching the ground between leaps. The lighter part of its eyes was visible because fear had pulled the lids far back to give it full vision. The antelope dodged between the trees as easily as a half-back at practice, heading straight for

All is turmoil in this photograph, also taken by Turnbull. An antelope has been trapped in a net, and the pygmy hunters have rushed forward to secure it before it can escape.

the patch of cover where the pygmies waited. If it saw the net, there wasn't time to change course, and it plowed head on into the mesh of liana vines. Before it could even think to struggle three little men threw themselves upon it. There was a frenzied instant of stabbing and slashing, and then it was all over."

The most common form of prey is the forest antelope, of which there are many varieties, though other victims include the forest pig and an occasional okapi. The latter, like the pygmy, was once considered an unlikely invention. Halfway between a giraffe and a deer in appearance, but with the black-and-white stripes of a zebra on its legs in irregular horizontal bands, the nocturnal okapi shared with his pygmy hunter the same shyness and the same forests. Unknown to science until 1900, the okapi preserved its anonymity a half century longer than the pygmy.

The arrow venom used by both net hunters and archer bands is much the same and is usually a strophanthus poison. According to Colin Turnbull, who has lived and hunted with the Mbuti, "When the poison is prepared, one test for its strength is to make a slight cut in the forearm and to allow the blood to trickle down for an inch. The poisoned wooden tip of an arrow is then touched to the blood below the wound. If, as the Mbuti say, the poison 'walks up the arm,' they claim to feel a tickling sensation and hurriedly wipe the blood away. If the poison does not 'walk up the arm' it is not strong enough." Since strophanthus poison is equally harmful to human beings and to animals, the Mbuti take care to carry the envenomed arrows sheathed in a bundle of leaves in order to prevent an accidental scratch. Using poisoned arrows, whether fire-hardened or metal-tipped, the archer hunters of the Mbuti either stalk their quarry or, more usually, lie in ambush and coax the game within range by imitating animal calls. In either case they wait until the prey is very close and then, holding a clutch of spare arrows in one hand, shoot a rapid succession of arrows from their small bows, depending more on scatter than on accuracy.

Because less cooperation is necessary in hunting with bow and arrow than with the net, the archer bands are less compact than the net-hunter bands. At the beginning of the hunting year, however, the archer bands come together for the "begbe," a driven hunt very like the standard net undertaking, but with a line of archers instead of a net barrier. In this form of hunting the beaters use petards made from magba leaves rolled into cylinders, which, when struck on the ground, make a sharp cracking sound. Elephant hunting, famous enough in travelogues, is in fact comparatively rare as well as extremely dangerous. A very competent hunter may tackle an elephant single-handed, tracking him down, then running up from behind and driving his spear into the animal's belly. His target is the animal's bladder, and if the urine is seen to spurt, the hunter will then return with his entire band to follow the animal until it drops dead some days later. Just as hazardous is the technique by which four or five hunters lie in wait along an elephant trail. One man stands in the path to attract the elephant's attention, while another hunter darts out of cover to slash and sever the tendon of one of the elephant's rear heels. As the outraged animal whirls to lash out at the new threat, a second hunter strikes on the opposite side, disabling a second tendon and immobilizing the animal. Naturally the killing of an elephant, particularly as it is so infrequent, is a major event for

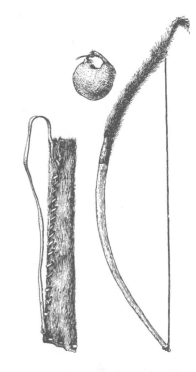

Pygmy artifacts, fashioned of local materials, are marked by their simplicity. At left is an antelope-skin quiver. The monkey-skin wrist guard, top, is used with the bow.

79

Honey, a favorite pygmy food, can be gathered only two months in the year. It is extracted with the adz (right) and stored in the bark pail.

a pygmy community. The entire band establishes a new camp around the carcass of the animal, and it is reported that the carving of the dish is attended with some ceremonial. A senior hunter climbs onto the carcass and slices away small pieces of tender skin to be chewed by the watching crowd. Then, carefully peeling back layers of flesh, the hunter exposes the final membrane of the, by now, bloated stomach. A small child is held up to bite through the membrane. A fetid explosion follows; and the entire band swarms onto and into the dead elephant to dismember it completely.

The gathering of wild foods in the forest is done mostly by the pygmy womenfolk. They search for edible mushrooms and fungi, sweet itaba root, eseli nuts, and berries. These are collected and placed in baskets slung on the women's backs from a tumpline across the forehead. Women, girls, and even quite young children will go gathering forest products, and as the Ituri is a bountiful provider, the collecting of wild products is a haphazard but successful operation. "Before I had walked a half mile," noted Anne Putnam on the way to a net hunt, "I was amazed to see the way in which the women gleaned food and other necessities from the jungle as they passed through on the way to the hunting grounds. They were never idle. They behaved like small birds searching through the trees for bugs and beetles. I was fascinated by their ability to spot things while moving at a fast pace. I decided to study one of the women exclusively and picked Tomasa as my subject.

"She had a container made of rattan and Mongongo leaves that was half basket and half bag. She wore it strapped around her forehead, which left her hands free. We went by a small Mongongo. Without slackening her walk Tomasa cut four or five of the leaves and packed them in the bottom of her bag. A minute or so later she passed a kola nut tree and a handful of nuts went into the container without any delay.

"Now and again the little pigmy woman stooped over to pluck herbs. How she spotted them amid all the greenery on the forest floor I couldn't imagine, but she saw everything, and knew its value. A short distance beyond the salt lick the path the hunters were following dipped into a small valley, darker than the rest of the jungle. Tomasa darted right and left of the beaten way and in less time than it would have taken most women to do nothing but cross the small depression, she had found and pocketed a pint of yellow mushrooms.

"Within the next half hour Tomasa had husked at least a pint of kola nuts, had found a few of the big gray mushrooms, and had picked from nearby leaves twenty or thirty caterpillars. These she rolled quickly in a Mongongo leaf to keep them from getting away while she was busy with other things."

Honey gathering, because it involves climbing trees, is usually done by the men. The Mbuti are superlative climbers and, being so agile and well-muscled, normally swarm up a vertical tree trunk simply by gripping it with arms and legs alternately and hoisting themselves up. If the tree trunk is too large, they place a vine loop around it and, holding the ends in their hands, clamber upward like lumberjacks. The honey season is the fattest time for the pygmies, two months in the middle of the year when life is particularly easy and the members of each band cooperate to reap the wild harvest. The honey is usually found high up in the rotten branches or hollow boles of the forest trees. The entrance to the hive is widened with a few strokes of an ax. A leaf tube containing smoldering embers is poked into the hole, and the pygmy puffs through the tube until the clouds of smoke drive away the bees. Then the collector puts in his arm, scoops out handfuls of honey, and after taking a few mouthfuls himself, drops the remainder to his waiting friends. There they share it or carry it back to camp to be divided among the band. Everyone has a portion of the honey and eats it ravenously, no matter what the quantity and never saving any. The forest always provides, and the honey season is always replete. Honey songs celebrate the occasion; honey charms aid the collectors to find the hives; and every pygmy is a honey connoisseur, able to appreciate the different tastes of different varieties, fresh or fermented, including the favorite maggot honey, full of white grubs and gently warmed over a fire until the maggots wriggle. Even the poorest grade of honey, clouded with dirt and broken bark, is salvaged. Wrapped in a leaf container, the honey is saturated with water, and the mead that drips out is caught in leaf cups and drunk on the spot.

Informal cooperation is the keynote of life in a pygmy encampment. The camp itself is a casual affair, quickly established at a suitable spot in the forest. The huts are erected by the women using saplings cut in the forest by their husbands. The ends of the saplings are pushed into the ground, and then they are bent over and their free ends lashed or woven together to form a low arch. A number of arches meet at their centers to form a frame and are girdled with horizontal hoops of wood to make a structure that resembles an upturned wicker basket. A hole is left as an entrance, and the frame is then clad with large rainproof mongongo leaves from the forest. Each leaf is hung exactly like a roof tile, held in place by its stem and overlapped like scales so that it forms a waterproof canopy. A single pygmy woman can build such a hut quickly and easily, but the work goes faster when there are two hut builders—one to hold the bent-over saplings while the other ties the ends together.

Cooperation is to be found in every level of Mbuti society. Most bands have a complex internal affinity by patrilineage, but each nuclear family, living in its own hut, has lesser importance than the band as a whole does. Nowhere is this more noticeable than in the treatment of children. Babies are almost communal property, handed around to be admired and fondled, suckled by other women, or casually cuffed by the nearest adult whenever the infant crawls into trouble. As the child grows up, so the bond of the immediate nuclear family weakens still further. Young children and youths form associations of their own age groups, each group behaving and learning what is required of it. For the young there is the "bopi," a special playground where they begin imitative games. Small boys and girls pair off to play "house," the girl pretending to gather food in the bushes or to build a crude hut while the boy hunts for small game, a rat or a snail or some grubs. Sometimes they will fish in a stream—though curiously enough, fishing is an activity that adult pygmies seldom do—or the boy, pretending he is an Mbuti raiding a village, will creep silently into camp to steal a morsel of food, which he and his "wife" will cook together before they lie down and pretend to make love. For the boys, in particular, there are games designed to teach them forest skills. One boy will tie a large forest fruit to the end of a length of vine and stand whirling it around him about a foot above the

Shinnying up a tree trunk, a pygmy makes his way to a honey deposit.

ground. His playmates gather in a circle to fling small spears at the moving target, and to dodge any unsuccessful casts that come ricocheting across the circle. If the spear misses and sticks in the ground, its owner must jump forward to retrieve it and, like unsuccessful medieval knights at quintain, dodge the next whirling stroke of the target..

Similarly, in preparation for the honey season, there is the "honey swing," which Colin Turnbull has described as "a long heavy vine that reaches up on each side of the clearing to maybe fifty feet, but certainly to a good twenty. If one vine is not long enough, two or three are knotted together. The youths line up, and someone sits in the loop of the vine, his feet just dangling above the ground. He swings back and forth until he is really swinging well, then the game starts. As he swings up over the heads of the waiting youths, and begins to come down, one of them starts running hard. He reaches up and catches hold of one side of the vine, and sprinting as fast as he can he holds on as the swing begins to rise on its backward stroke. He gets swept off the ground, but not before he gives a final push with his feet. As he flies upward he swings his whole body forward and does a somersault, still holding on to the vine, over the head of the youth sitting in the loop. At this moment, if the timing is right, the swing begins to come down again. The pygmy who was sitting drops to the ground, and the somersaulting youth lands in the loop which, with luck, has just been left empty for him. By then he is flying forward, and up over the heads of the next in line. To do this you not only have to be very strong but you also have to have a very quick eye and a sharp sense of time."

Sometimes an older youth or a semiretired hunter will supervise a mock net hunt. The children take castoff fragments of old nets and try to hunt and trap their instructor, who imitates the different behavior of the forest creatures, whether antelope, pig, or leopard. Only when the youth is competent enough to be of real help will he be allowed to join the adult hunters at the nets, and even then he is not necessarily apprenticed to his father, because it is the entire band that matters and the novice may learn from any adult who is prepared to teach him.

Authority and social control by community action are among the more remarkable facets of life in an Mbuti band. There are no formal chiefs or headmen to rule over the band. Instead, cooperative opinion settles disputes and arranges overall policies. A particular issue may invoke the advice of the relevant expert; for example, the most skillful hunter may recommend in a question of hunting. But it is still the band as a whole, women included, that makes the final decision. For the net hunters this total cooperation is clearly a necessity, since without communal agreement their net hunting would fail. It is noticeable that when there is a quarrel within a net-hunter camp, most hunting activity ceases until the affair is settled, in itself a considerable spur to quick agreement. Discussion and argument is frank and vociferous, and the weapons of debate range from invective and sulking to mild ostracism, though by far the most effective is ridicule, applied either as an offensive tactic or as a humorous device to gain the good will of the other listeners. Occasionally, however, the normal process of discussion breaks down, and a serious rift threatens to disrupt the camp. At this stage a mediator, usually a respected elder or an outsider from another band, may be called in to adjudicate. Alternatively, the camp buffoon may intervene.

A pygmy woman, with her baby and all the necessities of life, is prepared to break camp and move to a new location. Instant mobility is a prime requisite of daily existence.

Men take turns with women in caring for small children. This group is listening to a storyteller relate a legend.

Every band has just such a clown, usually a young unmarried man who is also a hunter of considerable skill and thus generally respected. (Turnbull, however, when he had just gone to live in the forest with the pygmies and was still an incompetent hunter, found himself cast as a buffoon simple, a role he turned to good use, enabling him to press on more quickly with his anthropological studies.) The pygmy clown needs to be a person who is a jester at heart, for his role in the dispute is to maintain social cohesion by lampooning both contestants and easing the tension with his antics, or simply by acting as a lightning rod, taking all the blame on himself and grounding the dispute. Once this is done, it is up to the entire band to enter the general discussion and reach a united agreement.

Puberty brings a time of great celebration to an Mbuti band. It is a season when the girls occupy center stage in a ceremony that rejoices in their potential motherhood as well as introduces the youth of both sexes to their choice of future partners. The puberty festival, the "elima," begins soon after a girl has her first show of menstrual blood. At that time she selects her "bamelima," the group of girl friends with whom she wishes to share the celebration. Some of them may have already had their elima; others, who have not, will count the festival as their own. Together they withdraw to the special elima hut where they will live during the festival. There they will wear garlands of vine, decorate their bodies with white clay paint, sing together the special elima songs, and eat and wash separately from the rest of the band. By day they cluster together around a campfire or go for walks in the forest, chanting their elima songs of happiness to the trees or receiving instruction from one of the older women in the mysteries of womanhood, the treatments and potions that bring on comfortable childbirth, ample breast milk, and abortion if necessary. Longer journeys are made to the neighboring bands of Mbuti in order to involve them in the elima ceremony and introduce the young people to each other. For the elima has an explicit purpose of sexual and social experimentation. The elima hut is a place where the boys and girls can spend the night together enthusiastically making love, though the choice of partners is exercised by the bamelima. When in their own camp or on a visit to a neighboring band, the bamelima may suddenly make a foray on the boy of their choice, chasing him and beating him with light sticks. Any boy treated in this way is required to present himself that same evening at the elima hut. There he may be beaten again before he can lie with the girl who chooses him, and even then he must ask her permission before they make love. Contraception is practiced, for impregnation during the elima is not recorded and, indeed, would run counter to the purpose of the festival, which is to allow a temporary and uninhibited sampling. Naturally, it is the ambition of most girls to find their future husband during the elima, and as the festival draws to a close with general dancing and singing in the camp, the girls return to the protection of their mothers, who fend off frivolous suitors and expect a serious offer of marriage, which, in Mbuti terms, is no more than a request from a young hunter of proven ability that he and the girl may live together in their own hut.

A boy who has taken a strong fancy to a particular girl may take the initiative during the elima and approach the elima hut on his own without first being pursued and whipped by the girls. But this is to lay serious suit,

A bridesmaid, being prepared for her participation in a wedding ceremony, is painted with a black juice extracted from the fruit of gardenias.

and he must run the gauntlet of the older women lined up to pelt him with pebbles and other missiles in an attempt to bar his passage. If he wins through to the hut, he must then ask the girl's consent, perhaps endure further whipping, and if accepted must stay within the hut for the rest of the festival because he is now regarded as formally betrothed.

Marriages can also be arranged without an elima celebration, but only with the approval of the entire band. As in the elima, it is really the mutual affection between the boy and girl that is valued most highly, though the band as an economic unit is also concerned. The band members must be satisfied that the boy can hunt skillfully, or when the girl is transferring to another band to join her husband, that she will fit in with her new colleagues. Group harmony, once again, is the overriding concern.

The final overseer of all Mbuti life is the forest itself. To the Mbuti the Ituri forest is a living, breathing, watching creation that can be pleased or piqued by their actions, generous if well treated, stingy if misused. Their forest is not a god, as it is not directly worshiped. Rather, it is a benevolent parent of a rather distant affinity and exceptional power. The Mbuti's whole lives are infused with an awareness of the forest's presence about them, an awareness that is acknowledged by the father of an Mbuti baby during the very first days of his child's life. "At that time," writes Turnbull, when the father sees that the delivery is near, "he goes off into the forest and selects the finest *esele* or *le'engbe* vine he can find, cuts off about eighteen inches of the bark, and goes to soak it in a clear stream. First of all he wraps it around his shin, as though his leg were the core of the vine, and

OVERLEAF: *A pygmy hunting party carrying nets, bows and arrows, and spears moves through the forest. At least seven families, each with its own net, usually compose a hunting group. Eventually all the nets are joined to create a huge game trap.*
COLIN TURNBULL

A scene during the elima, the happy puberty festival, when bamelima, or groups of pygmy girls, help one or more of their members celebrate their preparations for motherhood.

PHOTO RESEARCHERS, LOUIS RENAULT

with a long-bladed knife he scrapes off the outer bark. This leaves a soft, white, pulpy inner layer. After soaking it for twelve hours or so it is even softer. He then takes it and lays it on a fallen tree trunk, which has been prepared by careful scraping so that it offers a smooth, hard surface. He takes the solid end of an elephant tusk, which he uses like a hammer, and begins beating the bark. . . . After a while his narrow strip of bark is widened out to make a piece of beautifully white, supple bark cloth about two feet square. He makes sure it is perfect and that he has not hammered any patches too thin, then he stretches it out on the roof of his hut to dry. When it is dry his wife may take gardenia fruit and use the juice to draw simple patterns. The juice leaves a rich blue-black stain on the white cloth. When the baby is born, it will be lovingly wrapped in this cloth; its first gift, not from its parents, but from the forest.

"After birth, that very same day, the father goes off again and cuts three-foot lengths of another thick vine, and brings them back to camp carefully bound so that both ends of each length are pointing up. As he unties them and lets one end down, juice pours out just like water. The baby's first bath is in this forest water. Not from the sky, but water from the forest itself."

The guardian role of the forest will reappear again and again throughout the life of a young Mbuti. As an infant he is girdled with a belt of liana hung with small slivers of forest wood in order to place him in the correct relationship to the surrounding forest. The girls of the bamelima, when they sing their song of happiness in the forest, chant out a line and then wait respectfully for the echo. A young hunter with his first major success is marked with three tiny slits cut vertically in the skin of his forehead. The flesh beneath is gouged out, and into the cavity is rubbed a paste of ash and forest herbs, a visible sign of the presence of the forest within the body of the man. Unnecessary noise, needless destruction of plants, uncouth behavior — all are considered to be insulting to the forest. When a hunting party sets out, it is only courteous to light a fire of smoking leaves to announce the hunt to the forest; and when a pygmy is excessively happy, he sees nothing strange in going by himself to a woodland glade and dancing there with the forest as his partner.

Perhaps the most eloquent instance of the Mbuti's respect for their forest is their legend of the "Bird that Sang the Most Beautiful Song that the Great Forest had ever known." Told by Mbuti archer hunters to Anne Putnam, it recounts how "one day a pygmy child heard this Beautiful Song and searched for the bird that could sing so wonderfully. He found it and praised its song. The bird flew down and perched on the boy's head and the boy brought it back to the pygmy camp. His father saw the bird and praised it, and when it sang told the boy to give it some food. The bird then flew off. The next day the boy heard the song and searched until he found the bird again, and once again brought it back to the camp. This happened three times, and the last time the father took the bird away from the boy and said, 'Now you go off and leave me. Leave this camp and go away to another; go! go!' The young pygmy left his father, and went away to another camp. When he was alone, the father took the Bird, the Bird that sang the most Beautiful Song that the Great Forest had ever heard, and he killed the Bird. And he killed the Song. And no sooner had he killed the Bird than

Worn on wrists and ankles, bells like these from the Ekon district of southern Cameroon provide a jangling accompaniment to pygmy dances.

he himself dropped down dead, completely dead, for ever. *Basi* [That is all]."

The power of sound to communicate with their forest guardian is one of the strongest beliefs of the Mbuti. In times of distress—when hunting is bad, sickness is in camp, or a pygmy has died—the Mbuti turn to the "molimo," the ceremony of song, to call the forest's attention to their plight. They do not sing fearfully to appease the forest's wrath or to turn aside its malice, but happily in order to harmonize their relationship to the forest and draw its natural benevolence back to them. A hunting molimo may last from a couple of weeks to a month, with songs no more sophisticated than simple phrases like "The forest is good, the forest is kind," sung over and over again by the menfolk gathered around the molimo fire. In the usual course of events the game animals will return to the vicinity of the camp during this time when there is no hunting, and so the Mbuti are well satisfied with the results of their molimo. But after the death of a pygmy, particularly if the dead person was well loved by his companions and his loss is deeply felt, the band holds a more complex molimo and brings forth the molimo trumpet. The trumpet is, in effect, a large speaking tube made of forest wood, which uses the power of its sound to act as a medium between the forest and its children. The trumpet has a spirit of its own, and all year long, unless it is needed, it lies quietly hidden in the forest, submerged in a stream or concealed high up in a tree. Special pygmy signs, usually a vine draped across the path, warn the passer-by that he should avoid the trumpet's resting place; women especially should keep clear, as the molimo trumpet is reserved for male use. When it is needed, the trumpet is fetched from its sanctuary by the men and carried to the Mbuti camp. There it is aroused and encouraged by being rubbed with ashes and earth. It "smokes" when hot coals and smoldering leaves are placed near its mouth, and the smoke is inhaled along the tube. It "drinks" by being lowered into any stream it crosses.

Once the women have retired to their huts, the menfolk begin to "play" the trumpet, sometimes over the campfire, sometimes away in the forest in the hands of a young man with a particularly good voice. The trumpet relays and echoes the molimo songs that will awaken and rejoice the forest. Therefore, it must be played melodiously and well, and in such a way that the whole forest can listen and be pleased. In return, it brings the essence of the forest back to the men, who touch the trumpet to draw its strength and inspiration as they dance around the special molimo fire or gyrate wildly, holding it as a phallic symbol representing the power of the life force in the forest. As the festival approaches its climax, after several weeks in which the nights have been spent in dancing and singing, an extraordinary vision appears. An old woman, sometimes assisted by handmaidens, enters the circle of dancers and attempts to stamp out the vital molimo fire. Symbolically, she binds the men with light fetters of vine and, as they lie helpless, dances around and through the fire to destroy it. The men escape their bonds and dance wildly to revive the embers into flame with motions that are frantically erotic. Time and again the old woman and her assistants attack the fire and are defeated, because it is the crone who is now the symbol of the life force, a creature who gave birth to life and now seeks to destroy it.

At dawn, toward the end of the molimo, the trumpet reappears in a new

Amid the noise of drums, the ritual doctor arrives at an initiation ceremony to prepare eligible pygmy boys for their circumcision ordeal.
COLIN TURNBULL

89

COLIN TURNBULL

Pygmies help a villager build his house. The villagers like to hire pygmies for this job because the materials, like the pygmies, are of the forest. Thus the forest gods are not as likely to be disturbed.

role—as an impartial judge of the members of the band. Carried by young men dressed in forest leaves and hidden by branches, the molimo trumpet is taken around the camp. Symbolically, it visits each hut, and outside the huts of known troublemakers there is uproar. The youths beat on the hut with their branches, tear off leaves, and only retreat when the elders call out to them to go away. Diplomatically, the troublemaker himself is not directly chastised, but, by association, his misdemeanors are emphasized by the whole band together, using the trumpet to represent the spirit of the forest that rules their life. Finally, as the festival draws to a close after a month or more of singing and dancing, the trumpet retreats back to the forest. The molimo fire is finally stamped out, and the Mbuti go on with their lives, confident that the forest has been pleased and that life has been returned to a happy equilibrium. Mourning for the dead man, which good taste restricts to his own family, is over. His hut is pulled down over his corpse, and with their next move the camp will be abandoned to the forest.

The latest in a long line of misconceptions about the Mbuti was formulated by missionaries, administrators, and others who visited the forest.

Because they contacted the Mbuti via village intermediaries, they gained the impression that the pygmies were bondservants to the full-sized villagers. It was observed that when the Mbuti came out of the forest to visit the villages, they begged for food, particularly for plantains, which they themselves do not cultivate and for which they have a craving. In the villages they bartered meat and occasional offerings of ivory for iron knives, metal pots, and iron arrowheads; and they sold their labor, so that it was not uncommon to see Mbuti women pounding corn for village mistresses or Mbuti men cutting wood in the forest for village overseers. Even more striking were the ceremonies by which the villagers apparently formalized the servant status of individual Mbuti men or their families. Mbuti youths were encouraged to join in initiation ceremonies alongside village youths. Good service by a pygmy hunter was rewarded with special gifts; and with an excess of paternal benevolence, village "masters" even arranged marriages between pygmy "servants." Confident of a particular Mbuti's fealty, the villager would match him or his son with the unmarried daughter of an Mbuti family "owned" by another villager, pay the bride price, and confidently expect the union to produce children who would hunt and provide for the master.

But Turnbull's expedition into the forest with the Mbuti revealed that their master-servant performance was something of a sham. He found that the pygmies were not only duping the villagers, but enjoyed doing so. The pygmies regarded the whole matter of village initiation ceremonies and village-arranged marriages as something of a farce. They went to the villages because life there was a change from life in the forest, the diet was tempting, and the villagers were openhanded with their bribes. But as soon as the villagers began to demand real work in exchange for their gifts, the pygmies merely disappeared back into their forests where they could not be followed. In effect, the pygmies were prepared to stay only as long as it suited them. Moreover, if the villagers would not give them bananas, it was a simple matter for the Mbuti to raid the plantations and steal whatever they wanted. Few villagers even detected the raiders, let alone managed to track down the culprits. Tongue in cheek, the Mbuti were contracting marriages, undergoing initiations, and accepting servant status with different masters in different villages, all on an "exclusive basis." Being excellent linguists, they had even learned the several dialects necessary to communicate with communities in various parts of the forest.

More recent anthropologist opinion now believes that it is not so much the Mbuti who depend on the villagers, as the other way around. The Mbuti do not really need the village products at all. They can cook the forest food in leaf containers, use sharp bamboo or stone as cutting implements, and prefer fire-hardened poisoned arrows to the more expensive metal-tipped variety. If anything, it is the villager who is dependent: for meat from game animals to supplement his diet, for forest products that he is unable to locate or gather, and in time of war for advance warning of enemy movements from his Mbuti scouts. In fine, the villager stands on alien ground when he comes to the Ituri, and he needs the Mbuti to cushion the contact with the unfriendly forest.

Typically, the Mbuti see the deception they practice on the villagers as a source of lighthearted amusement. With impish delight, they boast of their

Pictures like this of a strong village chief and his pygmy vassal belie their true relationship. It is now realized that the villager is dependent on the pygmy, who requires only the forest for his survival.

91

ruses, and in their forest camps raise gales of laughter by imitating the gait of a villager or holding mock village initiation ceremonies. As Schweinfurth noted, there is a touch of the professional comedian in a pygmy, the shrewdness to capitalize on his strange appearance when in the company of "real people," as he calls them. But it is the controlled comedy routine of an experienced trouper, and behind his clowning antics the Mbuti is watching and calculating the effect of his performance. He is, above all, an opportunist who molds himself in the image expected of him—a grasshopper war dance for Schweinfurth or the apparently loyal retainer for a village headman. The secret lies in the Mbuti's adaptability and informality. When the villagers want to negotiate with the headman of an Mbuti band, the pygmies select their shrewdest businessman and obligingly promote him for the day. The moment the villagers are gone, the "headman" returns to his normal democratic status. Similarly, when in recent years a Hollywood film producer came to the forest to film pygmies crossing streams by the "pygmy method" of swinging across on a vine, the local Mbuti band, who had never in their lives seen such a thing, happily adapted their honey-swing technique for the occasion. Thereafter they gladly repeated the trick for any tourist who came to watch, though one skeptical observer calculated that to achieve a parabola sufficient to cross a river of any size, the pygmies would need to swing from a tree nearly as tall as the Eiffel Tower. This easygoing informality of the Mbuti can be surprising as well as misleading. A number of anthropologists had carefully expressed the notion that the molimo trumpet is made of special forest wood because it must embody the spirit of the forest. But then a band of Mbuti dumfounded the scholars by raiding a road-building site and stealing drainpipe to use as the molimo trumpet. The important factor, they blandly explained, was that the trumpet should make an excellent sound, not that it should be made of a particular wood.

Underlying this bantering relationship with the "real people" is the protective pygmy ethos that the advantage of wit and cunning lies always with the person who is small. The Mbuti point with devastating logic to the example of the forest, where the smaller animals survive by being cleverer than the larger beasts. Only the monkey, they say, can match the trickery of a pygmy, and in their folk tales even the most wicked demon is hoodwinked by his quick-witted pygmy opponent. It is this cheerful self-confidence, this pride in their ability to meet the situation, that is the psychological counterpoint to the physical protection the Ituri forest affords them. Since the 1930's the roadways in the Ituri have done much to break down the isolation of the region and have threatened to weaken the protective shield of the forest. But as yet the balance has not been altered too drastically. Recent observations suggest that the pygmies may have begun to cluster more regularly around the native villages, which in turn can draw confidence from the new roadways and no longer feel threatened by the encroaching equatorial forest. Inevitably, the pygmies have begun to absorb more outside influences, whether from the villagers or from curious tourists and scientists. On the other hand, they have also received benefits, particularly medical ones, and their culture, hardy and flexible, is neither so vulnerable nor so badly depleted that it may not yet survive the alien encroachment of the modern world.

The Life of Primitive Man

Vital Concerns

For some 400,000 years, since man first learned to use it, fire has been one of his most valuable possessions. Taken largely for granted by civilized peoples, it still plays a fundamental role in the day-by-day struggle for survival among less complex groups like the cave-dwelling Tasadays of the Philippines (above), providing such elemental necessities as warmth and protection against predator beasts. The satisfying of other needs—achieved with storehouses of knowledge accumulated by experience and sharpened by reason—is shown on the following pages. By the careful observation of nature, primitive societies so efficiently organized their economic pursuits that they were able to reach and maintain an equilibrium with their environments, no matter how difficult they were.

In some societies, anything edible and at hand is included in the diet. Other groups have traditionally limited tastes. But all hunting and fishing peoples have developed the weapons and skills necessary to keep their people fed. At right, a pygmy hunter, stalking a monkey in the African forest, takes aim with his short bow and poisoned arrow. On Little Diomede Island in the Bering Strait, at far right, an Eskimo, with a string of captured auklets as decoys, uses a hand net to snare another one.

The Camayura Indian of Brazil's Mato Grosso, left, got his fish by damming the arm of a lake to lower its level, poisoning the water with an extract of timbo bark, then using arrows and nets to catch the fish when they surfaced for air. With equal skill, combining ingenuity and a familiarity with the refraction of light by water, the Australian Aborigine at right goes after a deepwater fish with a long spear.

The ability to handle reindeer, the source of food and materials for articles of clothing, is all-important to the Lapps. The man at left, who has just cut one animal from the herd, began to learn the skill of lassoing in childhood games.

On the Great Plains of the United States, Indian hunters, as pictured by the artist George Catlin, learned to use coyote and other animal skins as disguises in order to creep close enough, downwind, to the buffalo herds to kill one of the animals.

The Japanese hand scroll of about
1840, above, shows Ainu villagers
watching somewhat warily as their
hunters capture a bear cub—the
central object of their traditional
ceremony, the Bear Festival, when
the animal is ritually killed.

At right, an early-nineteenth-century
print depicts the Australian
Aborigines' method of hunting
opossum. A fire is built in a lower
hole of a tree, its smoke forcing the
opossum out of an upper hole,
where it is then clubbed to death.

OVERLEAF: *Feuds or the need for prestige, captives, or booty often led to war, but a principal reason was the protection of a group's hunting grounds. The awesome battle scene of New Guinea Dani is really a posturing of neighboring groups asserting their territorial rights. Few, if any, casualties occur, and the face-off averts more serious hostilities.*

Agriculture, developed originally by primitive hunters and gatherers, is still regarded by the less complex societies as susceptible to supernatural influences. Yet the skill and the knowledge of soils, water, vegetation, and nature's cycles acquired by groups like the Hopis (hoeing corn in the Arizona desert, left), the Bororos (pounding sorghum in Nigeria, opposite), and the Cunas (gathering melons and nuts in Panama, below) have made them successful farmers and stewards of their lands.

The first clothing was skins, but by approximately 10,000 years ago, the weaving of grasses and other local materials was developed in many parts of the world to fashion finer garments as well as utilitarian objects. At left, a Maori woman weaves a cloak from dyed flax.

Among primitive societies, local materials, too, serve as cheap, accessible and functional building materials for homes and other structures. The Fiji Islanders at left are lashing woven palm fronds as roof thatching to the framework of a house, which they have built in half a day. At right is a complex long house of the Land Dyaks of Sarawak. Almost 1,000 people are sheltered in the individual family rooms within the huge structure.

3

The Cunas of Golden Castile

Pre-Columbian Coclé gold: a disk with a warrior and alligator god
BROOKLYN MUSEUM

Anthropologically as well as geographically, the Isthmus of Panama was something of a midpoint of the pre-Columbian Western Hemisphere. Situated between the high cultures of the Mayas and Aztecs to the north and the Incas to the south, its inhabitants and their ways of life shared links with the Circum-Caribbean cultures of the West Indies, and closest of all, with the Chibcha-speaking peoples of what would later become Colombia. Yet the native society that evolved in this unique pivotal location in the Americas was not quite like that of any of its neighbors. Aboriginal Panama was a pattern of small chiefdoms whose social and political form mingled a superficial flamboyance with what were, in the last analysis, very unassuming territorial ambitions. Compared to the empires of the Aztecs or Incas, the chiefdoms of Panama were very small indeed; but they had a pretention to grandeur that was successfully sustained until the coming of the Spanish conquistadors.

The isthmus was scarcely an encouraging region in which to found a great civilization. The narrow neck of Panama curves like a steel meathook, an S shape fallen on its back, with the Gulf of Panama caught within its south-facing bend and the Mosquito Gulf on the opposite coast. The spine of the land is a series of volcanic ridges so severely eroded and faulted that there is very little level ground fit for agriculture. These upland ridges lie closer to the northern, or Caribbean, shore of the isthmus, where the northeast trades blow steadily for eight months of the year, bringing almost daily rain showers. Dampness, all-pervading and constant, is the most noticeable feature of the climate. When a tropical cyclone or an easterly front hovers over the isthmus, the sky stays overcast for days on end, releasing prolonged rainstorms that saturate the countryside and turn narrow footpaths into mazes of rivulets. The short, turbulent streams that drain the cordillera—nearly five hundred of them—carry the surface run-off to the adjacent coasts, where the sudden influx of fresh water makes the sea water noticeably less salty.

The streams have dissected the terrain savagely, slicing into weakened rock strata and carving out a jumble of interlocking valleys and glens. The volcanic soils, their nutrients leached out by the sinkwater, offer poor

105

A San Blas Cuna Indian of today with a golden nose ornament

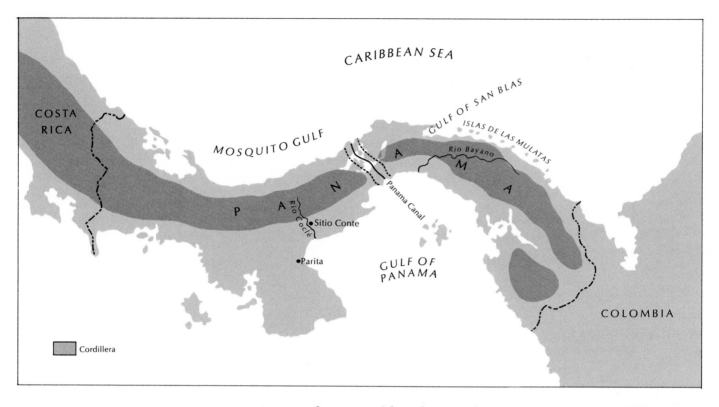

sustenance for crops. After three or four years, if it is not fertilized, the soil is too exhausted to give a good yield, and the fields must be abandoned. Much of the cordillera is still left to primary tropical forest, a close association of plant growth that rises story by story from the lowly ground ferns and shrubs through layers of softwoods, myrtles, rubber trees, and palms to a final canopy of majestic trees up to ninety feet high. The overall impression is an intense, shaded green, like the interior of a cathedral where shafts of green-tinted light penetrate to the buttressed roots of the larger trees, separated from each other by a carpet of dead and rotting vegetable debris. Overhead the branches are festooned with lichens, airborne orchids, and other parasitic growths, some with enormous fan-shaped leaves. In this unrelieved greenery almost the only patches of bright color are the occasional flowers of the climbing lianas, slowly strangling the host trees to death in their embrace.

The traces of the native society that once thrived in and around this unlikely environment have been difficult to unravel. Chroniclers of the Spanish conquest of the early sixteenth century spoke of elegant chiefs who traveled their domains in hammocks carried by teams of porters, of native noblemen dressed in gold-plated clothing, of towns and villages where now there is little more than scrubland. But the tales of the Spaniards seemed far-fetched, perhaps intended as propaganda to attract new settlers from the Old World. In succeeding generations, critics pointed out that few of the chroniclers had ever visited Panama. Even their name for the region was too bombastic: they had called it Castilla del Oro—Golden Castile—and the whole notion smacked of wild dreams instead of hard reality.

And yet there was always a nagging streak of truth to their stories. The writers had a habit of giving precise names to the towns and the Indian leaders of whom they spoke, of listing minute details of the golden loot seized in the four quick Spanish campaigns that subdued the native Panamanians, and of describing an aboriginal society whose habits were sometimes so unusual as to be difficult to invent. Over the years a few items of specific evidence turned up, hinting that perhaps the Spanish chroniclers had been right. In the 1850's the governor of the Bank of England noted a steady trickle of gold bullion flowing into London from Panama. It was a modest amount, several thousand pounds a year, but far more than could be expected from the poor and little-known republic. Then, too, there were reports of Indian graves known as "huacas," which were hidden in the hills and said to contain heaps of gold and jewelry. General Francisco Morazán, the erstwhile president of the short-lived Republic of the United States of Central America of the 1830's, even formed a company to exploit the graves, but the venture came to nothing when its employees found themselves unable to penetrate the interior.

Some of the rumors were undoubtedly exaggerated, but during a railway building boom in the second half of the nineteenth century, work gangs digging cuts for the new tracks reported several finds of gold jewelry buried in the soil. Other caches almost certainly were found and never reported to the authorities. Finally, in 1914, came the opening of the Panama Canal and its attendant publicity. Displays of early Panamanian pottery were organized; the intelligence section of the United States Army prepared a secret handbook about the isthmus for officers who might have to campaign there; and geologists, surveyors, and map makers started to probe the little-known cordillera. From an archeological point of view, it

Late in the 17th century, after they had fled from the Europeans to Panama's mountainous interior, Cunas were pictured, below, by the Englishman Lionel Wafer as they sat in council and smoked, while one of them reclined outside in a hammock.

A New Voyage . . . . , LIONEL WAFER, LONDON, 1699

was obviously high time for a serious investigation of Panama's aboriginal culture.

Fortunately for posterity, the spearhead of the inquiry—when it finally did come in 1930—was an archeological expedition that for its day was a model of care and scholarship. It was launched by the Peabody Museum at Harvard, and the site chosen for the dig lay on the banks of the Rio Grande de Coclé, fifteen miles inland and about seventy miles southwest of the Canal. There were strong indications that the project would be a success: minor archeological discoveries had already been made a little distance upstream, and a close study of the Spanish chronicles had revealed that the area had once been the center of a significant chiefdom. Most tantalizing of all, the Rio Coclé had periodically scoured its eastern bank, exposing native artifacts embedded in the wall of the river like currants in a fruitcake.

The Peabody team conducted three years of intensive digging, calling their site Sitio Conte after the local landowners, the Conte family. A series of trenches were cut near the riverbank at the point where previous finds had been made, and a number of isolated excavations were also undertaken. This work produced no less than fifty-nine Indian graves, some of them large enough to contain ten or fifteen bodies, and another thirty-two caches of assorted pre-Columbian material. It gave the most complete picture up to that time of a Panamanian chiefdom just prior to the arrival of the Spaniards.

The first point immediately obvious was that the chroniclers' Golden Castile was not such an inappropriate name at that. Sitio Conte's graves yielded literally hundreds of gold objects. Most of them were small gold beads, but there were also bracelets, rings, necklaces, nose ornaments, and headbands. There were golden greaves for men's shins, golden cuffs for their wrists, and gold helmets for their heads. Some items were inlaid with gold;

This Coclé grave, one of those laid bare at Sitio Conte by Peabody Museum archeologists, contained the remains of three persons, as well as coarse, undecorated pottery and a bracelet of shark's teeth on the wrist of one of the skeletons.

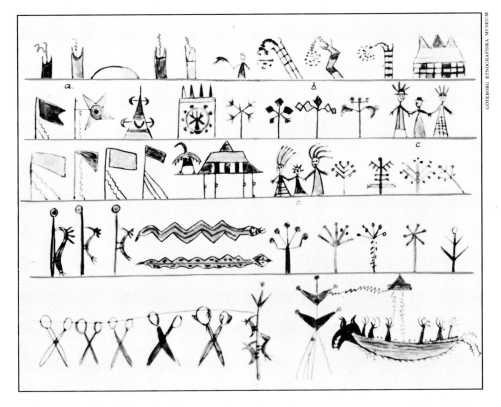

Cuna picture writing was formerly done on thin pieces of wood. Here, a deceased man is shown on his journey after death, being escorted through various obstacles by tutelary spirits in feathered headdresses.

others, particularly precious and semiprecious gems, were set in golden mounts. A popular form of jewelry had been pendants, apparently worn from chains hung around the neck or dangling from clothes and possessions. There were pendants shaped like human effigies, bar pendants, and winged pendants. Many of them were in the shape of animals, usually stylized, and some had agates, quartz, and emeralds set in gold. In these pieces the stone formed the body of the animal, while the gold setting represented the head. The animal motifs included frog-headed crocodiles, armadillos, toads, crabs, bats, curly-tailed monkeys, birds, and a strange-looking dog that seemed to be sitting on its haunches and begging.

When this treasure was taken back to the United States for chemical and microscopic analysis, the importance of gold to the original inhabitants of Sitio Conte became even more impressive. It turned out that nearly all the gold had been gathered locally, almost certainly from gold-bearing streams in the cordillera (though one item, a golden nose ornament, had probably come from Ecuador), and that the supply of Coclé gold nowhere near met the natives' demand for finery. The aboriginal goldsmiths had known how to harden or soften gold to their purposes and how to weld, solder, and clinch the shapes they wanted. But their main concern had apparently been to stretch their gold stock to its utmost limits. They had debased it with large quantities of copper to produce an alloy known as "tumbaga," and they had employed every device to display their bullion to best advantage. Comparatively worthless wooden cores had been given an illusory golden sheath, and the native jewelers had gold-plated less precious metals. It was sheer gilt acreage that mattered, not the quality of the workmanship. The reverse sides and the inner facets of gold ornaments were usually left raw and unfinished from the casting mold, but the out-

Surviving pre-Columbian works of gold, mostly found in graves, suggest the huge wealth in art melted down by the Spaniards. This ornament, with personal significance to its wearer, combines bird and animal features with human elements.

ward side was buffed and polished to a high sheen. How this superb polishing was achieved no modern expert could understand. Very possibly it was done with the help of a vegetable solution. Whatever the process, the result was that most of the objects retrieved from the damp soil of Sitio Conte had smooth and glittering surfaces.

The style and composition of the graves also told the researchers a good deal about the grandiose notions of the early Panamanians. The most important graves were massive undertakings. Up to ten feet deep and large enough to contain as many as twenty-two bodies, their digging with primitive stone tools must have required great toil. Even the Peabody workers had to use pickaxes to break up the solidified soil when they wished to refill the trenches that they had dug only a few weeks earlier. Clearly the burial of a Panamanian Indian chief had been a very spectacular affair. The graves were rectangular and fashioned with slightly sloping sides. The floor was covered with a layer of broken pottery and sometimes sprinkled with sand, while the sides of the grave were lined with cloth. Next, stone slabs had been lowered into the pit to form a crude flagstone floor, on top of which were arranged the bodies of the chief's sacrificial victims. It was not clear whether these victims, both men and women, had died previously or had been buried alive. Spanish reports spoke of high bacchanalia in which the dead man's entourage got so drunk on "chicha," the native beer, that they climbed into the grave and stayed there while the other revelers threw in piles of brushwood so that the befuddled victims suffocated to death. But in at least one of the Coclé graves the arrangement of the bodies, all face downward and laid out in neat rows, indicated that the victims, probably having taken poison, were already dead when they were interred with their chief. Their leader occupied the center of the funeral array and had apparently been seated on some sort of stool or throne under a canopy, because when the grave was opened up, the chief's bones were found to have collapsed in a pile in the middle of the pit among the skeletons of his retainers.

Funeral furnishings had been heaped into the grave in lavish quantities. Besides the jewelry worn by the chief and his followers, there were weapons and fabrics, household articles, pottery and food, tools and ceremonial objects. There was no special pattern to the way these offerings had been placed in the grave. They seemed to have been added merely in random manner, and in the case of pottery they sometimes filled the grave to a depth of five or six layers of broken jars. Oddly enough, no particular sanctity was attached to the burial offerings, and they were not regarded as inviolate. Several of the chiefs' graves had been dug up for later burials, reflecting the natives' desire to utilize their material wealth to the full. When this had happened, the old funeral goods had been deliberately salvaged and then reused for the new ceremony.

By a lucky stroke the Spaniards themselves had been able to witness a dead chief readied for his formal burial. In 1519 a conquistador raiding column surprised the Indian settlement near Coclé shortly after its ruler, the important chief Parita, had died. To the delight and amazement of the looting soldiers, they found the dead chief laid out in his golden funerary robes with two lesser chiefs beside him. The corpses were arranged in a sort of funeral parlor, and according to Samuel K. Lothrop, who led the Peabody investigations, the Spaniards found the three bodies "each enveloped in cloth bundles of many layers and slung in hammocks of straw. These hammocks were of very fine workmanship and themselves constituted the outer covering and were secured about the bodies with cords of agave. Next came wrappings of fine mantles with elaborate decorations, held in place by cords of cotton. Inside was another layer of even finer mantles secured with ropes made of human hair. Having torn off these coverings the Spaniards now beheld the body of Parita himself, as they were informed by one of his attendants. His corpse had been dried by fire.

"Parita had been laid out for burial in his finest array. On his head was 'a great basin of gold like a casque,' around his neck were four or five necklaces of gold, his arms and legs were encased in tubes of gold, his chest and shoulders were covered with plates and medals of gold, around his waist was a golden belt from which hung bells of the same metal. In short he appeared to wear a golden coat of mail. At his feet lay the body of a woman and at his head a second, both adorned with many fine ornaments of gold. The other two chiefs were wrapped up in the same manner and embellished with golden jewelry only less elegant than that of Parita."

Watching over these princely corpses were a score or so of unfortunate victims, warriors from the neighboring chiefdoms who had been captured,

In this 1590 engraving by De Bry, Balboa and his men quarrel over the division of a tribute of gold brought to them by Panama Indians.

trussed up, and lashed by the throat to the house beams to await their ceremonial death at the graveside the next day.

When the conquistadors arrived in Panama, they found that the customs and political structures on the isthmus were by no means all identical. Indeed, some of the peoples spoke different languages, and the Spaniards had difficulty procuring guides and interpreters to take them across tribal boundaries. Nevertheless, most of the native societies included four distinct classes. At the top were the great chiefs called "saco" in the Cueva language, or "quevi" in Guaymi, the second principal tongue of the isthmus. It was the saco who occupied pride of place in the graves opened by Lothrop and his colleagues of the Peabody. The saco had obviously lived in great style and considerable opulence. The archeologists found delicate carvings of bone and ivory made from the ribs of sea cows and the teeth of sperm whales; mirrors constructed of shards of pyrite set on a flat backing plate (sometimes with chicle gum for glue); bone combs, traces of featherwork, and piles of body jewelry made from shells, animals' teeth, and decorative stone. The chiefs, according to the Spanish accounts, had been surrounded by numerous wives and retainers. Their power was absolute. They decided all domestic and foreign policy, administered their own laws, and in certain cases even executed the convicted criminals, dashing their brains out with a club and perhaps thrusting one or two spears into the body as well. Every saco was usually based in his main township, which held several other settlements in fief. On his accession to the throne, usually by right of lineage, it was customary for all the saco's wealthiest subjects to parade before him and offer gifts, especially the gold items like those found in the huacas. One of the saco's first official acts was to select his personal emblem, which was often a symbolic animal figure such as a frog; this emblem was thenceforth marked on all his property, his golden regalia, his slaves and vassals, and in addition it was tattooed on the body of the king himself so that it became his personal livery.

Beneath the saco was a class of nobility or subchiefs known as "cabra." They were essentially a political-military caste, generally selected for their bravery in battle or for their outstanding administrative ability. Sons of cabra could inherit the same rank but had to devote themselves to the military service of their lord. Warfare, in fact, was endemic to the whole aboriginal culture. It was conducted in a mannered but bloodthirsty fashion. Challenges were issued and accepted by rival chiefs; native armies marched to war behind pipes and drums, equipped with clubs and long, vicious pikes, often embellished with cutting edges of swordfish or shark teeth or tipped with stingray spines, which caused a wound to fester. Bows and arrows were used only for hunting, the real war projectile being the dart. Made from cane or jet-black palmwood, the darts were hurled from spear throwers with enough force to run a man through. Some darts were pierced with small holes so that they gave a shrill whistle as they flew, in order to strike terror among the ranks of the foe. A form of body armor designed like a long quilted cotton coat was available but was not always used, since warfare was considered a method of enhancing prestige by conspicuous bravery (less sportingly the Spaniards adopted the quilt armor as cooler than and at least as effective against lightweight arrows as their own steel armor). Ambitious Indian warriors preferred to go into battle dressed in

Another De Bry view of the Spanish conquest shows treed Indians desperately holding off the Europeans with rocks, spears, arrows, and a bucket of water, as other Spaniards chop away at the tree.

India Occidentalis, DE BRY, 1590

112

brilliant finery so that they would catch the eye of the enemy as well as demonstrate their prowess to their own commander. The latter was expected to know his trade. Indian war leaders were trained in battle maneuvers and knew how to pick good ambush sites. Nor were they averse to sending special agents to be captured by the enemy in order to implant false information while they were being tortured.

Commoners, the third rank of native society, were seldom mentioned in the Spanish chronicles. But presumably they occupied themselves with the more humdrum affairs of life, building the wooden native houses with their steeply pitched thatched roofs like dunces' hats, and clearing the scrubland around the settlements to raise crops of maize, pepper, cassava, squashes, and yucca. Apparently they succeeded in destroying a considerable amount of the natural vegetation, for when the Spaniards passed by Coclé they noted that the land around the native settlements was open country, excellent ground for their cavalry, though the settlements themselves were usually fortified by a triple ring of thorn hedge and palisade and an outer defensive ditch.

Almost certainly the native artisans would also have been commoners. Sitio Conte yielded up a vast quantity of pottery, some of it quite finely made into bowls, plates, and long-necked pitchers. But the real distinction of the native ceramic was its color decoration. The vessels were coated with a varnish, probably copal, apparently intended to preserve the vivid designs of monstrous beasts and intricate scrollwork executed on the pottery in black and brown paints as well as shades of red, purple, and green. The effect was very arresting, a polychrome variety of patterns and shapes that enhanced the functional pottery of everyday life. The native textiles repeated this contrast between design and décor. The workmanship was a rather loose open weave, competent without being particularly outstanding. But the bright colors and bold designs greatly improved the appearance of such items as hammocks—which, it is interesting to note, were of solid cloth rather than open net—and the loose shifts of the chiefs, which were hung with gold plaques. Tradition rather than inability kept native cloth weaving at its relatively modest level, because skilled techniques were certainly not lacking. The Indians wove excellent wicker panniers and trays from pliant cane, and their basketwork was often watertight.

The pedestaled pottery vessel with a bird shape (perhaps a vulture), above, and the bowl with an alligator god motif, below, are from the Veraguas area of Parita's rule.
BOTH: MUSEUM OF THE AMERICAN INDIAN

Commoners, too, would have undertaken the other basic tasks of the natives' economy. They fished in the rivers with nets made from the bark of the mahoe tree, hunted in the forests with bow and arrow or used bird snares and nets, and gathered salt from the coastal swamps. Salt was a major article of commerce over short distances, and some long-range trade was also undertaken, the goods being transported in large dugout canoes or by files of porters with carrying poles placed like yokes across their shoulders. Gold, hammocks, raw cotton, and thread, as well as slaves, would have been well worth trading over considerable distances; and the trade evidently had an enormous scope, for the Spaniards found Central American Indians who had heard of the sailing rafts of Ecuador, and one chief actually modeled a miniature llama in clay to demonstrate to his interrogator the principal beast of burden in the Andes.

The lowest of the low in native society were the "pacos," the slaves. They formed the fourth and last category in the isthmian class structure

The unique Indian method of bloodletting by shooting small arrows into the flesh, hoping to strike a vein, appalled Lionel Wafer, although he was impressed by the Cuna shamans' use of medicinal herbs.

and were for the most part prisoners of war. Their life was a hard one because they were required to perform the most menial tasks and could be recognized instantly by the property mark of their master branded or tattooed on their faces, and perhaps by a missing front tooth deliberately knocked out as another indication of their slave status. Among the pacos were two special categories: the "carates," who were litter bearers trained to carry their master on his journeys and were recruited mostly from victims of a peculiar skin disease that left their skin rough and scaly; and a second group, the "camayoa," who were professional homosexual male slaves. These last were dressed in women's clothes and kept in their owner's house to perform traditionally feminine tasks such as spinning and housework. Overt homosexual behavior was apparently regarded as normal, for the chiefs expected personal loyalty from the camayoa and treated any infidelity as equivalent to adultery, which was punishable by death. Such recognition of homosexuality was apparently not unusual in Indian America. In Peru pottery jars were made showing two men engaged in sodomy, and Oviedo, the great historian and chronicler of the Spanish conquest of the West Indies, noted seeing a large gold jewel of Indian manufacture that graphically portrayed the same subject.

Nor was sex in its more usual form shunned by the natives in Panama. Chiefs were known to pick their wives from the commoner class for their physical beauty, and the Indian women were not coy about their appearance. Some wore brassieres made of gold bars held by shoulder straps to support their naked breasts, and it was said that they preferred not to bear children until later in life for fear of spoiling their fine figures. The pursuit of enjoyment, in fact, was an important part of Indian life. Day-long feasts were famous for the enormous quantities of chicha that were consumed until an entire community was thoroughly drunk; coca was chewed as a narcotic; and smoking was treated as a serious business. A huge cigar two or three feet long was carried around an assembled company by an attendant who puffed smoke into the faces of the participants, one after another. Swimming was a popular sport, and both sexes, with of course the children, spent much of their time in the water so that most Indians became strong and expert swimmers.

This, then, was the native society that Spain's conquistadors encountered in the isthmus during the early part of the sixteenth century. As a culture it was energetic without being outstandingly powerful, and it was probably as advanced as the resources of the region would allow. It was not a culture of great antiquity, for the constant wash of peoples to and fro across the Panama land bridge quickly dislodged any existing structure, and in a sense the arrival of the Spaniards was merely the latest in a long succession of such invasions. But the Spanish intervention was unique in that it was final. The conquistadors cut across the narrow neck of land and effectively severed the Indians of Central America from those of South America.

The trinkets and showiness of Panama's chiefdoms proved to be their undoing. The Spaniards located and dispossessed every chief who was worth the looting. It was not a quick process, but it was extremely thorough. Four expeditions were needed before the area around Coclé was satisfactorily depleted, and the Spaniards were fortunate to extricate themselves on one or two occasions from well-laid native ambushes when the white men incautiously entered the cordillera. But the shock of the conquistadors was far greater than any chiefdom could possibly survive. The prestige of the chiefs was irreversibly broken by their defeats. Their hoarded gold, symbol of their power, was confiscated, and the chiefs themselves were driven into the forests, killed or taken prisoner, or forced to acknowledge Spanish suzerainty. The invaders went about their task with an astringent mixture of greed and piety. They were eager to make their fortunes from looting native treasuries, but they were also genuinely shocked by what they considered the evils of native culture. Balboa burned alive or threw to his dogs more than fifty of the homosexual slaves, and the Spanish soldiery shuddered at tales of the devil worship, as they saw it, of the native shamans, who were simply dismissed as sorcerors. Actually the truth of the matter was that the Spaniards were no more cruel or vicious than a tribal army. Culturally, however, their impact was much more profound. Their way of life was so different that it lacked elements to serve as links between victors and vanquished. Isthmian culture had no chance to adapt to the new regime. The result was deculturation—a process of cultural decline. Aboriginal culture began to unravel like the hem of a garment, leaving it half finished and vulnerable. From the self-confident, squabbling

All but one of the Cunas' San Blas Islands lack water. So the women go to the mainland, fill their calabashes with water (below), and carry them back to their islands.

ELIZABETH KATZ AND NORBERT SPERLICH

A Cuna youngster plays in a dugout, which is similar to the hollowed-out logs used for "nigakannoets," or native "baths for strength."

little chiefdoms of the preconquest period, Indian culture went into reverse, turning back toward a more introvert, cautious, and simpler existence. In places the culture totally collapsed. Around Coclé, for instance, half the Indian towns were gone within a century. The land was divided into private estates owned by Spanish landlords and used for raising cattle; even the composition of the native population was altered by the import of other tribes as laborers. Up in the cordillera, however, a degree of native culture survived and began to adapt itself to the new conditions. The region was one that the Spaniards rarely penetrated because they considered the natives there wild and dangerous, and it was left to an Englishman, one of the notorious buccaneers, or "Brethren of the Coast," to provide the best description of the native culture during its transition.

Lionel Wafer was one of that remarkable breed of wandering surgeons who seem to have turned up in out-of-the-way corners of the globe throughout the seventeenth and eighteenth centuries. Literate and levelheaded, these Ishmaels were among the truest observers of the human scene that one could have wished for. Wafer not only wrote about the Indians of Panama, but actually lived among them, adopting their dress and customs and managing to learn some of their language. He was, as it happened, an ex-shipmate of that other buccaneer surgeon William Dampier, who described the Aborigines of Australia, and their writings helped mold Europe's image of two very separate primitive peoples.

Wafer fell among the Indians by accident. He and a party of buccaneers were returning across the isthmus from a raid into the Pacific in 1681 when Wafer was wounded by the accidental explosion of some gunpowder that a colleague was drying over a fire. The explosion tore Wafer's knee open to the bone and so badly scorched his thigh that he was unable to keep up with the marching column. So he and three sickly companions were abandoned to their fate, the other buccaneers never expecting to see them alive again because the forest Indians had a reputation for killing any intruders that they found and caught. But instead of slaughtering Wafer and his fellow castaways, the Indians rescued and cared for them, healed Wafer's wounded leg, and eventually guided him and his companions safely to a pirate rendezvous on the coast.

Wafer's guardian angels were members of the Cuna tribe, and their precise relationship to the Indians who had occupied Sitio Conte in the days before the conquest is not entirely clear. Because the Cunas shared so many cultural traits with the early Coclé Indians, it is reasonable to suppose that they possessed a common cultural heritage. On the other hand, the Cunas of Wafer's day seem to have been a physically smaller people than the occupants of Sitio Conte's graves, some of whom must have stood nearly six feet tall. Be that as it may, Wafer's Cunas can be judged on geographical rather than ancestral grounds, for they illustrate very well what had happened to Indian culture a century and a half after the shattering blow of the Spanish conquest.

In the first place, the Indians had moved from the area where they had once lived. The Cunas whom Wafer encountered occupied the deepest recesses of the forest-clad cordillera instead of the open foothills. They were, in effect, refugees who had found sanctuary where the Spaniards had not dared to follow them. Here the new environment had imposed fundamental changes in their way of life. Hunting had gained at the expense of agriculture as a means of obtaining food. The difficulty of clearing primary forest was so immense that the Cunas had resorted to slash-and-burn methods to make small holdings where they could grow only sparse crops of maize. Instead of relying on agriculture, they spent as much as three weeks at a time hunting for such forest animals as wild pigs, which they ran down with their dogs and dispatched with arrows. Their villages, too, had changed markedly. Except in one case, they were mere hamlets without the traditional defensive palisade, and the houses had been altered from their conical shape to a simple rectangle walled with cane and roofed with palm leaves instead of thatch. Only the "warrior's house" remained as a military feature; a large house with walls pierced for arrow ports, it was a training barracks for young men and stood in an open space by itself with the trees cleared all around it for a bow shot.

The only fortified settlement in the traditional Coclé manner belonged to a Cuna chief named Lacenta. He personally befriended Wafer, whose description of him recalled the great days of Coclé. Lacenta, wrote Wafer, was regarded with deep respect by the Cunas, and they treated him as a prince. He lived in comparative magnificence in his stronghold on a bluff overlooking the junction of two rivers. His village was protected by a fence of bamboos and prickly pears and was large enough to contain fifty Cuna noblemen. On his travels around his domain Lacenta was not as grand as his predecessors because he did not travel in a litter but had to walk like the rest of his attendants; nevertheless, he did manage to achieve something of a royal progress. Every settlement the chief visited was expected to arrange a feast in his honor, and one of his seven wives was sent ahead of her master to make his stay comfortable.

While Cuna women do most of the food gathering, cooking, and sewing, the men keep alive their ancient and intricate skill of cane weaving.

On his arrival, Lacenta and his entourage would be greeted by the village elders, and that same evening the chief and his followers would appear at the banquet dressed in their formal regalia, which had been specially brought with them in hampers carried by the women. This dress generally consisted of a loose cotton shift, reaching to the heels, with short wide sleeves and a deep fringe. Some of the robes were white and the others black, and Wafer noticed that in a procession those who wore black robes always walked in front of Lacenta while those in white robes went behind him, every man holding a lance in matching color. Some of the men were painted on the face; and all of them wore the characteristic Cuna nose plate, a flat half-moon either of silver or gold whose horns clipped the central nose cartilage so that the plate hung dangling over the upper lip and mouth. Noblemen, said Wafer, were always easy to recognize in a procession because their nose plates were larger and heavier, and the really senior attendants had in addition great pendant ear plates of gold—one hanging down on the breast, and the other hanging behind on the shoulder. Lacenta himself wore a nose plate and ear plates of gold, and on his head a golden diadem that was eight or nine inches broad and jagged at the top like the teeth of a saw. His personal counselors wore similar crowns, but theirs were made of wickerwork painted red and topped with tall, vividly colored feathers of jungle birds.

Love of decoration had obviously not left the Cunas. Even their informal attire kept up the old traditions. Men, women, and children all wore huge

This drawing by a Cuna Indian shows his village, with the council house and Panamanian flag at right and, behind it, the house of the principal chief and a flag of the Indian Republic of Tule, a short-lived Cuna state proclaimed in 1925.

necklaces of teeth, shells, or beads, up to thirty pounds in weight, which hung from neck to navel and if cunningly contrived looked like a single mass of bone. They were also inordinately proud of their long jet-black hair, which they spent hour after hour combing, oiling, and arranging so that it fell in a shining cascade down their backs. Nor was any toilet complete without a great blaze of body paints, which had replaced tattoo work because it allowed greater scope and opportunity for fashion.

"They make figures of birds, beasts, men, trees, or the like," wrote Wafer, "up and down in every part of the body, more especially the face, but the figures are not extraordinary like what they represent, and are of differing dimensions, as their fancies lead them. The women are the painters, and take a great delight in it. The colours they like and use most are red, yellow and blue, very bright and lovely. They temper them with some kind of oil, and keep them in calabashes for use; and ordinarily lay them on the surface of the skin with pencils of wood, gnawed at the end to the softness of a brush. So laid on, they will last some weeks, and are renewed continually."

Wafer knew what he was talking about because he himself abandoned his European clothing, and the Indians painted his body while he lived among them. He also wore the gold nose plate of the lighter, smaller kind that was used while hunting and presumably — since he took up all Indian male fashion — the other item of male attire: a conical penis sheath, made if possible of precious metal and shaped like a candle snuffer, which was tied securely to a string around the waist. How well Wafer took to this new garb can be judged from the fact that when he got back aboard a buccaneer ship he was able to squat down among his Cuna guides and for almost an hour pass for an Indian until one of his buccaneer shipmates took a closer

118

look at him and cried out, "Here is our doctor!"

Wafer's medical training was invaluable during his Cuna days, not only earning him the respect of the Indians, but enabling him to gain an insight into Cuna customs. In turn, he was enormously impressed by their skill with medicinal herbs. The Cuna shamans treated his own appalling wound with a poultice of vegetable paste well chewed before being applied under a plantain leaf bandage, and to Wafer's professional as well as personal satisfaction, the injury was completely healed within twenty days. He was rather less impressed with the Cuna method of bloodletting. This was to seat the patient on a stone at the water's edge and shoot miniature arrows into the flesh, hoping to hit a vein. When the blood spurted, the "doctor" skipped about with every sign of glee. This Saint Sebastian technique was being administered one day to Lacenta's favorite wife when Wafer offered to perform the bloodletting less painfully with his lancet. The operation was a success, despite Lacenta's misgivings when he saw the quantity of blood the surgeon enthusiastically drained off, and Wafer's position as a welcome guest among the Cunas was assured.

The other peculiarity of the Cunas that Wafer was uniquely qualified to record was the unusually high incidence of albinos among them. A satisfactory explanation is yet to be offered of why the Cunas should have had so many of them—estimates range from one in one hundred and fifty to one in four hundred—but Wafer's was the best firsthand description of their appearance and of the treatment accorded them by the rest of the Cunas: "They are white," he wrote, ". . . a milk white, lighter than the colour of any Europeans and much like that of a white horse.

"For there is this further remarkable in them, that their bodies are beset all over, more or less, with a fine short milk white down, which adds to the whiteness of their skins, for they are not so thick set with this down, especially on the cheeks and forehead, but that the skin appears distinct from it. The men would probably have white bristles for beards, did they not prevent them by their custom of plucking the young beard up by the roots continually. But for the down all over their bodies, they never try to get rid of it. Their eye brows are milk white also, and so is the hair of their heads, and very fine withal, about the length of six or seven inches, and inclining to a curl.

"They are not so big as the other Indians; and what is yet more strange, their eyelids bend and open in an oblong figure, pointing downward at the corners, and forming an arch or figure of a crescent with the points downwards. From hence, and from their seeing so clear as they do in a moon-shiny night, we used to call them moon-eyed. For they see not very well in the sun, poring in the clearest day; their eyes being but weak and running with water if the sun shine towards them; so that in the day time they care not to go abroad, unless it be a cloudy dark day. Besides they are but a weak people in comparison with the other, and not very fit for hunting or other laborious exercise, nor do they delight in any such. But notwithstanding their being thus sluggish and dull and restive in the daytime, yet when moon-shiny nights come, they are all life and activity, running abroad, and into the woods, skipping about like wild bucks and running as fast by moonlight, even in the gloom and shade of the woods, as the other Indians by day, being as nimble as they, though not so strong and lusty. The copper

Excavations of Coclé sites by A. Hyatt Verrill in 1925 revealed rows of 20-foot-high stone columns, many, like this one, skillfully carved.

119

coloured Indians seem not to respect these so much as those of their own complexion, looking on them as somewhat monstrous."

For the rest, Wafer's picture of the Cunas of 1681 evidenced the continued existence of many of their original traits. They were still a nation of great tipplers, indulging in enormous carousals after council meetings and tribal ceremonies. At a marriage feast it was a sensible precaution that the bridegroom disarmed all his guests beforehand and hid their weapons lest there be drunken bloodshed. The Cunas were also still very keen on water sports and spent much time in the rivers; and they still enjoyed dancing and music. "They will do anything to make a noise which they love much," Wafer reported, "and they keep everyone ahumming at the same time to themselves. They hum also when they dance, which they do many times, thirty or forty in a ring, men only together. They stretch out their hands, laying them on one another's shoulders. Then they move gently sideways round in the same circle; and shake all the joints of their bodies with a wriggling antick gesture as they move along the ring.

"They pipe and drum often, even at working times; but their dancing they use chiefly when they get together to make merry. When they have danced some time, one or other of the company goes out of the ring, jumps about, and plays antick tricks, throwing and catching his lance, bending back towards the ground and springing forward again, with many other motions like our tumblers; but with more activity than art. And when one is tired with his tricks, another steps out, and sometimes two or three together. As soon as ever 'tis over, they jump into the river, all in a violent sweat as they are, and there wash themselves clean; and when they come out of the water, they stroke it off from their hair and bodies with their hands. A dancing bout, if the meeting be large, lasts sometimes a whole day, seldom less than five or six hours, and 'tis usually after having a short drinking bout. But they don't dance after they have drank very hard."

Wafer's enthusiastic news of the Cunas helped to intrigue others. In the years that followed, many travelers visited the isthmus, though none of them was quite as observant as Wafer. An ill-fated Scots colony planted on the coast of Darien actually raised a band of irregular Cuna troops to scout against the Spaniards. Throughout the late seventeenth and eighteenth centuries Cuna men, renowned for their skill with boats, were employed as sailors aboard Caribbean merchant ships and served as pilots along the coasts of Panama. Only in their dealings with the Spaniards was the old reputation of Cuna hostility maintained. Despite repeated attempts to Christianize them, employ them, and even control them with a string of forts, relations between the Cunas and the dominant Latin American society of Panama remained bitterly antagonistic. Periodic Indian uprisings continued until modern times, culminating in a rebellion in 1925, when the Cunas declared themselves independent of the Republic of Panama. The dispute was patched up with the help of an American warship, which steamed to the coast and arranged for a parley between the Cunas and members of the Panamanian government. Thereafter the authorities decided that the best policy was to leave the Cunas alone, provided that they recognized Panamanian sovereignty.

All this time Cuna culture underwent a steady change. During the 250 years since Wafer's visit, a large majority of the Cunas had been on the

Shaman dolls were intended to cure almost everything. This unusual one, showing the white man's influence, has the wings of an angel but also a gun—the familiar weapon of the all-powerful tax collector.

YORAM KAHANA, PETER ARNOLD

move. They had gradually filtered down from the mountainous cordillera and onto the narrow coastal plain that fringes the Caribbean shore. Here, on the opposite side of the mountains from the pre-Columbian sites at Sitio Conte, the Cunas began to settle on the San Blas Islands, or Islas de las Mulatas, a long chain of sandy quays and islets that lie along the coast of the isthmus. It was a curious move because all but one of the islands lacked water, forcing the Cunas to carry it from the mainland in canoes. Yet the reasons for the migration were not far to seek. The previously desolate islands provided a natural stronghold against Spanish interference. At the same time, they were the traditional rendezvous for ships operating in the western Caribbean, permitting the Cunas to obtain employment and outside supplies. Also, the waterless islands were free of malaria, and it was possible to grow crops of coconuts for sale to trading schooners, enabling the Cunas to establish a cash base for their economy.

Even more remarkable was a profound change in Cuna culture. The physical retreat to the islands was matched by what can only be described as a protective mutation of their culture, a strengthening that reinforced it against further decay. The effect of the change was to bind the Cunas

Cuna women feed stalks of sugar cane into presses to extract the juice. Sugar cane, brought to the New World by the Europeans, is a principal Cuna crop, along with maize, plantains, and bananas.

121

closer together and present a united front against outside interference.

The most dramatic manifestation of their new regime was their attitude toward non-Cuna people. Beginning late in the 1870's, the Cunas were reported to be discouraging close contacts with visiting traders. Their womenfolk were bustled out of sight and taught that all foreigners were evil. Visitors to the islands were allowed to land only on sufferance and were constantly escorted by a Cuna guide. Above all, there was a strict rule prohibiting foreigners from staying on the islands after dark. The outward intransigence was matched by a new-found puritanism among the Cunas themselves. Their former carefree, mildly lascivious ways were replaced by a prudishness that dressed the womenfolk from neck to toe in heavy blouses and thick skirts and emphasized the occupational division between the sexes, which, having always been fairly stern, now became more pronounced. Young children received almost no sex education, and men and women were separated in such activities as bathing.

The political structure of the Cunas also changed to fit the new circumstances. Their chiefs dwindled in numbers and authority and became more democratic. Elected by popular decision, they wielded no more authority than the force of public opinion allowed them, and they could be deposed by popular vote. Fred McKim, an American military officer in the Canal Zone who became so fascinated by the Cunas that he spent most of his leaves with them and finally had his ashes buried in Cuna territory, described their government as a "household expanded into a tribe." Heads of families elected village chiefs who, in turn, voted for a paramount chief. Yet every Cuna retained the right of access to the supreme chief and the council, and the only real law of Cuna society was that no individual should behave in a way that would harm his fellows. The result, in McKim's words, was "a socialized democracy based on individual rights and individual responsibilities."

The authority and prestige lost by the chiefs seemed to have been gained in some measure by the Cuna shamans. They now played an increasingly important role in native society and in the main were of two types: those who had acquired the special chants and techniques necessary for contacting the spirit world, and the "neles," who had been born with so much wisdom and insight that they were natural shamans. Both types were invoked in cases of sickness and for all major ritual occasions, but their services were not sold cheaply. It is not clear whether payment for shaman help was a new development following the introduction of a cash economy, or a traditional feature of Cuna life. But whatever the historical background, the Cuna shaman now charged a stiff fee for his services.

To cure an illness, the Cunas believed contact had to be made with the spirit soul, which had wandered from the body. To help him achieve this, the shaman used special chants and gestures—sometimes consulting a primitive picture board as an *aide memoire*—and deployed numbers of small wooden fetishes carved in human shape, which in one or two instances depicted whiskered sea captains in blue caps. Bloodletting by bow and arrow had been abandoned, but the herbal treatments that Wafer had found so effective were still prescribed, though a puzzling emphasis—almost certainly new to the culture—was placed on treatment connected with water, preferably sea water. The "bath for strength," or "nigakannoet," for example,

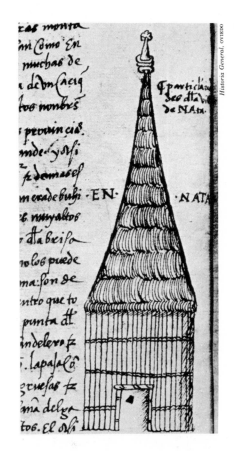

The houses are "round, like very tall turrets, and they are quite roomy and secure, because the wind and breezes . . . are thus unable to catch upon them as with square houses," wrote Oviedo, the Spanish chronicler of the Indies, in 1526. His drawing of a circular Cuna home is above.

123

Modern Cuna buildings are rectangular, though they still have steep roofs.

was given in a hollowed-out log much like a dugout canoe. "This," wrote McKim, "makes a tub in which the patient can lie at full length in comfort during the immersion, which lasts a number of hours. The liquid is usually, but not invariably, sea water. In this are placed a number of small pieces of wood, pointed at one end so that the quality of their strength may pass more readily into the bath. Their number is a multiple of four—the mystery number of the Cunas, which they see emphasized in nature in many ways. The bark of the wood used colors the water purple brown and has the appearance of tanning liquor."

Water in copious quantities was also a vital element in the rites for childbirth and puberty. When a mother gave birth, the newborn baby was lowered through a hole in the hammock in which the mother lay and splashed down into a canoe filled with water, a custom that may have been derived from a habit that Wafer noted in the cordillera days of taking a mother and her newborn baby to be washed immediately in a mountain stream. Wafer, however, made no mention of the Flowering Ceremony, in which a young girl at the onset of her first menstruation was subjected to a watery ordeal lasting several days. Placed in a small roofless cabinet made of plantain leaves, the girl was showered for four days by two specially designated women assistants who poured calabashes of water over her. On

Cuna musical instruments, prominently used in ceremonies, include pipes, drums, rattles, and flutes. The Indians in the photograph below are playing sets of Panpipes.

the fourth day a party of men went into the forest to a genipa tree whose fruit they collected while performing a strict ritual ceremony that "fed" the tree with eggs and plantains and the smoke of burning cocoa beans and protected its magic with sacred chants. The genipa fruit was then used to make an inky black stain, which was painted on the girl as a mark of her flowering. Finally the girl herself destroyed the leaf shower-cabinet and rejoined her people.

While there were no comparable puberty ceremonies for the boys, the Cuna girl had to face still another major ritual before she was considered ready for marriage. In this second rite, usually a year or so after her flowering, she was buried up to her shoulders in the ground, and small pieces of her hair were burned from her head one by one with a hot ember, interspersed with splashes of cold water thrown on her, while the shamans kept up their sacred chants. "I could not help contrasting the enjoyment of the Indians with the misery the poor wretched girl must be undergoing, buried up to her shoulders in the earth," stated Lady Richmond Brown, an Englishwoman who in the early 1920's tramped her way into the territory of the wild or bravo Cuna still living in the cordillera. "From first to last she [the Cuna girl] was in the position described for over six hours, while the hair was being slowly removed, ending at the nape of the neck, after which she was released from her cramped position. She was by then unable to stand, and had to be carried to a hammock when her part in the entertainment was over, and after this nobody took the slightest notice of her, but the real business commenced.

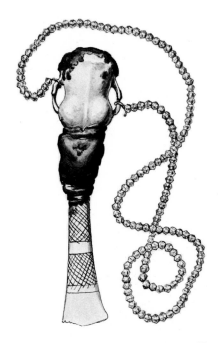

This Cuna flute, made from the skull of an armadillo and a bird bone, is suspended from the player's neck by the attached string of beads.
GÖTEBORG ETNOGRAFISKA MUSEUM

"It is difficult to put into words the mad scene which now took place. First of all a dance started—women advancing towards one another in lines, retreating with a curious jigging motion. Then the men followed suit, the contoolie [shaman] leading throughout. The flames—quite forty feet in height—from a gigantic fire that had been built roared upwards, and their lurid light added to the weird and uncanny spectacle, the witch doctors especially looking for all the world like fiends of hell, with their towering feathered head-dresses, masses of bone necklaces, and strange looking patch-work garments. The insistent noise of the rattles, the moaning of the reed pipes, added to the chanting, rose upwards, maddening the people until they lost all control of themselves.

"The dancing continued without a pause; as one group finished this queer jigging another lot took their place, while the previous dancers fell ravenously on the cauldrons of food. This continued till dawn, and only ceased when the people were so worn out and glutted that they could no longer stand."

Like Lionel Wafer before her, Lady Brown was intrigued by the Cuna method of performing a marriage. Neither bride nor groom had much voice in the matter, which was almost entirely arranged by the parents. Once the match had been decided, the girl's father arranged for a squad of six young men to seek out the unsuspecting bridegroom and oblige him to visit the girl's house. There the boy was forcibly placed in a hammock and the girl put in with him. The boy had the choice of jumping out and running away, in which case the kidnap squad seized him again and returned him to the hammock. If the boy repeatedly fled, he was finally allowed to go his own way, but group disapproval was so strong that he was well advised to leave the neighborhood. Indeed, many Cuna sailors first joined European ships as refugees from such marriages. If, on the other hand, the boy accepted the situation, he stayed a short time in the hammock with the girl and then went to take a bath with his escorts. The girl also bathed, though separately, and then the couple returned to the hammock. This hammock-and-bath ritual was repeated three or four times the same evening before the escort finally departed for the night, leaving the boy and girl together. They were allowed no sexual intimacies (some accounts state that defloration was performed ritually by a shaman or the girl's nearest male relative), and the young couple had to keep one another awake, for if either fell asleep it was an omen of an early death. The next morning the boy and his father-in-law went into the forest to chop wood, and the marriage pact was sealed when the youth, bearing the largest log he could carry, placed it at his mother-in-law's fireplace.

In McKim's time burials were no longer carried out with the magnificence characteristic of the Sitio Conte graves. The dead man was interred lying in a simple hammock after the grave had been dug widely and deeply enough for two posts to be set in it. Between these posts the hammock was slung, grave goods were placed in and on the grave, and the shaman sang the soul on its departure for the spirit world. Even the grave goods had become more humble than formerly. Pottery had been abandoned in favor of calabashes and gourds for water containers, and the Cunas preferred to buy their jewelry for cash from traveling vendors rather than go to the labor of finding, smelting, and manufacturing their own goldwork. Body paint, naturally enough after the adoption of clothing, had been reduced to a few dots and lines painted on the face, and red spots painted on palms, soles of the feet, and cheeks, though the old love of finery still lingered in the superb rainbow blouses of the women made by appliqué cloth of vivid colors on the basic shift. Albinos, too, were still found and treated with the same reserve that Wafer had noticed. As a method of discouraging albinism, the marriage of an albino was frowned upon, though albinos were shown the same special consideration in being excused from heavy labor that would cause them discomfort.

Today, almost thirty years after McKim's last visit, island life has turned out well for the San Blas Cunas. There are still some twenty thousand of them inhabiting the islands, and their economy and society have managed to achieve a measure of stability, though they receive much pressure for change from missionaries of four or five different sects. Their houses no longer stand haphazard and straggling in forest glades, but in neat, orderly rows on either side of the village high street. At sea their canoes are adapted to carry a mast and sails, and they successfully ply the offshore fishing grounds. On land they raise crops of bananas, plantains, maize, and sugar cane.

Yet the old ways are not entirely forgotten. The ceremonial feather crowns are brought out and worn for dances and festivals, even though the special occasions are now watched by boatloads of tourists from the mainland. And even if the once-naked Cuna men now wear jeans and shirts, their women still sport the traditional golden nose ring. It seems that suspicion of foreigners has, in the long run, proved a more effective shield against cultural invasion than force of arms. Deculturation seen in these terms has been a success, though at the same time the Cunas themselves harbor a sense of loss. They have their own ancestral mythology, and they recite the heroic epics of the chiefs who led them out to the islands, but there is still a nostalgia for the way of the mountains and for those Cunas who were left behind in the inland regions.

There, up in the cordillera, some twelve hundred tribesmen still live on the headwaters of the Rio Bayano, and their way of life is a little closer to the seventeenth-century style of Lacenta and his followers. But today the Panamanian government has new development projects for the hinterland. A dam is planned on the upper Bayano that will almost certainly disperse and destroy the mountain Cunas as a cultural unit, while it is the island Cunas, inoculated by centuries of exposure to outside contact, who stand the better chance of survival.

Cuna molas, familiar to present-day tourists, were conventionally slip-over blouses made by sewing tiny bits of varicolored cotton cloth on a cutout cloth base. This one shows a sick man in a hammock, a medicine man, and an incense burner.

4

Aristocrats
of the Ocean

In April, 1768, the frigate *La Boudeuse* of the French navy gingerly made her way into a lagoon off the island of Tahiti. Ignoring all the warnings to keep clear, a number of islanders, including women, succeeded in clambering aboard from their narrow canoes. *La Boudeuse*'s captain, Louis de Bougainville (in whose honor the flowering shrub bougainvillea would be named), was understandably exasperated. "How could one keep at work," he wrote, "in the midst of such a spectacle, four hundred Frenchmen, young sailors who for six months have not seen a woman? In spite of all our precautions, one young woman came aboard onto the poop and stood by one of the hatches above the capstan. This hatch was opened to give some air to those who were working. The girl negligently allowed her loin cloth to fall to the ground, and appeared to all eyes such as Venus showed herself to the Phrygian shepherd. She had the Goddess's celestial form. Sailors and soldiers hurried to get to the hatchway, and never was capstan heaved with such speed." When *La Boudeuse* sailed away from Tahiti nine days later, the island by common agreement was given the name New Cythera, in honor of Venus's own classic island of love.

A Hawaiian of the 1700's

In truth, this idyllic impression was somewhat misleading. Nine and a half months earlier, the first European ship to visit the island had not been met with the same ingenuous hospitality. The *Dolphin,* an English exploring vessel under Captain Samuel Wallis, had been obliged to brush off a determined attack from a large flotilla of Tahitian war canoes. The attack had been ruthlessly planned and executed. The attention of the visitors was distracted by the coquettish antics of a group of young women who went out with the trading canoes and smiled and waved alluringly at the visitors. Then, at a signal from a large double canoe that was hanging back on the fringes of the flotilla in a good position to give tactical orders, all trading activity suddenly stopped. The occupants of the canoes nearest the *Dolphin* picked up their weapons from a concealed magazine of rocks and slingstones, and the ship came under a wicked hail of projectiles. In a few seconds her deck was littered with rocks, and several of Wallis's crew had been cut and injured. Wallis had no choice but to open fire with round shot and grape, sinking a large Tahitian canoe. Temporarily rebuffed,

Outriggers at sunset on the placid waters of a Tahitian bay

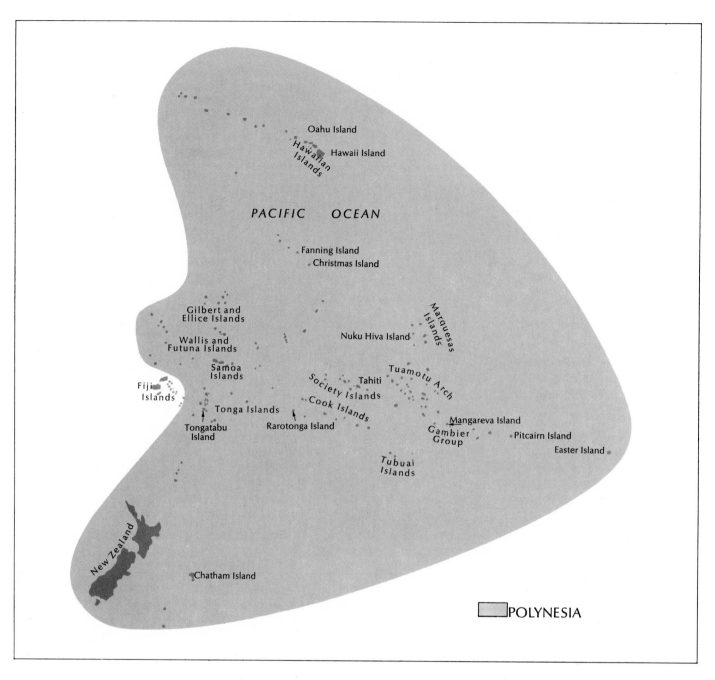

the attackers withdrew to what they thought was a safe distance, about a mile away from the *Dolphin*'s great guns. There, they were seen through the telescopes to be regrouping for a second attack under the direction of their leader. To prevent a further clash, the *Dolphin*'s gun layers succeeded in dropping a shot into the command canoe, bursting it in half. To the great admiration of the English gunners, the Tahitians were observed rescuing their leader from the water, and despite continued accurate bombardment from the *Dolphin,* two small salvage canoes managed to tow the shattered remnant of the great war vessel to safety. By that time a second wave of some three hundred Tahitian canoes had put off from the beach and was paddling to attack the *Dolphin* on the opposite quarter. Their furious charge was only stopped at three or four hundred yards' distance by a three-pounder loaded with some seventy musket balls.

Three days later the Tahitians were still sufficiently bellicose to muster an army near the *Dolphin*'s watering place on the beach and appear around

The nineteenth-century view, left, of natives of Tonga greeting Captain Cook with gifts, including a maiden and offerings of clams and fruit, idealized the islanders as "noble savages" dressed in togalike garments. The Hawaiian woman, below, with leis around her neck and in her hair, was pictured by John Webber, one of Cook's artists.

the headland with a large battle fleet. Once again the *Dolphin,* whose main battery had now been brought up from the ship's hold and mounted into position, broke up the assault with long-range gunnery. Determined to teach the Tahitians a lesson, Wallis ordered his men to keep firing at the fleeing crowds on shore as they retreated into the woods. Branches came crashing down around the Tahitians as the *Dolphin*'s shot went whistling over their heads. One group of natives retreated to the supposed sanctuary of a hill overlooking the beach, only to be awe-stricken when a cannonball plowed into the ground nearby, throwing up a great spurt of earth. "I really believe," wrote George Robertson, the *Dolphin*'s sailing master, "the shot which fell close by them on the top of the hill, frightened them more than anything which we did. Indeed none of us supposed that any of our shot would have gone so far: we only tried it for experiment's sake. The first shot that we fired at the top of the hill fell short about ¼ mile but the second fell within ten or fifteen yards of the crowd on the top of the hill—this shot, I suppose, made them think they were in danger of being shot anywhere in sight of the ship."

Robertson had come remarkably close to the truth, for the *Dolphin*'s marksmanship had persuaded the Tahitians that their visitors possessed supernatural power. It was an obvious conclusion for the islanders to draw. In their own culture they believed that all great men derived their ability from the gods; and this strange vessel, the astonishing destruction wrought by her weapons, even the pale color of her crew, pointed to a semidivine origin. It was not that the Tahitians thought the *Dolphin*'s men were gods themselves, only that they were imbued with a god-derived power. It was a quality for which the Tahitians had a precise word: they called it "mana." Their own chiefs had mana to a greater or lesser degree, as did these white newcomers. The white men, therefore, were to be treated in the future with much the same respect as high-ranking Tahitian nobles. It was an attitude that went a long way toward explaining the decidedly favorable impression later white visitors, Bougainville included, formed of Tahiti and her people.

The concept of mana was not peculiar to Tahiti. It was one of the fundamental beliefs of all the inhabitants of what would later be called the Polynesian cultural area (Greek: *poly* — many; *nesos* — island). This culture zone extended in a huge triangle, two of its sides more than four and a half thousand miles long, with its corners resting on Hawaii in the north, New Zealand in the southwest, and solitary Easter Island in the southeast. Within this immense territory nearly all the world's surface is water, the gently circulating vastness of the Pacific Ocean, stirred by a complex pattern of current whorls that, in places, encourage a teeming fish life. Spangled across the middle reaches of this oceanic triangle are other habitable island clusters, which are no more numerous than the first few stars that appear in the evening sky. Toward the western boundary of the triangle lie the Samoan and Tongan islands; at its center is Tahiti, the most celebrated among a cluster known as the Society Islands; and curving in an arc around the Societies are the scattered constellations of the Cook Islands, the

Illustrations of the native inhabitants, their catamarans, and one of their towns embellish this drawing by the Dutch explorer Abel Tasman of a bay he discovered on New Zealand's northern coast in 1642.

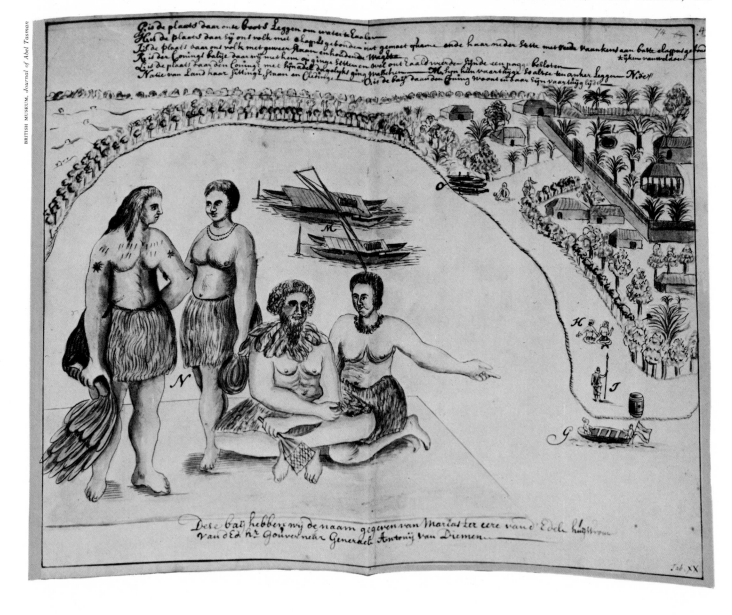

Tubuai Islands, the Tuamotu and Gambier groups, and the Marquesas.

One unifying factor for these central islands is their climate. Toward the extremities of the Polynesian triangle the winter months may be cold and wet, but here, in its maritime heart, the climate is remarkably stable and mild. The weather is excellent for growing tropical fruits of all kinds, and human habitation requires only the flimsiest shelter. On the other hand, the physical landscape is surprisingly varied. There are low-lying atolls like the sickle-shaped casts of giant sea worms; blunt and massive islands formed from huge blocks of coral uplifted by tectonic action; and most spectacular of all, the cone islands. These are the tips of submarine volcanoes rising thousands of feet from the ocean floor to appear above the Pacific water as soaring mountain peaks. Hawaii Island itself, the "big island" of the Hawaiian group, contains no less than five of these volcanic mountains, their lava flows combining to form a surface area of 6,424 square miles that rises to almost 14,000 feet, the highest point in Polynesia. Even so, the true base of the island is far out of view, resting on the ocean floor another 18,000 feet below sea level.

Gouged and eroded by the tropical rain, the lava and coral formations of these islands wash down as a rich alluvium to the shoreline. There, the combination of high, jungle-clad peaks, crescent beach, and blue sea creates a peculiarly striking effect. "From the verge of the water the land arises uniformly on all sides," wrote Herman Melville of the bay of Nuku Hiva in the Marquesas, "with green and sloping acclivities, until from the gently rolling hill sides and moderate elevations it insensibly swells into lofty and majestic heights, whose blue outlines, ranged all around close in the view. The beautiful aspect of the shore is heightened by deep and romantic glens, which come down to it at almost equal distances, all apparently radiating from a common center. The upper extremities of which are lost to the eye beneath the shadow of the mountains. Down each of these little valleys flows a clear stream, here and there assuming the form of a slender cascade, then stealing invisibly along until it bursts upon the sight again in larger and more noisy waterfalls, and at last demurely wanders along to the sea.

"The houses of the natives, constructed of the yellow bamboo, tastefully twisted together in a kind of wickerwork, and thatched with the long tapering leaves of the palmetto, are scattered irregularly along these valleys beneath the shady branches of the coconut trees.

"Nothing can exceed the imposing scenery of this bay. Viewed from our ship as she lay at anchor in the middle of the harbor, it presented the appearance of a vast natural amphitheatre in decay and overgrown with vines, the deep glens that furrowed its sides appearing like enormous fissures caused by the ravages of time."

The European visitors saw at once the cultural similarities among the various Polynesian natives inhabiting these remote and enchanting islands. From New Zealand to Hawaii, the natives all ate much the same diet, produced much the same sort of artwork, looked physically alike, spoke a broadly similar language, and observed many customs in common. Naturally there were differences of quality and emphasis. The massive carved-stone figureheads on Easter Island were unrivaled by anything on the other islands. The Maori peoples of New Zealand whittled the prows of their canoes into intricate double spirals, quite different from the simpler wood-

The best-made bark cloth, or tapa, a sample of which is seen above, was made in Hawaii. Used for robes and blankets, it was decorated by the use of small bamboo stamps that produced designs in varied colors.

133

work of the Hawaiians, who lavished more care on decorating feather cloaks or beating bark cloth with engraved mallets to produce a delicate water-mark in the fabric. Nevertheless, the entire Polynesian cultural area had a shared atmosphere, a feel to it that was all-pervading, characteristic, and distinctive.

The first item to impress the observant visitor, after the scenic splendor of his landfall, was that the culture had a strong maritime tradition. The Polynesians came out to greet the European ships in graceful craft of their own manufacture that were clearly masterpieces of local design and craft-manship. These vessels differed intrinsically from the European ships in being shallow-draft boats of light displacement intended to skim the sur-face of the ocean rather than drive through it. The maid of all work was the simple dugout canoe, usually improved by the addition of an outrigger float connected by spars to the main hull to provide greater stability. Such ves-sels could be quite substantial, depending on the size of the tree available for the dugout's main hull. By adding longitudinal planks along the gun-wale to provide increased freeboard, the Polynesians had improved the basic dugout into a deeper, more complicated vessel whose entire hull was made of planks carefully built up on a dugout shell that really served only as a keel. The carpentry in such work was of a remarkably high order, with tongue-and-groove joints and—as with Viking long ships—the planks lashed to the frames with cords so that the entire hull flexed and undulated with the waves. Polynesian vessels were at least as maneuverable as the Europeans' smaller boats. When the *Dolphin*'s cutter was chased by a num-ber of Tahitian canoes, she was lucky to sail clear, and this was only be-cause she had a newly cleaned hull. At other times the more ponderous ships' boats carrying water kegs to shore or taking soundings for the mother ship felt decidedly clumsy among the flotillas of Tahitian vessels skimming about them like water beetles.

But the pride of the Polynesian natives was the double-hulled canoe. For this, a pure catamaran design was used, a technique that was not to achieve full recognition in Europe for another two hundred years. First, two large main hulls were joined side by side, a few feet apart, by transverse spars. By

planking over these spars, a flat deck was constructed on which the boat-builders erected hutlike shelters. Here the crews could sleep and eat, cook and navigate, in comparative comfort. Power was provided by large lateen sails, usually of reed, and the steering was done by two enormous sweeps, up to forty-five feet long, one at each end of the vessel. When it was necessary to change direction, the boats could be shifted "end for end" simply by taking the sail aback and using the sweep at the opposite end of the boat as the new rudder. Under sail, or manned by highly disciplined teams of paddlers, these elegant double-hulled canoes were among the most superb spectacles of primitive Polynesia. Sometimes more than 100 feet long, and with their upswept bows embellished with intricate decorations, the sheer pageantry of these magnificent craft as they swept across the water invariably caught the imagination of the visiting European artists.

To match the ocean-going capabilities of their great canoes, the Polynesians had refined the navigational techniques necessary to guide them across the vast distances of the Pacific. Primary navigation was by observation of the stars, and the corpus of astronomical information that had been built up was carefully preserved and handed on from one generation to the next, sometimes by trained schools of priest-navigators. By day, the helmsman of an ocean-going canoe could steer by the fetch of the waves, by the slant of the prevailing winds, or by watching for the telltale passage of migratory birds, such as the Pacific golden plover (*Pluvialis dominica fulva*) or the long-tailed cuckoo (*Eudynamys Tahitiensis*), which followed established flyways between the Polynesian islands. Nearer land, he identified the cloud formations built by convection currents over the islands or recognized the refraction of the wave patterns disturbed by the land masses. To confirm these signs, land-homing birds were released that, like Noah's dove, pointed the way to the nearest shore.

To the European visitor, as he leaned against the rail of his high-masted ship watching the approaching natives, the Polynesians themselves were remarkable. Whether paddling their canoes, scrambling on board the European ships, or merely standing and watching from the beach, they were not at all like the fragile-looking inhabitants of the Indonesian archipelago

This proud New Zealand Maori warrior in a magnificent dogskin cloak was drawn in 1769 by Sydney Parkinson, an artist with Captain Cook.

Elaborately carved Maori canoes like this one, which was seen by Cook's men, were up to 69 feet long and carried as many as 80 warriors.

Forested peaks tower above Polynesian craft and Cook's ships in this painting of the explorer's visit to Tahiti in 1773–74.

to the west, nor were they like the scrawny and shivering inhabitants of the extreme tip of South America, often the last landfall the Pacific explorers had made if they had come around Cape Horn. Instead, the Polynesians were, by and large, a strapping and handsome people, big-boned and clean-limbed, with glistening copper skins. By comparison to the pallid and often scurvy-ridden Europeans, they must have seemed positively glowing with health. The visitors saw almost no cripples (they probably had been destroyed at birth, and minor defects were carefully treated by massage to straighten the limbs), and there was no evidence of hunger or malnutrition. Curiously enough, it was the men, rather than the legendary South Sea women, who first caught the attention of the Europeans. Nearly every visitor remarked on the extraordinary gracefulness of the young men, who had lithe, slender bodies, as elegant and supple as those of young girls. With age, a marked change took place: torsos thickened and filled out; limbs became more sturdy; and in their physical prime the Polynesian men were noted for their broad and massive bearing, powerful muscles, and dignified air of strength.

By comparison, the women seemed almost dowdy. Polynesian standards of beauty as well as nutrition tended to produce thick waists and ponderous thighs rather than the sylphlike elegance of Melville's fictitious heroine Fayaway. If Tahitian women were the Venuses whom Bougainville and his Frenchmen encountered, then they were built on a Titianesque scale. On Hawaii and Tonga some of the women, notably among the aristocracy, were positively massive. Outstanding heavyweights exceeded 300 pounds, and when they visited European ships, their very bulk was a menace. The Russian admiral Otto von Kotzebue, calling at Tonga, was dismayed when his cabin sofa collapsed beneath a portly chieftainess. Of course, the strapping physique of Polynesian maidens did not deter the European sailors from seeking the favors of the local women paraded on the beach for their inspection. An Irishman from the *Dolphin*'s marine guard was actually the first white man to take advantage of this offer, though his colleagues in the liberty party were shocked that he was so open in his behavior. They gave him a sound thrashing because he did not behave, in Sailing Master Robertson's words, "in a more decent manner, in some house or at the back of some bush or tree. Paddy's excuse was the fear of losing the Honour of having the first."

It was unlikely that the Tahitians saw anything untoward in the Irishman's eagerness. They themselves were never coy about approaching the sailors and offering sex in exchange for ironware. Robertson was among the last of the *Dolphin*'s crew to obtain shore leave, and while walking along the beach with two midshipmen, he was puzzled when "three very fine young girls accosted us, and one of them made a signal and smiled in my face. This made me stop to inquire what the young lady wanted, and supposing the young gentlemen better acquainted [than] me who had never seen any of the young ladies before but at a great distance, I desired one of them to explain the meaning of the signal. They both put on a very grave look and told me they did not understand her signs. I then supposed she had something for sale, made signs for her to show her goods, but this seemed to displease her and another repeated the same signal, which was this: she held up her right hand and first finger of the right hand straight, and laid hold

Paddles were important cultural elements in the sea-oriented Polynesian societies. This is a ceremonial paddle from the Austral Islands.

137

The European sailors often found the charms of Polynesian women quite accessible to them. But when local proprieties were not observed, angry scrapes with the offended natives, like this melee on Easter Island, usually upset the peace.

of her right wrist with the left hand, and held the right hand and first finger straight and smiled, then crooked all her fingers and kept playing with them and laughed very hearty, which set my young friends alaughing as hearty as the young girl. This made me insist upon their explaining the sign, and they told me the young girls only wanted a long nail each, but they never before saw them make a sign for one longer than their fingers, but they supposed the young girls thought I carried longer nails than the rest because I was dressed in a different manner. I wanted them to explain the other part of the signal, that I might understand the whole, but the young men begged to be excused. I therefore gave the young girls a nail each, and parted good friends. Then [I] walked down to see how the traders went on, and told the gunner what had happened betwixt us and the young girls, and he explained the whole matter in a few words and told me my young friends were not so ignorant as they pretended to be."

Significantly, the Tahitian girls had mistaken Robertson in his officer's uniform for the equivalent of one of their own aristocrats. It was an error to be repeated throughout Polynesia whenever the white sailors and their officers came ashore, so that at a native banquet on Tahiti the *Dolphin's* officers were ceremonially introduced to the other guests as the "chiefs" of the strangers. Everywhere in Polynesia the native societies recognized divisions of rank and status. These ranged from the humble headman and councilors on small atolls to an intricate pyramid of superaristocrats, lesser nobles, and commoners on the richer islands. Seeing this structure in reverse, the Europeans were quite happy to regard it as a reflection of their own social order, readily identifying "kings" and "queens," "high priests" and "generals." Indeed, taken together with their shared maritime traditions, the curious thing was not that the South Sea Islanders seemed so outlandish to the Europeans but that the two cultures could recognize — sometimes wrongly — that they had much in common.

In some ways the Polynesian ideas of status, rank, and privilege did in fact bear a distant resemblance to formalized European notions of the divine right of kings, of courtly precedence, and of noble chivalry and ostentation. Hawaii was the island (with Tahiti) where such social stratification had reached its most intricate state. In his survey of ancient Polynesian societies, Professor Irving Goldman distinguishes no less than eleven grades of seniority into which the Hawaiian ruling class, or *ali'i*, was divided. They ranged from the sacrosanct *niaupio* class, who were the offspring of a marriage between brother and sister of the very highest rank, to the *ali'i mak'ainana*, who were chiefs by lineage but lived incognito as commoners. As in most stratified Polynesian societies, the status of each Hawaiian nobleman was largely decided by the purity of his descent. The highest-ranking chiefs claimed unsullied descent from the great gods, and thus the rule of primogeniture was enormously important, the first-born of the first-born, whether male or female, being considered to bear the essence of heredity and accorded ritual honor. The inevitable result of this system was that the first families of Hawaii had branched out into complex lines of kinship, with the senior and junior branches of the noble families as aware of their correct relationship to the other as the senior and cadet branches of medieval European nobility. Like the Europeans too, the Hawaiian aristocrats considered depth of lineage as vital. King Kamehameha I, the great warlord of Hawaii who came to power after the arrival of the Europeans, was a comparative nobody, being from the fourth grade of nobility. But he recognized ninety-nine ancestors in direct line. On Tahiti, the Marquesas, and among the Maori of New Zealand, these concepts of nobility differed in degree rather than substance. Tahitian land disputes between chiefs were frequently settled by recourse to "memory matches," the winner being the man able to recite the most prestigious descent and land title.

In all such highly stratified Polynesian societies members of the nobility were a class apart, an elite. Mere commoners had to pay them the extraordinary respect due their rank, a behavior pattern that Captain Cook, the most conscientious of the early travelers, recorded faithfully throughout the islands. On Hawaii he saw commoners throw themselves prostrate on the ground in the presence of any person of high rank, and on an excursion into the interior of the island he found the natives doing exactly the same thing for him. Tahitians were required to strip to the waist when they appeared before any noble of high rank, and in Tonga Cook saw a native struck down and killed simply for coming too close to a chief. On one island it was considered disrespectful for any commoner to stand higher than his chief, and so there was a moment of panic when the local chief went below deck to Cook's cabin. To save their embarrassment, every commoner on deck promptly dived overboard into the water.

Mana was the source of a chief's special status. A force or energy, mana had capacity for good or evil. It could imbue either people or objects, and it was of the deepest significance, religious as well as practical, to the entire community, since it affected the well-being of everyone who came in contact with it. Mana was to be respected, protected, pampered, and—oddly enough —avoided. A really senior chief possessed mana to such a high degree that he was, in the brilliant analogy of Professor Douglas L. Oliver of Harvard, like a high-charged electric wire. Anyone who came too close to him was in danger of discharging the energy, and for this reason there had to be an elaborate code of avoidance in order to protect the weaker individuals from

The aristocratic bearing of this Samoan woman, photographed in 1910, suggests that she belonged to an island family with a noble status.

With its knees tightly pressed to its body for burial, the corpse of a Maori noble is carried to its interment site. When a Maori leader died, the people watched over his body for three days, allowing the soul to depart, then rubbed it with oil, attired it in the dead man's handsomest clothes, and carried it to its grave, which was called "udupa" (abode of glory).

Iconographic Encyclopaedia, J. HECK, NEW YORK, 1851

those who possessed mana in great quantity. It was this avoidance code that Polynesian societies had formalized into "kapu," a Polynesian word transcribed by outsiders as "tabu," and which has entered the English language as "taboo." Kapu was the reason for many of those remarkable customs noted by the European visitors as bizarre. Among the Hawaiians the supreme class of aristocrats, the inbred *niaupio,* were so hypercharged with mana that they could only move about the island after dark, for fear of disrupting the normal economic life of the island. Because his royal mana was contagious and could be transferred by contact, the mana-charged King Pomare I of Tahiti was carried by special attendants, lest he set foot on the ground and thus leave it kapu and useless for commoners. This performance led him to remark that while King George of England merely rode a horse, he, Pomare, rode a man. According to the Reverend William Ellis, a missionary in Tahiti in the early nineteenth century, "Everything in the least degree connected with the king or queen—the cloth they wore, the house in which they dwelt, the canoes in which they voyaged, the men by whom they were borne when they journeyed by land, became sacred—and even the sounds in the language, composing their names could no longer be appropriated to ordinary significations. Hence, the original names of most of the objects with which they were familiar, have from time to time undergone considerable alterations. The ground on which they even accidentally trod, became sacred; and the dwelling under which they might enter, must forever after be vacated by its proprietors, and could be appropriated only to the use of these sacred personages. No individual was allowed to touch the body of the king or queen; and everyone who should stand over them, or pass the hand over their heads, would be liable to pay for the sacrilegious act with the forfeiture of his life."

Mana and kapu were complementary, respectively the core and protective shell of Polynesian social organization. Mana helped formalize the duties and functions of the chiefs, because the possession of mana implied a responsibility to use it for the benefit of the community. Conversely, the obedience imposed by the code of kapu ensured the stability of the entire social order. It was, at first sight, a strait-jacketed and sterile society, but fortunately there were two other forces, "tohunga" and "toa," that allowed a certain amount of flexibility. Though far less important than mana, tohunga was of great practical significance. It was a quality that was acquired rather than inherited, and it implied a degree of professional expertise. Highly skilled canoe or hut builders, fishermen, birdcatchers, or even priests could possess tohunga by the evident excellence of their trade, and so too could any tools that a clever artisan might use to produce an outstanding artifact. It was this recognition of tohunga, some anthropologists believe, that allowed the genuinely talented members of Polynesia's lower classes to improve their position, though they could never rival the hereditary possessors of mana. Similarly, the quality of toa, named after the ironwood tree, enabled military valor and skill to be recognized, and toa in the form of a successful general could clearly challenge the rule of the mana chiefs.

Even more important, perhaps, was the apparent relationship between mana and the economic strength of the various islands. In the main, those Polynesian islands that evolved the most heavily stratified societies, with extremely formal recognition of mana, were the islands that could afford to do so. Hawaii, Tahiti, Samoa, and Tonga all had sufficiently large populations and the necessary resources to support a complex social hierarchy. Moving down the scale to smaller, poorer islands, the divisions of native society became weaker and less numerous. Finally, on barren atolls with only a few hundred people, mana could be recognized without affecting the straightforward regime of headman and councilors. Far to the southwest, the Maori of New Zealand were something of an exception. There, the much larger area of habitable land allowed them to spread out in a more scattered pattern of settlement. Like other Polynesians, the Maori recognized mana and kapu, and they too had a definite class system divided into aristocrats, commoners, and slaves (mostly prisoners of war). But they were also organized on a tribal basis, with each tribe occupying a defined territory and prepared to defend it by warfare, which was virtually endemic to the country, necessitating the construction of remarkable hill forts, known as "pas," complete with ramparts, ditches, and scarped earthworks with a military sophistication not found elsewhere in Polynesia.

Maori, Tahitian, or Hawaiian, every important nation in Polynesia shared similar religious beliefs. The common taproot of their mythology lay in the union of the great Sky Father and Earth Mother from whom had sprung a pantheon of major gods. Worshiped from one end of the Pacific to the other, each god was assigned his special province. Thus, among the Maori there was Tane, god of the forests and father of man; Rongo, god of peace and agriculture; Tangaroa, god of the sea; Whiro, god of darkness and evil; Tu-matauenga, god of war; and so on. In addition to these great gods, there were lesser gods and spirits contained in rocks and stones, animals and fish. All had to be worshiped, propitiated, and remembered. In the highly sophisticated societies there were specially trained priests attached to the royal courts. Everywhere one found minor necromancers and healers whose actions influenced the ordinary people. On Hawaii a

Polynesian religious leaders, like the one above, were part of the nobility and wore splendid raiment. White missionaries opposed them, as well as native dances, which—although often as sedate as the one below— were viewed by the Christians as heathenish and licentious.

cautious person took care to spit or defecate in private, and to hide such personal traces as nail clippings or worn-out clothing, lest black magicians use them to focus evil against their former owners. Above all, the worship of the gods involved the ancestors of the Polynesians themselves, and particularly of their great chiefs. Divine worship and the mana hierarchy were inextricably mixed. Among the Maori the holy places were no more than heaps of rock in the forest; but the temples of Tahiti and Hawaii, the "matae" and "heiau," possessed family as well as religious significance. There, at great open-air auditoriums usually built on some prominent headland, was concentrated the aristocracy's god-given power. There, the people worshiped their ancestor gods with sacred chants; made sacrifices, both animal and human; and placed the bodies of eminent dead to desiccate and disintegrate in the sun or to become the objects of future worship. Even Captain Cook himself, killed by natives on Hawaii, was very likely dismembered reverently at a heiau overlooking Kealakekua Bay. The natives thought that he was descended from the gods like members of their own aristocracy, and they gave him the honor of a royal funeral. Cook's men

Maori forts, usually built, like this one, on a promontory or headland, consisted of several sets of ditches and palisades. If an enemy captured one section, the defenders would retreat to another one.

recovered only a few bones and some salted flesh after the ceremony.

Material traits, as well as religion, linked the Polynesians. Soils and climate were suitable for growing breadfruit and taro, the latter a root that was cooked, pounded, and fermented into a paste the Hawaiians called "poi." Taro and breadfruit were the main staples of diet, relatively easy to cultivate and with a high yield. A taro patch forty feet square provided food for one man for a year, and a grove of breadfruit trees yielded edible fruit during a season of eight to ten months. Additional starch was obtained from a variety of yams, the kumara, or sweet potato, and—among the Maori of colder New Zealand—the pressed and grated roots of ferns. Tree fruits included coconut and varieties of banana, while seaweed was sometimes used as a garnish. Fish was the main source of flesh, particularly on the smaller islands, where plant cultivation was difficult in sandy or coral-derived soils. Fish pens and traps were constructed, but most of the catch was taken with hook and line (the hooks being intricately made of bone or shell), by trident, or with fiber nets. Domestic fowl and hogs were comparative luxuries, despite the fact that visiting European ships found it easy to trade for large numbers of pigs. The *Dolphin*'s crew, in fact, left no doubt as to what they wanted. When the ship was met by the Tahitians in their canoes, several of the *Dolphin*'s sailors pointed toward the land and hopefully crowed like cocks and squealed like pigs. Vegetable-fed dogs were a great delicacy on Hawaii, and when on Tahiti Cook was offered a picnic basket of cold dog, he was surprised to find that it tasted quite good, in his opinion second only to the flavor of English lamb. Even less choosy in their diet, the Maori enjoyed rats' meat.

Human flesh was also eaten, but never as a main source of food. Cannibalism was certainly practiced in New Zealand and the Marquesas, and to a lesser extent in Tuamotu and Tonga. But though there was human sacrifice in Tahiti and Hawaii, it seems unlikely that the flesh of humans was eaten. Even in the other islands cannibalism often had a ritual significance. Some islanders ate human flesh simply because they preferred the taste—in areas of the Marquesas, for example—but often cannibalism was conducted with much attention to ceremony and detail, invoking rites of victory or revenge over traditional enemies.

In two important ways, however, the apparent ease of subsistence in Polynesia was misleading. In the first instance, very little of the land surface was genuinely productive. On the atolls there was a very real shortage of cultivable land, and on the larger islands the arable surface formed only a small fraction of the total. Thus the population was obliged to cluster on the rich alluvium of the coastal strips, where population densities were extremely high. On portions of the island of Hawaii, for instance, there were possibly as many as 400 persons per square mile, while parts of the interior upland were virtually uninhabited. And on Tongatabu, in the Tongan group, it was said that a message could be passed from one end of the island to the other by voice alone, since the island was so densely populated. The second curious feature of the Polynesian economy, as Professor Goldman has pointed out, was that it lacked any genuine accumulation of capital. "Aboriginal Polynesia," he says, "had no entrepreneurship in goods, no systems of finance, no concepts of interest, no currency, no creditor-debtor relationships, no systematized trade, and none but the most elementary systems of

This Samoan chief posed for his portrait in 1910. His impressive headgear and other symbols of rank soon disappeared from daily use.

143

This nineteenth-century illustration purported to show the preparations for human sacrifice and cannibalism in Tahiti. Such an episode had deep cultural connotations, celebrating with ritual the defeat of an enemy.

Iconographic Encyclopaedia, J. HECK, NEW YORK, 1851

temporary accumulation." Instead, the islanders lived a strangely hand-to-mouth existence. Breadfruit and taro were harvested when needed rather than being stored for future use. Seafood was available in quantity only when the fishing was good. Thus, when a Tahitian chief wished to prepare a great banquet, he did not open his storehouse of wealth but imposed a *rahui,* or prohibition on his followers not to harvest certain types of food. By practicing this form of temporary conservation, a short-term surplus of the right foods was accumulated just before the banquet.

The primitivism of the Polynesian economy was matched by the comparative simplicity of most of the island artifacts. Domestic tools, such as adzes for woodwork, grindstones and files (sometimes of coral), digging sticks and carrying poles, were made of wood, stone, shell, and bone. There was no metalworking, though the Polynesians showed an immediate appreciation of the value of iron when the European ships arrived. Tahitian women demanded payment in iron nails from the sailors, and prices rose so high that the *Dolphin* began to fall apart as the sex-hungry sailors stole their currency. Sailing Master Robertson found half the cleats on the *Dolphin* loose from their fittings, and finally put a stop to the filching of iron by hiding in the galley during a meal break and eavesdropping on the crew until he identified the main culprits. More legitimately, the standard method of buying timber for replacement of spars was for the *Dolphin*'s carpenter to select the tree he wanted and drive a spike into its trunk. The delighted Tahitian landowner removed the spike to show his acceptance of the offer, and the sailors then felled the timber.

On the whole, the explorers were impressed with native architecture. The houses of the Polynesians were well suited to the mild climate, lightly built on wooden frames and thatched with leaves. Interiors were designed on an open plan, divided by light screens of latticework, and sparsely furnished

144

with a few sleeping mats and wooden headrests. Among the Maori and Hawaiians community houses achieved considerable size and elegance, the pataka of New Zealand having richly ornamented and painted rafters whose artistic merit was a source of pride to the community. Everyday dress in Polynesia was equally sensible. The standard loincloth or kilt was made from the bark cloth tapa, as were the short capes that Tahitian and Marquesan women wore over their shoulders. In their wetter climate the Maori preferred kilts and cloaks of flax to keep off at least some of the rain. In all the islands fiber and matting were worked into canoe sails, fishing lines, nets, and ropes, and in Hawaii there was a type of body armor made from coconut padding. One reason for Captain Cook's death at Kealakekua Bay was that he tried to drop a threatening warrior with a charge of shot from his musket, but the man's padded armor deflected the pellets harmlessly, encouraging the angry mob to press home its assault.

Polynesian warfare was conducted with weapons that bruised and bludgeoned rather than cut or pierced. The people's long-range arsenal was confined to spears and stones, which were thrown or slung at the enemy prior to the serious business of hand-to-hand fighting with a remarkable variety of clubs and cudgels. The Maori, who were possibly the toughest fighters of Polynesia and made a real business of warfare, were specialists in the use of a paddle-shaped war club that could be used both to slash and to stab as well as to crush the skull of an opponent. On Tahiti the ruling families engaged in internecine war, and interisland raiding parties were not always hit-and-run affairs. A serious raid could result in tremendous slaughter and the subsequent enslavement of all survivors and their families. This ferocity redressed the balance of what the early European visitors all too often saw as an idyllic society. Fortunately, the newcomers were protected by their superior technology, though for a hundred years the warlike Maori refused to be cowed, and it was never good policy for visitors to go ashore unarmed in the Marquesas. Crews of whaling ships were sometimes set

The skill of Maori woodcarvers was unsurpassed in Polynesia. The figures on this frieze appear to be monsters with the heads of birds.

upon and butchered, and men on exploring ships off the New Zealand coast were astonished when Maori warriors calmly paddled out to wave their war clubs and challenge the foreigners to step ashore and have their brains spilled.

Possibly it was the sheer novelty of the Polynesians' peacetime behavior that helped distract the visitors. Polynesian culture, with its sudden bursts of activity at harvesttime or when the fishing was good, was interspersed with long spells of leisure, ideally suited to the development of amusements and recreation. On Hawaii Captain Cook found the islanders attending boxing and wrestling matches, and gambling furiously on the outcome. They played a form of checkers with a board much the same size as the European version but using three times the number of counters, and they organized running and jumping contests among the children. The most curious of all, to Cook's eye, were their water sports. "Where there is a very great sea, and surf breaking upon the shore," he wrote, "the men sometimes 20 or 30 go without the swell of the surf, and lay themselves flat upon an oval piece of plank about their size and breadth. They keep their legs close on top of it, and their arms are used to guide the plank. They wait the time for the greatest swell that sets on shore, and altogether push forward with their arms to keep on its top. It sends them in with a most astonishing velocity, and the great art is to guide the plank so as always to keep in a proper direction on top of the swell, and as it alters its direction. If the swell drives him close to the rocks before he is overtaken by its break, he is much praised. On first seeing this very dangerous diversion I did not conceive it possible but that some of them must be dashed to mummy against the sharp rocks, but just before they reach the shore, if they are very near, they quit their plank, and dive under till the surf is breaking when the piece of plank is sent many yards by the force of the surf from the beach. The greater number are generally overtaken by the break of the swell, the force of which they avoid, diving and swimming under the water out of its impulse. By such like exercises, these men might be said to be almost amphibious."

Despite his quick grasp of the principles of surfing, Cook himself never actually tried the sport, though he did submit to two fierce sessions of massage at the hands of a dozen Tahitian women. It was a treatment then unknown to Europeans, and Cook, who suffered painfully from rheumatism, pronounced himself greatly eased. Even more bold, Joseph Banks allowed himself to be tattooed, a native Polynesian art that was a great source of diversion among the islanders.

Nowhere was the sophistication of Polynesian entertainment more evident than in the performances given by the arioi of the Society Islands. A category of traveling players somewhat similar to the peripatetic actors of Europe, the arioi went on regular theater circuits around the nearby islands. They are described by J. C. Beaglehole, the most eminent historian of Pacific exploration, as "combining the glamour of the secular stage with their religious functions; licensed satirists as well as, in some ways, children of the temple; highly skilled in mime and dance, with regular apprenticeship and grades of status, their practice of infanticide being perhaps the equivalent, for the dedicated life, of celibacy in more sexually inhibited culture-systems."

"Their origin," he goes on, "is suitably described in myth as the union of

The starchy breadfruit, seen in this eighteenth-century engraving, was the staff of life in Polynesia.

Oro, the god of fertility, with a maiden of earth. They existed, not merely in Tahiti, but throughout the Society Islands as well, and each district had its *arioi*-house and 'chief comedian.' There were eight orders or degrees, differing in dress and tattooing, the individual being advanced from one degree to the next with solemn ceremony. The chief *arioi,* male or female, were entitled *arioi maro-ura*—'comedians of the red girdle,' and wore girdles of *tapa* cloth dyed red and yellow. When acting, a whole troupe would dye their faces red and blacken their bodies with candle nut soot. Novices had to display their skill in dancing, and if approved, were sworn not to allow possible offspring to live, on pain of contumelious dismissal, and to entire obedience to the orders of their head. Children born to the highest orders, however, were regarded as descendants of the gods, and spared to enjoy their parents' titles . . . They toured the islands in fleets of consecrated canoes under the patronage of the gods, particularly of Oro as a god of peace; their progress was accompanied with offerings to Oro at all their stopping places, and the exchange of gifts with the local chiefs; and everywhere they were received with enthusiasm."

The fundamental regard for ritual and ceremony that lay behind the popularity of the arioi ultimately focused itself into the formalized existence of Polynesian aristocracy. Life among the nobility was not merely the code of the select but also had to be seen as such. Ostentation and status were immensely important. Chiefs prided themselves on their appearance—wearing sacred feather cloaks or holy girdles and bleaching their skin to appear whiter and therefore better-born—and went to considerable lengths to display and enhance their prestige. They might insist that they only be addressed in the special language of the chiefs, punishing by death anyone who accidentally spoke to them in the commoners' tongue. They gave ostentatious gifts to well-born neighbors, thereby implying a reciprocal gift

In a traditional way of fishing, a Tahitian close to shore casts his wide, circular net, one of various methods used to trap the different varieties of fish in shallow water.

147

Prior to great feasts, Maori often displayed the food gathered for guests—taro, fish, pigs, kumara, and pigeons—on "hakaris," or tall racks, like the gala one at right.

in the future, or they invited them to intricate drinking ceremonies of "kava," a mildly alcoholic and slightly numbing infusion of a pepperroot, which was taken with much eulogizing and proposing of toasts.

Power and importance, rather than material wealth, were the yardsticks of status. A chief's grand banquet, arranged after a *rahui,* demonstrated the efficiency of his food-gathering prohibition over his people as much as the fertility of his lands. Large numbers of people would gather to savor the massive repast—heaps of yams, pigs roasted in pits and eaten cold, piles of coconuts, fish, and vegetables. Etiquette and ceremony were carefully followed, whether sipping saucers of cold sea water as appetizers or honoring the most prestigious guests with careful orations. Any activity in which the chief employed large numbers of laborers showed that he could feed and command them, and thus increased his prestige. This effort might take a practical turn, such as the terracing of hillsides to make taro fields or the construction of fortresses on defensive sites in New Zealand and the Marquesas. But often it was no more than a matter of pure ostentation, as when large stones were heaped up to make a platform on which the chief's house could stand, the larger stones being set in the front of the pedestal to make it appear more impressive. By the same token, a high value was placed on any intricate or particularly painstaking labor. In Hawaii the chiefs prized above all else the handsome feather cloaks made of hundreds upon hundreds of rare colored feathers carefully tied in small bunches and then applied to a backcloth of fine net to produce a geometric design mainly in combinations of yellow, red, and black.

It was this intensity of labor, the infusion of mana and tohunga into an object, and the consequent association with highborn aristocrats, that gave material objects a spiritual value of their own. The feather girdles of the great chiefs of Tahiti had a special sacredness, and so did the English flag first planted on the beach by the *Dolphin*'s crew as an act of possession. Through their spyglasses the ship's officers saw the natives first shun the totem of the powerful white strangers, then come forward to lay offerings before it. Finally they took down the flag, only to carry it off and weave it into a chief's girdle as still another symbol of his power.

It was Georg Forster, the young naturalist with Cook's second expedition, who first proved scientifically that the languages of the Polynesian islands were closely linked. In his travels Forster collected and compared their basic vocabularies, and showed that key words, such as "pig," "fish," and "man," were all very similar. From this evidence he concluded that the Polynesians were a single race and that they probably derived their language from Malay. His reasoning, recognized as a breakthrough in linguistics, ignited a train of controversy that continues to burn and sputter two centuries later without being resolved.

It was never seriously thought that the Polynesians had evolved from the very beginning on their own islands. Indeed, their historical traditions told of long sea voyages by canoe from one island to another. Among the Maori the tradition was so strong that various tribes could even identify the names of the crew members within particular canoes. Later research was to show that Polynesia was the last major cultural area to be settled by human migrations, and most scholars came to agree with Forster that the ancestors of the Polynesians had originally migrated out of Asia, passed through the offshore islands, and finally come to rest in the Pacific archipelagoes, either because they sought better conditions or because they had been displaced by waves of later immigrants pushing in behind them. One romantic notion even had it that the Polynesians were a superrace from the Asian mainland, driven out as exiles and forced to flee overseas, taking with them a full-fledged culture in whose love of ornate ceremonial some observers detected links with the Chinese. Comfortable in this theory, paleoanthropologists concentrated their attention on trying to identify the actual routes by which the Polynesians reached their island homes, whether migrating in a relatively direct line or swinging in a great southward curve through Indonesia. One problem that had to be explained was why the Polynesians themselves did not possess pottery, using wooden vessels instead, whereas the people settled along their route used pottery extensively. A commonly accepted explanation was that the Polynesians either "lost" the art of pottery making as they migrated or, having arrived in Polynesia, had neither the use nor the correct clays for it.

But during the past fifty years this orderly interpretation of Polynesian prehistory has been thrown into a turmoil by a succession of sharp counterclaims. Scarcely a single theory has been left untouched. The most widely publicized dissent came after the remarkable voyage of the raft *Kon Tiki*, on which Thor Heyerdahl and five companions set out from the Peruvian coast to show that cultural influences could have been brought to Polynesia from the high civilizations of South America. Initial evidence, it was suggested, came from similarities in artifacts and blood groups, from the presence in Polynesia of the sweet potato, which is often held to be a South American plant, and in the discovery of other fossil seeds and plants that had South American origins but were also found in Polynesian archeological sites. The counterblasts to such theories were not long in coming. An aging French adventurer, Eric de Bisschop, sailed a raft in the opposite direction to prove that the same influences could have traveled the other way. The blood-group argument was dismissed as too vague; and a massive computer-assisted analysis of Polynesian linguistics (which has a remark-

Tattooed Marquesan islanders, like this one from Nuku Hiva, once had a fearsome reputation as cannibals.
AMERICAN MUSEUM OF NATURAL HISTORY

OVERLEAF: *Easter Island's mysterious stone statues are up to 70 feet high and weigh as much as 90 tons. Their origins and meaning are still debated by the experts.*
AMERICAN MUSEUM OF NATURAL HISTORY

The modern sport of surfing was introduced to the rest of the world by Polynesians, seen here showing off before shipboard tourists in the nineteenth century.

able ability to retain its protoform) has apparently confirmed that the language originated in the Indonesian archipelago. So, while the arguments still reverberate without conclusion, Polynesia remains a favorite area for further study among anthropologists.

Fresh mysteries are still being added. On Easter Island the decoding of the island's "picture writing" by cryptanalysts has failed as yet to explain the extraordinary profusion of religious sites or the history of Easter Island's famous statues, some six hundred of them ranging in size from small three-foot figures to a seventy-foot colossus. On Samoa recent excavations of early occupation sites have turned up traces of pottery where no pottery was previously thought to exist, and with every new shred of data the mysteries of Polynesian cultural origins seem to proliferate further. Today, the more cautious authorities will only accept that the Polynesians predominantly came from the west at least twenty centuries ago, that they spread outward in successive waves from island dispersal centers (probably in the sequence Tonga-Samoa-Marquesas-Tahiti-New Zealand, with direct transfers from the Marquesas to New Zealand and Easter Island, and from Tahiti to Hawaii), and that there was significant inter-island contact after the initial settlement. But as yet it is not known whether such voyages were accidental or deliberate, or whether there was any American influence. The case remains open.

On the other hand, while the origins of the Polynesians are still uncertain, there can be no doubt about their epilogue. The decline and fall of many of the island communities is amply documented. The islanders were riddled by foreign diseases, including syphilis, which the Tahitians knew as "the British disease" (though it is of American origin, and its early absence from the island is an argument against any pre-European contacts with the New World). They were decimated in bloody wars using the new, more deadly weapons provided by the Europeans. Their cultural identity was weakened by missionaries who frowned on such Polynesian pastimes as gambling and destroyed much of their artwork, which was considered profane. Whalers and merchant adventurers suborned the traditional

Western Samoan leaders discuss community problems in their thatched committee meetinghouse.

structure of Polynesian society to their own interests. Even the physical attractions of the islanders worked against them. The women so admired by Bougainville intermarried freely with the newcomers, to continue the process of racial intermixture that was part of Polynesia's heritage but in more recent times has led to the increasing rarity of full-blooded Polynesians.

In a sense, the very sophistication of Polynesian society seemed to hurt the islanders. They were too willing to adapt and identify with the newcomers. Their social structure was too ready to adjust to the white man's demands, and the Polynesians themselves were too quick to imitate. The *Dolphin* had scarcely arrived at Tahiti before her sailing master was astonished to see a native come aboard and take measurements of all the cabin furniture, observing the length and breadth of every joint of the chairs and even of the gunroom table, marking them off with knots in a piece of string. Estimates of the population of the islands when first discovered vary greatly. But everywhere the decline in numbers was brutally swift. Contemporaries of Captain Cook estimated the population of Tahiti to be at least 40,000 persons. Thirty years later, after bitter wars waged with European weapons, including some help from Captain Bligh and the men of the *Bounty,* the population of Tahiti had fallen to 16,000. Bligh himself noted the change of quality as well as of quantity. "Little of the ancient customs of the Otaheitans remains," he wrote in his diary on April 16, 1792, scarcely twenty-five years after the *Dolphin*'s pioneering visit. "It is difficult to get them to speak their own language without mixing a jargon of English with it, and they are so altered that I believe in future no Europeans will ever know what their ancient customs of receiving strangers were." Then again, on April 24: "The quantity of old clothes left among these people is considerable; they wear such clothes as truly disgust us. It is rare to see a person dressed in a neat piece of cloth which formerly they had in such abundance and wore with such elegance. Their general habiliments are now a dirty shirt and an old coat and waistcoat. They are no longer clean Otaheitans, but in appearance a set of ragamuffins with whom it is necessary to observe great caution."

On most of the other islands the situation was much the same, with the larger, more fertile centers taking the brunt of the white man's impact. The Maori, after bitter warfare to protect their lands from white settlement, were finally broken by colonial troops in the 1860's, though these superb warriors were never entirely defeated. Their population went into a slow decline for many years, reaching a low of 42,000 in 1896. Since then, the Maori have increased to about 7.5 per cent (over 200,000) of New Zealand's total population, with a noticeable move into urban areas. The Hawaiians, who may have numbered some 150,000 in 1820, had declined to 49,000 by 1853, though a century later they had increased to 86,000. Native Marquesans were virtually wiped out, and even on the smaller islands a low birth rate, combined with the exodus of the male population to look for work, produced drastic reductions. Census figures for present-day population levels are often vague or provisional, but even taking into account the influx of foreign, chiefly Oriental, labor, the total population of Polynesia is less than half the 3.5 million who, it is estimated, were living there when the white man arrived, enthusiastically claiming that he had stumbled on idyllic Cythera, home of Venus.

The Life of Primitive Man

Structure of Society

Primitive societies are usually small in scale (rarely more than a thousand people, often hundreds, or fewer). But the organization and rules required for their survival are frequently complex, even among simple-appearing groups like the South African Bushmen—seen above distributing meat, according to convention, among the families of the man who killed the animal, the man who owned the arrow, and a man who had shared an earlier kill with this group. Aggregations of people, like families and bands, are responses to the environment, biological needs, and limited resources. Further integration is achieved by clans and clubs. All must be group-oriented, and traditional roles, relationships, and behavior, based on age and other considerations, must be commonly accepted if the society is to live.

Many of the larger primitive societies develop into chiefdoms, whose complex hierarchical organizations include bureaucracies and specialists. Chiefs, like the West African king of Benin, seen below with his nobles and musicians in a 1686 print, are the source of authority and delegate necessary functions to other individuals. In such societies, various ranks of prestige usually derive from kinship statuses, based on heredity.

In the smaller groups, like those of the Lapps— one of whose families is seen at right in a summer camp in the Norwegian Arctic—the structure of society is more egalitarian. The leader is a person of influence who has achieved his status because of his wisdom, his skill as a hunter, or some other ability that the people as a whole recognize and acknowledge. There are no ranks or class divisions save those based on sex and age.

Description de l'Afrique, DAPPER, AMSTERDAM, 1686

156

IREFILM, STOCKHOLM

157

Order and cohesiveness are maintained in many societies by complicated kinship systems and clans, secret organizations, and clubs. These provide continuity between generations, and by regulating the conduct of interpersonal relations, help bind together the components of a society. The photograph on the opposite page shows a sick boy being treated in a clan kiva of the Zia Pueblo Indians in 1890.

Some societies are subdivided into groups whose members trace their ancestry to birds, animals, or other natural or artificial objects. They maintain an intimate relationship with them, often using visible signs like the totem poles of the Northwest Coast Indians (right) to display representations of the creatures and forces with which they, as individuals or as a group, are associated.

Myths and stories, sometimes providing the basis for cults, are often held sacred and are handed on from generation to generation, maintaining obedience to the moral law of a society. The Australian Aborigine members of a cult, below, are shown at a sacred ceremonial site overlooked by the image of the great snake, a totemic ancestor whose rules, conveyed in myths, guide many aspects of conduct.

Life in many societies is marked by advances from one age level to another. Each level changes one's social position and responsibilities. The bride in the pygmy wedding rites, above, will join the groom as an equal economic partner.

The roles and obligations of the different age groups are clearly defined. At first children learn group values within the family. Then older youths, like the Dani boys of New Guinea at right, practice skills they will need as adults.

The older people keep alive the traditional beliefs and institutions of the society. These aged Australian Aborigines are singing sacred songs preparatory to a ritualistic bloodletting and the decoration of their bodies for a corroboree.

Men and women in most—but not all—
societies have separate roles and responsibilities. Pygmy women join the men in
hunts, and pygmy men gather wild foods
with the women and help take care of
babies. But the Waura Indians of Brazil,
seen in these pictures, exemplify the more
common, separate obligations of the sexes.
Women, like the one below working manioc
flour into cakes, gather the wild foods,
prepare meals, care for the children, and
keep the home. The men make weapons
and, like those at right in canoes on the
Xingu River, do the fishing and hunting.

5

The "Click" People

A baboon and a Bushwoman: these were two of the more common status symbols to be found on the Dutch Boer farms of South Africa at the beginning of the nineteenth century. The baboon was usually kept on a tall perch, attached by a long chain so that its antics could amuse the family and at the same time by its barking serve as a watchdog. The Bushwoman, on the other hand, was a shy, elflike little person with wrinkled yellow skin and a triangular, wistful face. Usually she was the direct property of the farmer's wife, and in theory at least, the Bushwoman served as her mistress's tirewoman and kitchenmaid. But coming from the Stone Age of Africa's aboriginal peoples, it was seldom that the Bushwoman was of any practical use. She remained nothing more than a showpiece, and because she was liable to run away, it was common practice to shackle her to a table at night.

It is easy to see why the Bushmen were considered to be picturesque. To the North European eye they seemed like the apparition of some half-forgotten myth, a bushland Puck in the flesh, small in stature, with the graceful, fluid movements of a young animal and a wizened countenance that seemed as old as eternity. Averaging between 5 feet 3 inches and 4 feet 10 inches in height, they are among the smallest people in Africa. Indeed, at one time it was thought that the Bushmen and the forest pygmies must be closely related. But unlike the pygmy, the Bushmen have slender, almost fragile bodies. Their hands and feet are small and delicate, and they lack the pygmies' profuse body hair. The Bushmen's head hair is of the "peppercorn" variety, so tightly bunched in small spiral curls that it leaves patches of scalp exposed. Normally worn close-cropped, the hair is so brittle that it breaks off naturally on its own. Their skin easily forms wrinkles at quite an early age, and its color ranges from brown with reddish tinges to a more characteristic yellow. The irises of their eyes are brown and half hidden by drooping eyelids, which give the Bushmen a permanent rather sleepy expression. The nose is broad, with a low root leading up to wide-winged nostrils. Prominent cheekbones and deeply-lined faces give their countenances an Oriental caste, and inevitably the Bushmen were identified in the early days as a lost race of Chinese. But the Dutch gave them the

The gorah, a Hottentot instrument, is played by a Bushman.
Travels . . . , W. J. BURCHELL, LONDON, 1822

165

A Bushwoman carries her child on a cape fold filled with nuts.
LAURENCE K. MARSHALL

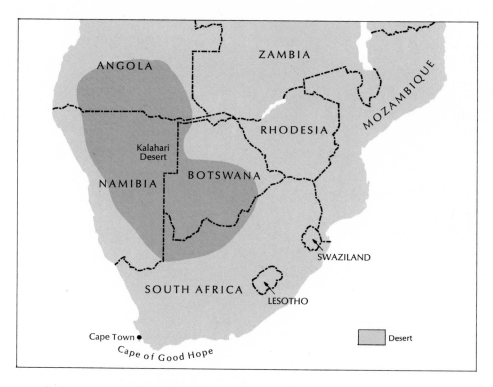

simplest name possible: the *bosjesmans*—people of the bush.

No other primitive people in Africa were so cruelly or consistently misused as the Bushmen—nor fought back with such bitter determination. The Boer farmers were by no means their first, or only, persecutors. When the Dutch settlers came to the Cape of Good Hope in the 1650's, the Bushmen were already fighting for survival against Bantu-speaking African immigrants from the north. The oldest of the living races in southern Africa, the Bushmen had been in the country at least 11,000 years, and perhaps longer. At one time they had occupied the country as far north as Rhodesia. They lived cheek by jowl with a taller people, the Hottentots, with whom they shared certain physical features and a broadly similar language. But the two races lived apart, for whereas the Hottentots possessed domesticated cattle and permanent habitations, the Bushmen remained pure nomads, traditional hunter-gatherers living off the wild animals and plants of their environment. Successive waves of tribal immigrants from the north pushed the Bushmen back into the cul-de-sac of the continent. In the mid-seventeenth century they were already living in scattered areas, seeking refuge in the inhospitable sand barrens and rock wastes.

By some grand design of history, the southern tip of the continent had become a living reliquary. It contained not only the Stone Age Bushmen but plants and animals that could not be found anywhere else in the world. In the mountains grew orchids and bulbous plants that were the last survivors of Africa's archaic plant associations; and across the plains roamed countless herds of wild animals whose profusion and variety were unparalleled since the last Ice Age. The arrival of the white man opened a second front in their war for survival. All the living creatures of South Africa were caught between two of the most aggressive migrations in history: from the northeast came a new invasion of the tall Bantu-speaking peoples, pressing down through the pasture lands with their herds of cattle, while from the south, after 1652, there was the growing intumescence of European Africa. Some species, such as the blue buck and the half-striped wild horse known as the quagga, would soon be extinct. The Bushmen, though driven from their ancestral hunting grounds, would barely manage to survive.

The African aborigines left a visual record of their plight. Scattered over the countryside are hundreds of rock paintings, many of them drawn in a style vividly reminiscent of the Stone Age cave paintings of Europe. The early scenes are peaceful, showing hunters and wild animals, such as gazelles and great herds of elands. But then appear troops of alien people, taller men than either the small Bushmen or the Hottentots, armed with spears and shields and driving horned cattle before them. The peace is broken, and there are battle scenes in which men lie dead or are seen fleeing from their enemies. Finally, the white man arrives, mounted on his horse, carrying his gun, and usually wearing a characteristic hat to protect him from the strong sun.

All the invaders looked on the Bushman as a menace. The newcomers trespassed on Bushman hunting territory, and the outraged aborigines struck back angrily. They were consummate guerrilla fighters and waged a campaign that was unparalleled for its tenacity and violence. They killed

Wary Bushmen hide behind rocks as Bantu-speaking immigrants, riding oxen and carrying poles for the frameworks of their homes, arrive from the north. This nineteenth-century reconstruction captures the drama of the invasions of the Bushmen's South African lands by outsiders.

An 1876 drawing depicts a Bushman camp in a rock overhang in South Africa's Drakensberg range. While hunters butcher a kill, a man at the rear works on a rock painting.

the immigrants' cattle, poisoned or blocked up the water holes, and ambushed stragglers. It was a war that had already been going on sporadically against the Bantu-speakers for five hundred years when the Dutch arrived. The Bushmen depended on game animals and water holes for survival and had strict notions of property rights. It did not matter to them whether it was the Boers or the Bantu who brought their cattle to the water holes and wild pastures and scared away or shot the game animals. The Bushmen were obliged to kill cattle instead of elands, and to complete the misunderstanding, cattle were accidentally destroyed when they fell into Bushmen game pits or drank at water holes that had been poisoned with euphorbia branches in the hope of catching wild animals.

The inevitable hostility between the races deepened and hardened into a hatred that was slaked with cruelty. Bushmen attacked and burned outlying Boer farmhouses, preferably with their owners inside. At night they sniped at travelers by lobbing poisoned arrows into Boer camps. François Le Vaillant, a French naturalist in the Bushman country, awoke one night to hear what he thought were raindrops pattering on the roof of his tent. Putting his hand to the ground, he touched a tiny Bushman arrow, one of several lying around his bivouac. A single scratch would have certainly killed him, and the "rain" was a continual hail of death. But the main target for Bushman attacks was the flocks and herds of the aliens. Partly for food and partly for vengeance, the Bushmen waged a regular campaign against the stockmen. Bushmen war bands traveled long distances across the desert, carefully preparing a trail by burying caches of water in ostrich eggs. Then they would raid an unsuspecting farmer at dusk and drive his cattle fifteen miles away by dawn. By the time the farmer had gathered a search party and picked up the trail of the raiders, it would be too late. Drawn into the desert, he would be forced to turn back for lack of water before he could close with the Bushmen fleeing along their prepared escape route. Even if the Boer managed to catch up with the raiders, he seldom recovered his cattle. In a last act of defiance, the Bushmen would cut the throat of every animal and then disappear into the wastelands.

So it was small wonder that most Boers regarded the Bushmen as little more than vermin, to be shot out of hand or crippled with a bullet in the knee. William Burchell, an English naturalist who traveled in South Africa between 1811 and 1815 and was one of the best early observers of the Bushmen, recorded meeting a Bushman chief named Goodheart who had sworn a feud against the Boer farmers for the rest of his life because they had wantonly killed his brother. (The latter had visited a Boer settlement in order to buy tobacco, for which the Bushmen have a great liking, and had been shot down in cold blood.) Similarly, if a Bushman village was located, the Boer farmers stamped it out as if it were a hornet's nest. They would organize a mounted posse, the famous commando. Encircling the Bushman settlement, the farmers would open fire with their heavy roer guns, huge muskets charged with black powder and a massive slug that was delivered with a thunderous report like a small cannon. In the final assaults the commandos concentrated on killing all the men in the village and taking the women and children alive as battle trophies. Under the law, one was allowed to take Bushman "orphans" into protection, which in practice meant their virtual enslavement. The captive boys and "tame" Bushmen were put to work as shepherds or cattle drovers and paid with one or two sheep carcasses every six months. The women and girls went to the kitchens, where they moped around the house under careful watch, for it was not unknown for them to try to poison the entire family. In 1774 a particularly successful anti-Bushman commando, the Roggeveld, killed 503 Bushmen and took 239 prisoners in a single campaign. It was calculated that between 1785 and 1795 some 2,500 Bushmen were killed, and 669 became serfs or captives.

When the British took over the Cape of Good Hope at the beginning of the nineteenth century, conditions scarcely improved for the Bushmen. By law any "wild Bushmen" beyond the frontier who did not surrender to the mounted troopers were to be killed. Scores of Bushman convicts were put to hard labor on the breakwater at Cape Town, the main penal workplace in the colony. There, many of them pined away to their deaths, though ironically it was among the breakwater prisoners that the first serious studies of the Bushman languages were made. Even casual visitors to South Africa, who otherwise considered themselves humane men, seemed to succumb to the temptation to treat the sullen Bushmen as scarcely better than dumb animals. Karl Andersson, a Swedish hunter and explorer, caught a Bushman while traveling in the Kalahari Desert. Because Andersson's expedition was desperate for water, and the Bushman refused to guide its members to a water hole, he lashed the man to a wagon wheel with a leather thong and dragged him from his territory until he cooperated. In the frontier districts that lay outside British jurisdiction, the Boer farmers kept up their old practices. As a result of one Bushman committing a murder, upward of one hundred of his people were taken and distributed as serfs among the Boers. Six Bushmen were killed by the punitive commando, and six more were executed almost immediately afterward by a frontier court.

A variety of styles are displayed in this rock painting. The action appears to flow in horizontal patterns, each with its story or idea.

169

The surviving remnant of all the Bushman peoples is now estimated at not more than 55,000 persons, and is probably less. The majority live in and around the Kalahari Desert, a huge 100,000-square-mile expanse of arid land that straddles Botswana, Namibia (South-West Africa), and southeastern Angola. Most of the Bushmen cling to the Kalahari's fringes, where they can find work on the farms of the Bantu and the Europeans; but in the almost waterless heart of the Great Thirstland, as the Boer trekkers used to call it, there still wander isolated bands of wild Bushmen, perhaps 2,000 in all. It is not known whether they have always lived there, or whether they withdrew to the desert to escape their enemies; but they maintain a traditional way of life as pure hunter-gatherers, without permanent habitations, without crops, and—in some parts—without a drop of rain or surface water for eight months of the year.

Technically a steppe semidesert, the Kalahari receives summer rainfall that turns the monotonous flat landscape into a short-lived pasture. Wild animals venture in from the margins to graze or to hunt before the grip of drought sears the vegetation into a semidormant condition. Then, as the days grow hotter and the rainfall dwindles, the retreat begins. Under a sky blue-white with heat, many of the larger animals leave; the water holes evaporate; the grassland parches and dies back to a few barren stalks poking through the dust-blown soil. Even the low thornbushes, adapted to extreme heat, become brittle and withered. Only the Bushmen and a handful of larger animals remain, in addition to the desert's usual complement of reptiles and insects. The Bushmen survive by eating water-filled roots and the wet centers of fruits, or by locating the permanent water holes that extend in a far-flung line down the axis of the desert. They are wary, isolated groups, usually named for some local characteristic, like the Sekhoin, whose name means People of the Plain, the Heikom, who are the People who Sleep under Bushes or Trees, and the lowly Naron, whose name for themselves means simply the People who are Insignificant.

It seems almost inconceivable that these shy, timid people, who are still so afraid of captivity and forced labor on the cattle ranches that they scatter into the bushes at the mere sight of a stranger, should once have been feared and loathed as deadly enemies. Their fighting skills and weaponry were no more than their standard hunting techniques adapted to human warfare. According to a sergeant of the mounted troopers, their bushcraft, or veld lore, was so good that a Bushman with nothing more than a fillet of grass bound to his head could creep within touching distance of a sentry without being observed. Their only effective weapon was a feeble-looking bow, which shot an almost child-sized arrow over a short distance. Seemingly so puny, this weapon was sufficient to kill or permanently disable a full-grown man if he was struck anywhere in the flesh. The arrow's potency lay in the reddish-brown layer of animal and vegetable poisons smeared on its foreshaft. Developed to kill large game animals, some varieties of the Bushman poison are still used by the surviving hunter communities. Depending on local availability, the gum of various poisonous plants provides the vehicle to bind the poison to the shaft. The best known of these vegetable poisons comes from the bushman's poison bush, a relative of the dogbane and periwinkle. The finely ground bodies of poisonous insects may also add strength, but the main virulence comes either from the poison sacs

A Boer woman takes her morning coffee while a native houseboy fans her. The Dutch colonists used Hottentots and Bushmen as servants.

AMERICAN MUSEUM OF NATURAL HISTORY

of venomous snakes or from the larvae of the small cladocera beetle. The Bushman cuts off the head of a poisonous snake, perhaps a puff adder or a cobra; trims out the poison sacs and dries them; then carefully pounds them into a fine powder. The beetle larvae are collected either from the leaves of the desert plant on which they dwell or after they have dropped to the ground and burrowed in the sand to make their cocoons. The latter are preferred by the Bushmen, because the poison is so powerful that they do not like to let it touch their skin and the cocoons form a ready-made wrapper. To prepare arrows for use, the beetle larvae is crushed to powder and mixed into a sticky paste with the vegetable gums. Then it is placed into a groove on top of a stone, and the foreshaft of the arrow is dipped and rotated in the solution until layers of poison have accumulated around it. The actual arrowhead is not poisoned in case the hunter or a child accidently scratches himself with it. The Bushman poison is brittle, so that a small speck is liable to chip off and fly into the eye, causing temporary blindness and painful inflammation. Any large game animal hit by a poisoned arrow will usually absorb sufficient poison in the blood stream to destroy its nervous system and render it helpless within a few hours. One of the native women with Andersson's expedition was hit in the buttock by a Bushman's poisoned arrow and died within thirty-six hours in considerable pain and without any hope of being saved, for there was no known antidote to the poison.

The remainder of the Bushman's hunting apparatus is meager. Wooden throwing clubs called knobkerries are used in much the same way as the

These women in a Bushman village have been gathering melons, which are used for water as well as food. The seeds are ground to flour or roasted, and the rinds serve as cooking pots or children's drums.

171

Missionary Labours . . . , ROBERT MOFFAT, LONDON, 1842

Disguised as an ostrich, with his legs painted white, a feathered saddle on his back, an ostrich neck and head in one hand, and his bow and poisoned arrows in the other, a Bushman hunter approaches his prey.

throwing stick of the Australian Aborigine—hurled at a bird just as it is rising from the ground. The Bushmen also have short spears and, in some northern areas, a fifteen-foot-long flexible pole with a barb at its point. This pole is carefully inserted down the burrow of a spring hare and gently twisted around any curves and obstructions in the burrow. By feeling the vibrations on the pole, the Bushman can sense when the tip is touching the spring hare. A quick thrust, and the animal is impaled. Then the hunter digs down from the surface to retrieve the carcass.

With the increasing rarity of large game animals in southern Africa, matched by the lessening number of hunters, it is no longer worthwhile for the Bushmen to dig the "hopos," or game traps, that caused the Boers so much trouble. In Burchell's day, and as late as the 1860's, it was not unusual for travelers to come across extensive lines of hopos built across the countryside like straggling trench fortifications. They were considerable constructions made of bushes and branches to form a fence pierced only in a few places by narrow passageways. At the exit of each passageway a pit would be dug and concealed under a flimsy lattice of branches and grass. The depth and width of the pit varied according to the anticipated size of the prey, and as the sides of the pit sloped inward, the unwary animal would be wedged into a helpless position. Piles of bones around the hopos indicated the success of the system and that when a large animal was caught, the Bushman community would live around the pit until the prey was consumed.

Today only a vestige of the old hopo technique still remains. Observing a game trail in use, a Bushman may casually throw a branch across the path. A few days later he checks to see how the animal has avoided the obstacle. A few more branches will be added, and when the animal becomes accustomed to passing through a particular gap in the haphazard barrier, the Bushman sets a snare in the gap. In the days when flocks of wild os-

172

triches could be found in great profusion on the veld, the Bushmen dressed in ostrich-feather cloaks to stalk them. Copying the gait of the ostrich, and with a shaped stick to imitate the creature's head, they would close within bow shot or lure the ostriches within range by exciting their curiosity. Now, however, it is more likely that the Bushmen will be snaring the much more humble guinea fowl. The guinea hen instinctively retrieves any egg that has rolled from her nest. The Bushman, on finding a guinea fowl nest, carefully removes a single egg and places it a few yards away. When the mother hen returns, she tries to roll back the missing egg with nudges of her head and beak. In so doing, she triggers off a noose concealed in the sand.

The subsistence pattern of the Bushmen has altered greatly since the loss of their hunting grounds, and there seems to be an increasing dependence on veldkos, the vegetable foodstuffs. An intensive study of the north Bushman group known as the !Kung has shown that only 37 per cent of their diet is provided by meat. Of the remainder, 30 per cent is provided by various plant foods and 33 per cent by the high-protein mangetti nuts, which grow wild and are a form of veldkos. It is mostly the women who gather the mangetti nuts, sometimes walking twelve miles a day to the sand dunes where they grow and then back to the camp carrying the heavy burden of the veldkos, in addition to any children who are too tired to walk. By contrast, the men only go hunting one to three days a week, and a major kill such as an eland is a rare event. Yet the same study reveals that the !Kung Bushmen have achieved a remarkably high state of efficiency in their environment. It has been calculated that their average intake of food, although only 2,140 calories, or 1.4 pounds, per day, in fact represents 60 per cent of the theoretical capability of the group, given their skill and level of technology. Thus an increased effort on the part of the Bushmen would bring very minimal additional rewards.

BLACK STAR, CONSTANCE STUART

Desert nights can be so cold that water turns to ice. At such times, Bushmen away from camp prefer to sleep in the warmth of the daytime sun (left), huddling close to their fires at night and telling stories.

In fact, the dominant theme of Bushman life is not the quest for food in the Kalahari but the supply of water. In Burchell's time the Bushmen preferred to camp some distance from the water holes so as not to frighten away game animals that came to drink. Today, game is much more scarce, and in the arid regions where the Bushmen now live, the supply of water is so vital that they are frequently found clustered near the water holes. Water is of such importance that stringent rules apply to its use and conservation. A single water hole may be shared amicably by two or more Bushman groups during a severe drought, though they will rarely agree to share the same areas of veldkos, which are regarded as the property of the band itself (it was this prohibition that the dead woman in Andersson's expedition probably transgressed, as she was shot while gathering veldkos). To carry water, the Bushmen still use ostrich shells, and sometimes bury caches of these shells while on hunting trips. In dire necessity a stranger may take water from one of the caches, but only on condition that he trace the owner immediately and offer compensation. As the seasons change, the condition of the water holes determines the size and movements of a Bushman band. In the rainy season the band may split up into smaller groups, each segment going off to live near a temporary water hole. But when these outlying water holes fail, the band concentrates around the few reliable water sources. In times of real drought, no source of liquid is overlooked: the contents of the succulent tsama melon, the blood and intestinal fluids of dead animals, or a subterranean silt hole carefully sucked dry through a hollow reed and dribbled sip by sip into half an ostrich shell.

Working in the shade of their summer scherm, a group of Bushmen prepare antelope skins for clothing.

Despite the fairly strict rules concerning water supply, the social regulations of the Bushmen are remarkably informal. Apart from the nuclear family, the only recognized social group is the band itself. This is scarcely more than a number of families living together as an economic unit. The size of a band is small, rarely exceeding eighty persons and sometimes counting less than a dozen members. For most of the year the band lives together in a shifting encampment known as a "werf," an insubstantial place easily overlooked by the passer-by, who may walk right through the camp without even noticing it. The Bushmen build small hemispheric shelters, four to five feet high, called "scherms." They are made of branches pushed into the ground and then bent over to form a canopy. More branches, grass, and reeds are tossed on top of the framework to form a roof, and in windy conditions these are weighted down with a heavier piece of wood to prevent the thatch from blowing away. In summer the scherm does little more than provide a patch of shade, but in the rainy season the Bushmen improve the construction, perhaps unrolling a reed mat on top of the roof to make the scherm more waterproof.

Inside a Bushman hut conditions can be quite comfortable. Small hollows are scooped out and lined with dry grass to provide nestlike sleeping places. Normally the Bushmen sleep in a curled-up position, knees drawn toward their chests, and covered by a "kaross," a leather cloak that doubles as a blanket. During the night the temperature may fall to freezing, and so a small fire burns on the hearth at the entrance to the scherm. The Bushmen keep their huts very clean, changing the bedding grass frequently and throwing any scraps and bones clear of the camp. Theoretically, the number of hearths around an abandoned Bushman werf will show the number of families it once contained. But anthropologists now studying the Bushmen as models for Stone Age excavations elsewhere have noticed that extra hearths may be added by the band simply to cook a particularly large game animal when it is brought into camp. This being so, the modern studies of Bushman hunter bands have cast some doubt on the traditional technique of assessing the populations of Stone Age sites by the number of hearths they contain.

Members of a Bushman band are related by blood and marriage ties. There is also a strong sense of interrelationship within a band, heightened by the repeated use of the same names within a family. Thus, the eldest son and daughter of a !Kung couple are always given the names of the paternal grandparents. The second son and daughter are named in honor of the maternal grandparents, and later children, if any, after other siblings. Since Bushman families seldom exceed four or five children, this means that the names are repeated over and over again as one generation succeeds another, until they become a hallmark of the band itself.

Marriages are arranged with the same informality that characterizes most of Bushman social customs. The young man may pursue a simple courtship, or merely request the girl from her parents. Formerly there was an element of bride capture, with a real or sham seizing of the bride, but this seems gradually to have been abandoned with the decline of the Bushmen themselves. Now it is not unusual among Bushman bands to find the parents arranging marriages simply by reaching a vague agreement between themselves when their children are still very young. If the mar-

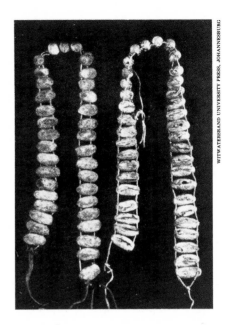

These dance rattles, tied around the ankles, are made of cocoons containing hard seeds or pebbles.

175

Women at a seasonal water hole fill ostrich eggs, which are used as canteens in the desert. In one area of more than 10,000 square miles, only three year-round water holes exist.

riage is made when the girl is still immature, it will not be consummated until she is physically ready. In any event, the young man is expected to provide bride service by going to live with the girl's family for several years, usually calculated as the amount of time in which she would be able to bear him three children. During this time, of course, his hunting skills are of great assistance to the wife's family. Marriages between young people are normally monogamous. It is only when a man grows older that he is likely to take a second wife, usually a woman who is widowed or divorced, for among the Bushmen divorce—like marriage—is achieved without formality or ceremony.

The small size of Bushman families is partly the result of economic pressures, for the Bushmen exhibit a high degree of social responsibility. They take care of their aged and infirm, and would not be able to support a large number of dependents. The birth of an unwanted baby therefore presents a problem that is sometimes solved by infanticide. The child is "thrown away," as the Bushmen euphemistically put it, by being buried immediately at birth. Any Bushman mother who is still suckling a previous infant (and Bushman children breast-feed until they are three or four years old) is extremely reluctant to take on the extra burden of a small infant.

The education of a Bushman child is an easygoing family affair based on imitation of parental behavior. At first, the small baby is carried about in a leather sling, hanging conveniently near the mother's left breast, or cradled in the hood of her kaross. When the child is old enough to walk, he accompanies the mother on food-gathering expeditions, gradually learning to use the pointed digging stick that is her main work tool. Boys are given a scaled-down bow at the age of eight or nine, but are not permitted to use poisoned arrows because they are too dangerous. They hone their skills on small game, such as hares, guinea fowl, and the miniature duiker deer, until they can be trusted with poisoned weapons to use against larger game. The emphasis of a boy's hunting education falls on the development of his veld lore, and in particular on his ability to follow the spoor of wild beasts. To find the game is difficult enough, but a badly placed arrow may mean

176

that a large animal like a wildebeest can travel for perhaps two or three days before it drops dead. The Bushman must be able to follow its trail over the desolate ground as relentlessly as any hyena, noting the signs of a furrow in the sand, a dislodged stone, or a single broken blade of grass. A superb eye for detail—coupled with a remarkable memory for shapes and spoor signs—becomes an essential aid for the skilled hunter. One notable side effect is that unsolved crimes are rare among the desert Bushmen. Any man's footprint is as recognizable as his face, and the culprit is almost certain to leave incriminating tracks by which he is immediately identified.

The return of a successful hunting party of two or three men and their dogs—an ill-kempt strain of curs that hunt without barking, though they snarl at strangers—activates the mechanism of Bushman social responsibility. The hunters have the privilege of eating the liver of the animal just after it has been killed, but the rest of the carcass is brought back to the werf. There it is divided up according to a system which ensures that everyone receives a share of the spoils. Among the !Kung Bushmen the deciding factor is the ownership of the first arrow that actually stuck into the animal. Each hunter carries arrows of his own manufacture, or which have been given or lent to him by other members of the band. If the successful hunter made and owned the lucky arrow that hit the animal, he is also the owner of all the meat and arranges its distribution. If, however, the arrow was merely on loan, the meat belongs to the real owner, even though he might have stayed in the werf and not gone on the hunt at all. In the third instance, when the arrow was a gift to the successful hunter, he is then expected to return a large counter-gift of meat to the original donor. But whatever the ownership, the carcass is divided and subdivided throughout the band according to a prescribed rule. The primary distribution is to the owner and the other hunters, each receiving a fore or hind quarter. In turn, they arrange a secondary distribution on a kinship basis, each giving food to his wife's parents, his own parents, the wife herself, and their children, in that order. A tertiary sharing follows between friends,

Bushmen youngsters at play use a cape for a sled ride on the dusty veld. Their usual swaybacked posture causes the distended stomachs.

Approaching cautiously from downwind, a lone Bushman hunter crawls quietly through the tall grass toward a herd of foraging wildebeests.

siblings, and any visitors who may be in camp. At this final stage the distribution is done without any sense of obligation and simply as a gift, but there is the implication that the recipient will make a gift in return at some future date.

Gift giving is a deeply ingrained ethos of Bushman life. Their material possessions are few: a kaross, hunting weapons, the characteristic shoulder bag in which the man carries small paraphernalia, a few scraps of net, and string. The women possess necklaces and bracelets of ostrich-shell beads, but their cooking pots are mere bowls of wood or clay pots bartered from the Bantu-speaking peoples. Only the most southern groups of Bushmen seem to have known how to make crude pottery, and these bands are virtually extinct. Yet all these small items constantly circulate within the band, given as a mark of favor or affection to a neighbor. There is very little surplus, for anything too cumbersome to carry when moving camp is left behind. Extra animal skins, traditionally prepared by the men as part of a hunter's duty, are traded away to the Bantu in exchange for scraps of metal or the dearly loved tobacco. In Burchell's day no expedition ever left for Bushman territory without first stocking up on an ample supply of rope tobacco and dagga (a cannabis plant), which was universal currency among the natives.

Property transfer does not, however, reach outside the band. The Bushmen have a rational sense of territorial ownership. They say that there is no point in owning the land itself, for one cannot eat the earth. But they do regard ownership as extending over the veldkos, the edible vegetable products within a given area. It is regarded as theft for an alien band to eat the vegetable foods from a patch of wild roots or a grove of mangetti trees normally harvested by another band. On the other hand, a hunting party will be allowed to enter territory belonging to a neighboring band when in pursuit of a wounded animal. It is considered a courtesy, however, for the

hunters to present a portion of the meat to the owners of the territory.

The question of ownership among Bushmen reaches its extreme among the Bushmen of the northwest Kalahari. Here the bands have headmen whose actual title is "Owner." In a sense the headman serves as the symbol of the united band, because in him is invested the possession of the veldkos and, in some cases, of fire. Among the Heikom, for instance, the hearths in a new werf are all kindled from a fire that is lit first of all in front of the headman's hut. But the headman's authority is severely limited. His role is to lead rather than to give orders. He controls or advises such group activities as when to move camp or switch away from a patch of veldkos that shows signs of being depleted. But even then he must act in accordance with the popular wishes of the adult men in the band, and in effect, he rules only by consensus politics. In the southern Kalahari the Bushmen dispense altogether with the notion of a headman and regulate their affairs by a council of all male adults, and even among the northern bands, the headman can be changed with ease. Normally the post is passed on from father to son. But if the son proves incompetent, the members of the band will gradually begin to ignore him and, quite informally, switch their attention to someone more respected.

This absence of a hierarchy has its counterpart in a system of justice that relies largely on self-help. In cases of individual injury it is left to the injured party to seek redress by his own actions or with the help of his immediate family. During the European expansion into Bushman territory, the violence of Bushman retribution among themselves was often cited as an example of their savagery. There were horrendous tales of how an aggrieved Bushman, catching up with his opponent's family, casually speared wife and child in the back and then carried on as if nothing had happened. Nowadays such blood feuds are extremely rare, as there seems to be almost no belligerence between the surviving bands. Instead, the emphasis is

Silhouetted in the dawn, two medicine dancers whirl before their audience. Such dances usually occur in darkness and last all night.

upon self-regulating law imposed through public opinion. Penal sanctions may still be exerted against anyone injuring the band as a whole—for example, by the destruction of water supplies—but individual complaints are settled as they are among the forest pygmies, by the pressure of group opinion. This attitude serves in turn as a positive stimulus for the correct behavior of the individual. Thus, although there is no definite rule that requires a man to go out hunting, he would find it very difficult to laze around the werf day after day in the face of public disapproval.

The Bushmen also manage their spiritual and medical affairs without the help of a special spirit guide or so-called medicine man. Their religious beliefs are still imperfectly known by outsiders, but the original moon worship described by early travelers, who spoke of moonlight dance ceremonies, appears to have been replaced or modified. Most Bushmen now believe in the existence of a supernatural being, variously named Cagn, Huwe, Hishe, or Thora. This god lives in the sky toward the sunrise, controls rain, lightning, and thunder (the sound of his horse's hooves), and gives good luck in hunting or in health. He is also the creator of all things, and the !Kung say that when a Bushman dies, his spirit flies to the east where the great god hangs it in a holy tree and smokes it over a sacred fire until it is ready to join his legion of spirit servants. This worship of Cagn is a personal matter between the Bushman and the god, usually a silent prayer offered up to him for his help when the men are about to leave on a hunt. In the opposite quarter of the sky, toward the sunset, dwells his counterpart and shadow, known as Gauwa, a smaller god with whom are associated such misfortunes as death and illness.

Among the !Kung the evil spirits of Gauwa's persuasion are held to be responsible whenever a member of the band falls sick. To cure him, the sickness must be plucked out by a "doctor." Any Bushman can aspire to be a "doctor" because the Bushmen believe that the healing power lies in the good spirit that is dormant in every man. But only in about half the men can this sleeping "cold" spirit be aroused and "warmed" into life. In a medicine ceremony the performers dance around the invalid until one man begins to feel his spirit awakening. Dancing up to the sick man, he leans over him and places one hand on his chest and one hand on his back to draw out the evil humor. Shrieking and yelling, the "doctor" extracts the sickness and throws it out beyond the circle of firelight, crying "Kai! Kai! Kai!" Then the "doctor's" trance continues to grow deeper and deeper. He begins to grunt and stagger; his breath comes in short gasps; and if he is a novice, he is liable to stumble into the fire or set his hair alight. He is held and protected by his companions as his spasms grow more and more intense, until finally his whole body goes rigid and he falls back into the arms of his attendants. Now he must be laid down to rest and rubbed and kept warm, for his spirit is believed to be wandering out among the spirits of Gauwa until it returns back to his body and he wakes up.

Apart from this medicine dance and an occasional dance simply to enjoy themselves, the Bushmen have remarkably little ceremonial. When a boy comes of age and kills his first large game animal, small lines of cuts are made in his torso, and a paste of the animal's fat and ash is rubbed in so as to leave distinctive scars. But the rite is performed with little preparation or fuss. Similarly, when a girl has her first show of menstrual blood, she is placed in a special relationship to the rest of the band, but without a great deal of ostentation. It is considered unlucky for any hunter to look at her, so she must stay hidden in a special scherm. It is also unlucky if she touches the ground of the werf; when she must answer a call of nature, she is carried out into the bushes by an old woman. Finally, at the end of her flow, the sacred eland dance is performed. No man is allowed to be present, except the two old men who play the main roles. Wearing eland horns, or wooden replicas, on their heads, these two dance among the lines of women imitating the eland with movements that are frankly sexual. The women, who are usually very demure, put off their karosses and dance erotically in reply, acting out their fertility ritual.

Modern Bushman music is a haphazard mixture of their own themes and instruments mingled with those borrowed from their neighbors. The African musicologist Professor Percival R. Kirby has identified several of their instruments, such as the water drum and a miniature reed flute, as having been copied from neighboring peoples. More typical of the Bushmen are their own quill whistles (also used as signaling devices), wooden bull-roarers called "!goin !goin," and delicate springbok rattles. The latter are made from the inner ear of the springbok antelope, sewed up as a purse and filled with dried berries or fragments of ostrich shells. They are worn around the ankle and produce, according to Burchell, "a sound that was not unpleasant or harsh, but greatly aided the general effect of the performances." Burchell himself was a great lover of music and actually persuaded a Bush-

A Bushman "doctor," at the climax of his trance, is supported by a helper during a medicine ceremony.

181

Many Bushwomen — more so than men — develop steatopygia. The extended, fatty posterior is an extra storehouse of energy, which shrinks during times of famine or drought.

man dancer to part with his ankle rattles. He also provided the classic description of a remarkable stringed instrument known as the "gorah," which probably originated among the Hottentots but was adopted by the Bushman. The gorah is shaped like a loosely hung bow, and its sound is produced by blowing on a flat feather spliced onto the string of the instrument. According to Burchell, the gorah when played by an expert had the tone of a violin and "with respect to the principle on which its different tones are produced, it may be classed with the trumpet, or French horn." In a rather more rudimentary form, the Bushmen even "play" their hunting bows by tapping them with an arrow while holding one end of the bow in their mouth to vary its harmonies.

A Bushman concert, with one man "playing" as many as half a dozen bows at a time, is one of the scenes depicted in the rock paintings of South Africa. In historical terms these rock paintings seem to be divided into two distinct phases, before and after the Bantu people's invasions. Art critics detect a more restful style in the former era, characterized by figures drawn in only one or two colors, with yellow, red, black, or white predominating. The main themes begin with exquisite pictures of a gazelle, beautifully drawn and evocative of Paleolithic art in other continents. Later, on top of the gazelles for want of space, the rock artists have drawn much larger but still highly proficient pictures of elands, which apparently played a large part in the artists' lives. It is difficult to define precisely who painted these rock pictures on the walls of cliffs and caves. It may have been the Bushmen, or their neighbors the Hottentots, or some vanished prehistoric people. But whatever the authorship of the rock paintings, there is no doubt that the arrival of the Iron Age pastoralists from the north had an immense effect. The whole style of the paintings alters. The movement quickens until it is almost frantic. Groups of men are seen fighting one another or running away. Bushmen are recognizable by having been depicted as small in size, painted brown, and carrying bows. Hottentots are drawn larger and with the characteristic projecting rumps of steatopygia (a word coined by Burchell); and the pastoralists are armed with spears and shields. Even the hunting scenes have a more bustling tone — stylized, rather spiky-looking lions and elephants, slain elands, and antelopes surrounded for the kill. Quite distinct from the paintings are scattered sites where the rock has been carved rather than painted. In these petroglyphs are found mysterious lines pecked into the rock face: geometric patterns of triangles, chevrons, and zigzags reminiscent of Australian Aboriginal art, and an interesting technique where the rock face has been etched by crumbling away the surface of the stone. Almost impossible to date, these petroglyphs have been tentatively ascribed to the Middle Stone Age, perhaps to the ancestors of the Bushmen. But no definite conclusions are possible because the whole question of the Bushmen's own origins has never been satisfactorily answered.

For years, it was accepted that the Bushmen, like other groups before and after them, were migrants who came down the length of the continent from the north. One of the strongest pieces of evidence to support this theory lay in the similarity of the languages spoken by the Bushmen and by the Hadza, a small tribe living in East Africa near the Olduvai Gorge. The Hadza, it was felt, were a linguistic castoff, left behind in the migration path. The strength of the clue lay in the fact that the Bushmen, the Hotten-tots, the Hadza, and the Sandawe (another East African tribe) all speak a unique form of language. The peculiarity of this language, which has no precise equivalent anywhere else in the world, is its dependence upon clicking sounds. These clicks serve as the main consonants, and not only seem bizarre to the alien ear but are also extremely difficult to imitate. Anthropologists have been so fascinated by the click language—Burchell wrote of "clacking" and "claps of the tongue"—that the four known examples of its use have been grouped together as the Khoisan family of languages. The term "khoisan" is itself an artifical word, created from the Hottentots' name for themselves, "khoi," and their word for the Bushmen, "san."

Strangely, for such a fundamental distinction, the click language was not studied intensively until the 1860's. Then Dr. Wilhelm Bleek, the librarian of the South African Public Library in Cape Town, persuaded the authorities to allow selected Bushman convicts from the breakwater at Cape Town to live at Bleek's home as houseboys. Bleek not only studied their music and physique but also made notes of their remarkable language. On the basis of his and later studies (his daughter also became a prominent expert on the Bushman), six different types of "click" have been identified. They include the dental click made by placing the tip of the tongue against the teeth and pulling the main body of the tongue down from the palate to make an implosive sound; the alveolar click, which starts with the tip of the tongue resting against the ridge of the upper gums; the palatal click, with the tip of the tongue against the roof of the mouth; and the lateral click, which produces a noise like the clucking used by riders to encourage horses and is made with the tongue spread out to touch the sides of the teeth. Finally, there is a retroflex click and a labial, or "kiss," click made off the lips. Not all the clicks are used by any single Bushman group. Indeed, the bands who use the labial click are virtually extinct. The use of the clicks is made even more sophisticated by the fact they can be made on a rising or falling note, as nasal or glottal sounds, voiced or unvoiced with controlled breathing, or run together with three or four consecutive consonants. This makes the language so tortuous for any outsider to learn that among Zulu children, whose Bantu mother tongue has adopted a few Khoisan words, these click words are usually the last ones the children are able to pronounce. To help them, the parents devise and make them practice nimble tongue twisters that increase their verbal dexterity. For Bushmen, by contrast, clicks are the very core of their language, and most words begin with one or another form of the sound.

It had long been known that all Bushmen bands did not speak the same language and could not understand one another. The new investigations showed that, in general, the northern and southern Bushmen spoke the san branch of the language, while the central groups had adopted the khoi branch, which they shared with the neighboring Hottentots. The two branches had some notable differences. In khoi there was a tendency for powerful, tall, or slim objects to be given a masculine gender, and weak, short, or round ones to be in the feminine. By contrast, the san branch was much more simple, scarcely using genders, and—like the tongue of the Australian Aborigines—lacking any numerals above one, two, and (some-

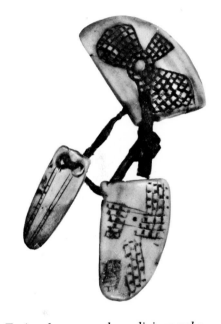

To invoke an oracle, a diviner rubs these ivory tablets in his hand until they are "jerked" away from him. The desired answer then comes from the person at whom they point.
BRITISH MUSEUM

183

times) three. A Bushman dictionary has finally been compiled, though not without immense labor in codifying the extraordinarily rich vocabulary of their veld lore. Today, research is mainly directed toward regional variations, the phonology and morphology, and trying to rescue the last vestiges of the pure san and khoi tongues before they vanish altogether.

The attention to the complexity of Bushman linguistics has been paralleled in recent years by a second look at some of their physical characteristics. It has been pointed out that Bushmen and Hottentots share many distinctive physical features. For example, the women of both groups may develop the unusual "Hottentot apron," an elongation of the labia minora that protrudes several inches beyond the vaginal entrance. If this is a specialized form of sexual lure, it is sometimes matched, especially among young Bushman girls, by the growth of the nipples at puberty so that they project like small orange spheres—a condition that is diminished after childbearing. Similarly, both Hottentots and Bushmen now exhibit striking instances of steatopygia, the accumulation of large deposits of fat in the buttocks which makes them project far backward. The reason for this physical specialization has not been established, though it is interesting that the artists of the wall paintings drew fat-buttocked people to represent the Hottentots, whereas they usually indicated Bushman physique by a characteristic swayback resulting from a forward curve of the lower spine. As both races now share these distinctive features, as well as the click language, it is reasonable to assume that in recent times they have intermingled greatly. Accepting this admixture as being almost impossible to disentangle by modern anthropometric techniques, the scholars have been looking at the archeological evidence to see which race, Hottentot or Bushman, is the older. The investigation is far from over, but from the existing evidence it appears that two separate archaic cultures have existed in South Africa for a considerable time. The dates are as yet uncertain, but there is a growing tendency to consider the Bushmen and the Hottentots as being inheritors, if not the direct physical descendants, of very ancient cultures of early man, who may have evolved in South Africa in comparative isolation.

At the opposite end of the time scale, in modern Bushman culture, the condition of the Kalahari hunter bands is becoming increasingly perilous. Physically they are showing more and more Bantu features, with longer heads, taller stature, and Negroid facial characteristics. Culturally the impact has been even more noticeable, despite the isolation of the interior Kalahari. It has been increasingly difficult to sustain life in a depleted environment. The hunting of spring hares and desert reptiles does not equate with the days when, as late as the 1870's, a single herd of springbok on the veld pasture was estimated at a million head and could be driven across the game pits. As their food supply dwindled, so the size of the Bushman bands diminished. Today there are no bands that would be able to resist, as in the early nineteenth century, a Boer commando. Moreover, the Bushmen's belligerence has gone. They have become so timid that on the desert fringes they are easily imposed upon. The Negro Bakalahari, for instance, have taken to "adopting" into semiserf status the Bushman families who gather around their villages. Some Bushmen have themselves begun to reside in semipermanent hamlets. In the wastelands of the central Kalahari the rest are impelled by the simple drive for survival.

The Life of Primitive Man

Rituals and Ceremonies

The sorcerers of Africa's Ivory Coast, seen above dancing with poisonous black cobras in a "rain-making" festival, exemplify the significance of rituals and ceremonies to the continued stability of a society. Carried out with precise rules of procedure and behavior, and often with special music and costumes, they reflect the people's beliefs in the powers and requirements of supernatural forces or beings whose help and approval are sought—generally or on specific occasions (such as the advent of the growing season, when rain is needed)—for the society's well-being and survival. But in publicly enacting sacred beliefs, they set the stamp on important cultural attitudes, teaching and enforcing acceptance of traditional moral rules necessary for the group's homogeneity and cohesion.

Many ceremonies, serving both social and religious ends, occur at the same time each year. In the Trobriand Islands, the people hold an annual festival after the yam crops have been harvested and stored in special tall, thatch-covered storehouses, right. Spirits of the dead return to the villages, and joyous feasting, drumming, and dancing continue for several weeks.

Among the Waura Indians of the Upper Xingu River in Brazil, the men observe a traditional rite of streaming forth in ceremonial procession, below, to present the women of the village with tools they have made for their use—digging sticks with which to harvest manioc, and wooden instruments, part spatula, part knife, to work and shape the manioc flour into cakes.

The water color opposite, painted by Edward Kern, an artist with an American exploring expedition in 1849, depicts Pueblo Indians at Jemez, New Mexico, performing the annual Green Corn Dance. Celebrating the harvest, it also honors the maize, the tribe's principal subsistence crop.

Wearing a ceremonial robe, a bearded Ainu elder in a dugout, left, returns algae plants to the waters of Lake Akan in Hokkaido. Part of a public festival to keep alive Ainu culture, the rite pays tribute to a water spirit, hoping to please it and prevent its ill will.

On the eve of the heavy rains, usually in September, Kraho Indians of the central Brazilian savannah, right, conduct a village ceremony to the fish that will supply them with food. The stick with a beak held by the man at center represents a heron, a successful fishing bird.

Somewhat like school graduations and weddings, numerous ceremonies mark a person's passage from one age status in life to another. The boys, right, of the Vachokue tribe in Angola are arrayed for their rites of initiation into manhood.

The ceremony below, held at the time of a birth, is occurring in a village of the Guere people in the Ivory Coast. In a nearby dwelling a chief's wife is striving to give birth. To ease her labor, sorcerers (one brandishing a knife to add to the drama) toss a hypnotized girl back and forth as they dance.

The ceremonies of life's stages—or rites of passage, as they are sometimes known—establish order by making clear each person's roles in a society. At right, Australian Aborigines enact the lessons of a creation myth in a dance during circumcision rites for the boys.

In Africa's Niger, a trio of young Bororo bachelors, right, waits to participate in the "yakey," a festival courting dance in which they display their manly elegance to eligible young women. Ridicule will greet the slightest deviation from tribal standards of beauty, which emphasize whiteness of teeth and eyes (heightened by the darkening of the dancers' lips and eyelids).

191

An Account of . . . New South Wales. DAVID COLLINS, LONDON, 1798

Among the most important ceremonies are those that follow death, for they hold societies together by counteracting the disrupting effects of fear. The Aborigines, left, are seen preparing a corpse for its ritual cremation.

Believing that men were created from fruit wrapped in straw mats, kinsmen of dead Umutina Indians of Brazil wrap themselves in straw, right, becoming the spirit of the deceased during the death ceremonies.

The mid-nineteenth-century drawing below depicts Hawaiians grieving for a dead chieftain, whose body is exposed on a scaffold. Afterward the bones will be preserved in sacred places or distributed to relatives.

Iconographic Encyclopaedia. J. HECK, NEW YORK, 1851

193

Technocrats of the North

A blurred photograph of five heavily clad men in front of an ice hummock is one of the milestones — and one of the oddities — in the history of human endeavor. The picture was taken on April 7, 1909, by Robert E. Peary, and the ice hummock represented the North Pole. A civil engineer in the U.S. Navy, Peary had devoted twenty-three years of fanatical preparation to this moment of triumph, so he arranged his little victory group with considerable care. His photograph is too indistinct, and the figures lined up by the ice hummock too swaddled in furs, for one to be able to distinguish that the man in the center was, in fact, a Negro. He was Matthew Henson, Peary's manservant and collaborator, who had spent almost as long in the Arctic as his master had, training for this moment. Now Henson stood cheerfully holding an American flag while the other four men in the group dutifully clutched an assortment of banners that ranged from the flag of the International Red Cross to the emblem of Peary's college fraternity. A faintly ludicrous quality was given to the scene by the fact that the four men flanking Henson were Greenland Eskimos who had not the least idea about the significance of their pose. As far as the Eskimos were concerned, they had merely brought the white man and the black man to this remote spot, and were prepared to humor their rather strange wishes.

The names of the four Eskimos, in Peary's rendering, were Ooqueah, Ootah, Egingwah, and Seegloo. Together with a long chain of Eskimo support parties stretching back to Peary's base camp, they had worked the dog teams and helped build the igloos that played such an essential part in getting the American explorer to the Pole safely. Peary himself had no illusions about the importance of the Eskimos' contribution. "It may perhaps be fairly said," he wrote in his account of the journey, "that it has been my fortune to utilize the Eskimos for the purpose of discovery to a degree equalled by no other explorer. . . . It has been a fundamental principle of all my Arctic work to utilize the Eskimos for the rank and file of my sledge parties. Without the skillful handiwork of the women we should lack the warm fur clothing which is absolutely essential to protect us from the winter cold, while the Eskimo dog is the only tractive force suitable for serious arctic sledge work."

A Siberian Eskimo ivory doll, incised with figures

A Canadian Eskimo, shown in 1916 piercing a bone with a bow drill

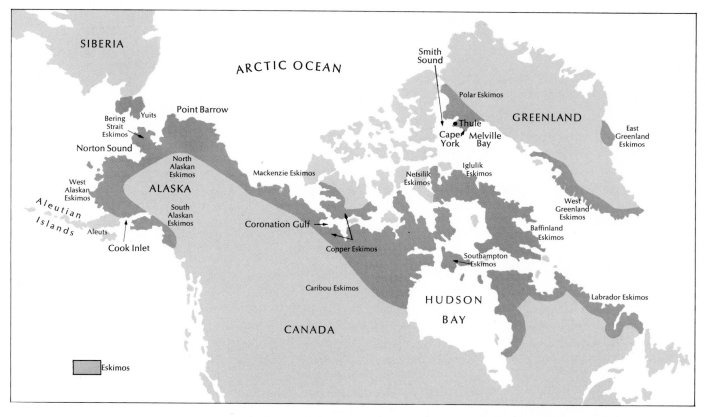

Peary's Greenlanders were but one small segment of an Eskimo population whose culture area extended in an immense arc from the eastern extremity of Siberia to Greenland and included much of Alaska and Canada's northern territories. This arc, subtended from the Pole itself, was neither smooth nor continuous. It was a jagged, erratic belt of heavily indented seacoast and undulating barren lands, of islands and polar sea. At three points — in the deep pocket of Hudson Bay and at Cook Inlet and the mouth of the Copper River in Alaska — the arc was penetrated by outposts of a more southerly forest Indian culture. Farther to the west the Aleutian Islands were a dangling appendix of another regional culture, the Aleut, which, though very similar to the Eskimo, was not identical. Nor were the Eskimos spread evenly across the arc. Recent figures of Eskimo population density probably reflect the earlier distribution patterns and give a total Eskimo population of almost sixty thousand, of which nearly twenty-five thousand are located in Greenland and more than sixteen thousand in Alaska. In the center the huge area of the Canadian Arctic accounts for another sixteen thousand Eskimos, and Russian Siberia has little more than a thousand of these unique people.

Across this huge sweep of land there were, and still are, variations in the cultural pattern. Some authorities distinguish between coast Eskimos, living off the produce of the sea, and inland Eskimos, who are mainly dependent on the caribou for food. Other, more historically minded scholars draw a dividing line between western Eskimos and eastern Eskimos depending on their cultural heritage. Still a third school of opinion emphasizes that many traits are shared by Eskimos of Alaska and Greenland, but are not present among Canadian Eskimos in the middle. Whatever the

The Private Journal of G. F. Lyon, LONDON, 1824

differences, however, the Eskimos all share broad similarities of culture that link them together whether they live in the U.S.S.R. or in Danish Greenland nearly six thousand miles away. It is this unity, together with certain notable characteristics from particular regions (such as the snow-house, or igloo), that has given Eskimo culture an unmistakable stamp, distinguishing it from every other culture pattern in the world.

To a visitor from an industrialized society the most immediately striking feature of Eskimo life, even in its most primitive form, is its astonishingly high level of technology. In craftsmanship, essential mechanics, and practical invention, the Eskimos excel most other primitive peoples. Their technological skill, it is generally agreed, was forced upon the Eskimos by the stern demands of their environment. They had to be both ingenious and meticulous if the equipment they prepared for their battle against cold and hunger was not to fail and leave them to die. The kayak that foundered gave a man only a few minutes' survival time in the icy water, just as surely as the collapse of his harpoon equipment for winter seal-hunting would condemn his family to death by starvation. Time and again the contacts between white men and Eskimos pointed up the Eskimo's quick grasp of new tools and techniques. In 1850, for example, when one Captain Ommaney asked a Cape York Eskimo in Greenland to draw the coast for him, the Eskimo calmly took the proffered pencil, a tool he could never have seen before in his life, and proceeded to draw with considerable accuracy the whole coastline of Smith Sound. Then he not only marked all the salient geographic features from memory but gave their names to his questioner. A century later, American technicians constructing radar stations along the Arctic DEW line were hugely impressed at how quickly the local Eskimos

This 1824 view of a winter village of Eskimos in northeastern Canada was drawn by Captain George F. Lyon, a British explorer. The cluster of igloos, averaging 14–16 feet in diameter and 6–7 feet in height, was occupied by thirteen families.

199

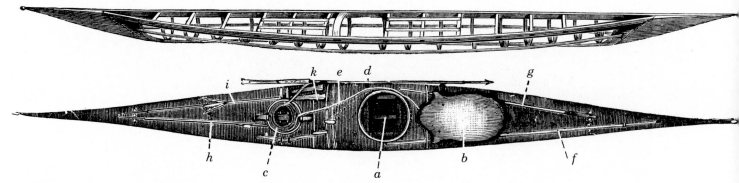

learned to run the motorized equipment. Very soon it was being said that only an Eskimo was capable of starting up a diesel engine in the very coldest temperatures.

A close inspection of an Eskimo's equipment for hunting seals in the water illustrates his original flair for bold and pragmatic design. In the first place, there is the kayak itself, one of the most maneuverable and beauti-fully sleek vessels ever invented. From one coast region to another the kayaks differ in profile and size, but everywhere they are essentially a light membrane hull stretched over an exceedingly narrow skeleton frame. The paddler sits with his legs outstretched inside the hull and his torso appear-ing through a cockpit in the upper deck. The whole assembly is so light that when an incautious Eskimo paddled out to inspect an Elizabethan exploring ship, her muscular captain, Martin Frobisher, was able to lean down from the waist of his vessel and seize the Eskimo by the hand, hoisting him and his kayak aboard in a single movement. Usually fifteen to twenty feet long, the skeleton of the kayak is made of arched ribs and longitudinal laths on much the same principle as an airship's cigar-shaped hull, though the upper surface of a kayak is usually left as a flat deck. The tightly stretched mem-brane is made of sealskin from which the hair is first removed, and then the skin is fastened into place with waterproof sinew stitching. In Alaska and around Greenland the kayaker completes his outfit with a waterproof skin jacket that has drawstrings around the hood and waist. When these strings are pulled tight and the waist of the jacket is lashed down to the cockpit coamings, the paddler is virtually sealed into his vessel and can survive a capsizal with equanimity. In fact, this is an essential precaution, because in rough weather the kayak is a cranky and unstable craft despite the balanc-ing effect of the kayaker's paddle, which may be either double- or single-bladed and acts rather like a tightrope walker's balancing pole. Perhaps the greatest polar explorer and traveler of all time, Fridtjof Nansen, in dis-cussing west Greenland Eskimos, was at pains to emphasize the importance of being sealed into one's kayak and knowing exactly what to do in a capsize.

"You cannot rank as an expert kayak man," he wrote, "until you have mastered the art of righting yourself after capsizing. To do this, you seize one end of the paddle in your hand, and with the other hand grasp the shaft as near the middle as possible; then you place it along the side of the kayak with its free end pointing towards the bow; and thereupon, pushing the end of the paddle sharply out to the side, and bending your body well forward towards the deck, you raise yourself by a strong circular sweep of the paddle. . . .

"A kayak man who has entirely mastered the art of righting himself can defy almost any weather. If he is capsized, he is on even keel again in a moment, and can play like a sea bird with the waves, and cut right through them. If the sea is very heavy, he lays the broad side of his kayak to it, holds the paddle flat out on the windward side, pressing it against the deck, bends forward, and lets the wave roll over him; or else he throws himself on his side towards it, resting on his flat paddle, and rights himself again when it has passed. The prettiest feat of seamanship I have ever heard of is that to which some fishers, I am told, have recourse among overwhelming rollers. As the sea curls down over them they voluntarily capsize, receive it on the bottom of the kayak, and when it has passed right themselves again. I think it would be difficult to name a more intrepid method of dealing with a heavy sea."

Even with such a high degree of skill, kayaking in icy water is a dangerous business. In Nansen's day the number of known Eskimo deaths in kayak accidents was large. In 1889, in south Greenland alone, twenty-four men were reported to have died in kayak mishaps, approximately a quarter of the total male mortality. This, as Nansen said, was "in a population of 5,614 of which 2,591 were males."

Lashed to the flat deck of a hunting kayak is an array of weapons demonstrating the mechanical side of the Eskimo's expertise. Usually there are short stabbing lances tipped with bone or, in later days, with metal; perhaps a small camouflage screen, rather like a tiny square sail, which makes the kayak look like a drifting ice floe; a spear-throwing board resembling the woomera of the Australian Aborigine; and several sealskin bladders on long lines, which, when attached to a wounded seal, serve to slow down or mark

A Russian engraving of 1793, based on a drawing by G. W. Steller, an artist with Vitus Bering, pictures somewhat crudely a village of Siberian Eskimos, with its inhabitants twirling long sticks to make fire.

the position of the prey. The most cunning contrivance, however, is the seal harpoon itself, the principle striking weapon of a kayaker's armament. In its most sophisticated form, the harpoon is a complicated tool designed not only to transfix the seal but to make sure that the animal cannot shake free and escape. As the harpoon strikes, it virtually collapses. The mainshaft, having delivered the impetus of the blow, sags limply away from the spearhead, to which it is lightly attached with thongs. The head of the harpoon is now embedded in the animal's flesh and is turned in the wound by a tug on the harpoon line that leads back to the kayak. Because the line is tied to a hole in the center of the harpoon head, the head is actually twisted in the flesh, anchoring it firmly. The hunter pulls in on the line, perhaps half-submerging the bow of his kayak against the weight of the struggling animal, until he is close enough to kill the seal with his lance and the hunt is done. In earlier days the Eskimos even used heavier versions of these harpoons to go after small whales. Operating from larger skin boats of an open design, called "umiaks" or "baydara" (and popularly known in Greenland as the "women's boats"), the Eskimo harpooners speared the whale and, as the creature sounded, threw overboard special drag floats on long lines that slowed down the animal's escape until it was too exhausted to avoid the hunters.

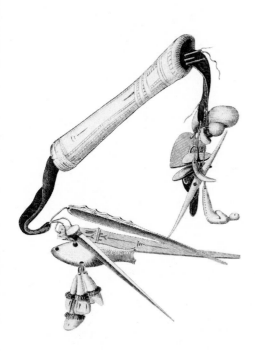

Canadian Eskimo utensils, depicted by Captain Lyon in 1824, include (top) a hollow bone carrying case with a leather strip, to which are attached small, easily lost articles like needles and spoons and (below) a long ivory nail to plug the spear holes in slain animals in order to save the much-prized blood.
Journal of Discovery, W. E. PARRY, LONDON, 1824

The other main feature of Eskimo life—on which nearly all the early observers agree—is that they are a remarkably cheerful and welcoming people. At first thought, this is surprising, for historic contacts between Eskimos and white men were not always peaceful. Some of the Elizabethan navigators who sought the Northwest Passage stirred resentments among several groups of Eskimos and were involved in bloody clashes with them. Despite such episodes, however, relations between the natives and the early visitors were actually more often characterized by a high level of friendship and good humor. In 1586, when John Davis's expedition reached Eskimo territory, the English crew found the natives willing to hold an impromptu sports meeting on the ice. To their chagrin, the Englishmen lost a wrestling competition to the Eskimos, though the visitors did win a very crude game of football by ferociously tackling any Eskimo who got near the ball and hurling him heavily to the ice.

The most detailed account, though, of the Eskimos' reaction to their first meeting with white men was recorded early in the nineteenth century, when John Ross's ships discovered the group known as the polar Eskimos, the people who lived farthest north in the world. Ross's two ships were coasting slowly along the edge of the pack ice when the lookouts were astonished to see several Eskimo sleds keeping pace with them, though at a safe distance. Scarcely able to believe that people could live at so high a latitude, Ross resolved to make contact and, after mooring his ships to the ice, waited for them to approach. But the polar Eskimos had clearly never seen a sailing ship before, because when the ships' yards were swung to the wind, the Eskimos took fright at the sudden movement of the great white sails and retreated. Eventually Ross was obliged to set on the ice a Greenland Eskimo named Sacheuse, who volunteered to walk unarmed up to four of the polar Eskimos hovering cautiously on the far side of a channel of open water. Watching through their spyglasses, Ross and his officers saw Sacheuse advance to the edge of the ice, where, "taking off his hat, [he] made friendly signs to those opposite to approach . . . this they partly complied with, halting at a distance of three hundred yards, where they got out of their sledges, and set up a loud simultaneous halloo, which Sacheuse answered by imitating it. They ventured to approach a little nearer, having nothing in their hands but the whips with which they guide their dogs; and, after satisfying themselves that the canal was impassable, one of them in particular seemed to acquire confidence. Shouts, words, and gestures were exchanged for some time to no purpose, though each party seemed, in some degree to recognize each other's language. Sacheuse, after a time, thought he could discover that they spoke the Humooke dialect, drawling out their words, however, to an unusual length. He immediately adopted that dialect, and holding up presents, called out to them, *kahkeite,* 'Come on!' to which they answered *naakrie, naakrieai-plaite,* 'No, no—go away'; and other words which he made out to mean, that they hoped we were not come to destroy them. The boldest then approached to the edge of the canal, and drawing from his boot a knife repeated 'Go away'; 'I can kill you.' Sacheuse, not intimidated, told them he was also a man and a friend, and, at the same time, threw across the canal some strings of beads and a checked shirt; but these they beheld with great distrust and apprehension, still calling 'Go away, don't kill us.' Sacheuse now threw them an English knife, saying, 'Take that.' On this they approached with caution, picked up the knife, then shouted and pulled their noses; these actions were imitated by Sacheuse, who, in return, called out 'Heigh yaw,' pulling his nose with the same gesture. . . . They now began to ask many questions; for, by this time, they found the language spoken by themselves and Sacheuse, had sufficient resemblance to enable them to hold some communication."

The most revealing moment of this whole incident, however, occurred

The scene below is based on Sacheuse's version of the 1818 meeting between Polar Eskimos and John Ross's men, the first Europeans these most northerly dwelling people in the world had ever seen. Note the Eskimo at rear looking into a mirror.

Voyage of Discovery, JOHN ROSS, LONDON, 1819

when the Eskimos were given mirrors as presents. For the first time, they saw their own faces reflected, and for a moment there was awed shock. Next they looked around in stunned silence at one another and at the white men. Then they gave a great shout, and immediately burst into peals of laughter.

The precise origins of the Eskimos and their culture remain something of an enigma. It is generally agreed that they were originally an Asiatic people and that they are comparatively late arrivals in North America, having crossed the Bering land bridge into Alaska long after earlier waves of migrants had pushed southward. But whether the Eskimos brought their culture ready-formed with them or developed it within North America is an open question, as is the manner and timing of their dispersal. At the moment, the oldest occupation sites showing Eskimo-type cultures are in Alaska and date from about 3000 B.C. This tallies with the notion that they came into North America from Asia and spread eastward, finally reaching Greenland. But the picture is complicated by the fact that there were obviously several waves of Eskimo migration, overlapping one another and surging irregularly, so that there were long pauses for cultural development in the intervals. Thus, southern Alaska appears to have been settled comparatively early and then have been by-passed, becoming something of a backwater while later waves of Eskimo dispersal took place along a northern corridor. In northern Alaska, especially at Point Barrow, where the essential archeological work has been done, the various horizons of excavation reveal a diverse pattern of Neolithic and Mesolithic cultures waxing and waning, and perhaps sending offshoots eastward, so that the Dorset culture, whose members possibly exterminated the Vikings in North America, has many similarities with early Alaskan cultures. Certainly there is some evidence for the idea that Eskimo culture finally spread to Greenland at about the same time that the Vikings reached Greenland from the opposite direction, an interesting hypothesis about two cultures that had both originated thousands of years earlier in Eurasia.

Many Eskimologists now prefer to qualify the notion of an overall west-east migration with the idea of cultural countercurrents. These, like waves breaking on a rock, set up a backwash, causing certain cultural influences to travel in the opposite direction. In some cases it has been possible to identify central dispersal points in Arctic Canada from which these countercurrents flowed. In rather the same way, the old notion that the Eskimos represented an entirely separate race has also had to be modified. Recent anthropometric studies comparing the northern forest Indians of America, the Eskimos, and the northern Asian tribes have shown so many similarities among them that instead of being an "Eskimo wedge" between the Asiatic peoples and the American Indians, the Eskimos are now seen as a linking people, sharing many characteristics with the races on both sides of them.

In fact, the physical characteristics of the Eskimos are by no means homogenous. As one would expect with waves of immigration out of Siberia, the Eskimos display a range of physical features that are most "Asian" near the Bering Strait and decrease as one moves across to Greenland. The outstanding example is the matter of skull shape. In Greenland the Eskimo skulls are outstandingly dolichocephalic, or "longheaded," with cephalic indexes of 70.7 for male skulls and 72.2 for female. The longheadedness is a distinctive characteristic of Eskimo cranial structure as far west as the

This complex painted Eskimo mask is attached to a cedar hoop and a staff that extends from its mouth. The mask is carved from a square of wood and has at its corners hands or claws holding fish and animals.

Garbed in their summer dance costumes (with fur side out), these Copper Eskimos of Canada were photographed in 1916.

Coronation Gulf Eskimos of north central Canada are seen in summer at a stone weir, spearing salmon trout that swam upriver and became trapped in an opening of the dam.

Mackenzie River delta, but in Alaska the percentage of mesocephalic and brachycephalic skulls, the middle and broad heads, increases noticeably. In height the Eskimos are a medium-sized people, averaging between 62.2 and 66.1 inches. To the casual observer they appear rather shorter, for they have long, stocky bodies and comparatively short arms and legs with small hands and feet. When clad in loose-fitting, bulky clothing, the general impression is of a sturdy, if somewhat plump, people, an outward aspect that is reinforced by the flat planes of their well-fleshed faces, giving them a distinctly Mongol appearance. Surprisingly, this layer of facial padding conceals an excessively narrow bone structure to the nose, the Eskimos having almost the narrowest noses in the world. These two features, the fatty layer of the face and the thin nasal passages, have both been explained as specialized adaptations against the extreme cold, though an alternative theory is that the shape of Eskimo noses and the large size of their jaws are the result of prolonged use of the jaws and teeth to masticate raw meat and as basic tools to chew leather and skins in order to soften and shape them. Certainly the teeth of many adult Eskimo skeletons are severely worn down, and in some cases there are bony swellings along the gum ridges, though it is debatable whether the entire skull shape can also have been modified.

According to Kaj Birket-Smith, the leading Danish authority on the Eskimos, their skin color varies greatly according to the season, from a basic yellow-brown or light olive to a deep sunburned tan as a result of exposure on the snow fields and ice. In Birket-Smith's observation, Eskimo women are consistently several shades lighter in skin color than the men, though both sexes have the same predominance of brown eyes and black hair. Curiously, as with the Australian Aborigines, there have been occasional rumors of "blond Eskimos," sometimes having blue eyes, who are considered to be descendants of European castaways. In the case of the Greenland Eskimos there has certainly been much racial intermixture with Danish settlers, but the tales of blond Eskimos among the more isolated groups have turned out to be either unsubstantiated reports or, in one instance, the result of Eskimos regularly drinking hot blood soup, which discolored the men's beards. As for the blue eyes, Birket-Smith is of the opinion that this is a pathological condition, an inner ring of blue color around the iris itself, which may be the result of frequent attacks of snow blindness. Yet the best description of an Eskimo is still Nansen's Greenlander, of whom he wrote: "He has a round, broad face, with large, coarse features; small, dark, sometimes rather oblique eyes; a flat nose, narrow between the eyes and broad at the base; round cheeks, bursting with fat; a broad mouth; heavy, broad jaws; which, together with the round cheeks, give the lower part of the face a great preponderance in the physiognomy. When the mouth is drawn up in an oleaginous smile, two rows of strong white teeth reveal themselves. One receives the impression, on the whole, of an admirable chewing apparatus, conveying pleasant suggestions of much and good eating."

The influence of the rigorous northern climate is never far from Eskimo life. The whole pace of their existence is geared to seasonal changes and to detecting the sudden variations of daily weather conditions, which can be extremely dangerous when one is living on the critical fringe of the earth's habitable environment. A kayak man fishing offshore with a hand line must be ready to paddle with all speed for the beach before a rising gale makes it impossible to come ashore through the raging surf. Knud Rasmussen, the polar explorer (and himself part Eskimo) who in the early years of this century did more than anyone else to foster Eskimo studies by his extraordinary long-distance Arctic journeys, recalled:

"Once, at the end of January, after a journey across Melville Bay, we drove in a party of twenty sledges along the land south of the Petowik glacier on our way to Thule. The weather was good, and as the day's journey consequently had been a very long one, I felt somewhat tired and stretched myself on the sledge to take a little nap, whilst a boy who accompanied me drove the dogs. Just before my eyes closed I noticed a swirl above some cloughs near the inland-ice, but as there were no other signs of bad weather on the sky, none of us paid any particular attention to it.

"My doze could not have lasted more than five minutes when I was awakened in the most brutal manner, being, as by a mighty grip, lifted up from the sledge and flung out on the ice. I received so violent a blow in the back that I was unable to get up for a moment, but when at last I succeeded in rising to my knees, I saw that all the many sledges which a moment ago had driven in a long string one behind the other, were swept together into one huge pile, like wooden shavings blown together by a breath of wind. With such suddenness and force the Föhn-Wind had sent out its first squalls as forerunners of the storm which was coming. As it was quite impossible to

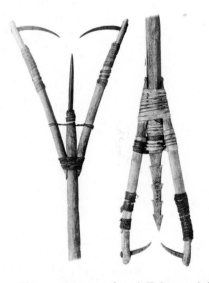

The working ends of Eskimo fish spears, or leisters, show the center point that jabs into the fish and the supple side prongs of antler whose sharp hooks hold on to the catch.

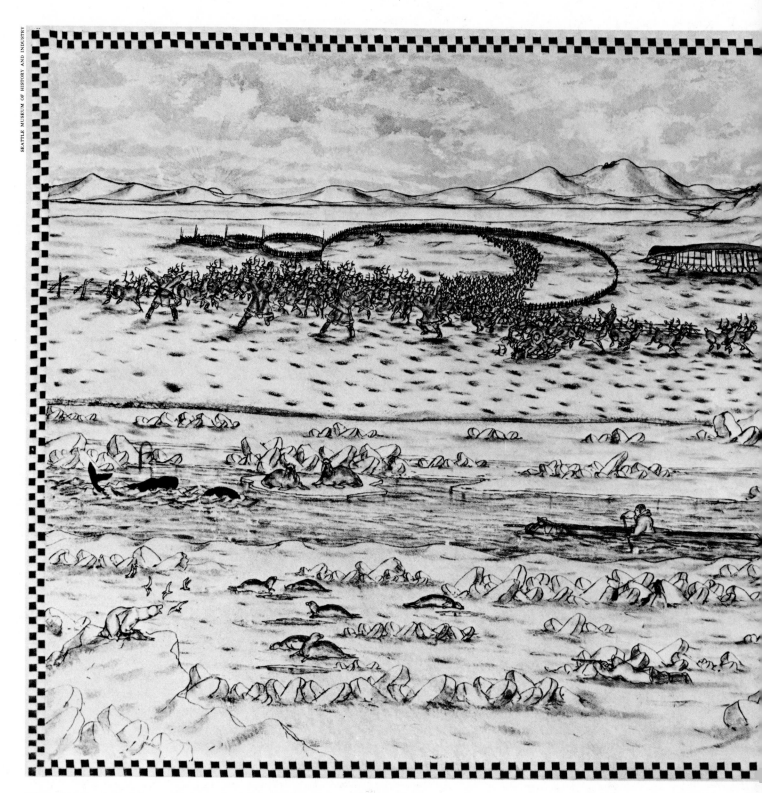

Many facets of the life of Alaskan Eskimos may be seen in this drawing on reindeer skin by George Aghupuk, a modern Eskimo artist. Food gathering includes caribou trapping (upper left), seal stalking (lower left), and ice hunting (lower right). Travel, dance, and camp scenes are above the ice hunters.

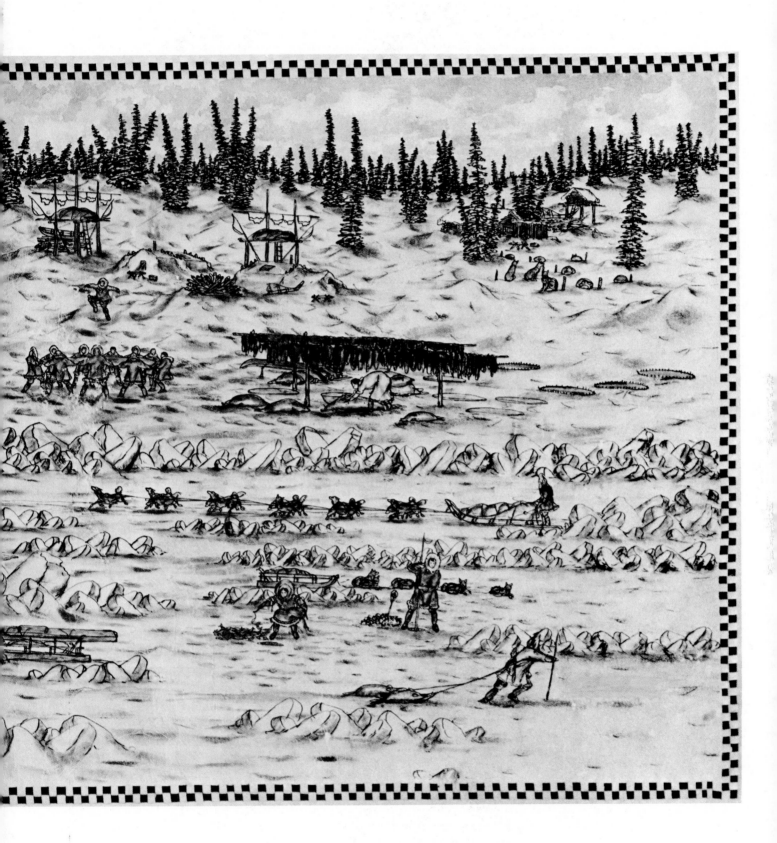

This sharp-bladed, planelike instrument, seen in two views above, is used by Eskimos to scrape skins for clothing and tents. Iron from white traders replaced the original stone or bone scraping blades.

stand upright, not to mention driving, we let ourselves be blown up on land with sledges and dogs, until we found some little shelter in a clough by a broad tongue of ice where the sledges could be anchored and the dogs tethered. Hardly was this done when the Föhn, with the roar of a hurricane, swept down upon us from the mountains and the inland-ice and made us suspect that the world itself was going under. It pressed its enormous weight down on the thick winter ice with such violence that the waves immediately burst up through the belt of the tidal waters. Half an hour later we saw through the darkness huge fissures in the ice, frothing white, and a few hours after the outbreak there was open sea where shortly before we had driven our sledges."

The effect of the changing seasons on Eskimo life is best illustrated by the Netsilik Eskimos of northern Canada. Here, northwest of Hudson Bay, live an Eskimo group whose habitat is partly on land and partly on the sea ice, depending upon the climate. Conveniently, too, the Netsilik fall midway between the Alaskan and Greenland extremes of Eskimo culture, sharing certain features with each and, as it happens, retaining their aboriginal culture long enough for it to have been studied in depth. They are in their own language "the People of the Seal," and until very recently they practiced the basic transhumance, the seasonal rotation of their living area, that was so characteristic of Eskimo life.

July was the key month when the Netsilik moved from the ice to the mainland, a time when the sea ice grew slushy and the Arctic spring brought new life to the interior. Initially the move was only halfhearted, the Netsilik remaining on the seashore to gather birds' eggs from the cliffs, hunt for a few last seals among the melting ice floes, and look for driftwood on the shore. It was now, working with small knives and simple mouth drills, that the new kayaks had to be made if they were to be ready for the fall hunting. As summer advanced and the char began to run in the rivers, the Netsilik moved more purposefully inland. Stowing their goods in backpacks—some of them strapped to their dogs—the Netsilik moved fifteen miles inland to fish weirs that had been built generations earlier at the spawning grounds. There, living in skin tents, they enjoyed the fattest time of the year, when the daily quest for food was no more than three excited periods of ten minutes each, fishing at the weir, stabbing at the moving fish with a tridentlike implement known as a leister. This weapon, shaped like a large tuning fork with a central barb, impales the fish and holds it fast with the two flexible side prongs long enough for the fisherman to whirl up his catch and fling it toward the women and children waiting ashore.

According to Rasmussen, who stayed at the Netsilik fishing camp, it was forbidden to approach the fishing ground until a certain signal had been given. "This cry was answered with glad yells from every tent, and a wild race started down the river, men, women and children from the oldest to the very youngest, some fully dressed, others half naked and most of them bare legged, despite the fact that the water in the river was icy cold. A short distance from the fishing place they all stopped; there all the leisters, with the long wooden shafts, had been left, and now four or five men moved stealthily, leister in hand, towards the lake from which the fish were to come. They had to take great care that their shadows did not fall upon the water; about twenty yards from the weir they suddenly jumped out into the water, and one could now see how the many fish that had collected about the stone barrier shoaled towards the weir a few leaped over it and continued their way out into the other lake, but most of them swam through the weir gate into the enclosure. As soon as there were no more fish in the lake, a man jumped in and closed the weir with a large flat stone. This was the sign that fishing could begin and, without regard for the cold water or their clothes, which became soaked through, the whole impatient crowd poured into the river and began to spear the fish that had gathered in it, and darted in and out between their legs. There was no system in their fishing; it was all a question of who could spear the most. It was always a mystery to me that in this scuffle, where the leisters rose and fell here, there and everywhere, apparently quite at random, several toes were not lost . . ."

With their supplies of fish safely cached beneath piles of stones out of the way of foxes, the Netsilik were able to spend their extra time idling and relaxing, gathering berries in a desultory fashion or perhaps snaring a few wild birds with traps baited with liver. Then, in mid-September, came the caribou-hunting season, the second high point in the Netsilik summer.

Eskimos of north central Canada begin the task of skinning caribou after a successful spring hunt. The photograph was made by the Arctic explorer G. H. Wilkins in 1915 at an Eskimo camp, where the animals were brought back for butchering.

The band scoured the neighborhood to round up herds of caribou and drive them toward the sea inlets. Frightened by the running shapes of the Eskimos and puzzled by strategically placed cairns that they mistook for men, the caribou plunged blindly into the water. There they were attacked by kayakers putting out from shore and spearing the exhausted animals as they swam for safety. A successful caribou hunt was immensely important to the Netsilik, for while their waterproof clothing is made from sealskin, the warm winter clothing is made of caribou pelts, which are unequaled for warmth because each hair on a caribou skin contains an insulating pocket of air.

In early December the trek back to the coast began, for this was the time when new sea ice formed and the seal hunting was particularly good. Several methods of seal hunting were used, depending on conditions, but the easiest was the fine-weather stalking of seals as they lay sunning themselves on the ice. Today most Eskimos use rifles to kill the animals, but a traditional Netsilik way was to imitate a seal itself by lying down on the ice and wriggling close enough to plunge home a short throwing harpoon before the animal took fright and disappeared down its escape hole. The Netsilik even used a bone instrument shaped like a small comb to scratch the ice and imitate the sound of a seal's flippers contentedly scraping the surface. Seal stalking by this method is surprisingly easy to learn, and Vilhjalmur Stefansson, a Canadian-born Eskimologist, managed to become quite an expert at it. "So long as you are more than three hundred yards away from a seal you need not be careful," he wrote. "He might see you at four hundred yards if you were upright, but you should begin crawling somewhat before the four hundred yard mark is reached. I crawl ahead on all fours while he is asleep, and when he wakes up I drop flat instantly and remain motionless until he goes to sleep again. This sort of approach will do until you are about three hundred yards away, but after that you must be more careful, for he now may see you at any time.

"When I felt myself well within the seal's range of vision, I began to crawl ahead seal fashion, which practically means snake-fashion. I moved as rapidly as I could while he slept and I stopped motionless while he was awake until finally, at a distance of 175 yards, he saw me.

"It was easy to tell when the seal first saw me. He stiffened up suddenly, lifted his head a little higher than ordinary and crawled a foot or two nearer his waterhole so as to be able to dive instantly if necessary. Being now in what he thought a safe position himself and considering me so far away that there was no immediate danger, he watched me carefully. Had I remained motionless for two or three minutes, he would have become restive, and in a few minutes more he would have dived into his hole, for he knew very well that no real seal would remain motionless for long. Accordingly I waited till he had been watching me about half a minute, which is the average sleeping spell in a seal. I then did my best to act like a seal waking up. I lifted my head about eighteen inches above the ice, looked around in all directions, and moved as if I were squirming seal-fashion on the ice. After spending about five seconds looking around, I allowed my head to drop on the ice. I then counted ten of my breaths and raised my head a second time, dropping it after a suitable interval. Occasionally I would flex my legs at the knee so as to imitate a seal scratching with his hind flippers.

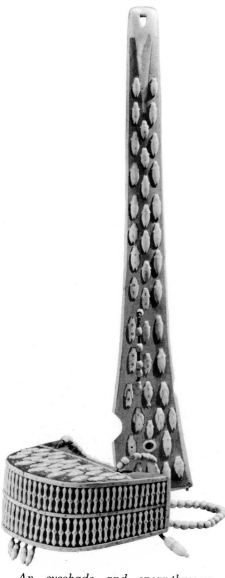

An eyeshade and spear-thrower, made by east Greenland Eskimos, are of wood decorated with human and seal figures of ivory and bone.
NATIONAL MUSEUM, COPENHAGEN

*These Coronation Gulf Eskimo arch-
ers, photographed by Wilkins in
1913, are dressed for summer, with
the hair side out on their long-
paneled coats. Their bows had a
range of 125 yards, but were most
effective at only 30 or 40 yards.*

"In about ten or fifteen minutes of this sort of acting I had the seal convinced that I was another seal. After that the whole thing was easy."

But when winter sets in, the snow lies on the ice, and the seals no longer
sun themselves, life is more difficult. The mainstay of seal hunting becomes
the long, patient vigil over a seal's breathing hole in the ice. Fanning out
over an area of four to five miles from their main camp, the Netsilik men use
their dogs to sniff out the breathing holes, then tether the animals at a safe
distance away from the spot, for the seals are wary of the slightest tremor on
the ice. Placing a thin bone wand with an attached twist of goose down over
the hole, the hunter patiently waits, watching for the warning quiver of the
down, which informs him that a seal is rising to the surface. As each seal
may have four or five breathing holes and uses them in rotation, it can be a
long and bitterly cold wait in temperatures that sometimes fall as low as
50 degrees below zero. A thick bearskin pad to stand on and a windbreak
of ice blocks give some small protection, but the hunter cannot afford to
grow stiff and clumsy. The breathing hole is a tiny aperture scarcely large
enough to admit a harpoon shaft, and as the seal surfaces, the loose-headed
harpoon must drive down accurately through the gap to transfix the animal
and tether it firmly while the hunter hacks out the hole large enough to
retrieve his quarry.

Despite their skill and patience, the Netsilik, like most northerly Eskimo
groups, find winter a severe test of survival. In a sense, the purpose of all
their hunting is to provide sufficient food to carry them through the nadir
of an Arctic winter. When blizzards rage, all hunting is impossible and the
Eskimo families are cooped up in their snowhouses. The center of their life
is the blubber lamp, a semicircular stone dish in which a carefully tended
wick burns steadily to provide light and warmth. When all food and oil

AMERICAN MUSEUM OF NATURAL HISTORY

A photograph taken inside an Eskimo dwelling at Cape Fullerton catches spectators enjoying a not too serious display of fisticuffs.

is expended, the family faces the genuine possibility of starvation unless there is a break in the weather. Not surprisingly, the annual ordeal of winter means that the Netsilik family cannot afford to be large. Superfluous infants, particularly girl babies, may simply be left to die of exposure if the mother cannot support the new child's demands. Eskimo women have a vital role in the maintenance of the family, not simply to cook and take care of the children, but also to provide the hunter with the essential clothing that protects him from the environment. Among Greenland and Canadian Eskimos it is said that a hunter is what his wife makes of him, and a poorly dressed hunter is at a severe disadvantage. Caribou skins must be cleaned and shaped; sealskin masticated to the correct suppleness; and even bird's down for women's finery needs to be scraped and cleaned and then carefully chewed. According to Nansen, "the operator takes the dry skin, almost dripping with fat, and chews away at one spot until all the fat is sucked out and the skin is soft and white; then the chewing area is slowly widened, the skin gradually retreating further and further into the mouth, until it often disappears entirely, to be spat out again at last with every particle of fat chewed away. This industry is for the most part carried on by the women and children, and is very highly relished by reason of the quantity of fat it enables them to absorb. In times of scarcity, the men are often glad enough to be allowed to do their share. It is a strange scene that is presented when one enters a house and finds the whole of its population thus engaged in chewing, each with his skin in his mouth."

Eskimo clothing is of a basically similar design everywhere, though style and cut may vary. Generally it comprises coat, knickerbockerlike trousers, stockings, and shoes or boots. The rule is that one set of clothing is worn in warm weather, and an extra set is added on top in winter. Indoors it is often so stuffy from the warmth of the lamp and the other inhabitants that the wearer strips off everything except his or her trousers or, in some cases, a

214

small loincloth. Eskimo babies are carried during cold weather in a pouch at the back of their mother's coat, nestling against her back, where they can easily be shifted around to be breast-fed or, if necessary, extricated quickly. Winter clothing includes heavy mittens and in many areas snow goggles made of wood or walrus ivory and with very narrow eye slits to reduce the glare and consequent risk of snow blindness.

In late March the Netsilik families, who have been seal hunting some distance apart, come together to build a great communal snowhouse. This is a large chamber with several connecting smaller snowhouses, intended to last the community until the end of April. Here, during these weeks, the Netsilik live together more or less as a cooperative. When a seal is killed, the flesh is distributed under the supervision of the hunter's wife, who divides the animal according to rigidly observed conventions. Songs and story recitals help pass the time, and shortly before the snowhouse is abandoned, a festival is usually held with dancing and singing to the sound of a skin drum shaped like a tambourine and held in one hand and struck rhythmically on alternate edges of the hoop.

Popularly known as an igloo (though the word means a house of any kind), the snowhouse of the Netsilik is one of the several ways in which the central Eskimos differ from the Alaskans and Greenlanders, who use tents or log-and-turf cabins. Another difference is that the Netsilik depend much more on caribou than do most other coast-dwelling Eskimos, who in the extreme case of some of the south Alaskan groups exist almost entirely on fish, to such an extent that when they were Christianized, they received special papal authority to substitute "Give us this day our daily fish" for "Give us this day our daily bread." In fact, modern dietary studies have shown that an all-fish diet, or one heavily mixed with seal meat, is sufficiently well balanced in vitamins and other necessities.

The Eskimo sledge also varies considerably from one side of the "Eskimo arc" to the other. To the Eskimo on land and ice the sledge is what the kayak is to him on the water: his most important hunting aid. Sledge design varies from a single ladder frame of two very long runners connected by crossbars, to a more complicated sleigh with upcurved runners, frame sides, and a central latticework. By and large, the central Eskimos use the simpler type, though their sledges are sometimes as much as ten yards long, and the Greenlanders use a slightly improved version with two upright bars at the back to help in steering. It is the western and Alaskan Eskimos who have the sleigh type, which, because it resembles sleighs used in northern Siberia, may be a cultural import. In all cases, whether simple or complex, the framework of the sledge is lashed together to give flexible joints, the better to ride the rough ice surfaces. Runners can be made of almost any material, from wood and bone to such rough-and-ready substitutes as rolled-up and frozen musk-ox skin or slats of frozen fish. Under favorable conditions a thin bearing surface of ice is applied to the runners—often dribbled out as melted water from the sledgeman's mouth during a rest stop—but when the ice and snow surface is broken and intermingled with rock, the runners are sometimes shod with bone or, in recent times, metal. Birket-Smith found that peat mold and even custard powder applied to the runners served as decent shoeing.

Similarly, the method of harnessing the dogs to the sledge varies geo-

The crescent-shaped "ulu," or woman's knife, has various uses, including cutting a chunk of meat into bite-sized pieces as the eater chews it.

graphically. In the west it is normal to have a single main towrope, to which the dogs are attached in pairs like an ox tow on a wagon. In Greenland and eastern Canada each dog has its own trace leading back to the sledge. In Greenland all these traces are the same length, and the dogs spread out fanwise. But in Labrador there is the refinement that each trace is a different length, with the longest attached to a chosen lead dog. Whatever the modification, the eastern system has the disadvantage that the dogs, as they mingle and change places, tangle their traces into a ferocious knot that must be undone at every halt. Driving a dog team by using a twelve- or fifteen-foot whip and voice commands is a considerable art, and Peary, who in his long siege of the Arctic did much Greenland-style sledging, stated that "a white man can learn to use an Eskimo whip, but it takes time. It takes time also to acquire the exact Eskimo accent to the words *How-eh, how-eh, how-eh,* meaning 'To the right'; *Ash-oo, ash-oo, ash-oo,* 'To the left'; as well as the standard *Huk, huk, huk,* which is equivalent to 'Go on.' Sometimes, when the dogs do not obey, the usual *How-eh, how-eh, how-eh* will reverse its accent, and the driver will yell *How-oooooooo* with an accompaniment of other words in Eskimo and English which shall be left to the imagination of the reader. The temperature of a new man trying to drive a team of Eskimo dogs is apt to be pretty high. One is almost inclined to believe with the Eskimos that demons take possession of these animals. Sometimes they seem to be quite crazy. A favorite trick of theirs is to leap over and under and around each other, getting their traces in a snarl beside which the Gordian knot would be as nothing. Then, in a temperature anywhere between zero and 60° below, the driver has to remove his heavy mittens and disentangle the traces with his bare hands, while the dogs leap and snap and bark and seem to mock him."

Fortunately for the novice Arctic traveler, the Eskimos are nearly always prepared to help and instruct in northern techniques. As noted, European and American pioneers, with only occasional exceptions, spoke highly of the welcome extended to them by the Eskimos. Birket-Smith quotes one post manager among the Eskimos and the Naskapi Indians in Labrador who said: "When you travel with the Eskimos, they try to make everything go as well as possible for you, because they know you are a stranger and to a certain extent helpless in their land. When you travel with the Indians, they try to make life a burden in every possible way until you have acknowledged their superiority. Then, and only then, they may perhaps

In this remarkable photograph, taken by Diamond Jenness in 1915, an Eskimo community is seen with its dogs and loaded sledges, migrating to a new winter location at Coronation Gulf in north central Canada.

change their ways." Peary is said to have been told by his Eskimos that they considered it too dangerous to push so far north and that they intended to turn back. One of them, however, agreed to accompany Peary so that he would not die alone. Nevertheless, in some ways, the Eskimos have perhaps been flattered by their visitors. There is no denying that life in a northern snowhouse can be cramped and incommodious. The conditions of life are not conducive to cleanliness, and the tendency for the caribou-skin clothing to molt leaves numerous hairs floating on the surface of any soup or greasy food. By others' standards the Eskimos have also seemed at times a rather vindictive people. Until recently, the family blood feud was quite common, and men boasted of how many of their rivals they had killed. Even the famous ridicule matches, where contestants mock one another in front of an audience instead of fighting, have a rather more serious result than is commonly supposed. The loser in a ridicule match may, in the long run, suffer a more enduring humiliation by group disapproval than if he had lost a physical contest.

It may be said that the Eskimos display a sense of good-natured fatalism and levelheaded pragmatism. They have strong unwritten laws and definite leaders, including recognized shamans who are able to communicate more effectively with the spirit world. Even their religious beliefs take a practical turn. To some Eskimo groups, there is a goddess at the bottom of the sea who must be pacified if the fishing and seal hunting is to be good. Fish caught through a hole in the ice are arranged in a circle to encourage their fellows to join them, and when the Netsilik catch a seal, it is customary to sprinkle a few drops of water in its mouth in order to appease the thirst of its spirit, for the Netsilik believe it is the same spirit seal that is caught again and again and must never be driven away. Similarly, when the Netsilik change camps in the winter, they range all the dead seal skulls from their catch in a line, pointing the way they are going so that the souls of the seals will follow them.

This practical approach characterizes much of Eskimo society. Small children may have to migrate on foot behind the sledges almost as soon as they can walk; and it is not uncommon to find toddlers of three or four years old accompanying treks of a hundred miles or more. By the same token, wife-lending is seen to be no more than a sensible arrangement. The Eskimos believe that if a traveler is without a woman, it is only natural to supply one. Similarly, if a hunter is leaving on a long trip, the woman he leaves

OVERLEAF: *Rectangular tents of hides, covering pole frameworks and held down by stones, provide summer shelter for a community of Alaskan Eskimos in this 1899 photograph by E. S. Curtis. Dead walruses hang from the tent in foreground.*
LIBRARY OF CONGRESS

A detail of the decoration on the sleeve of a parka, executed by the artist Una of Canada's Northwest Territories, depicts a drummer and other figures and is an example of the new Eskimo art of printmaking.

behind may, with the husband's permission, be taken in temporarily by a colleague. As the Eskimos see it, such behavior is no more than logical, for it maintains the social and economic equilibrium of all concerned. Clearly this social equilibrium is all-important in the close and sometimes claustrophobic environment of the north. Good humor, the willingness to collaborate, and the removal of all possible sources of dissent are vital if a community is not to fly apart in a blaze of anger. When all else fails, a curious phenomenon has been noticed, defined by some psychologists as "Arctic hysteria," in which individuals appear to behave irrationally for a short period, as if to provide a safety valve for their hidden tensions.

The language of the Eskimos remains one of their greatest puzzles, and in one instance provides a notable paradox. Although it has been the subject of intense study since the turn of the century, no one has yet been able to place Eskimo in the family of languages. To some ethnolinguists it is related to certain languages spoken in Siberia: to other authorities Eskimo (and Aleut, to which it is closely connected) are seen as forming a distinct, quite separate group of their own. One notion has even traced links with archaic European languages. Certainly there has been no lack of data, because the Eskimo language is too complex and too unusual to be overlooked. In the first place, it is divided geographically into two sections, with a linguistic watershed at Norton Sound. Around the Alaskan coast going northward and across the continent to Greenland, the Eskimos speak a branch of the language known as Inupik (derived from *Inuk*, a human being, and the singular of *Inuit,* the Eskimos' word for themselves), so that an Eskimo from Point Barrow can make himself understood to an Eskimo living in Greenland. But southward from Norton Sound and down around the coast toward Prince William Sound, as well as in Siberia, the Eskimos speak a southern branch known as Yupik, which is unintelligible to Inupik speakers. Secondly, the grammar and phonetics of either branch are supremely intricate and perplexing. Basically, Eskimo is a language of long centipede words, built up in sections by adding one idea to the next until a huge conglomerate is formed that packs an entire sentence into one word. The situation is further complicated by the fact that the ideas within the word do not follow one another in what is, to the outsider, a logical sequence. Birket-Smith gives as an example a *single* Eskimo word for "when he bade him go to the place where the rather large house was to be built," which in Eskimo comes out as "house-large-rather-build-place-to-be-go-bid-when-he-him." Add to this that Eskimo grammar likes to put all personal suffixes at the end of a word, that it revels in abstract terms, and that words are varied by stress on consonants as well as on vowels, and the language of the Eskimos becomes a veritable thicket of difficulties for the student.

The paradox of the Eskimos' language is that for so technically minded a people, who are able to produce such precise and well-thought-out artifacts, they have an astonishingly low mathematical ability. Indeed, in the first days of contact with white men, they could seldom count beyond five. It was a blind spot that, according to Nansen, was very difficult to eradicate. "All our ordinary branches of education," he wrote, "they [the Eskimos] master with more or less readiness. Arithmetic is what they find most difficult, and there are comparatively few who get so far as to deal competently with fractions; the majority have quite enough to do with addition and subtraction of integers, to say nothing of multiplication and division. The imperfection of their gifts in this direction is no doubt due to age-old causes. The Eskimo language like most primitive idioms has a very undeveloped system of numerals, five being the highest number for which they have a special word. They count upon their fingers: one, *atausek;* two, *mardluk;* three, *pingasut;*

Some Arctic customs (and costumes) have changed little in 400 years. The modern Eskimo woman below carries her child in the elongated hood of her outer coat in the same fashion as the woman at left, seen in a drawing made by the English artist John White at Frobisher Bay, south Baffin Island, about 1576.

221

four, *sisamet;* five, *tatdlimat,* the last having probably been the original word for the hand. When an Eskimo wants to count beyond five, he expresses six by saying 'The first finger of the other hand'; for seven he says 'The second finger of the other hand,' and so forth. When he reaches ten he has no more hands to count with, and must have recourse to his feet. Twelve, accordingly, is represented by 'Two toes upon the one foot,' and so forth; seventeen by 'Two toes on the second foot,' and so forth. Thus he manages to mount to twenty, which he calls a whole man (*inuk navdlugo*). Here the mathematical conceptions of many Eskimos come to an end; but men of commanding intellect can count still further, and for one and twenty say 'One on the second man.' Thirty-eight is expressed by 'Three toes on the second man's second foot,' forty by 'The whole of the second man,' and so forth. In this way they can count to a hundred, or 'the whole of the fifth man'; but beyond that his language will not carry even the most gifted Eskimo."

Within all four countries where the Eskimos live — Russian Siberia, American Alaska, the Canadian north, and Danish Greenland — education has been the key to more recent policies. To a certain extent this redresses the imbalance of the time when foreign whalers, sealers, and fur hunters plundered Eskimo territory and introduced such diseases as the influenza epidemic that in 1918 wreaked havoc in Labrador. In many ways the Eskimos survived the foreign invasion better than other primitive peoples. Their skills were useful to the newcomers: the environment discouraged permanent settlement by outsiders; and the Eskimos collaborated rather than resisted. They were often cheated or their economy knocked badly out of alignment, as with the change to fur trading instead of seal hunting in parts of northern Canada. But they retained a native identity long enough for the responsible governments to initiate specific programs of administration. In the U.S.S.R. the Eskimos now fall within the minority people's administration; in Alaska and Canada they benefit from government-directed training and supply programs; and in Greenland they have become increasingly integrated (and intermarried) with the Danish community. Of course, many of their old customs have withered away. The 1965 transhumance of the Netsilik was, in the opinion of some anthropologists, the last time that they hewed strictly to their traditional pattern of life. Elsewhere, motorboat and rifle have replaced kayak and harpoon, and in the American and Canadian territories the snowmobile often ousts the dog sled. Cash-bought goods are usually considered more desirable than subsistence items, and in some places reindeer herds have been introduced to turn the Eskimos into pastoralists rather than hunters. On the other hand, the introduction of new economic incentives and modern materials seems to have led to an expansion of Eskimo territory and numbers. In Alaska, where statistics are available, the Eskimo population is on the increase, and their occupation sites have actually expanded northward. In Canada the government has taken over many of the roles once monopolized by the Hudson's Bay Company, and the Eskimos appear to be prospering. In Greenland, too, government help has diverted the southernmost Eskimos into more stable occupations, such as dairy farming, reindeer and sheep raising, and commercial fishing. Only in the north of Greenland and in Arctic Canada do a few Eskimos continue a modified version of their traditional culture. But these, with benign official care, are likely to do so for several generations to come.

A Coronation Gulf Eskimo, in this Wilkins photograph, sings and beats his slender hand-held drum.

The Sky People
of Hokkaido

The great Louisiana Purchase Exposition held in St. Louis in 1904 cost an estimated $50 million, and its organizers were determined that it should be the grandest spectacle of its kind ever staged. The exhibition grounds covered 1,240 acres, and the surrounding fence stretched for nearly eleven miles. Dozens of important foreign exhibitors turned up, including for the first time at an American fair a representative from Imperial China, Prince Pu Lun, whose magnificent arrival in stunning robes of mandarin silk caused a great sensation. Above all, the St. Louis World's Fair was designed to be *modern*. It fairly bulged with the triumphs of technology. One whole building, the Palace of Machinery, was devoted to science, and it was only natural that the Palace of Electricity should have remained floodlit all night, regardless of expense. Among the scientific exhibits there was one gun, a monstrous sixteen-inch rifled coastal defense cannon, that would disappear ponderously on its mobile carriage into a subterranean pit after a discharge; and another, the German Luger Automatic Repeating Pistol, which, it was claimed, could fire more than one hundred shots a minute on the principles conceived by the renowned Hiram Maxim. Overhead—when the wind was not too strong—circled a prototype airship with its rider perched on a fragile ladder frame slung beneath its belly; and in one corner of the section devoted to "Instruments of Precision" was the spidery shape of a newfangled chloroform inhaler designed by a British inventor to provide patients with a carefully controlled mixture of air and laughing gas.

Tucked away, indeed almost lost, in the midst of this rumbustious carnival of an exhibition were nine bashful tribesmen from Japan. They were Ainus, popularly known to Westerners as the hairy people but informed by one of their own legends that they were Sky People, descended from ancestors who had come from the skies. In truth their racial heritage was, in modern terms, as bizarre and wonderful as any of the gimcrack inventions so glibly displayed at St. Louis. To their credit, the organizers of the fair had gone to considerable lengths to obtain the "Ainu Group," as it was officially dubbed. A special envoy, Frederick Starr, had been sent to Yokohama the previous summer with a young Mexican photographer to contact the Japanese authorities and obtain permission to visit Yezo (now Hok-

A conventional Ainu greeting

225

An Ainu elder wears a traditional crown of willow shavings.

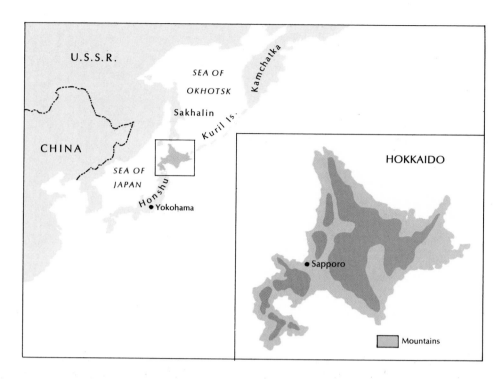

kaido), Japan's main northern island and the home of the surviving Ainu peoples. It was a considerable undertaking because the Russo-Japanese War was declared the night after Starr arrived in Japan, and Japanese troops were hastily transferred to Yezo, which was uncomfortably close to no man's land. Nevertheless Starr persevered, hoisted the American flag as his ship crossed the straits to Yezo, and successfully hired his Ainu Group to take back to St. Louis.

Of the nine Ainus, four were men, three were women, and there were two small children. One of the last, it must be admitted, was suspiciously Japanese-looking and could well have had Japanese blood in her veins. To observe the proprieties, Starr had arranged for the adult Ainus to witness their agreement to the adventure in the presence of policemen at the local Japanese police station, while he scurried around to several Ainu villages buying up Ainu bric-a-brac to display at the fair. At one hamlet he put down twenty dollars for an example of a square, reed-built Ainu house, which was to be dismantled and shipped, with a spare supply of reeds, to the Ethnological Compound at St. Louis. Then the entire party set off by steamer for America — just in time as it turned out, since Japanese troops were arriving on Yezo at such a rate that Starr was evicted from his hotel in Sapporo, which was being turned into a military barracks.

The nine Ainus whom Starr had hired were members of a race of primitive people whose origins remain to this day almost a complete mystery. Some Japanese scholars believe that the Ainus arrived in the islands by crossing out of Sakhalin and Kamchatka and entering northern Japan shortly before the ancestors of the Japanese arrived in the south. There is no certainty as to the date, but it would have been comparatively recently because the earliest Japanese artifacts have been traced back to only 2500 B.C. Quite a different school of thought credits the Ainus with being an aboriginal population that settled the Japanese islands many thousands of

226

years earlier. According to this view, the Ainus are an offshoot of an Upper Paleolithic or Mesolithic wave of migration that washed across Asia until it finally reached the offshore cul-de-sac of Japan. The crux of the evidence for this theory is that the Ainus are usually classified by physical anthropologists as Caucasoids and are considered to be quite distinct from the Mongoloid populations all around them. Certainly the physical appearance of an Ainu bears little relation to that of his Asian neighbors. Though fairly short in stature—with an average height of only 5 feet 4 inches for men and 5 feet 1 or 2 inches for women—the Ainus have a markedly Caucasian look about them. The color of Ainu skin has been described as white that has been turned to a brunet complexion, and they have strong planes to their faces and profuse wavy hair ranging from black to dark brown, the hairs being oval in cross section. Most noticeable of all, their eyes have a Caucasoid shape, which gives little suggestion of the epicanthic or Mongol fold. This eye shape is so characteristic of their appearance that the Ainus refer to themselves as people "of the same eye socket" when they wish to differentiate themselves from non-Ainus. As Starr put it, ". . . compare them [the Ainu's physical characteristics] with those of the Japanese. How profound the difference. The white skin, abundant body hair and beard, the hair wavy and of elliptical section. The horizontal eye full of expression and fire, the features combined into a strong relief—these are in strong contrast to the yellow-brown skin, hairless face and body, straight and round hair, oblique eyes and flat face of the Japanese. In all these respects in which the Ainu differs so profoundly from the Japanese, he resembles us, the whites of European race." Starr was, perhaps, a little overenthusiastic, but he may not have been very wide of the mark. Recent biological studies tend to show that the Ainus have physiological affinities if not with the Caucasoids, at least with the Australian Aborigines and perhaps

An Ainu altar, located on the east side of a dwelling, displays bear and other animal skulls positioned in the crotches of a row of forked poles.

A nineteenth-century drawing by an English visitor shows a dance of Ainu women, who keep time to their hopping by clapping their hands.

also with certain tribes of southern India that have been tentatively classified as the Australoid sub-branch of the Caucasoids. If this line of inquiry proves conclusive, it raises the interesting point that both the Ainus and the Australian Aborigines may be among the farthest offshoots of the prehistoric migrations of mankind.

The feature of Ainu culture that Starr wanted, above all, to illustrate to those attending the exposition in St. Louis was the Ainu Festival of the Bear. In strictly practical terms it was impossible to do this properly because the Ainu Bear Festival terminates in the ritual killing of a tame bear. Nevertheless Starr did make sure that one of his Ainu men knew the correct steps in the dance of the Bear Festival and even persuaded this Ainu to demonstrate the dance at a smoking party on board ship during the long, tedious voyage to Vancouver. In fact, the Bear Ceremony is another feature of Ainu culture that provides support for the theorists who link the Ainus with prehistoric migrations out of the Stone Age centers in Europe and West Asia. The Ainu Bear Festival, they claim, relates to the mysterious bear cult of the Neanderthals and to similar elements of bear worship found among indigenous peoples of the north—in Siberia, in Finland, and among the Lapps. All these traces of a bear cult, so the theory runs, link the cultures of the ancient hunting peoples who lived on the fringes of the ice sheets.

Few foreign travelers have witnessed the Ainu Bear Festival, and those who have usually differ in their descriptions of the precise style and form of the ceremony. The most faithful record is provided by a film made about 1931 by an expatriate Scottish doctor, Neil Gordon Munro, who moved to Japan at the end of the nineteenth century and worked and lived for many years among the Ainus.

In Munro's film, as in all the written accounts, the *primum mobile* of the ceremony is the bear itself. The animal has usually been captured as a small cub in the spring hunting season and taken to the village. There it is treated almost as a household pet until after a year or two it has grown to such a size that it must be confined in a wooden cage. Nevertheless it is still treated kindly, fed with tidbits, and pampered by the villagers. Well in advance of the day appointed for the festival the women of the village brew supplies of millet beer, prepare small rice cakes that resemble macaroons to be given to the children, and make dumplings of millet flour, which will be offered to the gods. The day before the main ceremony, guests and friends begin to arrive at the largest house in the village, which is to be the center of the festivities. With considerable formality their prayers are offered up to the gods, and a heavy post is firmly fixed in the ground outside the house. It is here that the bear will meet its ritual death.

On the day of the Great Offering, as the sacrifice is called, the village is packed with sightseers from neighboring Ainu settlements, dressed in all their finery. At the start of the proceedings an elder of the village approaches the bear in its cage, delivers up prayers to its spirit, and offers it ceremonial drops of drink. Two men then climb to the top of the cage and lower nooses of strong rope over the animal's head. Securely held, the bear is released from the cage and guided in the general direction of the execution post. Men run forward waving branches of evergreen to brush away evil influences, and the onlookers chant sacred songs in unison, while

The souvenir booklet of the 1904 St. Louis World's Fair, at which the Ainus were a featured exhibit

the increasingly puzzled and enraged bear is paraded up and down for all to see. Archers begin to shoot special decorated blunt arrows at it, and the animal, now roaring and struggling, is taken to the sacrificial stake and there tied up. A specially selected bowman steps forward, and after a brief prayer for the quick death of the victim, he shoots the bear with one or two sharpened bamboo arrows. A village elder invokes the benevolent regard of the departing spirit of the bear, and the animal's death coincides with a curving flight of arrows over its corpse. The village boys eagerly rush forward to pick up these arrows as mementoes.

Although it is already dead, the bear is now ritually strangled by having its throat squeezed between two long poles. The corpse is skinned, leaving the head attached to the pelt, and the meat is cut up and distributed. The blood of the bear is reverently treated, caught in cups lest it

This busy scene of Ainu life was painted by a Japanese artist. At bottom are seen stages in the construction of a house. At middle, right, is the finished house with its thatched roof. To the left is an interior view showing a family around a fire. At top, women weave and care for children, as men ready their fishing nets.

Traditional-style Ainu houses — with a storage shed on stilts as protection against animals — nestle against a hill on Hokkaido.

spill on the ground and be defiled, and drunk by the Ainus, who call it divine medicine. Ceremonially the bear's head and skin is then set up to observe the honor paid to it: libations are given; the guests courteously make offerings to the spirits before they drink any of the special festival beer or eat the sacred flesh; and the men dance the sacred Bear Dance. Gradually the formality oozes away. The small millet dumplings and rice cakes are thrown to the children, who scramble for them and then play tug of war. The women dance at the place of the sacrifice, and in the evening the bear's head and skin is taken indoors to a place of honor to watch over a great feast. The festivities culminate in singing, dancing, and much heavy drinking of the millet beer, whose intoxicating effects the Ainus claim are a sacred happiness and the true release of the human spirit.

Intensely dramatic though it is, the Festival of the Bear has baffled outside observers for a considerable time. Some critics have dismissed it as no more than a barbaric saturnalia. Others, including the Reverend John Batchelor, the greatest Western authority on the Ainus of his day, considered it a crude act of brutality. Batchelor, a member of the Church Missionary Society who liked to be known as the Apostle of the Ainus, devoted his life to ministry on Hokkaido and recorded an even more violent version of the festival. In the 1890's he wrote that, after the bear had been tied, struggling and raging, to its post, "all at once some brave young Ainu will rush forward and seize the poor brute by the ears and fur of the face, whilst another suddenly rushes out and seizes it by the hindquarters. These men both pull at the animal with all their might. This causes the animal to open its mouth. Then another man rushes forward with a round piece of wood about two feet long; this he thrusts into the bear's mouth. The poor beast, in its rage, bites hard at this, and holds it tight between its teeth. Next, two men come forward, one on each side of the bear, and seize its forelegs and pull them out as far as they can. Then two others will, in a like manner, catch hold of the two hind legs. When all this has been done quite satisfactorily, the two long poles which were laid by the *nusa* [sacred place of the offerings] are brought forward. One is placed under its throat, and the other upon the nape of its neck. Now all the people rush forward, each eager to help squeeze the poor animal till it dies. And so the poor beast is choked to death. It is indeed a brutal scene.

"As soon as the animal is dead, it is skinned and cut up; but it has to be carried into the hut and laid before the east window for two or three days before it is eaten. During all these days some of the men are dead drunk. But enough of this revolting cruelty and debauchery."

Batchelor's revulsion, understandable in a Christian missionary of his time, was only slowly replaced by a more sympathetic view of the Bear Festival. All who had seen the ceremony agreed that the Ainus had no hatred for the animal. Indeed, until the day of its death the bear was spoiled as much as possible, and the Ainus even claimed that they fired the blunt arrows at the creature in order to make it happy. To the Ainus the bear was always a creature to be admired and respected, and no greater compliment could be paid to another Ainu than to say that he had the strength or fearlessness of a bear. Today the most widely held explanation for the curious mixture of reverence and bloodshed in the Bear Festival is

An Ainu hunter in a tunic of woven bark is seen in this seventeenth-century Japanese scroll painting. Heavily bearded and barefoot, with his quiver slung from his forehead, he carries his long pipe and bow.

231

that the Ainus believe the spirit of the bear is immortal. They see it as a spirit messenger, which they are sending with full and correct ceremony to the spirit world. There, it is hoped, the powerful bear spirit will intercede on behalf of the Ainus, describe the punctiliousness of the ceremony and the pleasantness of life among the Ainus, and in due course return to Hokkaido as the spirit of another bear.

Frederick Starr actually met the Reverend John Batchelor on the train to Sapporo and enlisted his help in hiring the Ainu Group and collecting the various native artifacts that Starr wanted for St. Louis. But it had been another, quite different person who had first brought the Ainus to popular attention some years before and in a sense triggered Starr's quest. This pioneer was a noted Victorian lady traveler, Isabella Bird Bishop, who was—in the contemporary phrase—a "globetrotteress"; and her book *Unbeaten Tracks in Japan*, with its descriptions of the Ainus, had achieved great success. Isabella was a formidable character, physically as well as mentally. The adoring Dr. Bishop, who married her a few years after her Ainu adventure, said she had "the appetite of a tiger and the digestion of an ostrich," and indeed by the time of her marriage Isabella had already ridden elephants in Malaya, been decorated by the king of the Sandwich Islands, and enjoyed a flaming love affair in Estes Park, Colorado, with an Irish-American frontiersman known as Rocky Mountain Jim.

Isabella's descriptions of the Ainus were a tribute to her powers of observation and to the equanimity of her temper. Having commented on Ainu physique in much the same terms as Starr used twenty-five years later, Isabella went on to say, "The 'ferocious savagery' of the appearance of the men is produced by a profusion of thick, soft, black hair, divided in the middle, and falling in heavy masses nearly to the shoulders. Out of doors it is kept from falling over the face by a fillet round the brow. The beards are equally profuse, quite magnificent, and generally wavy, and in the case of the old men they give a truly patriarchal and venerable aspect, in spite of the yellow tinge produced by smoke and want of cleanliness. The savage look produced by the masses of hair and beard, and the thick eyebrows, is mitigated by the softness in the dreamy brown eyes, and is altogether obliterated by the exceeding sweetness of the smile, which belongs in greater or lesser degree to all the rougher sex."

Isabella was particularly intrigued by the Ainu custom of tattooing a broad band across the face of the women at mouth level, almost as if to provide them with a false mustache. The tattoo was built up stage by stage, and the process began at quite an early age in life, perhaps at five years old. "I saw the operation performed on a dear little bright girl this morning," wrote Isabella. "A woman took a large knife with a sharp edge, and rapidly cut several horizontal lines on the upper lip, following closely the curve of the very pretty mouth, and before the slight bleeding had ceased, carefully rubbed in some of the shiny soot which collects on the mat above the fire. In two or three days the scarred lip will be washed with the decoction of the bark of a tree to fix the pattern, and give it that blue look which makes many people mistake it for a daub of paint. A child who had this second process performed yesterday has her lip fearfully swollen and inflamed. The latest victim held her hands clasped tightly together while the cuts were inflicted, but never cried. The pattern on the lips is deepened

Since prehistoric times bears have been linked closely (and mysteriously) to the cultures of northern woods peoples, including the Ainus.

and widened every year up to the time of marriage, and the circles on the arm are extended in a similar way. The men cannot give any reason for the universality of this custom. It is an old custom, they say, and part of their religion, and no woman could marry without it."

Like the Bear Festival, the Ainu practice of face tattooing retains an element of mystery. In the opinion of most anthropologists, the face tattoo may have originated as a form of lucky charm, a prophylactic to scare away evil spirits who might otherwise enter a person's body via the mouth. But why it should be restricted to women—unless it was related to the extra risk of evil influences during pregnancy—or why women should also tattoo simple designs in bands and crossbands on the forearms have yet to find satisfactory explanations. Possibly both forms of tattooing are regarded simply as marks of beautification; the technique of tattooing may have been learned from neighboring Pacific peoples, several of which tattoo virtually the whole of their bodies.

Fortunately Isabella was a tenacious horsewoman and just the right person to describe to her readers the rugged countryside where the Ainus lived. Hokkaido, the stronghold of the Ainus, is about the size of Ireland and lies in the same latitude as Oregon. The cold Okhotsk Current and the mountainous terrain combine to give the island a subarctic climate with monthly mean temperatures varying between 41 degrees Fahrenheit and 46 degrees Fahrenheit. In sheltered places the snow may lie on the ground for six to seven months, which if anything pleases the Ainus, because they regard snow as almost a sacred blanket covering the earth. The natural vegetation emphasizes the wild grandeur of the countryside. There are forests of fir, spruce, birch, oak, and elm, and on the lower slopes are clumps of northern bamboo so thick that it is difficult to force a passage. Riding her half-broken Japanese pony along a forest path, Isabella got tangled up with a great forest liana, which, she ruefully confessed, "caught me by the throat, nearly strangled me, and in less time than it takes to tell it I was drawn over the back of the saddle, and found myself lying on the ground, jammed between a tree and the hind leg of the horse, which was quietly feeding . . . I was little the worse for the fall, but on borrowing a looking-glass I see not only scratches and abrasions all over my face, but a livid mark around my throat as if I had been hung!"

Within this wilderness, particularly in the high valleys leading up to a central chain of mountain peaks, the Ainus hunted bear and deer as well as smaller game such as otters, foxes, and hares. Their standard weapon was a comparatively feeble bow, some four feet long, made of yew. Arrows were fashioned from bamboo and fitted with an ingenious bone tip that broke off and remained in the wound. The tip was armed with a strong poison, usually made from pounded aconite root and sometimes bolstered with concoctions of animal gall, spiders' webs, and other venoms imagined or real. According to the Ainus, even so large an animal as a bear would die within easy walking distance after it had been struck by a poisoned arrow. For this reason much of Ainu hunting was done with spring bows set at the side of animal trails with a trip cord to release the poisoned arrow when the animal touched the cord. For deer hunting the Ainus also used hunting dogs and a form of deer decoy, much like a wild duck call, with which a hunter concealed himself downwind and imitated the cry of

Until recently, women's lips were tattooed to show they were of marriageable age. Like many other customs, it is no longer practiced.

233

射
禮
か
う
し
心
に
か
け
て
調
へ
た
り

三
匹
の
お
と
も
ベ
て

熊
り
首
球
木
の
上

に
お
し
上
す
る

木
そ
こ
あ
き
木
の
上

森
人
か
か
り
て
胴
も

起
返
ふ
商
長

時
有
は
刀
を
もく
て

右
に
も
ち
て
首
を
か
く

こ
の
時
こ
れ
あ
ん
さ
ん

き
ぬ
を
き
て
女
物
か
ら

そ
の
時
栗
と
お
き
て

栗
と
お
き
の
け
に

乳
を
あ
く
熊
を
を
し

て
メ
ソ
コ
に

沙
叫
ひ
掀
ろ
両

肉
じ
あ
つ
ち
か
ぬ
よ
う
し
て

み
ふ
り
小
見
ろ
よ
一
し
も
た

ふ
三
五
白
の
間
い
さ
ゝ
し
て

つ
み
を
ひ
り
と
と
て
玄
運
上
家
ち

ひ
か
り
て
係
を
抽
く

た
こ
と
を
賠
ろ
そ
く
一

此
時
支
酒
人
番
に

上
宿
た
り

Starting at upper right, the calligraphy on
these scenes from a Japanese scroll of 1840
describes the stages of the Ainu Bear Festival. First a bear cub, after being captured, is
put in a cage and fed, while the people
parade around it invoking the gods. Then
they secure and strangle the bear with poles
and cut off its head with a sword, while the
woman who had been wet nurse to the cub
cries. At bottom, right, the bear is skinned,
while the people sing songs and offer food
to the dead animal. Below, the carcass is
cooked, and the people partake of it.

イヨマンテ 又 イヨヂマンテ 俗 熊すつ と云

是頃者貧の大祭事なり 熊を殺して
神を祀るなり 光っ早十劣を深山は
那へ入積雲の中を熊の松を
さぐり熊を飼別したる狗を
今日チマンテせ 就て熊を
家帰ふさすけて乳味のへ
村育やと成長すし心
安へ入て食ふ鳥肉と
に乳せむ熊長大する
そにしてトへて
酒食とりて
親族用友と
いろくの曲を食せ神に
食しめて祝言して大物安を
めぐリムせをとなる又
イナ本を受くみいふ又
繒のぬき板つりたき倚
安り乳を受くむりつ
メンコれふ

ヌシヤサシカタ 祭ルコトナリ

みふく 左 ゆく 唄

我神
千コルカモイ   タ子ハツクノ
為神
カモイ二アヌソ
逆兄
チマシデコンルイ タハジ
再兄
シユカンナ   神而来
明年
オヤバ   カモイ二アヌソ
狀目
チコルナシコル
クシユ 今兄
タ子アナキ二ヲ子コタ
歌 サランバ
不解
ツキナンコンナ

そんより
皮を剥て
三人余のへ
加ぬせ
太刀を掌せ
酒食を
供ふるや
さの祝

Isabella Bird Bishop, a tireless world traveler, wrote perceptive and reliable accounts of the Ainus.

a doe until he lured curious bucks within range.

It seems likely that early in the seventeenth century before Japanese settlers began moving onto Hokkaido, the bulk of the Ainus on the island lived in hamlets near the coasts. Here they could combine inland hunting forays with some of the richest fishing in the world. They speared trout and pike, gathered a great variety of shellfish along the shallows, and from dugout canoes harpooned sharks and seals. At one time they may even have hunted whales and walruses. But the mainstay of the Ainu fishery was always salmon, enormous numbers of which enter the streams and rivers of Hokkaido in the spawning season. Henry Savage Landor, an even more eccentric British traveler, who wrote the splendidly titled *Alone with the Hairy Ainu, or 3,800 miles on a pack saddle in Yezo and a cruise to the Kurile Islands,* reported that while wading across Hokkaido's rivers in the salmon season he felt quite uncomfortable because of the numbers of large fish brushing against him or passing between his legs.

To catch salmon the Ainus used a special type of spear that had a pivoted hook designed to swing out and pin the struggling fish against the shaft of the weapon, so that the fisherman could stab his prey and whisk it out of the water in one movement. Other accounts spoke of trained teams of fishing dogs that were taught to swim out beyond a salmon shoal and then turn in a line and come back toward their waiting masters, herding the fish onto the beach. Landor, however, had no doubt that the bulk of Ainu salmon were caught quite easily with nets and because the salmon swarmed so prodigiously there was very little need for any skill. Exploring a small Hokkaido river with Unacharo, his Ainu guide, Landor glimpsed two Ainu dugouts disappearing on their way upstream. The guide assured him that in a few moments the dugouts would return, and, Landor continued, "We were not far from the river banks when shouts and cries of excitement reached my ears. I hurried on to the water-side and saw the two 'dug-outs' swiftly coming down with the strong current, parallel with each other at a distance of about seven feet apart. There were three people in each 'dug-out,' viz., a woman with a paddle steering at the prow; another woman crouched up at the stern, and a man in the middle. A coarse net made of young vines, and about five feet square, was fastened to two poles seven or eight feet long. The man who stood in the centre of each canoe held one of the poles to the upper end of which the net was attached, and attentively watched the water.

"'They are catching salmon—look!' said Unacharo to me; 'the salmon are coming up the stream from the sea.' The small net was plunged into the water between the two canoes, and nearly each time a large salmon was scooped out and flung into one or other of the 'dug-outs' where the woman sitting at the stern crushed its head with a large stone. If a fish escaped, yells of indignation, especially from the women folk, broke out from the boats to be echoed by the high white cliff. Both men and women were naked, and the dexterity and speed with which they paddled their canoes down the stream, working the coarse net at the same time, seldom missing a fish, was simply marvellous. On the other hand, it must be remembered that fish were so plentiful in the river, that it was really easier to catch than to miss."

Salmon was the staple diet for the coastal Ainus, who preserved their catch by smoking the fish over slow fires. Unfortunately for the Western visitor to an Ainu village, the pungent smells from the fish smokehouses and the natives' fish-stained clothing (in winter the Ainu wore boots made of salmon skin) combined with the swarms of body vermin to daunt even so persevering an observer as Isabella Bird. She confessed to being grateful that her Ainu host provided her with a bearskin mat to sit on and that this served as a barrier to the legions of fleas. Poor Landor, after a single night in an Ainu hut, took the trouble to investigate the number of insect bites he had received despite the liberal use of an insect powder. He counted up to 220 bites between the ankle and knee of one leg before he gave up the task.

The outsider's discomfort was usually increased by the very obvious need to maintain that formal gravity which characterized so much of Ainu behavior, particularly toward a guest. Anyone arriving at an Ainu home was expected to pause outside the threshold, make a low sound in his throat, and wait until his host came forward to invite him in. This was true even for close neighbors in the same village; and a foreign visitor had to be doubly careful to tread the prescribed path from the doorway of an Ainu house to the place of honor near the fire pit in the center of the floor, and to walk in the prescribed manner: a slow, half-stooping shuffle, with hands hanging limp before him. Luckily the interior geography of nearly all Ainu homes was identical, so that, once the design was learned, it was easy enough to observe the correct etiquette. An Ainu

The Ainu economy is helped by the harvesting of fish, shellfish, and seaweed. Here, an Ainu woman collects sea urchins, which Japanese customers prize as a table delicacy.

reed-built house, with its steeply sloping roof "in a series of very neat frills," as Isabella Bird put it, had an oblong floor plan with the shorter sides facing east and west. The door was at the western end, usually sheltered by a small lean-to porch called a "shem," which also served as a storage shed. Pushing aside the heavy reed mat that in wealthier Ainu homes did duty for a door, the visitor would see before him a single, rather gloomy room with a floor either of wood, or more usually, beaten earth. The center of the room was the "abe-shotki," literally the "fire bed." From 5 to 8 feet long and 3 to 5 feet wide, this fire pit was aligned squarely in the middle of the room, and there would always be a fire burning in it, or at night a heap of hot embers safely covered with ash. The home fire was regarded as sacred, and for an Ainu woman to let the fire go out was to provide her husband with grounds for divorce as surely as if she had committed adultery. Around the fire pit would be a heavy wooden frame, the "inumbe," which kept the burning wood from spilling out into the room, and above the two farthest corners of the inumbe projected the tops of two round posts driven into the ground. The one at the right-hand side had a particular significance, for the house owner customarily sat there, with the flat top of the post serving as his workbench. It was Ainu tradition that if the house owner died, this post would have to be uprooted and removed from the house.

Over on the opposite, or eastern, wall the observant visitor might notice a small hanging mat. Behind the mat was concealed the most important window in the house, the "rorun puyara," or sacred window. To the Ainus this window, sometimes scarcely more than a round hole in the wall, had a very special significance. Through it were handed any articles regarded as having sacred or magical properties, and the window, used for nothing else, acquired a sanctity of its own. Isabella Bird very nearly committed a terrible *faux pas* when she almost threw some used tea leaves out of the rorun puyara, being stopped just in time by the horrified looks of her host. Worse yet, after Frederick Starr's Ainu house was carefully reassembled in the Ethnological Compound in St. Louis, the gauping crowds could not refrain from using the sacred window as a convenient spy hole. Naturally the nine Ainus were most upset, and the fair's guidebook had to admonish the public that the Ainu home was not to be used as a vulgar peepshow.

The interior of a typical Ainu house was simple to the point of austerity. With almost no furniture, the main contents were ranged against the north wall in the form of the so-called household treasures. On closer inspection, however, these treasures nearly always turned out to be little more than Japanese storage jars containing cheap souvenir items of Japanese manufacture. Occasionally, it is true, there might be a few articles of better quality or the more practical paraphernalia of the feast such as lacquered feeding bowls, jugs, wooden ladles for pouring beer, and wine chalices. Nor could conditions within an Ainu house be described as comfortable. The reed walls offered very poor protection against the elements, and in winter the cold winds swept through the chinks to create fierce drafts around the occupants. Even in summer there was the problem of smoke rising from the central fire pit because Ainu houses lacked chimneys, and the smoke had to swirl about the room before escaping from the open gable ends. The only other domestic architecture of most Ainu home-

During September and October, salmon come up the rivers of Hokkaido. They are favored by the Ainus, who catch and bludgeon them, as above, smoking them for winter use and even worshiping them as divine fish.

Inside the "chisei," the traditional Ainu house, "inau," or prayer sticks, made of peeled willow stems with curled shavings, bring blessings to the fire. The sacred window, known as God's window and facing to the east, is in the background.

sites extended to two structures standing quite separate from the main house. One was the privy, usually in typical sentry-box style but built of reeds; while the other was the storehouse, which held sacks of grain and dried fish. The latter was invariably set a few feet above the ground on posts capped with wedges of overhanging wood to prevent rats from climbing up and ravaging the stores. To enter the storehouse the Ainus used an elementary ladder made from a log with notches cut in it to provide footholds.

The starkness of much of Ainu life was in strong contrast to the formality of their day-to-day existence. The Ainus behaved with a notable and very gracious decorum, which pervaded almost their entire existence. It was, for instance, considered a mark of rudeness to shout or to make any strident noise or even to bustle about unnecessarily. Very small children, as soon as they could walk, were taught the merits of obedience, speaking in a low voice and observing the rules of Ainu etiquette. Batchelor's mentor, the Ainu chief Penri, gave the missionary the following rules for good behavior: "Never enter a house with your shoes on; be sure to take your hat off; never rush in or out of a house, but go quietly and gravely; never look into a house through a window; treat the east end window as very sacred; never throw anything out of any window; never throw anything into the fire; do not touch another person's fire; do not go eavesdropping; never address a stranger unless he first speaks to you; if it is necessary to address a stranger, first say 'Your Honor'; when you meet another person step off the path and let him have the right of way; let a woman always, when she meets a man, take off her headdress, cover her mouth with her hand, step to one side and look upon the ground; let her even turn sideways; never strike a burning log upon the hearth; never turn the point of any edged tool towards the fire; never by any means allow human hair or nail parings to fall upon the hearth."

Batchelor (who spoke Ainu) had been startled when sitting in the chief's house to see the vehemence with which the chief and his wife reacted to an uncouth Japanese visitor who blundered into their home uninvited and failed to remove his muddy shoes, then began smoking without permission, and finally—when asked to leave—stalked out without a farewell. The moment the Japanese had left, said Batchelor, "Chief Penri gave the hearth a hearty tap with a stick and said, 'the beast!' This was as near a swear as he could get and implied a curse. The wife followed his example. Up she jumped, rushed as far as the door, turned her back towards the parting guest, and gave herself a hearty smack. I could not but laugh in astonishment at all this, and they laughed heartily when I asked if I also was supposed to learn and practice such etiquette. 'No,' the old man said, 'that was a bit extra.'"

In fact, Batchelor took lessons from the chief in the correct method of an Ainu greeting. The style was for two men to squat down cross-legged on the ground facing one another and begin by rubbing their hands together in a sliding motion so that the points of the fingers touched the palm of each hand alternately. All the while the two men quietly exchanged news about one another's affairs and the village. Finally, when the conversation was ended, each raised his hands to his face and slowly stroked his beard, simultaneously making a low rumbling sound in the throat. For the women there was a completely different mode of address. After being greeted by a man, the correct response was for the woman to wait for a few moments with eyes downcast, and then brush one hand down the hair and place the other hand over the mouth. Next the left arm was held straight downward by the side, and the right index finger was drawn up the arm tracing a straight line as far as the shoulder and then across in a sweeping movement of the same finger left to right across the upper lip under the nose. Finally both hands were used to smooth back the forelocks of the hair behind the ears. Graceful though this salutation was, Batchelor had to confess that it was also tediously slow, a delay likely to be exceeded only if two women, or

Formerly, Ainu couples were often betrothed in childhood (right). The bride was frequently brought up in the home of the groom, who presented her with a knife sheath (above, top), while she, in turn, gave him a girdle (bottom), both gifts symbolizing their special relationship.

indeed two men, had not seen one another over a space of some time. In this case the two acquaintances were quite liable to squat down, seize each other by the shoulders, and weep profusely upon one another while pouring out their whole personal history and that of their friends since they had last met. When such greetings took place, said Batchelor, the exchange might last for hours with the participants growing quite hysterical. On some occasions Batchelor and his wife were kept waiting several hours for their dinner because a servant had just encountered a long-lost friend.

Despite their stately notions of personal etiquette, the Ainus observed very few of those rituals often associated with life's major turning points. Childbirth was sometimes marked by a frenzied thumping of the mortar tub to drive away evil spirits during a difficult delivery, and in the last stages of the pregnancy the Ainu husband was expected to go into a state of semihibernation known to anthropologists as "couvade." This form of broodiness or withdrawal was usually justified by the belief that the father was spiritually involved in the exhausting business of childbirth. But coming of age among the Ainus went by without any sort of puberty ritual, and marriage was treated as a very straightforward affair, simply marked by an exchange of token gifts between the parents of the couple, followed by a wedding feast. At one time it seemed that child betrothal was common, but by the late nineteenth century, when travelers began to compile detailed reports about the Ainus, considerable freedom was allowed to both the young men and women. They were considered of marriageable age when they reached about nineteen or twenty years old for a man and sixteen or seventeen for a girl. Trial marriages were frequent, with the girl going to live for a time with the boy's family. Nor was it unheard of for the girls actually to make the first advances. Henry Landor, traveling through the Ainus' country on his pack horse, was agreeably flattered at one of his rest stops when he was lured into the forest by an Ainu belle who demonstrated that biting was the Ainu notion of kissing. "As we sat on a stone in the semi-darkness," he wrote, "she began by gently biting my fingers, without hurting me, as affectionate dogs often do to their masters; she then bit my arm, then my shoulder, and when she had worked herself up into a passion she put her arms round my neck and bit my cheeks. It was undoubtedly a curious way of making love, and when I had been bitten all over, and was pretty tired of the new sensation, we retired to our respective homes."

Death and burial were, however, treated very seriously by the Ainu, though even here a touch of matter-of-fact common sense was noticeable. For example, when an Ainu died, millet porridge and cakes were prepared by the womenfolk, though only the spirit essence of the food was expected to sustain the dead person, who, it was felt, had received little nourishment during the last illness. The actual physical food was eaten by the guests at a farewell meal in the presence of the corpse. Before this meal the corpse would be visited by sorrowing relatives and prepared for its last journey, the body being carefully washed and then dressed in clean funeral clothes. The normal Ainu attire was a loincloth over which a loose tunic made from elm bark fiber was folded in front, with the left side over the right, and on ceremonial occasions gorgeously embroidered with abstract motifs. But for the dead man the tunic, though of the best quality, was decorated only with

An Ainu woman works at her loom, which is fashioned from bamboo sticks. Today Ainu fabrics, often made from the inner bark of elm trees, are prized by collectors.

241

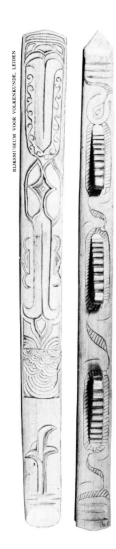

These carved sticks were used to lift one's mustache while drinking, for allowing even one whisker to touch the libation was considered bad manners. The stick at left was for everyday use, while the one at right was employed in ceremonies.

242

somber colors and was folded contrariwise, right over left. A second tunic was then placed on the corpse, back to front, so that the back of the gown lay across the dead man's chest. Sometimes the mourners themselves took up this theme of reversal, showing their grief by going home with their own tunics turned inside out. On the dead man's head was placed a special funeral "tara," or headband, and special mittens and leggings of deerskin or barkcloth were laid beside him. Next there followed the funeral feast, with mourners arriving from the surrounding villages to pay their last respects. Seating positions at the funeral meal were rigidly ordained by relationship to the dead man or woman, and every important visitor performed an act of mutual condolence with the relatives of the deceased. This action was very similar to the manner of falling upon one another's necks after a long absence, but the funeral style differed in that the relative of the deceased clasped the mourner below the armpits instead of putting his hands on the visitor's shoulders. A similar reversal of etiquette peculiar to funerals was that the rubbing together of hands in the customary greeting was done with slack wrists and with the palms facing downward.

After the meal, during which food was ceremoniously offered to the dead man and perhaps a pipe placed in his mouth, the chief mourner delivered a funeral eulogy, and the corpse was rolled into a mat that served as the coffin. A sacred black and white cord, the "utoki-at," was used to lace up the mat, and another special cord, the "para-muriri," suspended the cocooned body from the carrying pole on the way to the grave. At the graveside the various common artifacts of life were broken and laid beside the deceased: bow and arrows, spear and fishhook, knife, sword, tinder and flint for a man; spindle, loom, digging stick, and kitchen utensils for a woman. Both sexes were provided with clothing, feeding bowl, and chopsticks, and all the grave goods were deliberately damaged before being placed in the ground. Finally the grave was filled in, as each relative threw in a preliminary handful of earth; and a grave post, wrapped about with cord and sometimes ringed in black, was driven home at the head of the grave and tamped firm. Weeping relatives might kneel by the grave post for some time and daub it with sacred mud. Then the funeral escort returned to the village to attend the funeral breakfast. Very soon in the normal course of time the Ainu grave posts rotted away or fell down, and since there were no real Ainu cemeteries, only isolated burial places, the site of an Ainu grave was eventually grown over by the wild vegetation and lost to memory.

The Ainus believed that when a man died, his spirit walked down a path toward the underworld. There he came to a fork in the path and was met by a dog, which, if the Ainu had led a good life, escorted him to the village of the deities. An Ainu who had led a bad life was taken to the wet underworld, the haunt of evil creatures. The dog, according to the Ainus, was controlled by the most powerful of their deities, Kamui Fuchi, the Supreme Ancestress, and—it has been claimed—the god after whom Mount Fuji was named in the days when the Ainus occupied much of Honshu, Japan's central island. Be that as it may, Kamui Fuchi was so omnipresent in Ainu creed that before praying to any other god, it was customary to invoke Kamui Fuchi first of all. Furthermore, the Ainus assigned to Kamui Fuchi the most important location in the house—the hearth where burns the sacred flame associated with the Supreme Ancestress.

Ainu spiritual beliefs were imperfectly known by outsiders for a considerable time after the Ainus had been brought to the attention of the outside world. Isabella Bird went so far as to state flatly — and ignorantly — that "it is nonsense to write of the religious ideas of a people who had none," an attitude for which the Reverend Mr. Batchelor chided her without himself solving the complexity of Ainu beliefs. Instead, it was left to the Scottish doctor, Neil Munro, to come closest to explaining Ainu religion in a manuscript sent out of Japan not long before the outbreak of the Second World War closed all communication and Munro died in the following year.

According to Munro, the whole of Ainu life was imbued with animistic beliefs, and almost every act by an Ainu had to be performed with a meticulously correct ritual if the spirits were not to be displeased. The constant observance of proper ritual was all the more pressing because the Ainus lacked priests, and the head of each family conducted the formal ceremonies, so that the home was the place of worship. In Munro's understanding, the whole of Ainu belief turned upon three key concepts: the notion of "ramat" (literally, "the heart"), which was the spirit essence or universal soul found in every object; "kamui," the pantheon of gods and spirits; and the "inau," or offerings, which should be made to the spirits. Thus even a wasp possessed ramat and had to be killed with due ceremony; Kamui

This photograph of 1905 depicts the traditional Ainu seating arrangement during ceremonies. The men are grouped immediately around the food, while the women are seated respectfully in the background.

243

This assemblage of Ainu jewelry, including a bead necklace with a metal disk, reflects a fondness for simple design that is strongly reminiscent of Japanese artistic taste.

Fuchi took her name as part of the general kamui, or pantheon; and every traveler who visited an Ainu village noticed the inau, or offerings, that hung everywhere, from walls, from the pothook over the fire, and even from the headbands of the men.

These inau took a curious form. Usually they were small sticks or wands from which hung curled wooden shavings, so that they looked very much like children's stick dolls with pigtail shavings for hair. To the Ainus nearly all wood had special sacred properties, particularly if the inau was made from willow, lilac, dogwood, oak, or magnolia. Then, too, the method of cutting an inau was important—whether the shavings were whittled downward or with a backward stroke, whether cuts were made across the wands or short flaps or "wings" sprang out from the stems. It was *de rigueur* that all inau had to be made with the right hand, and those inau that achieved particular beauty or craftsmanship could even become effigies of the gods themselves, to be kept indoors and given offerings of their own. Similar, though without curly shavings, were the carved wooden spatulas dubbed "mustache lifters" by all the early travelers but described more correctly by Munro as "libation wands." In use, the libation wand was dipped into the sacred millet beer, and the drops from the tip of the wand were then offered to the spirit being worshiped. Afterward the wand was placed across the top of the cup while one drank from it. Finally, outside every Ainu home in a direct line with the sacred eastern window, there stood the "nusa," or place of the offerings. This was a strange assemblage of sacred sticks propped against a crossbar and looking, with their attached inau waving in the wind, like the racked pikes of a medieval army with bannerets flying from their staffs. Here and there in the forks of sticks among the ranks of the nusa would leer the somewhat menacing skull of a bear killed at some early Bear Festival and lovingly placed among the holy relics.

The strange feature of all this paraphernalia of Ainu worship was its impermanence. A basic tenet of Ainu faith was that ramat was mobile and could move from one object to the next. Thus a spirit essence needed constant worship and replenishing. An old inau, which had once represented a god, might well be retired after it had become metaphysically worn out; it was then given a spiritual dismissal, with the elder of the house holding

Willow shavings hung on sticks are spiritual symbols to the Ainus, who believe in many gods, as well as lesser spirits.

the correct ceremony before it. Once the ramat had departed, the worn-out offering was placed outside in the nusa or even burned. In much the same way, the dead bear was given his ritual dismissal at the end of the Bear Ceremony, and the bear spirit departed contentedly for the underworld until its eventual return in the shape of another bear.

The distribution of spirits in the Ainu credo was certainly all-pervading. There were spirits of the woods and waters, in the hills, and among every species of animal. There was even a spirit associated with the household privy. All had to be ceremonially honored with prayers and the presentation of inau. The selection of a new house site was attended with special rites to bring good luck to the future home and to drive away any evil spirits previously resident there. For the salmon there was one ritual at the beginning of the run of dog salmon, another rite after the first salmon were killed, and a final ceremony to return the spirit of the dead salmon to the underworld of the kamui. The greatest of all ceremonies was the Feast of Falling Tears, or All Souls, when not only was the entire pantheon of the kamui praised and honored, but the souls of the ancestors of the household were remembered, together with the ancestors of every member of their family.

It can be imagined how in the mid-nineteenth century this intricately formal and spirit-shrouded world of the Ainu culture quailed before a deliberate Japanese policy of intervention. Hokkaido had passed under the direct rule of the Tokugawa shogunate in 1799, and a half a century later it was decided officially to put an end to Ainu isolation. The lands were taken over by Japanese immigrants, and the Ainus were prohibited from hunting bear or deer or fishing for salmon. They were also forbidden to tattoo themselves or to practice Ainu traditions. Thirty years later, in partial compensation, the Japanese government established agricultural training centers where the Ainus could learn to become farmers instead of fishermen and hunters. But overall Japanese policy remained the complete assimilation, cultural and economic, of an aberrant population. Against all odds the policy was neither entirely nor rapidly successful. The coastal Ainus were soon assimilated, though in fact their gradual process of acculturation had begun generations earlier with visits by Japanese traders and fishermen. Up in the interior highlands, however, it was a different matter. The Japanese had difficulty policing their edicts, and the climate and terrain discouraged Japanese settlers. Disease, commonly the most destructive element in racial contacts, was of little consequence. The Japanese were unlikely to introduce into Hokkaido any disease that was not common already to all the Japanese islands. Rather, it was rice wine (sake) that in Batchelor's opinion did the most damage. Unused to so strong a liquor and positively delighting in intoxication, the Ainus suffered greatly from alcoholism. Even so, it was estimated as late as 1939 that there were living on Hokkaido as many as 160,000 Ainus reckoned by blood rather than by culture. At the present time, after a disastrous and as yet unexplained Ainu population drop during World War II and the years immediately following, estimates vary widely, partly because the Japanese census does not have a separate classification for the Ainus. Accurate knowledge continues to be so elusive that in 1960 one unofficial investigation claimed to have found 17,000 Ainus; yet four years later an outside researcher estimated that there were no more than 300 full-blooded Ainus left.

AXEL POIGNANT, LONDON

The Life of Primitive Man

A World of Faith

In the absence of science, which provides rational explanations, natural phenomena are viewed reverently, understood as the workings of supernatural beings and forces. Using rites and methods of magic, primitive societies try to control them for practical ends. But there are limits to magical powers, and appeals must also be made to gods and spirits that cannot be controlled. Since both avenues demand faith if the society is to survive, religion, a pervasive part of everyday behavior, is the cement of the group's culture, binding together man, nature, and the supernatural. In the ceremony above, Aborigines of Australia, who conceive of rainbows as a great serpent that brings rain to the water holes, push an imaginary snake into a well where it is thought to dwell.

Faith takes many forms, including the belief that by mimicry or the use of masks man may actually become the force or being whose attributes he wishes to possess. The engraving at left shows Aborigines imitating dogs to acquire their capabilities.

The creator, say !Kung Bushmen, gave their healers a supernatural potency that is increased by dancing themselves into trances, right, during which they lay hands on the people and drive away spiritual bringers of sickness and death.

In northern Luzon, the Philippines, the Ifugao people are dependent on successful harvests of rice, grown on the terraced mountainsides. An appeal to spirits for good crops, below, includes the ritual sacrifice of chickens and ducks.

These Clallam Indian medicine men of Vancouver Island were painted in their dance masks by Paul Kane in 1847.

The symbolic masks were believed by the Indians to transform their wearers into the spirit helpers that they represented.

Shamans, or medicine men, endowed with strong supernatural powers, intercede with the spiritual world, for good or evil, on behalf of individuals or a group. At left is a Karagass shaman of Siberia with his deerskin drum.

With special fetishes and chants, magic-working shamans may effect cures, divine the future, insure success, or cause misfortune, sickness, or death. The Cuna mnemonic picture writing at right is a shaman's fever-curing chant.

The faith of the people in the powers of their spiritual leaders is reflected by the sick child and tribesmen of a Meo village in Laos, below, awaiting the shaman's ritualistic sacrifice of a pig, whose blood will effect a cure.

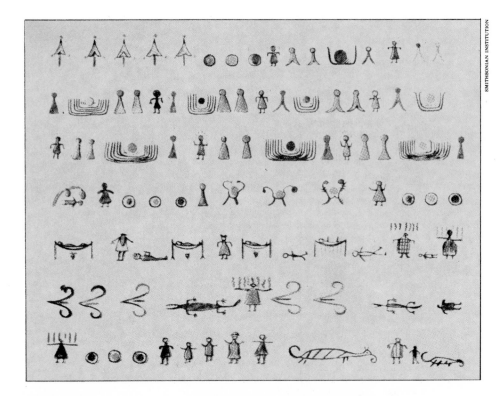

The worship of ancestors—including the society's founders, from whom the leaders claimed descent—reinforced the stability of hierarchical groups. In the New Hebrides the ancestral spirit represented by the clay figure at left was believed to be present when it was used by the people in ceremonies.

In an Ainu exorcism ceremony at right, an elder, trying to drive away a wicked spirit that has given a facial tic to the woman at picture's left, offers rice wine to the spirit of a "good" tree, before which prayer sticks with willow shavings have been set.

In all societies, charms, fetishes, and symbolic objects (like four-leaf clovers and rabbits' feet) help their owners achieve goals. At left is a wooden fertility charm of a religious cult in New Guinea's Torres Strait area.

Cannibals and Missionaries

A New Caledonia water spirit mask, with feathered costume

John Frum came to the Southwest Pacific island of Tana in the New Hebrides in the 1930's. He was a small man who had bleached hair and a high-pitched, squeaky voice, and he wore a coat with shiny buttons. He arrived, so he said, from South America, and he announced that Tana was soon to have a great apocalypse. The earth would tremble, the mountains would fall down and fill up the valleys with fertile soil, and the sea would roll back to connect Tana with its two neighboring islands. In this new land John Frum would be king. There would be no sickness, no one would need to labor, and all the ancient customs of the island from the days before the white man would flourish and prosper. John Frum promised to provide the money to pay the salaries of chiefs and teachers, to found new schools, and to arrange for the purchase of the white man's goods. Many of the islanders became his ardent disciples, and by the end of the decade almost the only people on Tana who had not heard about John Frum were the British civil agent, the Presbyterian missionaries, and a handful of traders, all of them white men.

Naturally they knew that something strange was going on. The missionaries saw their churches gradually emptying as the congregations drifted away. School attendance slumped, and the civil agent remarked on a sudden upsurge of goat killing, which, on investigation, turned out to be nothing more sinister than the preparations for a grand native banquet. But then the whirlwind struck. John Frum announced to his followers that his new kingdom would have a coinage of its own, stamped with a coconut. So the Tanaese rushed out to rid themselves of British currency. They went on a huge spending spree, literally buying every item in the storehouses, squandering their savings deliriously, and some even hurling their old cash into the ocean. The island's economy jerked to a halt, and the alarmed agent set out to talk to John Frum himself. Not altogether to his surprise, he found that John Frum did not really exist. He was a figment of the natives' imagination, a prophet who appeared to his believers only by firelight and in the shadows. One opportunist islander had dressed up in a coat with gold buttons—how he got such a garment no one could fathom—and he and a few other leading devotees were promptly arrested and shipped off the island.

A Dani sentry, left, stands guard on a watchtower in West Irian.

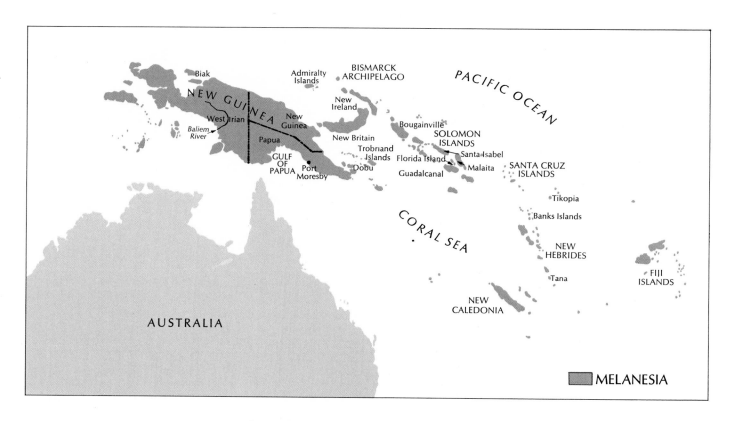

MELANESIA

But this policy soothed the trouble only temporarily. When the Pacific war began, Catalina flying boats of the Royal Australian Air Force were seen by the Tanaese, who reported that John Frum's three sons, Isaac, Jacob, and Lastuan (possibly a corruption of "last one"), had been landed by them. The three sons were reputed to be half-castes, dressed in robes and jackets, and they would rule as subkings in the islands until John Frum himself, now rumored to be king of America, sent enormous quantities of material aid.

The arrival of a regiment of black American soldiers to help in the war against the Japanese caused wild excitement on Tana, and the John Frum movement soared to new heights. No islander had ever before seen black-skinned men dressed as whites and casually handling such vast quantities of desirable goods. Jubilantly the islanders began clearing an airstrip where John Frum's Liberator planes were prophesied to land with their cargoes. Squads of enthusiasts drilled with imitation bamboo rifles and dressed in singlets that had "T.A.," for Tana Army, written on them over the legend "U.S.A." The movement spread to other islands in the New Hebrides and became a well-established cult. In 1957 two thousand natives actually assembled on a beach to wait for John Frum's personal arrival—much to the embarrassment of the skipper of an American barkentine on a world cruise, who accidentally arrived at Tana some months later and had to explain that he was not the expected messiah. All over the island the natives had erected John Frum emblems of red-painted crosses and small effigies of John Frum himself, with arms outstretched like Christ and beside him a carved wooden model of the long-awaited cargo plane, its U.S. white star lovingly painted on its fuselage.

John Frum was only one among dozens of similar mystical phenomena that sprang up on the islands of the Southwest Pacific. The first local

258

messiah had been recorded as early as 1885 on Fiji, where a "prophet" announced the impending reversal of the world order, when chiefs would serve as commoners and white men would obey blacks. Like most of the subsequent cults, this first Fiji manifestation eventually collapsed with a little help from the white administration, but not before it had caused considerable alarm. Since then there have been movements which told their devotees that they would slough their black skins and become white, or set up crude ladders pointing into the sky so that Jesus could descend to them in person. One cult group, in a fit of violence, killed and ritually ate a white planter. Some cults forecast the millennium, perhaps heralded by a rainstorm of flaming kerosene; others, the so-called cargo cults, believed in the coming of enormous quantities of outside aid sent by an all-powerful benefactor. Their true believers confidently built wharves and docks and enormous storehouses in which to place the expected wares. They erected "wireless masts" of wood, strung with "aerials" of lawyer cane, and then started talking hopefully into tin cans as if to make radio contact with their sponsor. Native prophets included those who spoke in incoherent tongues when they fell into trances and leaders who erected miniature pulpits in the villages and required their followers to carry walking sticks like white men. The actions of some groups were deeply sad, like that of one whose members launched a flotilla of native canoes armed only with wooden rifles, attacked a Japanese gunboat, and were blown out of the

Village houses, built on stilts for better ventilation and protection against floods, line a weeded, well-swept street in Kerepunu, New Guinea. The men's, or bachelor, clubhouses have front gables up to 80 feet high.

All Around the World, W. F. AINSWORTH, LONDON, 1869

World War II engulfed most of Melanesia, establishing close contacts between native peoples and outsiders and hastening acculturation. In New Guinea, above, Americans used tribesmen as stretcher-bearers.

water. Others were impressive. In the Solomon Islands a postwar movement known as Marching Rule was dedicated to creating an entire native civil administration complete with districts and subchiefs. Some of its leaders—one of whom had received the Silver Star for heroism against the Japanese—were sent to school by the appreciative Australian colonial government to take courses in civil administration.

Of course, such extravaganzas are by no means confined to the Southwest Pacific. They are related to Adventist movements and millenary cults that have occurred all over the world, whether among the ghost dancers of the American Indians or in medieval Europe, where prophets proclaimed the end of the world and caused widespread panic. What is peculiar to the Southwest Pacific, however, is the sheer frequency of such phenomena. They amount almost to a regional characteristic, flickering sporadically in the small islands and flaring up again and again among the larger populations. New Guinea, for example, has witnessed more than fifty such manifestations, and a weighty literature has grown up on the subject with contributions by anthropologists, psychologists, and churchmen, who ascribe the native cults to everything from outright pagan savagery to mass hysteria and hypertension. Most agree, though, that the underlying cause involves cultural stress, the result of an abrupt collision between the Stone Age and modern material culture in the area collectively known as Melanesia, where the last major concentration of Stone Age peoples was brought face to face with modern technological life.

Melanesia, conveniently for the student of mankind, is one of the few major world regions to have been delineated by cultural, rather than geographic, criteria. It is the territory of the black islands (Greek: *melos nesos*), whose native peoples possess much darker skins, on the whole, than the rest of the aboriginal population of the Pacific. Their archipelago extends in a broad lozenge shape from New Guinea to Fiji and includes the Solomon Islands, New Caledonia, and the New Hebrides—areas now familiar as a theater of operations in the Pacific war, with such names as Guadalcanal and Bougainville. But during the previous century they were much better known as the Cannibal Islands, where the natives were reputed to pick their teeth with dead men's bones and eat any sailor unlucky enough to be cast away among them.

The ethnic history of Melanesia's population is still far from clear, and the archipelago's racial makeup is certainly not as simple as its Greek name would indicate. Essentially three quite distinct types of people inhabit the region. In the first place, there are a handful of pygmies, most of them in the mountains of New Guinea. They are probably the original inhabitants who retreated into the mountains under pressure from invaders. Secondly, there are the Papuans, who also dwell principally in the highlands of New Guinea. They have heavy brow ridges, large jaws, and high receding foreheads sometimes taken as evidence that they are an early migrant wave, perhaps related to the Australian Aborigines. Thirdly, there are the Melanesians themselves. They are found throughout the smaller islands and on the seaboard of New Guinea, and it seems reasonable to assume that they were a sea people who spread from island to island, absorbing, overrunning, or mingling with the more isolated Papuan communities. Shorter in stature than the Papuans, the Melanesians may be a mixture of the dark Papuans and their own lighter-skinned forefathers, as these coastal peoples range in color from light brown to almost black. Their distinctly frizzy hair, another characteristic shared with many Papuans, is accentuated by careful curling and dressing so that in some cases the coiffure stands out like a wired wool halo.

The immigration theory to explain the presence of the lighter-skinned Melanesians is reinforced by an examination of the languages of the region. By and large, the coastal and island peoples speak languages belonging to the Austronesian superfamily of languages that also includes Polynesian, Micronesian, and Malay. The Papuan people of interior New Guinea, on the other hand, use an entirely different Papuan group of languages, about which very little is known at present because the linguistic landscape is so complex and fragmented. It is possible for native communities to have a radius of outside contact of less than twenty miles, sometimes reaching no farther than the next inhabited valley, and the result is a plethora of mutually unintelligible but related languages that may be restricted to a single village of a few hundred inhabitants or extend to as many as sixty thousand speakers. Linguistic research now in progress seems to indicate that this confusion of Papuan tongues may, for the scholars at least, be resolved into a dozen or so major groupings. Nevertheless, throughout Melanesia as a whole the impression is of a grand Babel. Tana Island, for example, has a population of about ten thousand but boasts no less than seven languages, while Omba, another island nearby, shares five languages

A mask and cover of leaves hide a Duk-duk, a combination policeman, judge, and hangman in New Britain.

Wanderings in a Wild Country, WILFRED POWELL, LONDON, 1883

among seven thousand people. There are parts of the region, as Austin Coates points out in his survey *Western Pacific Islands,* where there is actually one language for every two hundred thirty people. Nor are the differences between one language and the next necessarily trivial. The people of Abelam in New Guinea use only two genders, masculine and feminine, but their Arapesh-speaking neighbors just to the north employ no less than twelve noun classes. Elsewhere on the island some Papuan-type languages run up to fifty distinguishable classes and subclasses of nouns. To make matters worse, many of them are also tonal. That is, they resemble Chinese in using a change of pitch in word or syllables to alter their meaning.

To impose some sort of order on this chaos, common trade languages have been used for centuries throughout Melanesia, but even here the picture is far from simple. In New Guinea people in the western half once used a plain form of Malay as the lingua franca, but this is now being replaced by standardized Indonesian. At the same time, the lingua franca of the eastern half of New Guinea is contested between police Motu and Pidgin English. Both languages, as it happens, have good historical claims. The former is a dialect from the region around Port Moresby first used by native traders and then adopted by the Royal Papuan Constabulary for their patrols inland. By comparison, Pidgin English is derived from Bêche-la-Mar, the earliest form of barter English of the Pacific traders. This was based, in turn, upon the original Portuguese-Chinese trade talk of the South China coast—the word "pidgin" actually means "business" in Cantonese—and so has a complex syntax, grammar, and vocabulary of its own. In fact, Pidgin is the stronger of the two trade languages and is taking over from police Motu on New Guinea, while Pidgin in one form or another also serves as the interisland language among the natives throughout Melanesia except where the speakers can use English.

If the languages of Melanesia are a nightmare of complexity, the geography of the region is scarcely less confusing. The land surfaces include both New Guinea—which, fifteen hundred miles long, is the world's second largest island—as well as minute pimples of coral that are liable to go awash during a bad hurricane. The climate allows permanent snow fields on the New Guinea mountains, and less than three hundred miles away a sultry equatorial stability at Biak, where the monthly variation of temperature throughout the year is just one degree. Melanesia's topography ranges from "eggbox" limestone country so crisscrossed by erosion that it defies human exploration, to dangerous and still-active volcanoes. In 1951 Mount Lamington in Papua suddenly released a cloud of burning gas that rolled down the hillside, smothering to death the people of the nearby government station. Nor, indeed, are the regional boundaries of Melanesia very clear-cut. Culturally, the eastern fringes overlap with Polynesia, and several small islands like Tikopia, where the eminent anthropologist Raymond Firth made his studies on community life, are often considered Polynesian rather than Melanesian in character. Politically, the area is divided among Indonesia, Great Britain, France, Australia, and independent islands. Geographically, when the territory is not hazily classified as part of Oceania, it may be regarded as an appendage of Australia or Southeast Asia.

Yet certain generalizations can be made. The total land surface of this

This striking helmet mask of wood, straw, tusks, and glass, utilizing a figure, is from the New Hebrides Islands, one of the most productive centers of Melanesian art.

region is some 370,000 square miles, of which 90 per cent is the giant island of New Guinea. The total native population of Melanesia late in the 1960's was a little less than two and a half million, more than two million of whom lived in New Guinea. Some comparative idea of these figures can be gained from the fact that New Guinea is about three times the size of Great Britain but has almost the same population as Kentucky, while Bougainville, the largest of the Solomon Islands, is almost the size of Jamaica but has a population of only seventy-eight thousand inhabitants. Topographically, the larger islands have much the same type of terrain. They all rise fairly sharply as one proceeds inland, so that the traveler wishing to visit the interior must surmount a succession of difficult, heavily dissected hill crests. The natural vegetation is a thick cover of primary tropical forest, and the climate is hot and humid except where altitude gives some relief from the enervating mugginess. Curiously enough, there is not nearly as much sunshine as the temperature and latitude would indicate. Weather pictures from satellites show that Melanesia has a more frequent cloud cover than any other comparable tropical area. The unique combination of heavy overcast, dense vegetation, and rugged and closely arrayed hills

The view below of the interior of a large "Stranger's House," or inn, in Fiji shows the architectural use of horizontal tie beams to counter the pressure of the roof timbers. The cooking area in the room's center is surrounded by sleeping mats.

has had a noticeably limiting effect. Man's horizons in inland Melanesia have stayed strangely constricted, so circumscribed by environment that large areas were unexplored and uncharted until very recently. It was not until the 1930's that the interior highlands of New Guinea were effectively penetrated by white men, who found there almost a million previously unknown Stone Age inhabitants. On a smaller scale, isolated valley communities still exist that have yet to be contacted by government patrols. Naturally enough, such an extraordinary patchwork of isolated native communities has proved an anthropological bonanza. Fieldwork in Melanesia has helped to make the reputation of scores of renowned anthropologists and has provided the materials for such works as Margaret Mead's studies of growing up in New Guinea and Bronislaw Malinowski's *Argonauts of the Western Pacific,* which describes the native trade pact of the Trobriand Islands. So vast is the scholarship that a basic bibliography for Melanesia includes considerably more than four thousand items, with entries ranging from "Artificial cranial formations in New Britain" to "Papuan cats' cradles"; while a more specialized bibliography for the island of New Guinea now has more than ten thousand items.

The vast majority of Melanesia's indigenous peoples live by gardening, a simple process of clearing the natural vegetation with stone axes and adzs, and then breaking up the soil with sharp digging sticks. Their most important crops are yams and taros, both of which are easily propagated and need little attention apart from periodic weeding. As many as eighty different varieties of yams are recognized, and as a general rule they are found growing on the drier upland sites, while taro cultivation is practiced

A New Guinea family in the Western Highlands, changing to a cash economy, which requires income for needed goods, picks pyrethrum flowers, used for an insecticide.

in wetter areas, sometimes with the help of irrigation. In mountainous districts bananas and plantains are also cultivated, and at the opposite end of the scale, coconuts provide starch and oil for people living along the coasts. Perhaps the only unusual tree crop—apart from breadfruit, which is grown in Fiji and the New Hebrides—is sago, because the plant grows wild and requires special harvesting and processing techniques. Twenty to thirty feet high and fifteen to twenty inches in diameter, the sago palm is ripe to be cropped just before it flowers, when the tree has stored up a large reserve of starch in its trunk. The tree is cut down and the hard outer rind of the trunk is removed and discarded. This reveals the starchy inner core, which is cut into chunks and battered with a special hammer to help separate the starch from the coarse pithy fibers. The morsels are then washed in a trough usually made from a large sago leaf, and the water carries the starch out into a settling pan. Once the starch has fallen to the bottom of the pan, the water is drained off, and the sago meal is packed in leaves ready for use. Unavoidably, the flavor of meals based on such bland crops as yams and sago is remarkably tasteless, and the sheer dullness of Melanesian cooking has been a frequent complaint of visitors. It is aggravated by the fact that the starch foods are generally served as a baked or steamed pudding with no more piquant flavoring than a dish of sea water, or, in the interior, a few grains of smoky salt laboriously obtained by burning brine-soaked plants and extracting salt from the ashes.

Flesh and fish in real quantity are reserved for special occasions, and here the traditional earth oven does justice to the raw materials. Of this cuisine R. H. Codrington, a nineteenth-century missionary and a Fellow of Wadham College, Oxford, who wrote the pioneer ethnographic study of the Melanesians, stated nostalgically that "there are differences in detail, but the method is generally the same, and the result admirable; the food being cooked by steam in its own juices. The hole in the ground which forms the oven is mostly permanent, with its heap of stones that will bear the fire lying by it. The fire lighted in the hole which has been lined with stones heats those and others heaped upon it. When the fire has burnt down, these latter stones are taken out with wooden tongs; the food wrapped in leaves is arranged within, hot stones are laid between the larger parcels, and the rest of the hot stones above all. The whole is shut in with leaves, or maybe covered in with earth. Water, salt or fresh, is poured in to make steam, and every escape of the steam is watched and closed. The process is lengthy, and gives much of the day's occupation to the native men, who cook for themselves. It is a pity, perhaps also because it takes less time, that the introduction of iron pots and saucepans is changing the native cooking for the worse."

To a certain extent the blandness of many Melanesian dishes is compensated by the widespread use of stimulants. Tobacco is grown and smoked in New Guinea, where one unusual form of pipe is a gourd or bamboo tube in which the smoke is trapped before being inhaled by the smokers. Rather more general are the habits of betel chewing and kava drinking. The former was almost certainly introduced from mainland Asia, because it occurs most frequently in the adjacent parts of Melanesia, where a considerable paraphernalia of betel-chewing equipment is maintained. The basic betel mixture is the unripe nut of the areca palm together with the fruit

Harvested yams in the Trobriand Islands are protected from animals and the elements in special storehouses like the one pictured above.

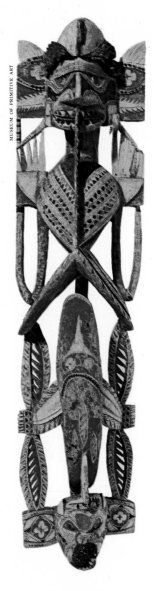

In New Ireland, the unveiling of a special carving is the highlight of the "malanggan," a funeral memorial festival honoring a dead person. This malanggan carving of a double human figure has eyes of shell, which was once used as currency in the islands of Melanesia.

or leaves of the betel pepper and a dash of lime made from burnt coral or limestone. The areca nut is first chewed to the correct consistency, or if the teeth are inadequate, pounded up with a special wooden mortar and pestle. Then the pepper is added and also chewed, and finally a taste of lime is carried to the mouth on a special spatula until the right flavor is achieved. This equipment—the pouch or bag holding the areca and pepper, the areca mortar, the gourd container for the lime, its special stopper, and the lime spatula—is often intricately carved and decorated. Equal care is taken with the utensils used for drinking kava, the beverage made from the roots of *Piper methysticum,* a variety of pepper. Kava is probably a cultural import as well, this time coming from Polynesia, in the opposite direction. Traditionally, kava root was prepared by young men who chewed up portions of the root and spat the masticated cud into a large, often beautifully carved wooden bowl. Water was then added; the mash was stirred; and the kava fiber was sieved out, the bowl and drinking cups often acquiring in the process a distinctive kava patina.

The kava drink itself, looking somewhat like watery milk, has aroused mixed reactions in strangers. Christian missionaries banned the drink as intoxicating and vicious; medical opinion stated that taken to excess, it led to skin troubles and feeble-mindedness. In recent times the most balanced judgment is from Austin Coates, who went on a kava-drinking binge to test its effects: "Many attempts have been made to explain what kava tastes like. It has been compared with all kinds of things in the chemical and medical world. It was not thus that it struck me. As I drank it I was conscious of earth after a shower of rain at dawn in a wood, and of the green of young shoots in a primeaval spring. Never in my life have I been so conscious of man's descent from his own antiquity. If anyone had told me that I had by magic been transported back in time a million years, I would not have been surprised. As far as man today is capable of conceiving what it was like to be the first human beings in the world, living in the forests, this was what the liquid conveyed. It is, I feel sure, the most ancient drink on earth." After four half-coconuts filled with kava, Coates felt that his legs had turned to jelly and that his mind had reached a state of euphoria. After another three nutfuls he staggered home, caroming off every tree and not sobering up until the next morning.

By an odd stroke of history, almost the first outside organization to recognize the distinct social and cultural unity of Melanesia was the Christian mission movement. With the intention of converting the islanders, the Melanesian Mission, as it was forthrightly called, started work in 1848. Initially the idea was to recruit young Melanesian boys and ship them to New Zealand, where they would be baptized, trained, and then returned to preach the word of God to their compatriots. This plan was based on the assumption that no white missionary could possibly survive the climatic rigors of Melanesia. But this attitude soon changed when it was discovered that the real risk was the hostility of the natives rather than the climate. Numbers of dedicated missionaries flocked to the islands fully prepared to find martyrdom there—as several of them did, including Bishop John Coleridge Patteson, founder of the mission, who was killed in 1871 in the Santa Cruz group and his corpse floated out in a canoe to his waiting companions. Ironically, it is from the reports of the missionaries that one finds the best record of the native life, which was soon to be altered in such a drastic manner by their teaching.

Let us follow for a moment the reactions of the Reverend Alfred Penny, M.A., recently volunteered to join the Melanesian Mission and sent to its then mostly northerly limit, the Florida Islands, adjacent to Guadalcanal in the Solomons. Penny's first impression was of the scenic beauty. He found it "very lovely," particularly the "queer-shaped hills with their fantastic peaks, their slopes covered with long yellow-green grass and crowned with coco palms or nut-trees; the long streak of sandy beach, dazzlingly white, meeting the pale blue water, of the tint of an Italian sky. . . ." But there was no escaping the sheer savagery of the place. Bishop Patteson had been dead scarcely three years, and Penny was disturbed to learn that Solomon Islands head-hunters were raiding as far as two hundred miles in their canoes to capture human trophies. The inhabitants of nearby Santa Isabel Island lived in dread of these raiders and built special refuges in the trees to which they fled at the first warning of an attack.

"I went up into one of these tree-houses when I landed at Ysabel," wrote Penny. "The tree in which the house was built must have been 150 feet high. The lower branches had been lopped off, leaving a bare straight stem below the platform on which the house was built, eighty feet from the ground. It was reached by a ladder, made by lashing rungs across a stout pole spliced in lengths, the ends of the rungs on either side being made fast by a rope of

On November 20, 1839, the zealous career of missionary John Williams came to an abrupt end when he was clubbed and speared to death by the natives of Eromanga just after his arrival in the New Hebrides Islands.

twisted canes. This description does not, I know, tend to give an impression of security, while contemplating the thought of this ladder; and I shall be believed when I say that the ladder did not feel a bit more secure than the description reads. The rungs had a most uncomfortable trick of giving way in a slanting direction beneath one's feet; and the whole ladder creaked and swayed about in an unpleasant manner, so that I was very glad when I scrambled up on to the platform and entered the house. Here a surprise awaited me: I had no idea from below of the skill and neatness which the construction of these houses would display. The floor — smooth and flat, and perfectly clean — was made of split bamboos closely plaited; these had been laid upon a layer of soft bark, which again rested upon the woodwork of the platform. The side walls were made of bamboos firmly lashed together, and the roof thatched with the leaves of the sago palm. In the centre of the house was a small circle of stones keeping in its place a layer of sand, on which the fire was made. In a corner of the house was piled a heap of yams for food, and a large bowl of water stood beside it. The interior of the house measured thirty feet by fifteen, and I was told that forty people had once taken refuge there. When an attack is expected, the women and children go up into these houses, or into the forts, and the men keep watch. The news of one of the flotillas being in sight is sent down the coast by a peculiar cry, once heard never to be forgotten."

On the whole Penny found it difficult to believe that his new wards were distant cousins of the cannibals. The natives of the Floridas were not particularly warlike. They looked after their yam plots peaceably enough, worked together in large communal labor forces to build their box-shaped thatched houses, and took great pride in the craftsmanship of their canoes. These vessels were very well made. Their planks were lashed together with fiber twine like the lacing on a boot, as Penny put it, and the seams were caulked with the pulp of a reddish-brown nut. This set so hard that the side of a canoe was often stove in and the planks smashed without the seams giving way. The canoe of a great chief was also fantastically decorated with inlay of mother-of-pearl. The inlaying process was tedious, for each piece of mother-of-pearl had to be hand rubbed to the required shape with a file or stone and then, under the direction of the artist in charge, glued into place with seaming caulk. A chief could requisition as many as one or two thousand pieces of inlay from his dependents in each village, and a really grand canoe could be decorated with up to fifty thousand separate segments of mother-of-pearl. Such a vessel, however, was considered almost legendary. It was used only for prestige voyages to visit other chiefs, whose people would sometimes pay to see such a marvel.

The ingenuity of the islanders astonished Penny. They had learned to fish, for example, with the help of a kite made of palm leaves. The bait was a ball of cobweb, specially made by spiders kept in a small casket. The cobweb was attached to the tail of the kite, and the fisherman in his canoe kept the kite hovering in such a way that the bait skipped over the surface of the water until it was seized by a garfish, whose long, scissorlike jaws became so enmeshed in the glutinous cobweb that the fisherman could haul in his catch without difficulty. Another equally effective device was to turn a live fish into a lure by boring a hole through its lower jaw, threading a fine line through the hole, and making it fast. The tethered fish was then

Tree houses in New Guinea were often pictured by European explorers. In fact, they were usually emergency quarters for times of danger.
Pioneering in New Guinea, JAMES CHALMERS, LONDON, 1887

269

New Guinea villagers, in mud masks and make-up, represent spirits and ghosts.
MAGNUM, BURT GLINN

To assert their manhood during initiation ceremonies, young men in Fiji joined their elders in walking barefoot on stones over a bed of fire. The traditional rite has become an island tourist attraction.

returned to the water, where its antics attracted other fish within range of a long-handled scoop net.

Less than thirty miles from the Floridas, Penny noted also, a particularly astute native community on the island of Malaita purchased much of their food with money that they had made themselves. The raw material for this native mint was a special type of seashell retrieved from the waters off the island. "The women," wrote Penny, "dive for the pink and white shells, from which is made respectively the gold and silver currency. Another set of people break them into small pieces, which are passed on and rubbed smooth between two hard stones. Then more skilful workmen round them off and bore them through piece by piece. The drill used is of the whorle and spindle pattern, tipped with flint. The bits of shell, smooth, rounded, and pierced, are now strung in fathom lengths, and stretched upon a board. Two men, one at either end of the board, rub the string with a grooved stone till it is quite smooth and even, and about the thickness of a cedar pencil. Another party finish off the strings with tortoise-shell ornaments, and make them up into bunches of two, three, four, and up to ten strings in a bunch. The money is now made. When a sufficient quantity is prepared, a trading party set out for the Floridas, Ysabel, or other islands, to buy food. The canoes they build for this trade are very large, some large enough to ship two or three tons of cargo—pigs, yams, and coconuts, with which they will return home. Custom has established a regular tariff for yams and coconuts, fifty of the former and a hundred of the latter being the equivalent for a fathom of a single string of red money. The white will only buy half as much. . . . It is a noticeable fact that the Malanta men, from smartness in this business, acquired by long practice, almost invariably get the best of the bargain. So much so, that when the money passes into circulation at Florida, it soon depreciates in value fully fifty percent."

It was to the missionary's credit that Penny's observations during his ten years in Melanesia touched upon most of the elements of Melanesian culture that anthropologists would later define as important. The gorgeous mother-of-pearl canoe belonging to the chief was a case in point. Very few Melanesian chiefs inherited their position or wielded genuine despotic power. Instead, they were elevated to the front rank of their community by a mixture of ability and showmanship. Initially, the aspiring leader had to win the respect of his colleagues by demonstrating his superiority in amassing wealth, or in diplomacy, or in some other branch of activity such as warfare. He then took under his protection his close relatives and dependents. These, in turn, showed their gratitude by providing services when called upon to do so and thus enhanced and increased their leader's position still further. So, ring by ring, the ambitious and talented Melanesian could extend his patronage and control until it embraced so many followers that the manufacture of fifty thousand pieces of inlay was possible. On the leader's death or decline, however, the entire political structure usually fell apart and had to be rebuilt by a new contender. Only on Fiji was there a self-perpetuating autocracy living in the grand style (probably a cultural link with the neighboring Polynesians), and even there the chiefs felt obliged to give periodic feasts to demonstrate their influence and gratitude to their followers. Another Christian missionary, Thomas Williams, recorded a banquet given by a Fijian prince at which two hundred men were employed for nearly six hours in collecting and piling up the food, which included fifty tons of cooked yams and taros, fifteen tons of sweet pudding, seventy turtles, five cartloads of kava, and about two hundred tons of uncooked yams. A single baked pudding at another Fiji banquet was estimated to be twenty-one feet in circumference.

Ostentation, in fact, was an essential element of Melanesian culture. Besides the ostentation involved in organizing a banquet or arranging a dance display that might be as long as a year in rehearsal, there was an extreme showiness in personal appearance. The dress of very few native cultures made such a stunning impact as did the masks and headdresses of Melanesia—whether those of the mud men of New Guinea, who plastered enormous helmets of clay over their heads and shoulders, or the wig-wearers of Fiji, whose enormous artificial perukes of coir (an elastic fiber extracted from the husk of a coconut) and human hair sometimes extended to include a complete set of built-in false mustaches. Body decoration had many motives, not the least of which was the sheer love of display. In some parts of New Guinea a fully accoutered warrior was a fantastic apparition: his decorated bark girdle was cinched in tight; a penis sheath of rolled leaf extended a full three feet from his loins; and an enormous sunburst headdress of bird-of-paradise feathers nodded and swayed on his head, until the

A splendidly ornamented New Guinea bride wears colorful bird-of-paradise feathers and a high-tiered necklace of mother-of-pearl plates.

A common experience in the Solomon Islands is conveyed by this carved house post: a man in shark's jaws.
<small>MUSEUM FÜR VÖLKERKUNDE, BASEL</small>

man himself appeared like some enormous, spindle-legged bird of the forest. Display could have financial significance, with rolls of shell money worn as necklaces, but often it was flamboyance alone that counted. A plume would be discarded as soon as it looked bedraggled, and many days would be spent hunting the elusive birds of paradise in order to find a replacement.

Often, of course, there was a distinct magical or ritual importance to self-decoration. A man who painted his face with stripes, picked out the lines of his ribs with white clay, or donned a fiercely scowling dance mask of bark could be protecting himself against unseen spirits or actually impersonating them and thereby drawing some of their power to himself. The cult dancers in particular were incarnations of spirits and wore elaborate headdress disguises and long capes of grass to heighten the visual effect. The "Toberran" dance of the New Britain cultists was described by a globe-trotting fellow of the Royal Geographical Society in 1883 as "really a very impressive sight. . . . we saw some sort of creatures creeping out of the bush in all directions; they did indeed look like devils, which the word 'Toberran' signifies. Some wore masks composed of skulls cut in half, and filled in with gum to represent a human face; these are held between the teeth by a stick, fastened across at the back of the mouth of the skull; on their heads they wore long black wigs composed of coco-nut fibre, and their bodies are covered with dead leaves. Some that had no masks had their faces painted an unearthly green colour, and on their shoulders were fastened a kind of wings (on closer inspection I afterwards found these were actually fastened through the loose skin in the side of the neck). On came these unearthly figures, creeping from the bush on every side, some with tails, some with spikes all down their backs, all keeping step and beautiful time, no matter what position their bodies were in. Suddenly the tom-toms stopped, and all the Toberrans rushed to the centre of the open space with a fearful yell; then the music strikes up again, and there begins a dance that defies all description; heads there, arms here, legs one way, tails another, and yet in perfect unison, for if there was an arm one side there was a leg to correspond on the other. The shrieks and yells grew louder, and the singing became shouting; and as they dance, the fires are lighted and blaze up. . . . demon faces showing here, toothless skulls there, the air above them seeming full of arms smeared with blood, and below legs apparently in the last stages of mortification, and above all this a moon that sends a fitful light through the overhanging trees, whilst the huge fires alternately blazing up and dying down casting strange shadows which suggest things even more horrible than the frightful reality. Indeed, however terribly we might try to put a 'Dance of Death' on one of our stages, we could never equal this in its diabolical and hideous effects."

What the observer had witnessed was the dance of a "ghost" society deliberately engineered to instill a feeling of awe into the uninitiated audience. Formerly found throughout the islands, but especially in the Banks Islands, the Solomons, and New Britain, these ghost societies had a semimagical function and impressed their spiritual laws on the rest of the community as well as protecting the members' power. Much less ghastly, but similarly endowed with the trappings of masks and display, were the civilian men's clubs of Melanesia. In New Guinea these were really all-male congregation halls where the menfolk of a village could meet to talk

A New Guinea sailing craft, photographed in 1919, is decorated with shells and inlaid mother-of-pearl.

over their business, smoke, or eat. Bachelors often lived on the premises, and women were specifically excluded except to prepare and bring food to the threshold of the club. Indeed, in some cases a woman risked death if she happened to see the sacred cult objects kept in the clubhouse. More formal were the rules of the male clubs existing on some of the lesser islands. There, not only the clubhouse but also a large area around the building was off limits to women and children. Moreover, while the New Guinea clubhouses were available to almost any initiated male adult, the clubs on the smaller islands were frequently organized into rigidly exclusive grades within themselves. Just as a newcomer to a medieval European trade guild had to serve or pay his way through the grades of apprentice, freeman, liveryman, and member of the court, so the Melanesian clubman was required to purchase his advancement through the ranks of his club. Like the guildsman, the Melanesian had to display his cash worth or trade skill, which made it possible for him to buy his promotion. To be elevated in rank, he had to pay his seniors with lavish gifts of pigs, shell money, or garden produce. In the end, when he had reached the highest rank, the Melanesian, like the guildsman, acquired power and prestige among his fellows.

Nothing was more indicative of the importance and strength of the men's clubs than the clubhouses themselves. In general, Melanesian villages

Standing on piles in a lagoon at Malaita in the Solomon Islands, the isolated men's house, where bachelors sleep, is off limits to all women.

This New Ireland wood carving of a bird and snake typifies a wealth of masks, objects, and figures made for display during rituals and festivals.

were modest affairs, a straggle of small thatched houses sometimes built on stilts and usually arranged in seemingly haphazard fashion among gardens and yam patches. The basic architecture was quite varied. "In one district," said Williams about Fiji, "a village looks like an assemblage of square wicker baskets; in another, like so many rustic arbours; a third seems a collection of oblong hay ricks with holes in the sides, while in a fourth these ricks are conical." But there was no mistaking the clubhouses. Often they were enormous structures, soaring many feet into the air with complex frameworks of ridgepoles, rafters, tie beams, and wall plates, all clad with perfectly watertight thatch. One New Guinea clubhouse was measured and found to be 827 feet long and 40 feet wide. In some of the hangarlike buildings the various grades of the society were restricted to special areas. In others there were shelves where the young men stacked their weapons, using the building as an armory. Many of the clubhouses, especially those associated with spirit cults, had row upon row of multicolored stylized faces of spirit and clan ancestors, or a façade of carved boards, around the doorway to catch the eye of the visitor and make the front elevation more impressive.

The Melanesians felt that they lived perilously. Their world was peopled with a multitude of spirits and ghosts that could do them harm if they were not treated correctly. The ghosts of the ancestors might be offended if the old traditions were not upheld; and the animistic spirits dwelling in rocks and trees and other natural features were by nature malevolent and needed to be guarded against. The surest shield against such troubles was to adopt or associate oneself with a particular form of magic—which was one of the functions of the ghost societies, whose members drew strength from their rituals and ancestry. Throughout Melanesia some communities believed in the Polynesian notions of the spirit force, mana, and the code of conduct, tabu. In the west, toward New Guinea, the concept of magic became more and more intimate. On the small island of Dobu, where anthropologist R. F. Fortune conducted studies of the social behavior of its few hundred inhabitants, there was intense competition to employ what the natives considered a very limited supply of magic. The Dobuans vied with one another to weave magic spells that would insure a good yam crop, for they believed that even the growing yams were living creatures that could be charmed away by a rival. Just as vital to them was the need to guard against the malign attacks of witches and warlocks, often hired by a jealous enemy to do them harm. "If a man has a grudge against another," the

275

Towering front gables, carved and painted, characterize the houses in the Sepik district of New Guinea where the men meet and conduct ceremonies. The buildings are held sacred, and no woman may enter them.

Reverend Alfred Penny had written half a century earlier, "he tries to possess himself of what he can convert into a charm. A fragment of food is generally the thing used, but a lock of hair will do as well, or a piece of tobacco cut from the twisted roll with which the man has filled his pipe. The charm is then taken, with the fee, to the Sorceror, who places it inside a shell in the haunt of his Tindalo [spirit force] on whom he calls to consume the victim. The next thing is to send word to the man that he is being bewitched, the result of which message almost invariably is to make him feel ill. Events may then take one or other of two courses. The Sorceror may be 'squared' by a heavy bribe, and induced to give up the charm; in which case, such is the power of mind over body, the victim will recover; or else, if the Sorceror himself is the enemy, or if he has been heavily paid to push matters to the bitter end and allow no compromise, the victim dies."

Understandably, it was felt that diseases caused by magic could be cured only by similar magical antidotes, and so the great bulk of Melanesian medicine involved incantation and counterspells to heal the sufferer. Among the Dani of the Baliem River in western New Guinea, a man honorably wounded in battle had to be cut and scarified about his torso to release the *mep mili*, or dark blood, which would otherwise place his life in danger. And the Dani were such ardent believers in ghosts and spirits that they shunned going abroad after dark and built in their villages tiny wooden structures, almost like dolls' houses, which were kept furnished and in repair as lodging houses for wandering ghosts.

Death, when it came, almost always aroused a formal ceremony to dispose of the corpse in a manner befitting the newly created ancestor, whose spirit was now a force to be reckoned with. Some communities like that of the Dani cremated their dead. Others dried the body and kept it mummified in the house, or affectionately preserved the dead man's skull, enclosing it like some large jewel of bone in a carved casket. In some of the Solomon Islands, this casket was shaped like a streamlined fish; in others it was a miniature cane-thatched house. The most lavish funeral rites were observed by the autocrats of Fiji. In August, 1845, missionary Thomas Williams, who had labored hard to bring Christianity to Fiji, was disturbed to hear reports that the great chief Tuithakau of the Somosomo district was being "prepared" for death. Hurrying over to the royal household, Williams was appalled to find two women actually in the process of being ritually garroted. Each was seated under a veil and held down by female attendants, while gangs of eight or ten strong men were cheerfully pulling against one another on stout white cords tied around the victims' necks. Even as the missionary sank against the palace wall in horror, he saw the struggles of one veiled bundle cease. An attendant called out gleefully, "She is cold," and the veil was pulled aside to reveal the contorted face of one of Tuithakau's favorite wives. To add to Williams's distress, he found that Tuithakau himself was not yet dead, but only convinced that he was about to die. The chief was complacently allowing mortuary attendants to paint his body with a thick coat of black powder and tie his arms and legs with ceremonial white scarves, while the chief's son and heir looked on with good-natured professional interest. Taking Williams to one side, the future chief tried unsuccessfully to calm the agitated missionary with the assurance that had it not been for the Christians on the island, every one of the king's women would have been similarly put to death.

Cannibalism, by far the most celebrated of Melanesian native customs, was also the least understood by outsiders. Cannibal stories gave a tingle of horror to accounts of the region; and undoubtedly there were men, such as the Reverend James Chalmers of the London Missionary Society and his companion the Reverend Mr. Tomkins in Papua in 1901, who were murdered, cooked, and eaten by the natives. But there were many communities that not only refused to eat human flesh but abhorred cannibalism as much as any Christian. Generally speaking, the custom had a magico-ritual significance. Human flesh might be eaten in order to imbue the feasters with a special degree of mana; or a cannibal banquet might be called to celebrate some great occasion that had spiritual overtones, such as the completion of a secret-society clubhouse. The body of a convicted criminal was sometimes eaten as a final gesture of punishment to the dead man, and the eating of a slain enemy was often a combination of thank offering and victory celebration. Williams witnessed one Fijian raiding party bringing

The spirit images in this detail from the gable of a Sepik district men's house, like the one on the opposite page, are meant to influence and impress the supernatural.

New Guinea funerals, lasting several days, are communally observed with traditional meals and gift giving to impress the dead person's ghost that everyone is concerned. The climax, seen here, is the cremation of the body in a funeral pyre.

back the corpse of a dead enemy whom they had killed on a revenge raid. The two canoeloads of warriors arrived to the beat of a special victory drum, and they could be seen striking the water with poles to signify that they had killed a man. When they were near the beach, the men in the canoe began a special war dance that was answered by a similar performance by the women on the shore. Next the corpse, which had been exposed on the prow of the canoe, was cut free and tossed into the water, where it washed back and forth in the waves. It was then retrieved by vines tied around its wrists, and dragged face downward on the ground by an exulting crowd, who presented it to their chief while singing the successful warrior's song. Finally a young man, whose skill as a carver was obviously based on long experience, cut the corpse into several pieces using a sharp bamboo knife, and the pieces were wrapped in leaves and placed in an earth oven. Sometimes, said Williams, the dead man was cooked whole, placed in a seated position within the oven.

Head-hunting and cannibalism were frequently confused by outside observers, though the two were not necessarily connected. Some head-hunters, it was true, were also cannibals and were known to consume their victims on the spot. But more often the head-hunter was concerned with the prestige he gained by taking and displaying human heads. Again, not all the islanders were head-hunters. The practice seems to have been concentrated in the Solomon Islands and New Guinea, where certain tribes

278

like the Kiwai were notorious for the custom, or where heads were hunted as part of the initiation of boys to manhood. Inveterate head-hunters often took special equipment with them for their task. For the actual man-catching, they devised a type of gaff with a loop on the end of a long spiked pole. As the victim fled, the pursuer caught him in the loop, jerked sharply, and pulled the victim back on to the spike of the pole, which neatly stabbed him between the vertebrae of the neck. To carry the trophy home, there was another loop of cane that was threaded through the mouth and out the windpipe of the trophy head, and then slung over the shoulder. Once back in the village, the head was usually put on display, perhaps with artificial vegetable hair and a set of false eyes made from white seeds, or after its face had been mummified by the removal and drying of the skin and its replacement over the skull with a stuffing of dried bark fiber to fill out the features.

Warfare, with or without head-hunting, was common throughout the whole of Melanesia, and again the main motives were prestige or the prosecution of a feud rather than territorial advantage. Even on Fiji, where the chiefs employed Tongan mercenaries, battles seldom lasted after the death of one or two contestants. A surprise raid, a sharp skirmish, the precipitate flight by one side or the other, and then the looting and months of boasting were the sequence of most Melanesian hostilities. The weapons employed were club, spear, bow and arrow, and daggers in offense; and various shapes of wooden shields, with—in some areas of central New Guinea—body armor of plaited rattan in defense. Warfare was such a constant factor of Melanesian culture that in some regions it became highly institutionalized. In their investigation of the New Guinea Dani, an expedition from the Harvard Peabody Museum found that the inhabitants of the Grand Valley of the Baliem River were accustomed to formalized inter-village fighting. Although the different villages occupied the same valley floor, they each maintained a complex system of frontier zones with guard posts and high watchtowers manned by sentries on the lookout for hostile raiding parties. Every so often, groups of rival warriors would meet at recognized battlegrounds to hurl spears and shoot arrows at each other from a distance of as little as fifty feet. Injuries were common, but deaths were rare enough to bring an immediate end to the day's fighting—as did nightfall, because the Dani, fearful of ghosts, had to get back to their villages before dark.

Not all strangers were regarded as enemies by the Melanesians. Peaceful trade links existed among many communities, particularly between coastal and inland tribes exchanging maritime produce and imported goods for the feathers, raw materials, and specialized products of the mountains. The Motu of Port Moresby sent out an annual trade fleet of large sailing vessels known as "latakoi." Designed as bulk carriers, the latakoi had as many as fourteen hulls rigged in parallel and decked over so that they provided a massive carrying platform. Their fleet took an estimated thirty thousand specially made clay pots up to the head of the Papuan Gulf, where the cargo was exchanged for sago. Even more important was the "kula" trading ring of the offshore islands and nearby coast of eastern Papua, where an intricate commercial organization became one of the most intensively studied native trade systems in the world. Fundamentally, the kula ring was a circular trade route defined by the passage of two special

A Dani warrior in New Guinea exults after an engagement with the enemy, shouting for himself and his fellow tribesmen, but also to impress the ghosts who ordered the battle.

280

The personal adornment of this proud New Guinea man includes a pig's tusk and cassowary quills.

The Melanesians, R. H. Codrington, Oxford, 1891

A drawing by a Melanesian islander depicts the belief that a fisherman struck by a flying fish will die because the fish had been shot at him by the ghost of a dead one.

commodities: arm rings made of conus shell, and necklaces of red Spondylus shell. The odd feature was that neither commodity ever stopped circulating. Both were simply handed on, stage by stage around the ring, giving brief prestige to the temporary owners. To keep the system in operation it was necessary for the two commodities to continue to rotate in opposite directions—clockwise for the necklaces, and counterclockwise for the arm rings—and the pattern never varied. Meanwhile other articles came in and out of the kula ring and were carried around to different sectors as they were needed. Pottery, axes, sago, canoes, and coconuts were all piggyback riders, so to speak, of the two essential products.

The kula ring and one or two other native trade systems still function as exchange mechanisms, though modified, within various areas of Melanesia. Clearly they still have a useful contribution to make in a region so fragmented by geography that a sizable proportion of Melanesia's aboriginal culture remains. Of course, great changes have taken place since the days when the ill-famed "blackbirders," the white slaver captains, first raided the islands for plantation labor and sometimes transported allied head-hunters with them as auxiliary troops. Also, the missionaries soon put an end to wife slaughter and the secret societies. But there are tribes in the New Guinea highlands that have yet to give up head-hunting; and on several of the smaller Melanesian islands the subsistence pattern is virtually unchanged from that of the traditional way of life. In such places it is still possible to find native plutocrats who count their wealth in the possession of pigs whose tusks grow in spirals, or artists who maintain the vivid and powerful artistic traditions of their regions. Indeed, it is Melanesian artwork that best enshrines the atmosphere of the former cannibal islands—squat figures boldly carved in dark wood; faces adorned with staring eyes, white-rimmed teeth, or birds' beaks; incised canoe prows, and a profuse variety of bows, hatchets, and weirdly shaped weapons of war. They are the relics of a turbulent and spirit-haunted heritage that has still to succumb fully either to the sermons of the missionaries or to the instruction of the government officers seeking to educate and prepare the Melanesians for political independence.

The Ski Runners of Lapland

Lavish and hand-adorned, the atlases of the seventeenth century portrayed Europe's far north with a festive flavor that would not look out of place on a Christmas card. There, in an icy region, according to the map makers, began a vast plain, eternally covered with snow and dotted at intervals by clumps of evergreen trees. Among the trees rode trim sledges drawn by prancing deer with enormous branching antlers and escorted— for pursuit seems unlikely—by friendly-looking animals that could have been either domestic dogs or at worst benevolent wolves. In a few places were the rotund and sleeping forms of hibernating bears, obviously in little danger from a species of hunter who slid nimbly along on curiously misshapen skis, carrying bow and arrow at the ready and dressed in a strange garb of loose blouse and tight leggings that made him seem for all the world like a pixy turned Cupid.

Of course such maps were built on years of accumulated cartographic lore and established convention. The same antlered deer are found on early charts of North America; the same bears and sleds appear on maps of Russia. And yet the little hunter on his skis was, in his own way, a mark of real authenticity, for this was how seventeenth-century cartographers envisaged the Lapps, the natives of northern Europe, after nearly fifteen hundred years of knowledge about them.

Tacitus, the historian of Rome and an amateur anthropologist by inclination, had first brought the Lapps to the attention of scholars. "They are remarkably wild and horribly poor. They have no weapons, no horses, no permanent homes. They live on grass, they dress in skins, they sleep on the ground. Their one hope is the arrow. Lacking iron, they use bone to give it a sharp point. Their hunting provides food for men and women alike, and in fact the women follow the men everywhere and demand their share of the prey. The children have no other protection from storm and tempest than a few interwoven branches. In such a refuge the young gather together, and the old men retire. Yet," Tacitus continued nostalgically, "it is this people's belief that in some manner they are happier than those who sweat out their lives in the fields and exhaust their strength in houses, trafficking with their own fortunes and that of others. Disregarding either

Land of the Midnight Sun, PAUL B. DU CHAILLU, NEW YORK, 1882

A 19th-century image of a Lapp

In the mist of the Arctic: A Lapp couple and their reindeer

283

IREFILM, STOCKHOLM

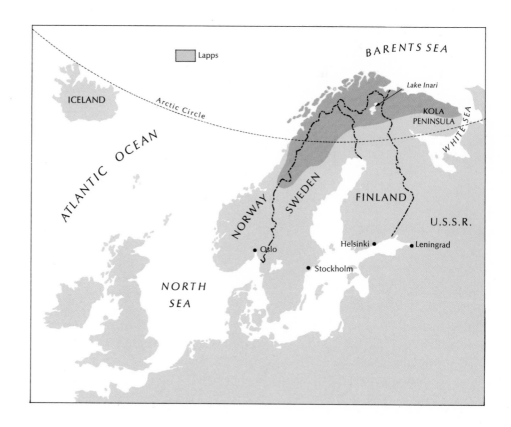

men or gods, they have the most difficult thing of all: they have ceased to feel the harrying of men's desires."

Over the next thousand years various scraps of information were added to Tacitus's original description. The Lapps were reputed to wear animal skins sewn together with sinews and to nourish their babies on animal marrow, hanging their children up in trees so the women could leave them and go hunting with the men. King Alfred of England described these strange people as "Scridefinnas" (the ski-running Lapps), and it was commonly asserted that they could move so fast on their skis that they literally ran down the wild animals they hunted. The Lapps also built up an international reputation as magicians. Tsar Ivan the Terrible kept Lapp shamans at his court as soothsayers, and sailors on voyages to the White Sea thought that Lapps were able to control the winds. The sailors bought lengths of magical knotted cord from them and believed that the untying of the first knot would bring a gentle, fair breeze. On the unraveling of the second knot, the wind would freshen; but the third and last knot must never be untied, for this would raise up a terrible hurricane that would founder the ship. Neighboring peoples to the Lapps—the Norwegians, Finns, Swedes, and Russians—reported that Lapp shamans could foretell the future, and that when the shamans fell into their trances, their souls flew through space to visit distant places and came speeding back with news of events far away. Swedish peasants hired Lapps to tell their fortunes and to predict the sex of their future children. Lapps and Lapland also fascinated scholars of a more scientific inclination. Carolus Linnaeus, the father of botany, traveled north to visit them in 1732 and had his portrait made wearing Lapp dress. And Thomas Malthus, the celebrated authority

Travels in Sweden, Finland and Lapland, JOSEPH ACERBI, LONDON, 1802

This 1802 print depicts a group of Lapps who fish for their livelihood. Plying the ice-free coasts in the spring, they migrate to rivers in the summer and get their food from lakes during the autumn and winter.

on population, made a point of staying in a Lapp encampment, where he counted heads and studied the northerners' mortality rates. There were missions to Christianize the Lapps; several Lappish dictionaries and grammars were written; a system of orthography to write down their language was developed; and dozens upon dozens of books were written about Lapp ethnography. In short, the Lapps became the most thoroughly studied aboriginal people of the world, for the very good reason that they lived so close to their investigators. By the nineteenth century it was possible to leave the University of Uppsala in Sweden and be among the Lapps within a week, exchanging the world of the steam age for a culture that was still essentially rooted in the Ice Age.

Yet the first question in Lapp studies has still to be answered—namely, where exactly did the Lapps come from? There is no lack of theories, but none of them has proved entirely acceptable. Linnaeus classified the Lapps as an Asiatic people. Later proponents of this popular theory went on to maintain that there are cultural and biological similarities sufficient to link the Lapps with the Samoyed peoples of northern Siberia, and more tenuously, with the Mongols proper in Mongolia. According to this idea, the Lapps are the remnants of a people who trekked westward out of Asia in paleoarctic times and settled the extreme northern cul-de-sac of Europe. Fundamentally opposed is the notion that the Lapps are related to short, square-headed Alpine peoples of prehistoric times who migrated northward at the end of the Ice Age, following the fringes of the melting ice sheet and its attendant reindeer herds. Another theory, once laughed out of court but now revived on the basis of recent archeological discoveries, is that the Lapps represent a unique relic of a human stock that was trapped in a

285

habitable pocket behind the glaciers of the last Ice Age. It is argued that because these glaciers spread down from the mountain centers and did not form a single ice sheet, they may have left certain lowland areas in the far north free of ice. In the opinion of this school the Lapps survived in these pockets as the marooned cousins of the rest of the human race, and may therefore be a very early crossbred stock arising from contacts between the proto-Europeans and proto-Asiatics. The truth of the matter is that the mystery of Lapp origins may never be solved. With each passing generation the genetic purity of the Lapps is diluted by intermarriage with their neighbors, and the physical evidence is fast dwindling. Skeptics have also pointed out that the Lapps themselves do not represent an altogether homogenous physical type. In the north of Lapland, for example, the Lapps have mongoloid features such as slanting eyes; while in the south they have triangular, elfin faces without the flat features of central Asians.

The compromise has been to classify the Lapps as a separate group, and on this basis try to identify a median physical type. Karl Wiklund, one of the great authorities on the Lapps, has identified their essential characteristics as "low stature (150 cm [4′ 11″] or a little more for the males), short legs in proportion to the trunk and arms, small hands and feet, very

Lapps of the Kola Peninsula are pictured at a winter encampment outside St. Petersburg in 1874. They appear to have adopted the Orthodox religion of their Russian onlookers, as evidenced by the icon at the tent.

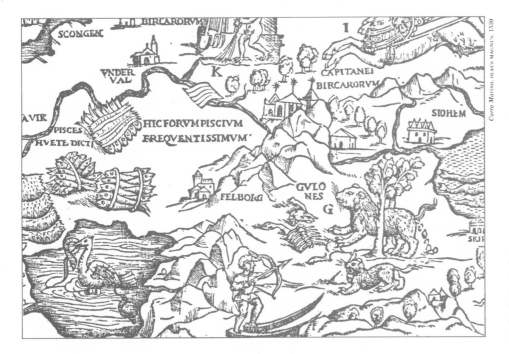

In this detail from his Carta Marina of 1539, Swedish map maker Olaus Magnus portrayed the Lapp as a hunter pursuing his prey on skis. Another section revealed that Lapps had already domesticated reindeer.

short skull in proportion to the breadth (average index about 82), and broad and low face, prominent cheek bones, feebly developed lower jaw with pointed chin . . . brown eyes, hair dark to black, lank, coarse, beard or moustache straggly or scanty." Medical as well as popular opinion recognizes the Lapps as an outstandingly fit and healthy people. Disease among them is rare, and their muscular strength and stamina are almost legendary. In 1883, when the polar explorer Baron Nils Nordenskjöld reached the ultimate limit of one of his expeditions in Greenland, he asked two of his Lapp scouts to make a flying dash into the still-unexplored wilderness. The two men set out on skis, and in 57 hours through totally unknown country they covered 290 miles. When Nordenskjöld returned home, there was some doubt that this feat had been physically possible, so he arranged a long-distance ski race in which one of his scouts, Tuorda, completed the distance of 137 miles in 21 hours and 22 minutes. Similarly, during the Second World War Lapp skiers proved invaluable as scouts in Arctic campaigns and as runners to carry messages for the Norwegian resistance.

Linguistically the Lapp heritage is extremely rich, and if anything it sustains the theory that they may have been a people who originated somewhere in Asia. The Lapp tongue belongs to the Finno-Ugric group of languages, which includes Finnish and Hungarian as well as the Vogul and Ostyak languages spoken in northwestern Siberia. But to the frustration of ethnographers seeking to find the answer to Lapp origins, it is not clear whether the Lapps have always spoken their present language or whether they adopted it from their Finnish neighbors, for there are certain archaic Lappish words that hint at an even earlier language. Moreover, the Lapps have borrowed heavily from Norwegian and Swedish and have acquired some three thousand loan words, some of which are obsolete Old Norse, so that present-day Lappish has become a remarkable storehouse for otherwise extinct vocabularies. For example, the Lappish words for items connected with fishing and the sea depend noticeably upon Scandinavian

287

Amulets, like this charm adorned with bells, were carried for luck by Lapps on bear-hunting expeditions.

A Winter in Lapland and Sweden,
ARTHUR DE CAPELL BROOKE, LONDON, 1827

vocabularies, chiefly Norwegian, and indicate that along the coasts there has been much cultural contact.

To confuse the linguistic maze still further, the Lapps speak various regional dialects, so that the different Lapp groups cannot necessarily understand one another. As early as 1840 the Honorable Arthur Dillon, an avid traveler who spent a winter in Lapland, found the Lapps speaking at least three dialects, and modern scholarship now distinguishes up to seven different linguistic groups. Also, local vocabularies reflect local needs. Among the reindeer-herding Lapps of the interior there is a whole lexicon of words to describe the differences among their reindeer. Besides the usual designations for an animal's age and sex, there are more than a hundred different ways of describing a reindeer's color and the shape and pattern of its antlers. No one was more impressed by this facility than Linnaeus, who was himself something of an expert, the inventor of a binary system of nomenclature to classify the entire animal and vegetable world. "They [the Lapp herders]," he wrote after watching a large herd of reindeer milling about, "told me that all the reindeer have their specific names, which they know quite distinctly. This seemed to me most strange, because the shape (of the animals) is the same, the colour is similar, and varies from one month to another. The size differs according to the age, and to know such a muddle, like ants in an anthill, seemed to me to be a most puzzling thing."

Linnaeus's *Iter Lapponicum* took him to visit the Lapps of Jokkmokk in north central Sweden, a little off center from the main area of Lapp occupation. Today Lapps are found in a broad swath of territory running across the most northerly parts of Norway, Sweden, and Finland. In the extreme east they spill across the Russian border into the Kola Peninsula above the White Sea; and in the west the Lapp territory follows the high mountain core of Norway and Sweden as far as 62 degrees north. Thus Lapland has a shape something like that of a horse's head facing east, with its muzzle in the Kola Peninsula, Lake Inari as its eye, and the irregular fringe of the outer skerries and islands standing up as a bristling mane. The topography of this huge area is diverse—the severely bleak mountains and fells of northern Norway falling away gradually eastward toward the undulating forest-clad plains of Finland with their lakes and swamps. At one time Lapps lived even farther south in the Swedish mountains, and certainly in Finland they once ranged over a much larger area until they were driven back by incoming farmers and woodsmen. On the whole, however, this was a slow process of encroachment, for Lapland lies on the outer limits of land that can support cereal crops or cattle successfully. Not until the Middle Ages were the traditional homelands of the Lapps unduly threatened, resulting in the first of a long series of border agreements that demarcated the areas where the Lapps could still hunt and fish and graze their herds of reindeer. To this day Lapp herdsmen retain their right to migrate across the frontier between Norway and Sweden while moving between their winter and summer pastures.

Contrary to popular opinion, only a minority of Lapps are true nomads of the reindeer-herding type, and these are largely restricted to the central and northern parts of Norway and Sweden. Much more numerous are the coastal Lapps along the Norwegian shoreline, who live by fishing and some herding; while a third category, the forest Lapps, are more characteristic of the Finnish and northern Swedish woodlands, where they breed small reindeer herds, do a little hunting, and fish in the rivers and lakes.

Yet it is this last—and most often overlooked—division of Lapp culture that most closely resembles the traditional way of life depicted on the early maps. Paul Du Chaillu, an American traveler who had explored in central Africa before deciding on a trip to Lapland, visited a Lapp encampment in the 1880's, and his description serves well for the scene at a forest dwelling in deep midwinter: "We followed a well-furrowed track, each of us leading our animal [a sleigh reindeer]; we soon heard the barking of dogs announcing our approach to a Lapp encampment, and found ourselves before a kåta (tent). The people were friends of Herr Gustaf and we were heartily welcomed. They could talk Lappish, Finnish, Swedish, and Norwegian. Several women were inside the kåta, seated on skins, and all were, as usual busy. Lapp women are very industrious; upon them devolves the labor of making the clothing for the family. One was weaving bands of bright colours, another was giving the final touches to a garment, while a third finished a pair of shoes . . . there was a blazing fire in the centre, the smoke escaping by an aperture above. Two kettles filled with meat were boiling, for they were preparing the evening meal; and the tent was so crowded that I wondered how we should all be able to sleep comfortably. Numerous pulkas and kerres [types of sledges] were scattered around, snow shoes were either lying on the ground or standing upright against the trees. Harnesses were hanging here and there, and quarters and pieces of frozen reindeer meat were suspended from the branches. A kind of rack had been built about six feet from the ground, where frozen meat was piled. There was also a store of smoked

Explorer Paul Du Chaillu recorded this congested domestic scene inside a Lapp winter tent in the 1880's. The family circle includes the dog, an invaluable aid in reindeer herding.

meat and tongues, buckets full of frozen milk—for some of the deer are milked until Christmas, as was stated by the host himself—and bladders of this congealed milk or blood, and reindeer feet. The skins of animals recently killed were drying, stretched on frames so that they could not shrink. Saddles, empty pails, kettles, iron pots, wooden vessels, and garments were scattered about."

Strictly speaking, the forest Lapps can be described as seminomadic, because they travel short distances between their winter encampments, spring hunting grounds, and the lakes where they spend the summer fishing before moving to the areas where they round up their small herds of reindeer in the autumn. At one time these forest Lapps were much more dependent upon hunting and trapping, and the most frequent glimpses of them occur in the account books of medieval traders and landowners who collected taxes—paid in fish, beaver skins, wolf and fox pelts, and other furs—from the Lapps. Wild reindeer, at least in early times, were more important than the domesticated variety, and the forest Lapps would build extremely long "lead in" fences that funneled the wild deer into a suitable killing ground such as the edge of a lake or against a cliff. Elsewhere, they planted snares to catch the animals' feet, dug pitfalls, or employed tame reindeer as decoys. The latter were very valuable because they could be trained to entice numbers of wild deer into a corral. The antlers of a male decoy would also be draped with noosed cords so that when a wild buck challenged the animal to a fight, the contestants became hopelessly entangled and the hunter could run forward and kill his prey with a dagger thrust. Only one Lapp hunting bow of early design has survived, and it is a formidable weapon. Almost six feet long, it is made of composite wood with the outer arc of birch glued to an inner layer of pine. The whole weapon was then

Armed with long spears and crossbows, Lapp hunters close in on a cornered bear. This dangerous activity, pursued only by the most physically fit, was conducted according to a precise ritual and was followed by elaborate ceremonies.

sheathed in coils of fiber to give it additional strength and tipped at one end with iron to make it a useful lunging weapon at close quarters. Later the Lapps adopted metal crossbows and firearms to make their hunting more efficient; though even with their traditional weapons of knife and spear they were quite prepared to tackle wolf and bear.

Bear hunting, according to the disapproving accounts of the early missionaries to Lapland, was the supreme form of chase. Like the Ainus of Japan, the Lapps attributed near-human intelligence to the bear and regarded it as semisacred, enveloping the animal in a web of ritual and taboo. They believed, for example, that a bear could distinguish between men and women; that it was frightened only if two brothers went together to hunt it, knowing that one brother would avenge the death of the other; and that the bear could understand the Lappish language. Therefore all bear hunters used a special language (now identified by linguists as mainly a borrowed Scandinavian vocabulary), and they never referred to the bear directly, preferring to use such euphemisms as "the winter sleeper," "woolly one," and "honey paws."

The proper season for bear hunting was early spring, when the bear was just about to emerge from its winter hibernation. First, a Lapp hunter would identify the lair and "ring" it by marking a circle around it in the snow, thereby claiming for himself the right to kill the animal. On the day of the hunt the shamans would be consulted for favorable omens; then the party of hunters would set out dressed in their brightest clothing, decorated with ribbons and amulets, and carrying special bear pikes, each with a heavy metal head and a thick foreshaft so that the animal could not bite through it. On the way to the den the party would be led by the chosen executioner, who carried a staff tipped with a sacred brass ring. Once there, he would station himself in front of the lair; two heavy poles would be set across the mouth of the den to impede the bear's furious charge; and a couple of the bravest hunters would slip quietly into the den to rouse the animal.

The actual technique of bear spearing required strong nerves and a steady hand. As the animal lumbered forward and rose on its hind legs to attack the hunter, the Lapp sank the butt of his pike into the ground behind him, and holding the weapon firmly, fell back so that the lunging bear literally impaled itself with its own momentum on the head of the pike.

Once the animal was dead, an elaborate ritual began. First, the hunters sang a verse of congratulation to the animal, thanking it for not damaging their spears or harming the hunters. Next—and the reason for this is not known—the hunting party would lash the corpse with twigs. Then they would shake their spears at the animal and place their skis across its body, presumably to bring good luck in future bear hunts. Sometimes the hunters would cover the corpse with spruce twigs and leave it for twenty-four hours; on other occasions the bear would be taken straight to the camp. In either case the carcass was loaded on a sledge and hauled along to the accompaniment of a special hunter's song that culminated, on arrival at the tents, in a description of the day's events. Later, the women responded by singing a paean of congratulation to the hunter's skill. Going around to the back of his tent, the man who had killed the bear would beat three times upon the tent cloth with a thin whip of plaited birch twigs, which was later wrapped in linen, decorated, and carefully put to one side. At this stage—though ac-

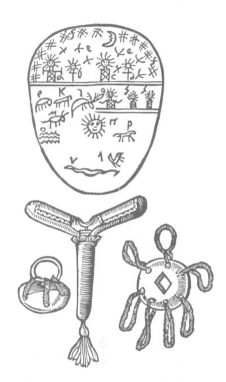

Painted with symbols and figures, the head of a "kobda," or shaman's drum, is shown at top. A reindeer-horn drumstick, below, is flanked by "arpas," copper pointers that bounced on the drum's surface as it was hit, guiding the shaman's divinations.
Lapponia, JOANNIS SCHEFFERI, 1673

OVERLEAF: *A present-day Lapp watches over reindeer during an annual summer move from the forests of northern Sweden to grass-covered pastures in Norway.*
IREFILM, STOCKHOLM

This 1673 woodcut illustrates a traditional mode of Lapp worship at a "seide," or shrine, consisting of a stone, weirdly shaped by the elements and partly circled by antlers.

counts vary—the hunters would raise the back of the tent cloth and enter the tent, where they would be greeted by the womenfolk peering at them through sacred brass rings held up before them like monocles. At the same time the women would spit on the hunters' faces a sacred concoction of alder bark that they had chewed until the saliva had become stained blood-red.

The bear was then skinned and cut up, the butcher taking great care not to break any of the bones and as far as possible to keep intact the main tendons. The meat was cooked in a pot and doled out in a solemn banquet, each piece being distributed according to strict rules, while the men and women sang alternate verses of a banquet song. It was important that no morsel of bear meat be left over, and so the feast could last as long as three days. Afterward the skeleton of the bear was carefully buried, together with its head, genitalia, and tendons, the skin of its muzzle, and a cup of red alder juice. In the grave the vertebrae of the bear's spine were threaded in their correct anatomical order upon the birch whip of the successful hunter. Finally, the bear's skin was stretched against a tree trunk, and the women, their faces covered with veils, came out of their tents and threw birch branches or shot arrows toward the skin, which they could not see. When one of them by a lucky accident first hit the skin, her husband was considered to be the next hunter most likely to find and kill a bear. If the woman was unmarried, it was believed that she would one day wed a famous bear hunter.

The exact form of the Lapp bear ritual varied from one group to another, but there seems little doubt that the ceremonies were linked with a spirit force that was very powerful and had sexual connotations. The brass monocles used by the women have been interpreted as sexual symbols. Also, no hunter was allowed to sleep with a woman for three days after a bear hunt lest the woman become sterile. For the same reason the man who had killed the bear had a sexual prohibition placed on him for five days. Moreover, the sledge that had brought the bear's carcass to camp was avoided by the women for the rest of the season, and during the banquet certain parts of the bear were forbidden to women, even the pieces they were allowed to eat having to be handled very cautiously with pointed sticks that served as forks. Only after a ritual cleansing ceremony was the potentially malign spirit force of the bear considered to have left the camp. In this cleansing ceremony the men ran around the hearth fire one by one, holding on to the chain of the hanging caldron while the women sang a final purification verse and sometimes threw hot ashes behind the men as they ran out the door.

The shaman was the most important figure in Lapp ceremonies. Usually he was a man in whom the mystic forces had been recognized at an early age, perhaps because he was prone to vivid dreams or had been singled out as a child by some strong omen. The spirit world of the Lapps was not so much a forbidding place as the synthesis of animistic beliefs and minor creed through which the shaman was expected to steer an intelligent course. He needed to know how to read the auguries of birds and animals, how to prepare medicines with magical properties, and how to enter the spirit places. This he did by falling into a trance so that his spirit was released to go on its journeys to the other world. In many of these feats the shaman was helped by sacred drums. "That which they principally depend upon in their magical mummeries," observed Dillon, "was a drum . . . made of one entire piece, the tree being cleft asunder and hollowed out in the middle so as to resemble a bowl. The flat or upper part was covered with skin; the convex side had two holes cut in it, and the space between served as a handle. The rim upon which the skin was stretched, was not exactly circular, but nearly an oval. They were, in fact, small oblong kettle drums. On the drum head were painted several figures in red, which represented their god, our

The Lapps. ROBERTO BOSSI. THAMES & HUDSON, 1960

Executed in ineffaceable red ocher and dating from about 1500 to 2000 B.C., *these rock paintings in Swedish Lapland were probably precursors of the magical drum paintings of the Lapps. Represented are two elk, with reindeer above and below.*

Saviour, the Apostles, and the animals they were acquainted with. . . . The hammer with which this drum was struck was generally made of reindeer's horn, about the thickness of a man's little finger. The other instrument, without which the apparatus would have been incomplete, was the 'Arpa.' It was the mark that pointed out the answers to their enquiries. It was a large copper or silver ring with other smaller ones attached to it in a variety of fashions. One of those represented is a thick plate, perforated in the middle, and surrounded with small chains. The other is a ring with a circular plate attached to it by little brass bands. In use of the drum, the magician was not so solicitous about producing a great noise as about the motion of the 'Arpa,' and the position they took on the hieroglyphics painted on the skin. . . . During the ceremony, the operator and all those present remained on their knees. The sorcerer took the drum by the handle, and laid the ring on the part where the sun was delineated. He then struck the drum with his hammer, and sung a song called in their language 'Jorke,' the rest of the company joining in chorus. As the song proceeds, the violence of the singing and drumming increase. At last he raises it above his head, and drops down like one in a trance, and his soul is supposed to have abandoned his body, and conveyed itself to the country from which intelligence is required. Meanwhile, the whole party keep up a chorus, and watch, lest anything should disturb him. Not a fly is allowed to approach him lest he should die from the effects of being aroused before the proper time. When he recovers his senses, he gives the required information."

Already by the time of Dillon's northern tour only a few Lapp shaman

Lapps erected small log huts, like this structure in Finland, to serve as storerooms and emergency shelters. Elevated above the ground, they provided protection against winter snowdrifts and scavenging animals.

This contemporary photograph shows how Swedish Lapps utilize reindeer as beasts of burden during treks. Encumbered with panniers of up to 40 pounds each, the animals also carry young children.

drums still survived. The Christian missionaries regarded these drums as the very root of Lapp paganism and tried hard to destroy them all. Almost every Lapp family had once owned a drum, and the missionaries insisted that they bring them to church to be burned in huge public bonfires. Luckily a few drums were saved by zealous curio seekers and scholars, and a few more were hidden away by the Lapps themselves, so that more than eighty shaman drums have been preserved.

There is a good deal of evidence to show that the work of the Christian missionaries, who began to have a real effect in Lapland at the end of the seventeenth century, was by no means the first of the foreign influences on Lapp religious beliefs. Several of the existing Lapp deities were obviously derived from Norse mythology, including a god of thunder who demanded a sacrifice of a reindeer buck buried alive, and many of the hieroglyphics on the sacred drums can be recognized as copies of runic symbols. Ironically too, the Christian missionaries were sometimes gratified instead of shocked by manifestations of Lapp paganism. The phenomenon of "Lapp panic," or "Arctic hysteria," when entire groups of Lapps fell into ecstatic trances or lost control of their senses in a frenzy, was seen — when it happened in Christian churches — as evidence of deep and total conversion to Christianity; though at the same time no missionary priest could ignore the fact that out in the wilderness the casual traveler might stumble across a "seide," the personal Lapp shrine with its ring of antlers, or an odd-shaped stone surrounded by twigs where a Lapp was accustomed to worship his age-old gods.

The social fabric of the Lapps stood up remarkably well to the pressures of outsiders. Fundamentally, early Lapp society was based upon the family group, in which men and women played an almost equal role and brought up their children with much indulgence and affection. The young received most of their education through mimic games. For example, they learned to saddle and pack reindeer by practicing first on smaller animals such as dogs and goats, and one of their most popular games was to run around holding up a set of antlers while their playmates tried to catch them with toy lassos as if they were reindeer. When they grew older, Lapp children

These 17th-century water colors depict important seasonal occurrences in the life of the Lapps. During the winter (top) they pay taxes of pelts and dried fish to the king's commissioners and receive in return a spoonful of brandy (1). They also travel and trans-port goods in reindeer-drawn sledges (3, 4); train their reindeer (8); smoke their highly prized tobacco (7); and prophesy with magic shamans' drums (10–11). One of the summer scenes (bottom) portrays Christianized Lapps in a wedding procession at a church (1,3–7).

Inside, a basin of brandy has been substituted for the traditional holy water. Other Lapps are shown making baskets, rearing their children, stocking an elevated storehouse with provisions for the winter, drawing wire for the decoration of their coats and boots, eating, and lying in bed inside a tent. On the right they may be seen imaginatively adhering to various ancestral forms of religious worship (16–20). The use of animal sacrifices is depicted, as well as the Lapps' "way of praying to death that it would be pleased to spare them a while."

Young Lapps have little opportunity to indulge in childish play, but are trained from an early age to engage in useful activities. The boy in northern Norway, above, cleans codfish.

began gradually to participate in the real-life activities of their parents and to contribute toward the family economy. Because most Lapp families in their early culture lived in loosely associated groups, sharing their territory according to its natural resources such as rivers, pastures, and good hunting grounds, there was usually opportunity for young men and women to meet and select marriage partners from neighboring families. Later, as trade fairs and churchgoing became more common, these served as the centers for youthful members of the opposite sex to encounter one another. Courtship involved the boy in giving presents of silks and jewelry to the girl and—in the early days—a cash gift to her parents, which could be recovered if the marriage did not take place. This gift was, in effect, a down payment on the girl's economic value, because every Lapp child was an owner of reindeer and personal property in his or her own right. The formal request for a girl's hand in marriage was a carefully arranged affair. The suitor would assemble a large caravan of friends and relatives and drive up to the tent of the girl's family. In some regions the approaching caravan would announce its presence by firing a fusillade of shots. In other areas the suitor was expected to drive three times around the tent in his reindeer sleigh and wait for the girl to show her interest in him by unharnessing his reindeer. Then the suitor entered the tent accompanied by his spokesman, or "head of the wooing," a friend with a glib tongue whose task was to argue the suitor's case for him while the bride's relatives, usually the elderly female ones, disparaged the suitor's character, skill, or prospects. Throughout the entire negotiation neither suitor nor girl was allowed to intervene. If the suit was successful, it was customary for the young man to move in with his bride's family until he could set up a household of his own, though this seldom took long because the girl's inheritance, together with the man's property, was often sufficient to start a new reindeer herd.

All in all, Lapp households were really very democratic. Even if a man had too few sons to manage his reindeer and so needed to hire servants, the latter had a voice in his domestic affairs. They were paid in reindeer and could acquire a fair-sized proportion of the total herd. Nor was there a social barrier that prevented a servant, man or woman, from marrying into his employer's family. Servants could also expect the same care and treatment as any other member of the household, though in fact, the vigorous outdoor life of the Lapps meant that there was little illness apart from rheumatism. There were reports that in early days the Lapps killed their aged and infirm by plunging them into freezing lakes or throwing them over cliffs, but in historical times euthanasia was seldom necessary. Elderly Lapps simply died in their everyday occupations—the old women in the tents, the men while traveling, hunting, or herding. There, with little ceremony, they were buried, usually in a birch-bark shroud, in a simple hole dug by their family.

Like the forest Lapps, the coastal, or fisher, Lapps were essentially semi-nomadic, though their range of movement was even smaller, little more than short treks from the inland hunting grounds to the heads of fjords, or when the fishing required it, down to the mouths of the fjords. How old this pattern of life might be is, once again, a matter of conjecture. Half-buried and abandoned hearthsites on the northern fjords date back at least four thousand years, and in Tudor times English navigators who sailed to

Russia to pick up furs at the White Sea spoke of seeing numbers of wild, half-savage "sea Finns," as they called them, who scoured the shoreline for birds' eggs, shellfish, and anything else edible. Unlike the Eskimos, who must contend with the hazards of winter pack ice, the coastal Lapps have the overwhelming advantage that their strip of coastline — unique in northern Eurasia — is kept free of ice by the last swirl of warmth from the Gulf Stream. Here they can fish all year round, taking whale, walrus, seals of various kinds, and a great variety of saltwater fish. In the Middle Ages they used planks sewn together with sinew to make boats, which were so famous for their seaworthiness that the Norwegian kings placed special orders with Lapp boatbuilders. Today the fisher Lapps, who account for the great bulk of the surviving Lapp population of Fennoscandia, have modified their original culture drastically.

The basis of the economy of the third category of Lapp culture, the mountain Lapps, is, of course, the domestic reindeer, a relative of the New World caribou and a migratory creature of unusually finicky appetite. To breed and benefit from this unusual herd animal, the mountain Lapps have devised highly specialized techniques of animal husbandry that are matched only by those of a few of the northern Asiatic reindeer-breeding tribes, whose methods resemble, but are not always the same as, the ways preferred by the Lapps.

The principal problem of reindeer breeding is how to control an animal that remains only one step from its wild state, retaining its migratory instinct, its seasonal mating pattern, and its preference for special wild foods such as moss and lichen. The Lapp solution is to direct these instincts rather than to block them, and to employ as their chief ally the reindeer itself. Thus the foundation of any reindeer herd is its cadre of neutered, trained animals, which act as Judases for the half-wild herd. In all probability these lead animals are a development from the former decoy reindeer, which were once used to trap wild reindeer. Now they are found at the tip of the characteristic arrowhead formation of a Lapp reindeer herd on the move. First comes a "haerge," a castrated male deer led by a Lapp herdsman in the direction the herd must go. Next — and the key to the entire reindeer formation — walks a reindeer ox that has no halter but has been trained to follow the leader. On this animal is ultimately focused the group instinct of the remainder of the herd, which will usually follow docilely enough, particularly if a troop of trained reindeer is stationed immediately behind the two leaders. At the base of the arrowhead formation, and scouting along its flanks, come the rest of the Lapp herdsmen, urging stragglers along and chasing mavericks back into place so that the herd remains relatively compact; for should the herd begin to disintegrate, the process quickly accelerates as individual reindeer lose their herd instinct and run off singly or in small groups, which must then be rounded up with great labor. In all these operations the Lapps rely greatly on the help of their herd dogs, which, said Du Chaillu, "somewhat resemble the Pomeranian breed; they are not large, and are covered with long thick hair. Some look very much like small bears, and I have seen a few with the same dark brown color and without tails . . . it is wonderful to see how these dogs can keep a flock of reindeer together; occasionally, for some unknown reason, a panic seizes a herd, and it takes all their cunning and a great deal of running to prevent the deer

Lapp girls are taught to assist their mothers in such womanly tasks as preparing reindeer skins to be made into clothing. This girl in Finland is photographed scraping a hide.

Domesticated reindeer must depend on their Lapp herdsmen for protection against wolves and other predators, as seen in the drawing above.

from scattering in all directions."

The routes taken by the Lapp reindeer herds were, until very recently, dictated largely by the migration trails traditionally used by the wild reindeer. Zoologists have yet to analyze fully the migration instinct of reindeer, but it seems to be a combination of factors, including some degree of sexual drive possibly triggered by a change in the seasonal weather. To the Lapps, however, the movements of their reindeer herds come down to the vital quest for suitable feeding grounds where the animals will keep healthy and fit. In winter the reindeer prefer to eat "reindeer lichen" (*Cladonia rangiferina*), which grows in the deep forests. To reach this food, when it is submerged beneath a blanket of snow, the reindeer will paw away the snow with their broad hooves and dig down into the holes, presenting the extraordinary sight of a crop of reindeer rumps, along with tips of antlers, projecting above the snow. As the climate warms, the heat soon dries out the forest lichens and makes them inedible for the reindeer. Moreover, the spring brings swarms of midges and gadflies that infest the reindeer, laying their eggs in the animals' coats, nostrils, and mouths, where the larvae hatch and burrow into the flesh, damaging the skin and causing the reindeer great distress. So the onset of spring weather sees the start of an annual migration away from the forest and up toward cooler grazing lands in the high mountains, a migration that also answers the hereditary urge of the pregnant female reindeer to drop their young at their customary calving grounds en route to the uplands.

The start of this migration is usually in April, when the ground is still covered with snow, and it is the most colorful and cheerful episode in the Lapp calendar. The winter encampment is dismantled; goods and chattels are packed and stowed in the sledges; and while some of the men keep an eye on the restless herd, the others assemble the sledge caravan that will accompany the trek. Nowhere else in the world is there anything quite like the "pulka," or reindeer sledge of the western Lapps, and it attracted the admiration of every early traveler to Lapland. Shaped like a small boat cut in half, it is drawn by a single trained reindeer harnessed with a thong leading from a halter around its neck, back between its legs, to the prow of the little "boat." The driver sits in the vessel with his legs outstretched and controls the animal with a rein attached to the base of its antlers. Driving a pulka requires great skill, for at high speed the sledge rises upward on a narrow "keel" some four inches wide, which acts like the blade beneath a skate, and the whole conveyance goes tearing along in the reindeer's track, bouncing over ruts, caroming off rocks and trees, and occasionally spilling the careless driver headlong into the snow. Some pulkas are designed as load carriers and are so broad and flat as to be virtually sledge-boxes, but the real fliers are the lightweight, one-man posting sledges that most European visitors had to learn how to drive. Said Du Chaillu: "The rider seats himself, holding the rein twisted around the right hand. The line must not be held tightly, and the middle part should not quite touch the snow, for it is dangerous should the rein get under the sleigh; in this case the driver's arms may become entangled, and he be dragged some distance before he can loosen the cord around his hands. A novice, therefore, must be constantly on the watch. If you want the reindeer to stop, the rein is thrown to the left; if you wish to go fast, then to the right; as for

302

myself, I have never been able to make a deer go slow—they never walk unless very tired. You must make up your mind to be upset a great many times before you learn to drive a reindeer.

"The most difficult and dangerous time in driving is when descending steep hills, as the speed of the sleigh is greater than that of the reindeer. The Lapps sit astride with their knees bent, using their feet as rudder and drag. To a novice this practice is very dangerous, and might lead to his breaking his legs. They never would allow me to try to come down in this manner, and even they, with their constant practice sometimes ruptured themselves from this cause. In going down I used a short stick, the point of which I would force into the snow with all my might, this acting as a drag. But sometimes the hills and mountains are too steep even for the Lapps. In that case the reindeer is tied behind the conveyance; they cannot bear to be pulled by the horns, and consequently make strong efforts to free themselves, and in so doing greatly lessen the speed. It is also very difficult to learn how to balance one's self, so as to keep the equilibrium of the *pulka* and prevent upsetting; the greater the speed the more difficult is the task. For example, when a deer, after swiftly going down a hill, turns suddenly

Before moving from summer pastures to winter quarters, the Lapps sort out their reindeer flocks into smaller groups, weeding out the strays. They use sticks and lassos to drive the animals into corrals.

A well-trained lead reindeer, wearing a harness, pulls a sledge—the favorite form of Lapp transportation in winter—while others follow.

in a sharp curve, the rider must bend to the other side, or he will be overturned."

Du Chaillu learned just how exhilarating a downhill pulka ride could be sometime later, when his party was obliged to make a forced descent of a steep mountain slope in sub-zero weather. Pehr, the leader of the caravan, halted the group at the lip of the descent and made very careful preparations. The sleighs were linked together in tow lines of eight or ten apiece, one behind the other, with the reindeer fastened at the tail of the convoy. Only the lead sledge had an animal in pulling harness, and its task was to guide the whole caravan snaking down the icy slope like a runaway freight train. When every Lapp had taken his position seated astraddle his pulka with his feet outstretched, ready to dig into the snow like a racing tobogganist, "Pehr looked back and gave the signal, and started his reindeer down the hill in a zigzag course. This required great dexterity, as we flew over the snow with astonishing speed. At times the sleighs would swerve on the declivity, but we went so fast that we were soon out of danger. I was anxious in the highest degree. If one of those cords had broken we should have been precipitated far below, or dashed against the rocky sides. I admired the simplicity of the arrangements, which were dictated by the fact that reindeer cannot bear to be pulled by the head, especially by the horns; each one, therefore, makes an effort to disengage himself, and by so doing acts as a brake on the ones in front, so that no sleigh is likely to be overturned. But what a speed, with a precipice on our right! In two or three places we went for a short distance over the bare rocks; I was afraid the reindeer would miss their foothold, and was intensely excited, for I might at any moment have been thrown out headlong. Pehr and my other companions were accustomed to this route, and knew what they were about. After reaching the bottom of the ravine we allowed the panting animals to rest. We were now on the western shed of the mountains, and had just ended the most thrilling ride I had ever taken."

The spring trek of the mountain Lapps out of their forests is, in fact, performed mostly at night, when the harder snow surface makes sledge travel easier. One important stop is made en route at a special staging camp, where unwanted winter equipment is placed in storage, and summer equipment is gathered up. Then the herd and its accompanying caravan continue, with a halt at the calving grounds, up to the high pasture, where the deer will feed on young grass and buds. During the summer it is sometimes possible to keep the reindeer within a well-defined area, perhaps on a coastal peninsula whose neck can be patrolled by the Lapps, or, best of all, on an island. Reindeer are good swimmers and can be swum out to the islands by their owners, but they are reluctant to try the return journey on their own. For the most part, however, the reindeer herds are on open fells where they must be watched constantly by squads of herdsmen working in shifts, ready to head off stray groups or contain sudden, apparently mad rushes of the animals. Johan Turi, a mountain Lapp who in 1910 published his remarkable memoirs of the nomadic life, described how "when it grows hot, the reindeer run up into the high ridges where men can't get, and because of the heat and the mosquitos they sprint higher and higher up the fell sides, and the reindeer on the top set the loose stones rolling, and when one stone begins rolling it starts others, and thus many reindeer are killed, and if a man is underneath, the danger is as great for him. A fell top that is very high and covered with grass is called a *ride*. In the heat, the reindeer run up on to the fell slopes and in between the tall cliffs till they can get neither up nor down, if they have not got the sense to turn back the way they came. The tame reindeer still have the same nature as their ancestors . . . and reindeer will kill themselves, sometimes whole flocks."

Some Lapp groups milk their herds during the summer, preventing the young calves from suckling by tying a short stick across their mouths like a bit. But reindeer milking is a considerable chore, for the animal must be lassoed and held steady by a man while a woman milks the animal into a special wooden scoop rather like a large soup ladle. Moreover, the yield is low—Malthus claimed scarcely half a pint on the average per animal—and the milk is almost nauseatingly fat, rather like liquid butter. Mostly it is used for cheese, which is molded into fiber pots or kept fresh in the membranes of reindeer stomachs turned inside out. Summer is also the time for marking reindeer calves so that they can be identified by their owners. Instead of brands, the Lapps today use a complex system of ear notches, every Lapp—even the children—owning his own reindeer mark, which is registered with the state reindeer-breeding authority to prevent reindeer stealing and quarrels during the separation of the herds. Throughout the summer, too, the Lapp herdsman will be culling and training his animals. Selected reindeer are gelded (traditionally the genitals were bitten off, but now forceps are used), and the castrated reindeer begin their training either to pull sleighs, as lead animals, or to carry pack loads.

Autumn brings the early frosts, which shrivel up the young grass of the alpine pastures and oblige the nomads to begin their return movement down toward the lowlands. Summer utensils are loaded onto pack reindeer

Le Magasin Pittoresque, 1834

This 19th-century print depicts the difficult task of reindeer milking. A man steadies the animal, while his wife extracts the extremely fatty milk, which is used mainly in cheese.

Lapp men, at a market in Jokkmokk, Sweden, sport their regional styles of headgear.

in special panniers that hold about forty pounds apiece and are slung on each flank, and the very young children are placed on top, clutching the high pommel of the pack saddle for support. The herd, now roughly divided into separate groups, is taken down below the timber line and turned loose in the birch woods. There, between late September and early November, it is the rutting season, a difficult time for the Lapp herdsmen, who are liable to be attacked by enraged bucks while trying to prevent their animals from straying too far. At the end of the mating season the herds must be collected and then broken down into even smaller units before being driven to the shelter of the pine forests for winter. The animals are gathered in a main corral and separated into side pens as required by their owners. As they are now in peak condition, the autumn slaughtering is done, a bloody business in which the victims are stabbed in the heart so blood will collect in the chest cavity, whence it can be removed and turned into blood pudding.

As one would expect, very little of the reindeer's carcass is wasted. The meat is eaten fresh or is dried and smoked for winter food. Sinews are used for thread, and the pelt is either traded or turned into clothing. The skins are rubbed with fat made from boiled reindeer bones, or if the pelt is to be fashioned into chamois leather, the hair is removed with a special instrument resembling a paint scraper. Then the skin is softened by being rubbed with fat and drawn backward and forward over an iron hoop before it is stitched into garments. "This dress," wrote Dillon after donning a Lapp costume for his sleigh journeys, "combines great warmth with the advantage of being light, and leaving sufficient freedom to the limbs. The principal piece is the mudda or fur gown, closed all round, and resembling a shirt of sufficient length to reach the calves of the legs. The skins of young deer are chiefly used for this part of the dress, and when attention is paid to appearances, the backs only of the darkest calves are selected. The collar, and sometimes the cuff, is ornamented with stripes of red cloth; the sleeves are rather short, as long gauntlets cover the arm halfway up to the elbow. The 'Poussa' or breeches are worn by both sexes, and are confined round the ankle by woollen bands that connect the shoes with the rest of the dress, and prevent the introduction of snow. These bands are generally variegated, and measure from twelve to fourteen feet in length. Custom has devoted particular parts of the hide to the different articles of the Laplander's costume; thus the gloves are always made of the skin that covers the feet as the cleft of the hoofs answers in shape to the part of the hand between the thumb and forefinger. The skin of the hocks, being toughest, is made into leggings, and gives the same protection to the legs of the master that it had given during life to those of the deer. The face undergoes a great change, being transferred to the man's feet. To make a shoe, the head of the deer is flayed, and the skin sewed up on each side, and it thus forms a buskin, with the tip of the nose for a peak at the toes."

These Lapp moccasins with their peculiar turned-up toes are admirably suited for wearing with skis, and to keep their feet warm the Lapps formerly stuffed their shoes with a certain type of sedge grass. This grass had a special property that under most conditions kept the feet dry as well as warm (Fridtjof Nansen specified it for equipment on his polar expeditions), and if it became wet, the grass could be dried out in front of a fire more quickly than wool. Today, however, the Lapps prefer to wear woolen socks,

This woman's vest is elegantly trimmed with geometric shapes and sun motifs, patterns popular in the Swedish part of southern Lapland.
The Lapps, ROBERTO BOSSI, THAMES & HUDSON, 1960

307

and even in winter they use a cloth jacket with an upstanding collar, a swashbuckling flare to the skirt, and bright bands of color at throat and wrist. Oddly enough, this jacket is scarcely Lappish at all; rather it is a medieval fashion, complete with fine embroidery of gold and silver wire filigree — almost certainly copied from the Vikings — that found its way up to the Arctic Circle. The Lapps' dandyism is also evident in their choice of headgear. Most Lapps wear a cloth cap that is either conical or flat, but the style varies so greatly region by region that it has become a good way of identifying the different Lapp territories. In Tornio, for example, a red pom-pom — so big that it covers the whole edifice — is worn on top of the cap, while in the far north of Norway the crown is pulled out into four flapping points, making a square cap like a jester's hat. Women too may wear special hats, perhaps with an embroidered brow band and deep ear flaps or a peak stiffened with wood. But styles and tastes alter, the biretta that Linnaeus is shown wearing in his Lapp portrait is no longer in style, and in fact it may have been a now-outmoded woman's headdress.

The changing costume of Lapland reflects an underlying shift that has been taking place in Lapp culture for a very long time. Unlike most aboriginal peoples, the Lapps have had the advantage that their confrontation with alien ideas has been spread over a period of at least five hundred years. The resulting changes have been drastic but not fatal to them. One reason seems to be that the Lapps enjoyed an unusually good reputation with their neighbors. They were sometimes thought to be nuisances, unruly or childish in their behavior, but they were seldom hated, even by the farmers who usurped their reindeer-grazing lands. Equally, it appears that Lapp culture contained elements that could be modified to new conditions, not merely in fishing or reindeer herding, but on a social level. Thus the original Lapp grouping of five or six families working together as a commune at first suffered decline in the early days of cash nomadism, when reindeer were regarded as individual property to be bought and sold, but it has now been successfully revived as an elementary form of farming cooperative. Nor has the cultural challenge from outside always been destructive. Reindeer milking is almost certainly a cultural import from the pastoral peoples to the south, and present-day Lapps, of which there are about thirty-two thousand, have been quick to adopt modern equipment wherever it has helped them. Now they use rifles and binoculars against wolves, build chain link fences on the fells to contain their reindeer, and navigate little boats with outboard motors on the fjords. Most important of all, though, they have managed to rescue their sense of cultural identity, partly through government help and partly by their own tenacity. After World War II there was a great blossoming of Lapp cultural enthusiasm. National Lapp federations, dedicated to the preservation and strengthening of their own heritage, sprang up in Sweden, Norway, and Finland and formed links across national boundaries. Today there are Lapp radio programs, Lapp schools, and newspapers and pamphlets devoted to Lapp affairs. Doubtlessly regional variations will continue to fade away. For example, the dialect of Finnmark, in the north of Norway, has become the most widely used form of Lappish at the cost of its rivals. But there is also a happy irony in the fact that a primitive culture, which has been under pressure for so long from its overweaning neighbors, now seems to have found a *modus vivendi.*

The Life of Primitive Man

The Language of Art

For a people who lack writing, art has been called a language in plastic form. Often conceptual rather than representational, a primitive group's art and artifacts convey its beliefs, as well as its knowledge, oral literature, and moral code. The works are functional and usually serve—and draw inspiration from—the community's religious tradition. Like the Aborigine painting on the roof of a rock shelter in Arnhem Land, above, they may reflect a ritual activity associated with a sacred myth. Or when integrated in ceremonies, they may evoke or placate supernatural forces, becoming, indeed, their actual repositories. Visible reminders of convention as handed down from one generation to another, they are a strong force for cohesion, helping to bind the people together as a social unit.

Body painting, an elemental art, has profound social or religious meaning. Acting like a second skin on the Xicrin boy in Brazil, left, it symbolizes the subordination of his physical life to the cultural values and social behavior of his people.

In Melanesia, as elsewhere, masks represent ancestors, spirit beings, and divinities. The figure below, from New Guinea's Sepik River district, is a dance costume, with a carved wooden mask attached to a fiber-covered frame that is slipped over the wearer for use in secret clan rituals.

This striking mask of the Guere tribe in the border country of the Ivory Coast and Liberia in Africa invested the wearer with the supernatural powers of an ancestor and helped him to communicate with the supreme being. The mask is fashioned from wood, fiber, cartridge cases, and metal.

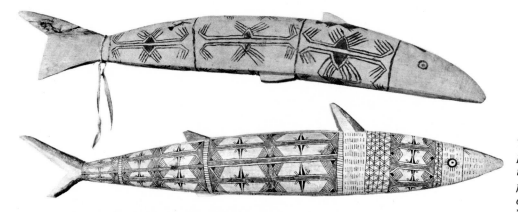

These elegantly carved sharks, with patterns repeated in the divided sections of their surfaces, had a magical function for the Santa Cruz islanders, an ocean-oriented people of Melanesia.

The stylized designs and symbols of bark paintings are expressions of the religious attachments between Aborigines and real and imaginary elements of their environment. The one at left relates the story of a mythical bird.

The wood sculpture below is a product of Easter Island's cult of the Bird-Man, usually a chief who possessed a certain egg that was won in a race and gave its owner strong magical powers.

Charms with special powers aided shamans' rites. This ivory canoe, shaped like a seal and an octopus and filled with spirits, was used by a Tlingit shaman on North America's northwest coast.
MUSEUM OF THE AMERICAN INDIAN, HEYE FOUNDATION

Wooden medicine figures called "nuchus," below, were carved in the image of Europeans and used by Cuna shamans to drive off demons of illness.

313

The impact of Japanese cultural influences on the Ainu people of Hokkaido is seen in this cotton kimono with decorative patterns, worn by Ainu chiefs at festival ceremonies.

Even utilitarian objects, carrying out familiar designs and motifs, reinforced tradition. The wooden arms to which Tlingit Indians tied their halibut hooks, below, were carved with figures of shamans and spirits.

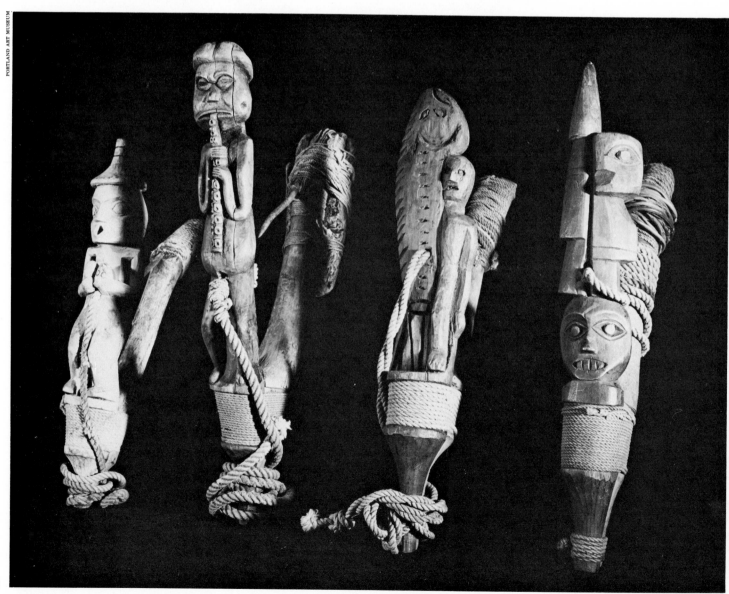

The powers of a churinga, a board containing the spirit of an ancestor, right, let Aborigines contact the eternal dream-time and share the sacred life of their tribal heroes.

Ashanti tribal artisans of West Africa cast in brass miniature figures of animals—creatures of their familiar natural environment—to adorn the cross-shaped box at far right, in which traders kept their gold dust.

Tapa cloth, like this sample, is made throughout Polynesia for use as clothing, night coverings, and decoration. Its manufacture is entirely women's work; men formerly did not even watch as vines or the inner bark of trees were gathered, kneaded and beaten, glued together in patterned strips, and colored and stamped with geometric designs.

Influenced by Europeans, traditional arts underwent many changes. Combining Western styles with tribal motifs, and losing their original functions, some were pursued only to market to outsiders. Others, employing fresh ideas, blossomed into something new with an artistic validity of their own. Encouraged by James Houston, a Canadian white man, Cape Dorset Eskimos developed the making of prints, like the one below, drawing on traditional themes and using sealskin stencils and brushes of polar-bear hair. At bottom, in contrast, is an example of the art of a tribal woodcarver in Angola after white men exerted dominion over his people: two African bearers carry a European in a hammock.

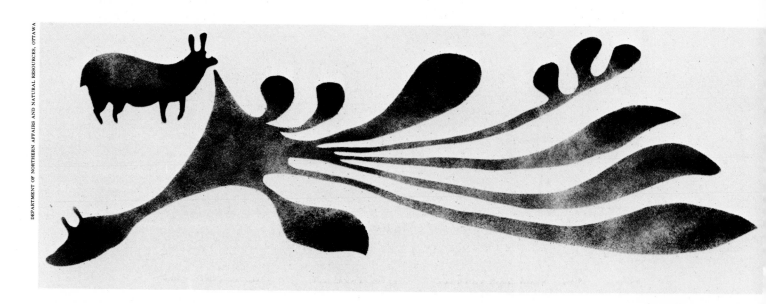

Among the Indians of the Northwest Pacific Coast, traditional arts reached a flourishing climax after the arrival of European fur traders, for their ironware, taking the place of bone, antler, and stone, put more effective tools into the hands of people already skilled as woodcarvers and led to an outpouring of house posts, totem poles, and other wooden objects. A more subtle influence, according to some students, is shown by tops of hats of Nootka whalers on Vancouver Island, right, reminiscent of onion-shaped domes on Russian churches in the area. The modern-day mola, the traditional textile of the Cunas of Panama, below, speaks for itself: a salute to the men of an Apollo moon flight.

10

The Spartans of the Mato Grosso

Of all the many Indian tribes of Brazil the Xavante have held possibly the most fearsome reputation. They were alleged to attack any expedition that ventured into their territory and to slaughter white settlers who infringed on Xavante hunting lands. They spurned the overtures of the Brazilian Indian Protection Service, disdainfully ripping open sacks of salt and scattering piles of presents left for them by the side of trails. Enterprising journalists from the big Brazilian cities, in search of a good story, would hire small planes in order to fly low over the Xavante villages and bring back photographs of naked savages rushing out of their huts to hurl war clubs at the intruding aircraft. One low-flying journalist even returned triumphantly with a dent in his aircraft where an angry Xavante had scored a direct hit. Suitably, the frontier of the Xavante's land, in almost the geographical center of Brazil, was marked by the sinister-sounding Rio das Mortes, the River of Deaths, and Brazilian pioneers in the outback were reluctant to cross this barrier, pleading that they were sure to be ambushed and killed. They and "pacified" Indians of this interior region spread all manner of wild rumors about the Xavante: they were said to be immense—eight feet tall—with the minds and muscles of brutes. They could carry tree trunks on their shoulders, run at top speed for days on end without tiring, and would attack without warning or mercy. One yarn, reminiscent of an old medieval traveler's tale, said that the Xavante had feet that could point backward. Thus, after the Xavante had raided an outpost, they could confuse all pursuit by running away with their feet turned around so that their tracks led in the wrong direction.

There was a modicum of truth behind all this flummery. The Xavante were, indeed, a brave tribe. They fought valiantly to protect their territorial integrity, and they did so without respite. It was not the case of an isolated encounter or two when bands of white prospectors stumbled upon the tribe and were slain for their ill luck and ignorance. Rather, the Xavante waged open warfare against all comers. Beginning in the early part of the nineteenth century, they fought not only white settlers but also the powerful Indian tribes who were their neighbors. Formerly the Xavante had been linked with the Xerente, another tribe of very similar culture and

Earplugs: symbol of manhood
BLACK STAR, ANTHONY HALIK

319

Facing the white man's threat: Xavante hunters in central Brazil
BLACK STAR, FLAVIO DAMM

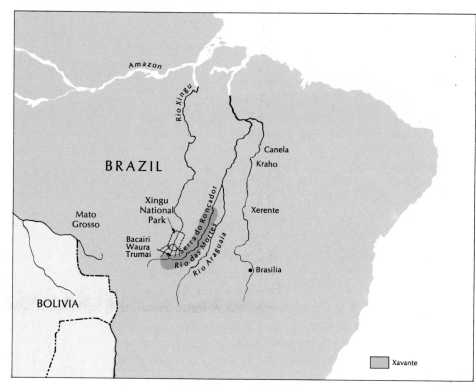

language. But when the Xerente gave in to the advancing white men and were pacified, the Xavante withdrew across the Araguaia River to continue their struggle. From this new stronghold Xavante war parties kept the settlers who penetrated the area in constant fear for almost a century. In 1887 a Xavante war band successfully rebuffed a Brazilian military column that tried to invade their land. In addition, they launched a series of raids against groups of pacified Indians who were clustered around neighboring mission posts. Xavante hostility toward strangers grew more virulent as time passed. In the 1930's, with pressure on their stronghold from the surrounding white settlements growing more intense, the feud moved toward a climax. In 1934 two Salesian priests, members of a religious order that had successfully contacted several of the nearby tribes, landed from a canoe on the Rio das Mortes and walked up to a group of Xavante on the riverbank. In full view of their horrified companions, the unarmed priests were clubbed to death. Later the Xavante came back to the place to tear down a cross that had been erected to mark the spot where the priests had fallen. Relations with the Xavante became more tense a couple of years afterward when a posse of irate Brazilian settlers invaded and shot up a Xavante village, murdering perhaps thirty Indians, including women and children; and the lowest ebb was reached in 1941 when a Brazilian pacification team from the Indian Service was massacred by the Xavante on the day after preliminary contact had been made with the tribe. The Xerente guides of the expedition were the only survivors of the slaughter, which, ironically, took place after the Indian Service commander had ordered his men to lay down their weapons because he was afraid that they would create an unnecessary incident.

So there was, then, a genuine basis for the Xavante's notoriety, though for the most part it was greatly inflated. Any unexplained death among the frontier settlers tended to be laid at the door of the Xavante, and there was an understandable inclination to magnify the dangers from them, while at the same time ignoring less melodramatic realities. The forbidding Rio das Mortes, running through the heart of their land, was a case in point. Early maps show that the river was called the Rio Manso, or gentle river, because of its slow current compared with the other mighty rivers of the area. Its name was changed to Rio das Mortes before the Xavante had arrived in the area; the change was almost certainly derived from a bloody battle that had occurred there between rival groups of white prospectors looking for precious minerals. Nor was anyone in any hurry to point out that the Xavante's land embraced the peaceful-sounding Serra do Roncador (literally, the mountains of one who snores), a name scarcely calculated to strike terror into the heart of a listener. Similarly, there was only a muted fanfare of publicity late in the 1940's when the first bands of Xavante gave up their habit of disemboweling the propitiatory sacks of salt and instead showed a willingness to exchange gifts with the Indian Protection Service, which finally persuaded several Xavante groups to settle down near their protection posts. Not until 1958 did the non-Brazilian world have an opportunity to understand the Xavante's way of life, for it was only then that a young anthropologist, David Maybury-Lewis, accompanied by his Danish-born wife and their one-year-old son, managed to arrange to live in a Xavante

This 1519 Portuguese map depicted the flora, fauna, and Indians of Brazil. The natives, some of whom are shown gathering the hardwood that became a prized colonial export, were subsequently assimilated, wiped out, or driven into the interior.

JOHANN MORITZ RUGENDAS ALBUM, 1835

In 1835 a German artist, Johann Rugendas, toured Brazil's rain forest and painted this view of an Indian camp and vine suspension bridge.

settlement so that he could examine their social structure.

The Xavante village where Maybury-Lewis did his research was São Domingos, on the Rio das Mortes. It was a desperately isolated place, a ramshackle Indian Protection Service post clinging weakly to the fringe of the Xavante's land and reached only by an occasional river craft or by one of the small airplanes flown by Brazilian military pilots who were experienced in landing on the tiny homemade airstrips carved out near the posts. To the east, between the Rio das Mortes and its parent river, the Araguaia, lay low, swampy ground. To the west rose the escarpment of the Serra do Roncador, mostly a poor scrub-dotted savannah scarcely fit for grazing animals, let alone human settlement. Here and there lines of semijungle growth marked the courses of small rivers and streams, but for the most part it was a bleak region of baked earth, meager grassland, and a monotonous repetition of clumps of thornbushes and trees. The Xavante who occupied this unpromising territory were, at the time of Maybury-Lewis's visit, still more or less a law unto themselves. The Indian agent at the post took good care to intrude as little as possible in the everyday affairs of the Indians, who meted out their own rough justice to their fellow tribesmen.

The Xavante in the immediate area had settled on a site barely fifteen to twenty minutes from the protection post. Their village of eighteen leaf-and-branch huts was arranged in the traditional horseshoe Xavante shape, and the Indians were a band of the Akwe-Xavante under a chief named Apewe, who was recognized as one of the more powerful of the Xavante leaders. Elsewhere along the river were similar, though usually smaller, Xavante communities; and farther out toward the headwaters of the Xingu River were two more Xavante settlements. These few groups, numbering perhaps fifteen hundred to two thousand people, were all that remained of a tribe which during its earlier struggles with the white man may have numbered twice as many.

Biorn, the one-year-old white child, provided the anthropologist's entrée to the Xavante village. The Xavante were fascinated by the little boy. They made a great fuss of him, fondling him and "borrowing" him whenever possible, and partly because they wanted to see more of him, they agreed to build a hut in their village where the white child and his parents could stay. There at every turn it was apparent to Maybury-Lewis that Xavante children were the most privileged members of their society. They were very seldom scolded or smacked. They were allowed to run free and to poke and pry into the affairs of everyone in the village, acting as its eyes and spies whenever a stranger approached. Their childish tantrums were ignored, laughed at, or even encouraged by their parents, and the fathers would egg on their children to strike back at their mothers or even take the toddlers to sit in their arms during formal council meetings. When Biorn's mother went so far as to slap her child for misbehavior, the shocked Xavante hurried off to report the outrage to his father. Only in matters of physical pain were the young Xavante children expected to submit. The boys would engage in mock duels, punching one another until the weakest burst into tears, and sometimes their elders would lacerate them with a sharp animal claw, ostensibly to improve their health by bloodletting but also to imbue them with strength and fortitude.

Most of the indulgence vanished when the boys were between seven and twelve years old, for at that time they were ceremonially inducted into the first of a series of social classes, known to anthropologists as age-grades, or age-sets, which would thereafter dominate their lives. This initiation was a formal affair. On an appointed day each boy prepared for it by painting himself scarlet from head to foot with the bright red stain of the urucú plant and putting on a broad collar of white cotton above which he arranged a necklace of beads and macaw feathers. One by one, the boys were fetched from their homes by a master of ceremonies and taken to the assembled men of the village, who stood by a special "bachelors' hut." In the presence of the adult men the boy's collar was removed, after which he entered the bachelors' hut and seated himself facing the rear wall. Next he was handed his sign of manhood, a Xavante penis sheath, a tiny cone of palmito bark that he, like all Xavante men, would thenceforth wear as the only item of dress. From that moment on, all the boys in the bachelors' hut were, in effect, members of a special male training school, being prepared for their entry into the community as full adults. It was a curious education—part relaxation, part instruction, and part harassment. There were long periods of enjoyment, spent splashing in the river or playing group games together, but these were interspersed with bursts of hard work. The mature men of

A Brazilian Zaparo Indian was idealized in this lithograph, accompanying the report of a U.S. Navy expedition to the Amazon River in 1854.

Reflecting her people's warmth for children, a Xavante woman fondles Biorn, the son of anthropologist David Maybury-Lewis, who lived with the tribe in 1958 and wrote an authoritative account of their society.

the village could come to the bachelors' hut at any time, day or night, to order the boys out on a singing tour of the village, leading in the chanting of ceremonial songs and making sure that the youths learned the words correctly. Or a Xavante man might take the boys on a hunting trip or show them how to catch fish or make weapons. From time to time, if the village council so decided, the boys were led from the bachelors' hut in two groups and lined up facing each other. They were armed with light wooden batons, about two feet long and stained red with urucú, and after a harangue from one of the older men, the youths would be paired off so that they were roughly matched in weight and size. Then each pair of boys would take turns doing battle, clubbing one another over the head and shoulders. Neither contestant was allowed to show any sign of pain or weakness. When the battle had gone on long enough or one of the fighters broke down, the duel was stopped by the village elders and the next pair began. On the whole the boys' lives were relatively carefree, for they were not confined to the bachelors' hut and could wander around the village, visiting their homes and expecting to be fed by their families. But after about four years, as they approached their graduation, the pressure began to intensify, and they had to spend most of their time rehearsing dances and preparing special regalia for the great ceremony that would mark their entry into the next level of the Xavante hierarchy. More and more frequently the boys could expect to be called out for a clubbing duel to show their warrior spirits or for wrestling with mature men in order to demonstrate their newfound strength. They rehearsed the traditional songs that they had learned, and under the approving eye of their seniors, they practiced the admired style of Xavante dancing, an athletic stamping of the feet on the hard ground accompanied by rhythmic chanting.

The first phase of their actual graduation-cum-initiation was a water ordeal, in which the boys were supposed to relive the myth of the Xavante culture hero who made the water his habitat and there grew sleek and stout and beautiful. Every day the young Xavante boys had to go down to the river and enter the water. Standing in the river, they had to leap upward, throwing water over their heads with their hands and bringing their arms back down on the river with a resounding smack. Again and again they had to repeat the action until their supervising elders got bored and wandered away. But should the boys attempt to creep out of the river to dry themselves, their seniors came rushing back to cuff them and order them back into the water. Two or three times each day the boys had to endure this ordeal. Between plunges they would retreat to the bank to build a fire and crouch shivering around it. After some three weeks of these repeated baths, they were judged ready to wear the coveted Xavante earplugs. The lobes of their ears were pierced with a bone needle and tiny cylinders of wood inserted. Little by little the size of the cylinders was increased until the boys wore the full-sized ear ornaments that marked an initiated male Xavante.

The second phase of the boys' graduation followed a few months later. Once again it was an ordeal of a sort, this time concentrating on foot races along a specially prepared track that had its starting line outside the village and led into the main square, where two posts were erected as finishing markers. First, however, the boys had to prepare their "no'oni," the huge grass capes made of stripped palm fronds that were essential items in the ceremony. Then they and the men of the village painted themselves on belly and back with urucú red. The calves of the adult men's legs were also painted, but in black, and against this dark background they drew two or three vertical white lines to represent their particular ceremonial moiety. Next a master of ceremonies appeared, painted red all over and having his

DAVID MAYBURY-LEWIS

Apewe, the prestigious and powerful chief of the Xavante community of São Domingos, anoints young initiates—one of many ceremonial duties of his status—in this photograph taken by David Maybury-Lewis.

hair bound up in a ceremonial-style sheath. He wore a grass cape suspended from his forehead by a loop and moved with a queer swaying of his body back and forth between steps. He led groups of runners up to the starting line, and at his signal they raced down the track toward the village, not competing directly with each other so much as showing off their agility and fleetness to an appreciative audience of spectators. At the finish line the runners touched one of the marker posts and rejoined the crowd to wait for the master of ceremonies as he came hopping back, bending his body low and with each jump slapping the grass cape with his hand like a strange, one-winged stalking bird. Group by group, the members of each age-set who had graduated together at five-year intervals in the past performed this ceremonial run; but the boys' group of initiates had to do it most often, perhaps seven times on the opening day. Thereafter, and beginning before dawn, the boys were obliged to run the course several times daily, morning and afternoon, watched by the senior men of the village. In the afternoon session the master of ceremonies in his grass cape reappeared, and sometimes in the evening two adult Xavante played a pair of special double-barreled flutes that were kept in the bachelors' hut. Even when most of the men were away from the village on hunting trips, the boys kept up their daily runs until the final day, more than a month later, when this phase of the initiation was closed. Then, decked out in an even greater finery of headdresses and ornaments and with their bodies painted black instead of red, the adult males ran a last set of races. A few virtuoso per-

New Xavante initiates clip the hair of the next age-set of boys, who are about to enter the bachelors' hut to prepare for their adulthood. The hair-dressing rite is a symbolic demonstration of the graduates' power.

During the period of their initiation, Xavante boys are seen preparing their ceremonial no'oni, long capes made of stripped palm fronds.

formers did an exultant stamping cape dance between the finishing posts, eventually flinging their grass capes to the ground between the posts and tying crossbars into place, thus closing the entrance and signaling the conclusion of the running ceremonies.

Then came the formal induction of the boys as young adults, a five-day ritual of singing, dancing, and formal processions around the village with intermissions for rest and food. Even the women were involved from time to time, appearing in body paint and symbolically challenging the men for possession of their dance masks. Some boys were singled out for special treatment as future patrons of specific ceremonies. They were dressed up with stripes of latex applied to their bodies and dotted with tufts of cotton wool, or with crowns of brightly colored feathers. One dance, performed on the second night, had to last from midnight to sunrise; for this marathon dance the boys were painted with a pattern of crisscross stripes that made them look like cavorting skeletons, while their faces were colored half red and half black, with their eyes circled in opposing colors. On the fourth day the initiates destroyed their bachelors' hut and made a last formal run, each youth escorted by a cluster of adult men "running him in" as he loped down the track toward the village to the accompaniment of the cheering women. That night the boys were given permission to establish their own council fire for the first time, and the next day they formally clipped the hair of the age-grade below them, the new batch of young boys who were entering a bachelors' hut of their own for the five-year training period. So a new age-grade passed into adult male Xavante society, and their replacements moved in behind them.

For the next few years the members of the newly graduated age-set were cocks of the walk. They epitomized the Xavante ideals of good physical condition, watchfulness, and fleetness, and not without a certain amount of self-pride. Maybury-Lewis on his first evening in the Xavante village could not help remarking on this age-set as its members assembled for their evening conference. "It was no ordinary group [of young men]," he wrote. "They were painted scarlet on their backs and bellies. Their fringes were plastered down on their foreheads with some sort of oil, and one or two of them had put scarlet paint on the coronal tonsure which every male Xavante wears. They wore hawk's feathers at their necks and clean wrist and ankle cords. Each of them had planted a speckled club in the ground behind him, so that they looked like warriors resting on their lances, and it transpired that that was exactly what they were. It was the young men's age-set gathered in all its finery for their evening council. They were men between the ages of seventeen and twenty-two who had completed the initiation ceremonies necessary for full manhood but who were not yet mature enough to be admitted to the councils of their elders. They made an impressive sight and they were conscious of the fact."

To an anthropologist this regular succession of age-sets is an intriguing feature of Xavante society. It explains why the Xavante villages, when they were first spotted from the air, clearly showed several quite distinct council fires in their centers. At first it was thought that the Xavante were divided into two separate moieties, each with its own meeting place. However, now it is known that the mature men of the community used one hearth, while the young men had another. Here at their respective circles the two groups met every evening: the young men to strut and preen, sing and dance, the mature men to gossip and thrash out village policies in the peculiar Xavante style of oratory, in which the lead speaker declaimed his view, sonorously repeating phrase after phrase, while his opponent interjected and overlapped his counterarguments until the two speeches virtually ran into one. In fact the Xavante were very quarrelsome, readily breaking into factions that cut across the group loyalties of age-sets and created bitter internal feuds. The mature men of the main village council fire were less interested in physical prowess and display than in politics and the search for prestige. They formed cliques and coalitions against one another and established factions based on personal loyalties and family ties, and deep animosities soon set in. The headman of a Xavante village was really no more than the leader of the strongest faction within the community, and he had to tread carefully. Should he accidentally weaken his own faction by ill-advised decisions, rule with too heavy a hand, or—worst of all—alienate the members of the young men's age-set, the chief faced a danger of revolt. He might be assassinated, as happened to a community chief in Maybury-Lewis's day, or a party of his more disgruntled followers might strike camp and move away to join another Xavante village. The bad blood tended to travel with them, and they would continue their grudge with the help of their new hosts, waiting for the time when they could avenge themselves on their former leader with a surprise attack. As a result, the Xavante villages were often potential enemies of one another, warily guarding against ambush from their neighbors.

At no time was this possible threat more evident than during a hunt. When a Xavante hunting party was in the field, its members took care to light fires and make smoke as a signal that their intentions were peaceful. To travel without such a warning sign was to arouse the suspicion that they were a war party and so invite counterattack. Yet the Xavante, essentially a seminomadic people, always spent a good deal of time away from their

This Tapirapé Indian wax effigy, crowned with feathers and covered with fluff, represents one of the topu, anthropomorphic spirits associated with lightning and thunder.

ROYAL SOCIETY/ROYAL GEOGRAPHICAL SOCIETY, 1971

villages. The latter were really no more than semipermanent bases from which to make regular forays into the surrounding countryside to hunt and gather food. These treks could last from six weeks to three or four months, and the journeys were carefully planned by the village council to utilize the natural resources of the region to the maximum. The entire community would be on the move, visiting localities rich in animal life, or areas where fruit-bearing trees could be harvested in certain seasons or where they could find prized materials such as vegetable beads for necklaces or special types of wood for bowstaves.

Xavante men, armed with bows and long cane arrows (today the Xavante use .22 rifles if they can get them), frequently went off on side trips, hoping to come across such prey as tapir, peccary, armadillo, deer, and almost any of the savannah birds save carrion eaters. Since they seldom used hunting dogs, the Xavante relied on their own tracking skill and speed to locate and run down their quarry. The hunting trips were fast-moving, exhausting affairs, covering mile upon mile of territory at a distance-eating lope. The men would drink at streams and rivers, or in an emergency uproot a clump of grass and quickly dig a narrow hole that filled with muddy subsurface water. Only before major ceremonies that required much feasting were special driven hunts organized by an entire community in order to build up stocks of meat necessary for the festivities.

Yet it was a hard fact of Xavante existence that on a day-to-day basis

Indians in the headwaters region of the Xingu River lock hands with one another in a wrestling bout, one of the activities of a "kuarup," an intertribal festival that ends a period of mourning for the dead. Other males will soon join in the bout.

331

there was never any guarantee that the men would have the time or good fortune to supply their families with enough food. So, as with many other hunting communities, the burden of providing the staple diet fell upon the Xavante women. They had a difficult life, beginning when scarcely more than toddlers to copy their mothers in collecting wild roots, nuts, and fruit and doing most of the cooking on the ashes of a fire. Seldom invited into the mainstream of Xavante ceremony and ritual, the women were scarcely more than drudges. On the march their duty was to carry baskets of possessions from one camp to the other, and they also had to build the low beehive-shaped huts of branches and fronds that were arranged in the traditional horseshoe shape at the temporary hunting camps. "Trekking was a dirty business too," Maybury-Lewis reported. "Xavante often cleared the ground by directing a ragged bush fire over the site they planned to move to and then they camped in the ash so that living in their shelters was like living in a chimney. Everything in them, including their inhabitants, got covered in grime. Often the only water to be had was from water holes so that washing had to be restricted to taking a mouthful of it and squirting it in a thin stream over one's hands. For the rest the Xavante titivated themselves by chewing nuts, spitting the oily juice into the palms of their hands and anointing themselves liberally on the body and hair. I got used to the smell in the shelters and to the offal that littered their entrances where the cooking fires burned. I found that I did not much mind that the starchy roots which were the basis of our diet were pulled out of the fire, covered in earth and ash and casually thrown over to us in this state. But it took me a long time to get inured to the fact that they always plumped into that patch of ground just inside the shelter which was invariably covered with garbage and mucus, to be retrieved, dusted off and eaten. Still, though it turned my stomach, I was glad to have food tossed over to me just the same as the other men. It made me feel accepted."

A typically tonsured member of the Kaxinaua tribe, a fishing people living on forest streams in western Brazil, prepares an alligator in palm leaves for cooking on a grate.

HARALD SCHULTZ

Despite their basic mobility, the Xavante were also agriculturalists after a somewhat unenthusiastic fashion. Though they much preferred to go hunting, the men allocated three or four weeks every year to the rather desultory preparation of plots of maize, beans, and pumpkins. Fortunately, there was little real need for cultivated crops because the wild game and plants of the savannah provided an adequate diet; but an occasional surplus of food from the gardens was useful for ceremonial occasions when there was no time for hunting or gathering. Indeed, special maize pies were customarily prepared for the young boys' initiation ceremony. Nevertheless, when a Xavante community decided to abandon its base village and move elsewhere, it did so without the slightest regret about deserting its plantations.

The Xavante also gave limited value to the family as a social unit, preferring to regard it as an economic and prestigious asset. Thus an important Xavante who eventually acquired two or three wives looked upon them as useful helpmeets who would enhance his reputation among his tribesmen and increase the amount of wild produce brought into the household. By contrast, for the first few years a young Xavante regarded his wife as something of a social embarrassment. His marriage was a group affair conducted on the same day that the boy initiates destroyed their bachelors' hut. That event was followed by the entire group entering a special shelter where everyone lay down facing the wall. The young girls of the village, some of them scarcely more than small children, were brought in by their mothers and made to lie down briefly behind the boys whom their parents had chosen for them. All the time the young initiates kept their eyes averted and generally behaved as though they were acutely ill at ease. The "marriage," in fact, was then over, but a considerable time passed before the young men would even approach their brides, because the boys regarded having anything to do with women as unmanly and shameful. Only when the bride was physically old enough to consummate the marriage, and the luster of the young men's age-set had worn off, did the husband begin to visit his wife in her family hut. Even then he was at a disadvantage because his in-laws made fun of him, and he was, in effect, acknowledging to his peer group his dependence upon a member of the opposite sex. To make matters worse for the young husband, he also had to take up residence in his wife's family house, where he was considered subordinate to both his father-in-law and his brothers-in-law. Sexual satisfaction and the procreation of the much-pampered children were the main reasons for putting up with this humiliation, and here the Xavante men believed not only that frequent sexual intercourse up to the fifth month of pregnancy was necessary to "make" a baby properly, but that a man's potency was greatly increased if he wore red plugs in his ear lobes while making love to his wife.

Relatively little is known of the spiritual beliefs of the Xavante. Their most important ceremony was the "wai'a," which was performed in three different versions, to cure the sick, to bless the newly prepared arrows, and to bless the dance masks, which symbolized the whole process of initiating young men. There were two types of power communicated to the wai'a participants, generative power, symbolized as sexuality, and destructive or bellicose power, symbolized as aggression. After prolonged bouts of singing, warlike dancing, and—for the initiates' age-set—fasting, the participants indulged in the ceremonial rape of selected women of the village, indicating

A Xavante woman has packed her possessions in baskets, which she will carry, slung from her forehead by a tumpline, during a communal food-gathering trek.

OVERLEAF: *Kaxinaua Indians, having poisoned the water of the upper Curanja River with toxic leaves, rush through the stream with bows and arrows to secure the stupefied fish.*

sexual potency and aggressive power that they had acquired from various classes of spirits in their dances. The exact relationship of the various spirits to each other is not clear, because the spirit world of the Xavante is only hazily understood by outsiders. They believed in a powerful, warlike spirit-creature that was ritually attacked and defeated by the wai'a dancers, and there was also a Village of the Dead somewhere in the far eastern sky where the souls of deceased Xavante went. The abode of evil spirits lay in exactly the opposite direction, the farthest west, whence the wicked spirits could return to earth to threaten and terrify lonely hunters and scare men who were foolish enough to roam after dark, sometimes carrying them away never to be seen again.

Before the second type of wai'a the Xavante would organize a log race, the most dramatic of their rites. To prepare for it, the young men of the village went into the forest, where they cut down and shaped two massive logs of buriti palm that were to serve as huge relay batons for the runners. Each log was bulky and weighed up to two hundred pounds. They were left beside the start of the village running track, and there, on the scheduled afternoon, the most athletic of the Xavante assembled, while

A log race in progress: Kraho Indian relay runners in the Tocantins Valley, with the heavy logs on their shoulders and teammates keeping pace with them, hasten down the racetrack toward their village.

the older and less vainglorious men took up stations along the track. After the runners had divided into two teams, four men picked up the logs and balanced them on the backs of two of the runners. The pair of racers then set off for the village as fast as they could go, each man stumbling and struggling under his load, clutching the enormous baton to his shoulders like an ant fleeing its broken nest. As soon as a man began to flag under the strain, a teammate ran into place alongside him. The log was transferred from one man's shoulders to the next without a break of step, and the new runner spurted forward until he too had to be replaced. As the two racers came careering down toward the village, the older men joined in to take their brief turn in the ordeal, and with excitement rising to fever pitch amid the whoops and yells of the exulting runners, the logs were brought thundering over the finish line in the village center, where they were thrown triumphantly to the ground.

The races were literally solidarity rites in which the society organized into two complementary teams that performed a ritual whose message of balance and harmony, expressed in the athletic idiom they favored, was clear to every Xavante. In one form or another log racing was practiced among other tribes, including the Canela, who had racetracks up to ten miles long, and the Xerente, who made something of a fetish of the buriti logs themselves, carefully weighing them before the race so that they were exactly equal and often painting and decorating the timber with special designs. Most, if not all, of the log-racing tribes belonged to the same linguistic group, namely, the Ge-speaking native peoples of Brazil, and log racing was a cultural tradition among them.

When the Portuguese explorers and colonizers came to the country, many of the first inhabitants they encountered were fierce coastal tribes whom they called Tupinambas. These tribes spoke the Tupi language and seemed to have been immigrants themselves, having spread along the great river valleys and down some two thousand miles of coastal strip in search of a legendary idyllic homeland associated with an ancestor or grandfather figure. The Tupinambas had a reputation as ruthless fighters, and they raided one another's villages as well as those of neighbor tribes in order to gain martial glory and seize slaves, whom they later ate in cannibalistic orgies. Among their enemies were the Ge-speakers of the interior, who had presumably occupied the central block of Brazil some time before the Tupi-speakers arrived. But the situation was confused still further by pockets and seams of peoples speaking tongues of at least two other language stocks, Arawak and Carib, who were also to be found scattered throughout the Brazilian plateau, apparently without any particular pattern. Thus at least four different linguistic heritages had intermingled in Indian Brazil, and because the various tribes were seldom stationary, but like the Xavante, tended to shift their territory, the result was—and still is—a huge mosaic of tribes and subtribes of different languages and backgrounds.

Nowhere was this intermingling of native peoples more noticeable than in the very center of the Brazilian plateau, near the watershed where the rivers flow north to join the Amazon or drain south to the Paraguay River. Here, close to where the Xavante lived, coexisted other tribes of Carib-, Arawak-, Ge-, and Tupi-speakers, and even a group called the Trumai, who had an undetermined linguistic affiliation. All of them, when first discovered,

This gaily painted clay figurine of a hunter with his quarry was made for sale to tourists by an artist of the Caraja tribe, which lives on the Araguaia River and is noted for its many artistic skills.

337

An imaginative woodcut, published in Germany in 1505, attempted to illustrate Spanish and Portuguese explorers' accounts of cannibalism among the Carib- and Tupi-speaking tribes along the coast of Brazil.

were somehow managing to retain their separate identities in a population pattern that extended to scarcely thirty-five Indian villages with an estimated total of twenty-five hundred to three thousand inhabitants.

This unique Indian enclave occupied the gallery forests, lakes, and broad grasslands of the headwaters region of the Xingu River in the remote west central part of Brazil. On the east it was shielded by the Serra do Roncador and the dangerous cordon of the Xavante's land, and on the west by vast tracts of jungles and savannah. Its only feasible access was up the Xingu River from the Amazon, and it was along this general route that there arrived in 1884 Karl von den Steinen, the first anthropologist to penetrate the Upper Xingu. He found an extraordinary richness and diversity of Indian culture. Along the banks of the five feeder streams of the Xingu, which splay out like the fingers of a hand, he came across tribe after tribe, whose villages were usually established some two or three miles from the river and linked to it by footpaths. Their houses were substantial affairs, generally containing several families and built to an elliptic ground plan measuring about thirty by sixty-five feet. In the middle of each house rose three main supporting posts, their bases set solidly in the earth and their tops joined at a height of about twenty-five feet by a long ridgepole. From the ridgepole down to an outer supporting wall arched long, thin rafters reinforced by heavier beams, and the entire structure was covered over with a light framework and thatched with grass. Viewed from a dis-

338

tance, these houses looked like nothing so much as large, neatly made haystacks with smoke holes at their peaks.

Though not as sturdy or muscular as the Xavante, who were built like the professional warrior-athletes they strove to be, the peoples of the Upper Xingu area were well set and healthy. All of them (again like the Xavante) shaved a central tonsure on the pates of their heads, and most had a characteristic Indian "sugar bowl" hair style that was cut to the right length with a sharp piranha tooth or singed with a red-hot ember. The men had pierced ear lobes, and one or two of the tribes also made a hole in the nasal septum through which they wore nose ornaments of wood or stone. Clothing was kept to a minimum or was nonexistent. The men usually wore a belt, with which they supported the penis, while the women either went naked or in most instances wore a minute triangle of plaited straw held between the legs by a string girdle. By comparison, their body decoration was lavish. Some tribes wore armbands and anklets of straw or cotton; others put brightly colored feathers in their ear lobes or on special occasions donned elaborate headdresses made of skin, fur, and plumes. Several communities went so far as to keep harpy eagles in cages, magnificent monkey-eating predators whose tail feathers were greatly prized by the tribesmen as decorations. The Indians plucked out the feathers and then rubbed a special unguent on the bare patch to promote the rapid growth of new plumes. In addition, the tribes of Arawak descent kept up their traditional use of tattooing, and all the peoples of the Xingu area painted themselves lavishly with urucú and oil-based colors.

On the whole, the day-to-day life of the Upper Xingu was simple and not very strenuous. Hunting was done by all the men in the village in short treks through the neighboring countryside, where they would sometimes be joined by the women harvesting wild fruits and berries. Far more important to most communities was the food that they took from the rivers. There the Indians built traps and weirs, went fishing after dark with long spears and torches, and hauled dragnets through the smaller pools and tributaries. One specialized technique employed the bow and arrow. The fish would be tempted to the surface with a floating bait of wild fruit and then shot as it swam into view, a tricky process because the marksman had to allow for his refracted vision of the target in the water. Unlike the Xavante, who were essentially savannah dwellers, most of the Xingu villagers were accomplished watermen. They regarded the rivers as their main source of life, knowing how to make canoes from tree bark in less than a day and how to live off roasted turtle eggs that they gathered on the sandbanks in the dry season. Indeed, the lives of some tribes were so closely related to the rivers that there is reason to believe that they originally came to the Upper Xingu area by water, migrating along the rivers as natural routeways leading into this isolated heartland.

Compared to the somewhat Spartan Xavante, the Xingu peoples were much more like the gentler inhabitants of Greek city-states. Of course, there was some local fighting between tribes, sometimes escalating into bloody engagements fought with clubs and bows and arrows. But neither the blowgun nor the poisoned arrow was used, and there was a much more sedentary pace to village life. Most villagers preferred to devote their energies to cultivating their small patches of tobacco, sweet potatoes, manioc,

Among many Brazilian tribes, an ideal body is a hairless one (save for hair on the head). Here, a Uruku woman plucks her son's eyebrows.

339

During a grueling and perilous expedition down Brazil's previously uncharted Rio da Duvida (River of Doubt) in 1914, Theodore Roosevelt, sighting no Indians (but at times aware of their presence in the jungle around him), wrote that the fertile area should not be permitted "to lie as a tenantless wilderness."

and maize, laboriously preparing the soil with a digging stick. Many villages had orchards of wild fruit, and the more ambitious gardeners transplanted whole avenues of fruit trees to the outskirts of their settlements. Then, too, there was a degree of specialization to their activities. One tribe became more proficient at manufacturing axes and beads of stone; another at working cotton into hammocks; a third at turning out bows. Inevitably, therefore, trade links were established between the various settlements and became so regularized that it was not unusual to find visitors in each village, men from other tribes who could speak more than one language and who had come with articles to barter. Most villages had guesthouses to accommodate these commercial travelers, and in some instances there were official intertribal gatherings, when entire delegations from different tribes would be invited to come together to trade, share in festivals, and attend banquets. At such times there might be intertribal sports, notably a wrestling match on a catch-as-catch-can basis, when the men took turns wrestling with each other, singly or in groups, until the entire male population was grappling in formal combat.

Despite this advanced state of relationships between tribes, the social structures of the Xingu tribes were probably originally quite dissimilar. In coming into close contact with each other, these peoples from differing language groups had eventually developed common cultural patterns and institutions, so that explorers in the Upper Xingu noted a certain resemblance between life in one village and the next. The evening palaver of the men was a typical feature. Every evening in almost any Xingu compound, the menfolk gathered together by the campfire to smoke and gossip or talk over the plans for the next few days. Everywhere, too, one tended to come across the same political organization, with a village chief, whose power was usually limited to organizing group activities. And there was the same recognition of a kinship system whether in one place it paid more heed to brothers as the most important relatives or in another area to cousins or maternal uncles. Of course, there were differences in etiquette and style — among the Carib-speaking Bacairi tribe, for example, it was considered offensive to eat in public, and so meals were taken privately or else people turned their backs while eating. The Bacairi also disapproved of loud singing and showed their displeasure by spitting. Among the Trumai, on the other hand, many of the social conventions were related to the various stages of the life cycle: sexual intercourse was forbidden until the previous child was old enough to walk; at his initiation a boy had his body scratched with a fish-tooth comb, and, if possible, was required to wrestle with a boa constrictor; and when a Trumai man wished to divorce his wife for adultery, it was customary for him to stand in the village square and shout out his accusations against her lover.

Perhaps because of its remoteness, or because its native culture was so striking, the Upper Xingu exerted a powerful fascination on explorers in interior Brazil. Colonel Percy Fawcett, a British mystic and adventurer who dreamed of finding in the Xingu the ruined metropolis of a once-great native empire, tried to enter the Xingu from the south. Fawcett, his son, and another white companion vanished in 1925, almost certainly killed by the Indians. The expeditions that went out to search for him during the next seven or eight years enhanced the Xingu legend by bringing out scraps of information to add to the existing knowledge of the geography and ethnography of the area. Though in an indirect fashion, two even more famous travelers in Brazil also helped to drum up the Xingu's attractions. In February, 1914, ex-President Theodore Roosevelt, his son Kermit, and a number of American scientists passed some distance to the west of the Xingu headwaters in the train of Colonel Candido Rondon, a Brazilian explorer who did more than any other man to open up the plateau country of the Mato Grosso, the "Thick Brushland." True to form, Roosevelt was keenly on the lookout for wild Indians and was cruelly disappointed when the only incident was that some members of an unknown tribe shot Rondon's dog and left its corpse stuck with arrows lying by the side of the trail. A generation later Claude Lévi-Strauss, one of the most brilliantly intellectual of anthropologists, covered much of the same territory, visiting the Bororo tribe to the south of the Xingu and the Nambikwara, nomadic hunter-gatherers of the plateau, who lived to the west. The journeys of these two men not only helped to define in anthropological terms the extent of the Xingu culture area, but in the interval pointed up the rapid changes that were taking place in the interior and the consequent breakdown of native societies as they disintegrated on contact with the white man.

A "second skin" of black paint, symbolizing the imposition of his people's cultural values upon his biological make-up, is painstakingly applied to a young boy by women of the Xicrin tribe in central Brazil.

Xingu men, joined by women at a kuarup festival, blow sacred flutes to exorcise spirits of the dead.

Despite this, the Upper Xingu still retained something of the nature of a haven, an Indian refuge that was relatively untouched either by the terrible epidemics of disease that were afflicting the other aboriginal populations in Brazil or by the steady erosion of tribal lands by aggressive prospectors, rubber tappers, and squatters.

The credit for preserving the Upper Xingu as an Indian sanctuary right up to the present day lies with three of the most remarkable men in the history of the Brazilian Indian Service—the Villas Boas brothers. Former colleagues of Colonel Rondon, who was himself part-Indian and who set up the Indian Protection Service, Orlando, Claudio, and Leonardo Villas Boas were responsible for the peaceful penetration of the Upper Xingu late in the 1940's and for the defense of the Indians still living there. The brothers' difficulties were monumental, not the least being the eventual wreck of the first Indian Service, which was suborned by landowning and other economic interests seeking to get rid of the Indians in order to take over their territories. Yet by patience and tact the Villas Boas brothers managed to preserve at least the main strands of the tribal culture of the Upper Xingu. It was a long and often heartbreaking task. The Indians, as had been found elsewhere in Brazil, were exceptionally vulnerable to diseases brought from outside. A minor epidemic of measles or influenza could suddenly flare up as a deadly plague, wiping out the entire population of a hamlet. In addition, several Xingu tribes had become so terrified of contact with the whites that they fled from their settlements, preferring a slow decline in the jungle to the dangers of communication with the white man. These tribes had to be persuaded to return to their old settlements or to establish new ones, and at the same time the Villas Boas brothers needed to be on constant watch to stem the twin threats of disease and foreign interference.

The establishment in 1968 of the Xingu National Park, some eight thousand square miles in extent, was a triumph, but it was not a final one. As created, the park set aside for the Indians (and for the protection of its flora and fauna) an area about the same size as Massachusetts, though it was still a very modest land grant from Brazil's total area of more than three million square miles. Nor did the park include the territory of all the threatened Indians of the cultural area, so that even as they were protecting their wards on the Xingu, the Villas Boas brothers had to mount expeditions to contact tribes outside the park and persuade them to move within its boundaries. In several cases this policy contradicted the everyday values and wishes of the Indians. Tribes were asked to abandon their traditional homes and hunting grounds. They were expected to remove to a strange area and often to settle near their erstwhile enemies. As a result, intertribal fights broke out within the park, and sometimes the cultural dislocation was severe. Hunter-gatherers had to concentrate on becoming horticulturalists and learn about new and unknown crops, and where tribes had shrunk in numbers below their replacement level, it was necessary to persuade the few survivors to go to live together with another group in similar plight. Nevertheless, a great deal was achieved. In 1971 some fifteen hundred Indians from fifteen different tribes were living within the park, mainly divided between Posto Leonardo (named in honor of the deceased brother of the trio), where lived mainly the traditional Xingu dwellers, and a post at nearby Diauarum, in whose vicinity had settled at least

Painted with snake designs, this bark-cloth anthropomorphic mask was made about 1900 by an Indian of a Tukana linguistic group in the Upper Rio Negro area of Brazil.
BROOKLYN MUSEUM

343

one tribe brought in from outside the park. In some cases the plight even of these luckier survivors was hopeless. Of the Trumai, whom von den Steinen had first classified as a unique subgroup of their own, only 26 members remained, scarcely enough to occupy two huts at Posto Leonardo. From the Arawak-speaking Waura, an early Xingu people who had learned to make beautiful colored pottery and sell it to the other tribes, there were just 115 survivors.

Yet, in context the Xingu National Park is a success story. Something between 1 million and 2 million Indians are believed to have formed Brazil's aboriginal population when the white man came, and perhaps 200,000 were left at the beginning of this century. Today there are only an estimated 60,000 to 100,000 survivors, and the true figure may be considerably less. A few Indian bands have not yet established contact with foreigners and prefer to withdraw and remain mobile deep within the forests and bush. Others are in the Xingu Park and the newer parks like it, which are attempting—usually with sad lack of success—to emulate the Villas Boas' achievements. Many more Brazilian Indians are on the verge of total cul-

tural assimilation or extinction. There is the comparison between the slender, but still vital, shadow of the Xingu peoples who live on their own territory and are slowly adapting to modern conditions, and the Xavante who are outside the Xingu Park and not thirty years ago first allowed friendly contact with the white man. Today the Xavante, the Spartans of the Serra do Roncador, are trapped on the land that they fought so hard to defend. They cannot move westward away from the settlers as their fore-fathers did. Instead they have to try to deal with the invading cattle ranchers and real estate companies through the unfamiliar channels of an alien government, or they have found shelter with the Salesian mission-aries, members of the same order whose priests they once killed. With the Salesians, at least, the Xavante are learning to farm and mend machinery, and they still run their splendid log races in the mission compound. But even so, there is an ironic footnote to their story, for the Salesian mission posts that are now their refuge were originally set up not to protect the proud warrior Xavante, but to proselytize the Bororo Indians, whom every Xavante formerly regarded as a cowardly and inadequate neighbor.

Caraja men, wearing feathered masks with long bast fringes, keep time with gourd rattles during an "aruana," or fertility dance, which is performed daily during the summer months on the sandbanks of the Araguaia River.

11

Exodus, Judges, and Lamentations

In 1972 Orlando and Claudio Villas Boas, the two Brazilian brothers responsible for the foundation and success of the Xingu National Park, were nominated for the Nobel Peace Prize. As matters turned out, the committee decided not to award the prize that year, but the two brothers' names are certain to be put forward again by the growing number of admirers, conservationists, and ethnographers who are convinced that the Xingu experiment is of fundamental importance to the future of the world's surviving primitive peoples. Simultaneously, however, a new Brazilian highway, the BR80, has been heading as if to slice the Xingu Park in two. Under construction by pioneering battalions of military engineers, the BR80 will be a technological triumph, a monument to Brazil's conquest of its interior plateau, and—very possibly—a catastrophe for the fifteen hundred Indians who are sheltered in the park.

These two events, the Nobel Prize nomination and the threatening BR80, symbolize a dilemma that is not peculiar to Brazil but is found wherever primitive peoples still survive in their aboriginal state. Even while public opinion is growing more sympathetic to the plight of primitive man and pondering a solution for his woes, the pressures that are likely to destroy him are growing increasingly sophisticated and final. That a modern highway could possibly change the vast, inhospitable expanse of the Mato Grosso is almost as inconceivable to some Brazilians as it is to the Indians who live in its path and flee before its head, which is eating into their countryside like an enormous hookworm. The truth of the matter is that the last refuges of primitive peoples are coming under what may be a conclusive attack. Whether in the Mato Grosso or in the Arctic of the Eskimos, there is every likelihood that within another generation less than a third of surviving primitive cultures will be left.

From necessity, therefore, we must turn to the history of contacts between primitive societies and more developed civilizations in order to read the entrails and learn the processes of cultural contact. Only in this way are we likely to foresee how the world may avert the loss of the last remnants of primitive cultures. Moreover, a historical perspective enables us to glimpse these other cultures as they existed in their pristine state, before

A South African Hottentot servant, degraded by his European owner.

347

Brazilian road builders push into the last Indian homelands.

they were irrevocably changed by outside influence. The narratives and descriptions of the explorers, missionaries, seamen, and all the outer fringe of travelers who first made contact with primitive peoples suffer from many faults. They are often superficial, nearly always ethnocentric (that is, they look upon the "natives" from the subjective viewpoint of another culture), and they invariably offer an incomplete picture of native society, ignoring perhaps the local religion, the art forms, or the social structure. In short, the narratives of the early travelers do not meet the modern demands of sociologists and anthropologists. Nevertheless, they constitute most of what we are able to recover of the full blossom of other cultures. The modern field anthropologist can observe the fine details, get himself accepted as a fellow tribesman, and live in the native huts for months on end, patiently gathering notes, photographs, and tape recordings. But very rarely can he retrieve the exact way of life of the halycon days, when primitive existence was not such a struggle to survive, and the native felt neither puzzled nor threatened by the alien mechanized civilization that had appeared on his horizon. The Xavante of Maybury-Lewis's day or the Bushmen who still shelter in the sands of the Kalahari Desert are intriguing in their own right, but their cultures are pale relics of what they were formerly. Before one can seek to cement together the cultural past with the anthropologist's modern techniques, it is necessary to cull the early travel narratives for data that show why life among primitive peoples was so complete and so stable, to collect the artifacts that have survived, and to rearrange the paintings and sketches that constitute the pictorial legacy of the explorers.

The first result of this process is a somber one. Inevitably a sense of regret intrudes. The evidence of cultural collapse among native societies is too frequent and too tragic to be ignored. Like the roll on the plinth of a war memorial, it is a long roster of premature death. There are those primitive peoples who have vanished forever in a great exodus, whether the aboriginal Tasmanians who were wiped out entirely; the Yahgans, who formerly inhabited the most southerly tip of Tierra del Fuego in South America; or the many extinct Indian tribes of North America. In Brazil the demise of the Indians has been so far-reaching that when the *Handbook of South American Indians* was published recently, its map of Indian tribes had to include special symbols for those tribes whose names and customs were recorded but whose peoples were no longer in existence. Then there are the people of the twilight, the tribes that are already so reduced in numbers as to be on the verge of extinction. They include the Ainus of Japan and the Xavante, the desert peoples of aboriginal Australia, the Veddas of Ceylon, and fragments of native cultures on every continent. These peoples occupy a position midway between those tribes that have already gone and the primitive societies that seem likely to survive. But the difference between the survivor and the doomed is impossible to foretell, because the process of extinction is volatile. A government may decree to end a tribal sanctuary, or a sudden epidemic of sickness may sweep away a whole people. Only those societies that are still healthy and numerous can be said to stand a genuine chance of survival. Among them one can number the pygmies of the Ituri, the Maori of New Zealand, the majority of the Melanesian peoples, the Lapps, the island Cunas, and — perhaps

The beginning of the end: Xavante Indians in the 1950's shoot arrows at a plane that has discovered their village in the Brazilian jungle. Soon they were reached by ground parties that "pacified" them and put them on reserves. In 1973 the tribe was again on the defensive, threatened by white settlers who were crowding onto the reserves.

—the Eskimos. Yet even these people are changing, for they have no other choice. The Eskimos have their motorized snowmobiles and government schools; the Maori are integrated into white New Zealand society; the Cunas of the offshore islands have drastically altered their original way of life. And everywhere the hunters use modern weapons, or the gatherers are tempted into agriculture.

One might suppose that such native cultures will never again be subjected to quite the same destruction that their defunct cousins suffered. The brutal suppression of a handful of "natives" seems a nightmare of the past. It is difficult to imagine, for instance, a repetition of the deliberate shelling of a Pacific island by a French warship in order to punish the natives for their belligerence, or another driven hunt like the one that the British governor organized on the island of Tasmania in 1830. He sent lines of soldiers as beaters marching across the island to try to sweep the last Tasmanian Aborigines into a cul-de-sac, where they could be placed under guard or deported from their homeland as nuisances to the settlers and farmers (only two, in fact, fell into the net). Yet, unbelievably, such injustices do still occur. An investigation between 1968 and 1971 of the former Brazilian Indian Protection Service produced a scandal-ridden seven-thousand-page report, which found that employees of the service had been rounding up and killing Indians instead of defending them. The directors of the Protection Service were summarily dismissed and stood trial along with three hundred of their employees. Extermination had reverted to techniques that were prevalent over a century ago. Then, as now, the most efficient ways of killing were to lace supplies of flour with arsenic or to infect an unwanted tribe with smallpox virus carried on clothing left scattered temptingly on the ground. Indeed, in earlier days cast-off clothing was collected from the fever hospitals especially for that purpose. In twentieth-century Brazil a more novel system made use of airplanes, not simply to lob hand grenades on unwanted Indian villages but to drop gifts of food and clothes into the central clearing, and once the Indian populace had gathered in the dropping zone, to follow with a home-made dynamite bomb.

But the situation of the surviving primitive peoples is not the same as that of their vanished peers. At one time the hunters and gatherers and neolithic farmers occupied prize lands coveted by the agricultural and industrial societies that took them over. Or, just as dangerously, primitive

Anne Putnam, one of the first anthropologists to study the culture of the pygmies of the Ituri forest, records the movements of a dance demonstrated in an Mbuti village.

man lived on coastal lands whose flanks were vulnerable to the seaborne invaders of the colonial area. Thus the mysterious Guanche, a race of tall men with blue or gray eyes and fair hair who may have been relics of a Cro-Magnon civilization, lived harmlessly on the Canary Islands until early in the fifteenth century, raising goats and pigs and probably cultivating local fruits. But it was their misfortune that the Canaries lay athwart the sea routes that Portugal and Spain used when they sent explorers and colonizers to the New World and the Orient. So the Canaries were overrun and occupied, and the Guanche vanished forever. They left behind the deep caves that seem to have served as mass mortuaries where lines of dead Guanche were laid out in their final tomb, a suitable remembrance of the first overseas civilization to have been destroyed by Europe's westward course of empire. Similar seaborne destruction was wrought upon the South Sea islanders, the Yahgans, and the Indians of New England who were carried off as curios by European mariners. They were all coastal peoples, and their downfall did not result from a deliberate process of extermination so much as from a casual sideswipe by the newly arrived culture.

By contrast, most of today's primitive societies are to be found in interior, submarginal lands that were formerly regarded as unusable by the Europeans and therefore served as sanctuaries for their inhabitants. Now these same refuges have turned into traps. The outsiders are beginning to exploit these previously neglected barren lands for space in which to build, to irrigate, or to mine, and their indigenous inhabitants have nowhere else to go. They have already withdrawn as far as possible, and they are threatened by the very frailty of their existence in these marginal areas. The basis of their life is so precarious that the slightest disturbance can do terrible damage. The loss of a single reliable water hole or the disappearance of a particular type of game animal can be the death knell for a people already living on the edge of survival. Moreover, the shroud of obscurity that once helped to keep these primitive societies remote and inaccessible has also become a liability. These little-known primitive communities would stand a better chance of survival if they could be identified and counted, and the nature of their problems recognized and made public so that help could be given them. But no one knows exactly how many Stone Age hunter-gatherers and farmers are left, and thus the problem of their preservation is made even more acute, for it is doubly difficult to protect what one cannot identify or define. Instead, the doubt and mystery only feed the distrust of frontiersmen who live alongside these exotic peoples. The atrocity tales of the Xavante or the traditional dislike of Bushmen among South African farmers is rooted in misunderstanding, which is, in turn, based upon ignorance. It becomes one of the paradoxes of primitive man that while we have the knowledge and skill to penetrate into the last marginal areas of the world, almost no one has seen fit to apply other sophisticated techniques to identifying, counting, and explaining the cultures of their human denizens.

Naturally it is valid to ask whether these fringe peoples either can be saved or are worth saving; or whether it would not be more sensible to integrate, say, an Amazon Indian totally into industrialized society as a bus driver or a mechanic than to make him a tourist guide, dressed up for visitors in occasional paint and showing off for the tourist's camera in a

When the pygmies were still mysterious to the outside world: an illustration in Henry M. Stanley's In Darkest Africa, *a vivid account of his 1887–89 expedition, depicts a group of pygmies trying to outwit his Sudanese bearers by darting off with one of his ammunition cases.*

351

In 1907–8 an explorer in Tierra del Fuego, the windswept southern tip of South America, painted these Ona Indians clad in guanaco hides. By 1960 only seven members of the tribe were known to be still alive.

plastic-feather headband as he dances a spring planting ceremony five months out of season in order to supply a colorful celluloid image. Sadly, though, experience has shown that total integration is seldom a success unless it is done very gently. In case after case, the trauma of cultural dislocation is too shattering to be endured. The transition from one culture to another is like a man leaping from a wrecked ship onto the rocks that have destroyed his vessel. The preliminary jump may take him to temporary security, but the castaway soon grows tired, his grip loosens, and the surge of the sea licks him off to destruction. In the same way, a jungle Indian who leaves his wrecked culture and moves to a town to look for work finds the strains and difficulties of life too great, and like the castaway, his grip loosens and he is pulled down by the countercurrents of circumstances that he neither understands nor can control. The result is usually a pathetic figure, foundering on the fringe of an alien civilization.

An alternative solution, which is sometimes mooted, is that surviving primitive peoples be placed off limits. Their territories would be marked out, and no one (including anthropologists) would be allowed into the reservations. There, so the argument runs, indigenous peoples could continue to live out their lives as they had always done. Something very similar to this policy was, in fact, achieved by the government of British India on the northeast frontier where it lapped against Burma and the Himalayas. By government decree the tribes in those regions, some of whom were head-hunters, remained virtually untouched and formed a convenient and virile buffer zone for imperial India. But such policies are no longer practicable. Pressure on land has grown too great, and there are qualms about creating "human zoos," where man is condemned to a deliberate backwater. More realistically, too, it is very doubtful that such a rigid reservation could be kept intact. The difficulty of policing its margins would be immense, and disease in particular would be hard to exclude. A

Exterminated, or interbred with whites, as above, Tasmania's Aborigines no longer exist.

BUFFALO BILL'S WILD WEST
AND CONGRESS OF ROUGH RIDERS OF THE WORLD.

COL. W. F. CODY
"BUFFALO BILL"
WILL APPEAR
AT EVERY PERFORMANCE

A CONGRESS OF AMERICAN INDIANS, REPRESENTING VARIOUS TRIBES, CHARACTERS AND PECULIARITIES OF THE WILY DUSKY WARRIORS IN SCENES FROM ACTUAL LIFE GIVING THEIR WEIRD WAR DANCES AND PICTURESQUE STYLE OF HORSEMANSHIP.

Wild West shows, such as the one produced by Buffalo Bill in America and Europe, used conquered Indians as performers to exploit the myth that red men were ruthless savages.

sudden epidemic invading a helpless native group that lacked doctors or modern medical care would have disastrous effects. Nor are primitive societies always sedentary. As often as not they are mobile hunting populations or seminomads who abandon one area after it has been hunted or cropped out and move on to the next. The attempt to keep such a peripatetic group within circumscribed frontiers would be doomed to failure and equally harmful to their culture.

Advanced societies, therefore, are left with the moral obligation of devising for primitive man the best transition from his aboriginal state to a condition in which he can survive alongside more modern cultures. Many people would also argue that primitive societies should be valued for the contribution they can make. In strictly technological terms it must be admitted that this contribution seems modest. It is true, for instance, that certain South American and Asian tribes make use of vegetable-derived drugs that could be of considerable value to medical science. In *Mato Grosso,* an excellent book on the work of the joint Royal Society–Royal Geographical Society expedition to Brazil, the zoologist Anthony Smith lists a dozen plants used by the Xingu Indians for various purposes from oral contraception to insect repellent that have yet to be analyzed by scientists. But many of the technological contributions of primitive societies have already been made and can be recognized by the native terminology, which has also entered our culture with such words as *catamaran, kayak,*

354

quinine, parka, moccasin, hammock, and *barbecue.* Rather, it is in the field of sociology and psychology that primitive man has much to teach the outsider. Native societies, their laws and behavior, their fears and ambitions, are among the finest clinical material available for study by experts today. Margaret Mead's work on adolescent education systems in Samoa and New Guinea has already become required reading for child psychiatrists; Maybury-Lewis's account of the pampered infancy of Xavante menfolk may be equally relevant in the future. Nowhere is it possible to duplicate the conditions that gave rise to functioning societies of this type, any more than it is possible to synthesize the complexity of the Australian Aborigine's ideas of moieties, ancestors, clans, and totems, each assigned to its fourth-dimensional place relative to the rest of creation. So, despite the romantic overtones and the extravagant dreams of those who envisage primitive society as a return to Mother Earth, the study of primitive man retains a broad area of mystery, of unexplored psychological and social territory that will grow more valuable as the stresses on industrial society increase and techniques for investigation improve.

Yet here again there is a danger. The very inquisitiveness of outsiders has always tended to destroy primitive societies, one after another. As we poke and pry, hoping to find the links and discern the internal structure, we are like fumbling surgeons dissecting a living body. All too often our probes carry infection. They are too brutal, and they often cut essential linkages that can never knit together again. Indeed, if a sense of curiosity and enterprise was responsible for carrying industrialized man into the territory of other cultures, the same curiosity tended to blight whatever was found there. Perhaps the first lesson that must be learned from primitive man is that curiosity is not universal, nor is it always beneficial. Among the highlanders of New Guinea a sense of curiosity happens to be applauded. The questing cameraman with his battery of long-range lenses is welcomed and understood. Magnificently dressed dancers from the Stone Age will strut and show off because they appreciate his curiosity. But among tribes of Brazilian Indians there is quite the opposite reaction. Curiosity is frowned upon more severely than an inquisitive child is disciplined in a Victorian household. Decorum demands that no one show interest or pry into the affairs of another man, even if he arrives in the village girded with parachute harness and dragging a sackful of Bibles, as do the more daring and fundamentalist Christian missionaries who train as parachute evangelists.

Broadly speaking, the causes of cultural breakdown in primitive society have been either physical or psychological, and while the former is more easily diagnosed, the latter is equally damaging.

The most spectacular of the physical annihilators has been outright warfare. Whether it was the Spanish conquistador in steel morion, mounted on a charger and brandishing a metal sword, or his latter-day counterpart, the United States cavalryman attacking with saber and firearm, the military paraphernalia of the invader was crushing. He brought with him all the gadgetry of "civilized" warfare and was prepared to deploy it if threatened or obstructed. The gross inequality of armed clashes between invader and native can be judged from the fact that these conflicts were usually finished in a few minutes and seldom repeated. Weight of numbers

FUNDAÇÃO NACIONAL DO ÍNDIO, RIO DE JANEIRO

Forced into dependency on the cash economy of Brazil's industrialized society, Indians from the Ilha do Bananal, near the Mato Grosso, peddle pottery souvenirs to tourists.

rarely mattered, unless poor judgment or exceptional circumstances canceled out the imbalance. Captain Cook would probably have survived at Kealakekua Bay if he had loaded both barrels of his gun with man-killing ball instead of putting bird shot in one barrel; and Custer need not have lost at the Little Bighorn if he had used more sensible tactics. The very fame of such defeats shows them as the exceptions that prove the rule. The multitude of victories over indigenous populations are not sung loudly because they scarcely deserve the praise, and even less honorable were the consequences of giving weapons to native warlords so that the balance of power within a primitive society was upset and the engines of destruction were set in motion against traditional foes.

Even more ruinous was the scourge of disease introduced by outsiders. Epidemics killed more widely among native peoples than any form of man-made weapon, and sickness was an enduring danger because it could linger among the survivors of one epidemic to emerge again and again as a killer. The chief culprits were smallpox, measles, yellow fever, typhus, and typhoid, the venereal diseases of syphilis, gonorrhea, and chancroid, and leprosy and malaria. The identity and virulence of each affliction varied from one area to the next. In Tahiti it was venereal disease, rightly or

The once independent Ainus of Hokkaido, now a prime Japanese sightseeing attraction, perform in costume for the cameras of visitors.

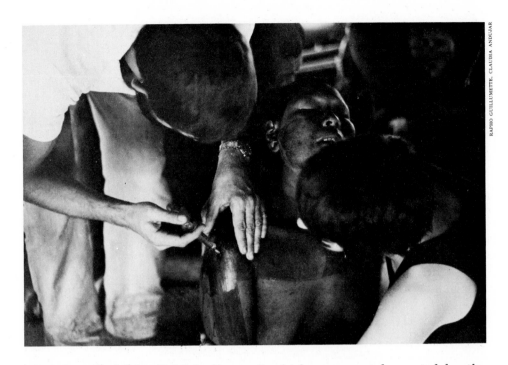

A Xicrin Indian woman in the trop-ics of central Brazil is inoculated against malaria, a disease intro-duced in the Americas by Europeans.

wrongly called "the British disease," which was most lamented by the natives. In Mexico of the Aztecs it was smallpox, originally an African and Indian fever introduced there by a pox-ridden black soldier in Cortés's army. According to one estimate, three and a half million Indians perished in the epidemic that then raged across the country. Moctezuma's imperial successor sickened and died, and illness is reckoned as having been more effective in reducing the Mexican population than all the attacks of the soldiers. But disease was a "moving frontier," as A. Grenfell Price, the geomedical authority, has called it. Once introduced into a contact zone, a particular illness could seldom be halted in its progress through an entire population. Often, in fact, it ran ahead of the human invaders like a deadly miasma. The smallpox that Cortés brought with him outstripped the ranks of Spain's colonial armies and went ahead to Peru. Smallpox ravaged and weakened the Inca empire ten years before Pizarro put in his appearance and toppled the enfeebled structure. Among Australian Aborigines, three centuries later, the effects were much the same. Smallpox, which was imported into Australia late in the eighteenth century, reached the natives of southwest Australia well ahead of the white man, so that the explorer Charles Sturt found cases of the disease among tribesmen who had never even seen a white man before. Similarly, in Alaska a smallpox epidemic that occurred between 1836 and 1840 killed hundreds of Eskimos before it could be brought under control, because although the white settlers had been vaccinated, the Eskimos were entirely vulnerable to the ravages of the virulent disease.

Nor did a disease have to be flamboyant in order to be a killer. Quite commonplace maladies were disastrous if they occurred among native peoples who lacked the relevant immunity. The European childhood dis-ease of measles became a calamity when it spread up the Amazon in 1749–50, killing an estimated thirty thousand Indians. Measles also cut in half the native population of Hudson Bay in 1846, virtually put an end to

357

JOHN CARMICHAEL, SYDNEY, 1839

Besotted by alcohol and wearing Western rags, these Australian Aborigines, caricatured by an unsympathetic white man, were shorn of all dignity by contact with "civilization."

the Yahgans at the southern tip of South America, and was a noticeable disaster in Fiji when it was introduced there by men from H.M.S. *Dido*. It also sent the death rate soaring among the Hottentots of South Africa, the Maori, and the Australian Aborigines. Geography, meanwhile, combined with illness to produce totally unexpected results. As far as one can tell, the most frequent ailments developed by Eskimos brought back from the Arctic by Elizabethan explorers were debilitating colds and influenza, presumably contracted from their English hosts and nurtured in that island's damp and dreary climate.

The loss of land was, of course, the most tangible of the injuries that befell primitive man. Certainly it was a calamity that the foreign invaders could have understood at first hand. Land, its possession and use, its inheritance and partition, were ideas that were basic to the societies of Portugal, England, France, Holland, and Spain. Indeed, the possession of land was probably more important to interlopers from these countries than to many of the native peoples they encountered. The famine, demoralization, and emigration of the agricultural Scots following the clearances in Scotland, when the great landlords evicted their tenant-farmers and turned the land over to sheep instead (beginning a wave of migration to the United States), had its parallel when the sheep farmers of Australia pushed back the Aborigines in order to acquire pasture for their imported flocks. Similarly, the speed with which the Spanish conquerors of Central America established vast feudal estates over native peoples and took to themselves the grand landowning titles of Europe indicates the priority given to the ownership of land. But to many primitive societies the notion of personal ownership of land was incomprehensible. As the Bushmen put it, one could not eat the soil itself, and so all that the Bushmen valued were the fruit-bearing bushes and the game animals that the land supported. Other primitive societies considered that ownership of the land was vested in the community as a whole. The notion that it could be given to or purchased by an outsider was totally mystifying. They envisaged a land grant as a temporary arrangement, allowing the newcomer to hunt or farm as long as he needed but never to claim the land for his heirs in perpetuity.

This land question took many different forms. In some cases there was a genuine conflict over living space. The settlers simply did not like rubbing shoulders with the natives and therefore did away with them. This distaste underlay much of the malice directed against native peoples wherever cultural contacts occurred, and the fate of the Tasmanians was a clear example of such bigotry. The natives on the island were never really numerous or warlike enough to threaten the whites, and so the ponderous efforts made by the colonists to herd and corral the natives were largely inspired by the plain intention to be rid of the native Tasmanians as neighbors. Just as commonplace were clashes between native and foreigner over the physical resources of the land. They contested with one another for good grazing lands, suitable building sites, key routes, and — above all — water supply. The Bushmen fought with Boer farmers over the ownership of water holes; the Australian Aborigines were similarly at loggerheads with the stockmen of Australia; and in a backhanded fashion, even the better-known watering places of the Pacific became battlegrounds when visiting ships habitually filled their water casks and cleared the beaches of resentful natives with musketry. Neither could the Stone Age hunters and gatherers and Neolithic farmers agree with the new-style planters, graziers, and modern farmers on how the land should be used. The two sides wanted to exploit the land in wholly different ways, and their two

Tamati Waka Nene was the first of 500 Maori chiefs in New Zealand to sign the 1840 Treaty of Waitangi (below), ceding his sovereignty and tribal lands to the British crown.

Nagas in India learn the dominant Hindi language—and thereby undermine a foundation of their own culture—at a government center hastening the assimilation of minorities.

systems of land use could not coexist. Game animals competed with stock animals for food and pasture; tropical plantation crops ousted the small gardens of the natives; and intensive agricultural techniques changed the entire landscape familiar to its original population. Such conflicts of interests still exist. In the New Hebrides 40 per cent of the land is owned by French plantation companies, and the New Hebridean natives are still being dispossessed from their small holdings and pushed back toward the central uplands; while in Brazil the savannah, when it is cleared for cattle ranches, is thenceforth denied to the Indian tribes who formerly hunted and went on trek there.

Alcohol and clothing were the fifth column of physical damage. The indictment against western-style clothing, so blithely handed out to native peoples, is easily made: it encouraged vermin and dirt, and, ironically, it brought about colds and pneumonia. Primitive communities often failed to grasp the uses and limitations of fitted textile clothing. Because they had never needed to wash or repair clothes, they allowed their garments to become filthy and tattered, breeding grounds for vermin and germs. Untutored in the purpose of clothing, which was frequently regarded as a status symbol, they failed to throw away their old rags. Worst of all, they continued to wear clothing even if it was wet or soaked with sweat. The skin of an unclothed jungle Indian who had waded across a river soon dried off. But the Indian who crossed the river and failed to dry his clothing afterward was liable to catch pneumonia. Of course, such dangers threatened only the naked societies, and peoples like the Eskimos or Ainus who knew and appreciated the use of clothing were not at risk, even if they accepted the white man's garb. Regrettably, the same discretion did not apply to previous knowledge of alcohol. Many communities, such as the Polynesians, Cunas, and Ainus, knew all about alcoholic drinks and brewed their own; others, like the Aborigines and the Xavante, were totally ignorant of alcohol. Yet in both cases the excessive use of alcohol supplied by the newcomers could be catastrophic. The new beverages were usually stronger than anything brewed before, and sometimes they were actually poisonous. The French *voyageurs* of Canada sold to the Indians a ferocious homemade "cognac," which they doctored up with raw spirit, turpentine, and pepper to give it bite, and this firewater probably did physical damage to anyone who drank it. On Fiji, on the other hand, heavy kava drinking was already causing skin diseases and early senility long before demon rum was imported. Thus the contribution of the developed civilizations was to make alcohol more widely available and to supply it in greater quantities. Primitive men who had never known alcohol developed a taste for it and lacked any traditional restraint against excess. Those who already knew of strong drink took the opportunity to indulge themselves and quickly overstepped their former limits. The result was alcoholism, with all its attendant mental, economic, and physical disorders.

But alcoholism was a disease that harmed the psychological as well as the physical health of primitive peoples. As a rule, their cultures leaned heavily upon the three factors of regular observance, general acceptance by the community, and the passing on of tradition. Anything that challenged or weakened these factors damaged the culture as a whole, whether it was a drunken native who mocked his fellow tribesmen for their traditional ways, an age-set of young men from one locality all taken off to be taught Christianity in mission schools, or a bad epidemic that swept away a growing generation, which was then unable to hand on the legends, chants, and technical skills of its forefathers. These sudden strains were all the more dangerous because they took place in communities that were usually weak and small. Primitive society was seldom organized on a large scale, because any unit that became unwieldy tended to break up into smaller self-sufficient cells. Cultural clash then obliterated these cells one by one.

This trauma of the psychological invasion entered every crevice of native culture. It challenged primitive man's gods, traditions, society, and even his very existence. Some primitive peoples had never even imagined that there were other human beings, and they were thrown into confusion by the appearance of aliens. Other societies had never questioned their way of life and were appalled by the notion of considering, let alone adopting, any alternatives. These societies had occupied their particular niches, established satisfactory perimeters, and were content. They found it pointless and inexplicable that the newcomers should seek to change the traditional ways, and in return the foreigners grew exasperated with natives who, they complained, were stubborn blockheads. In this context the role of the missionaries was crucial. The missionary spirit was at the very root of overseas expansion from the days when explorers first went out to discover and annex new lands that, as their charters put it, were neither

A boomerang thrower competes in an annual "Olympics" held for Australia's Aborigines, several of whom have become world-famous athletes.

Earnest English missionaries impose their garb and Gospel on New Guinea natives early in the 1900's.

occupied nor claimed by any Christian ruler. From there the missionary movement went forward, and by a quirk of history it was the missionaries who were generally given charge of the indigenous peoples in new-found lands. During four centuries of cultural contact, the missionaries served as advance scouts for their own culture. They negotiated with chiefs, preached to the common people, established hospitals and schools, taught new ways of building or farming or social behavior, and in some cases were the natives' only experience of the outsider. Yet, as their vocation demanded, the missionaries were also concerned with saving souls. To a primitive society nothing could have been more culturally challenging than the Christian mission with its new rules for everything from cradle to coffin and into the spirit world beyond. The dedication of missionaries was beyond question—their very presence in a primitive society was proof of their calling—but as cultural shock troops they were unequaled.

So in the long run it was the psychological decline among primitive societies that was the most difficult to arrest. Whereas lands could be given back, diseases checked or allowed to peter out, and hunters retrained as farmers, nothing could be done if the natives abandoned hope when their culture needed revival. Some lost the will to live, refusing food and committing suicide by self-starvation. More often they simply became apathetic, mere shells of humans, men who were stupefied by the drug of psychological defeat.

But the picture is not one of total gloom. There are indigenous societies that have survived the cultural impact. Their record is as valuable, if shorter, a lesson for the future as the post-mortems on their extinct neighbors. With the hindsight of history, for example, one can see that the pygmies and the Eskimos were lucky that their habitat was so thoroughly hostile to foreigners. Most primitive societies had only a temporary advantage in their isolation, which was quickly lost as the foreigners appeared. But the Ituri forest and the ice and snowscapes of the Arctic continued to repel outsiders far longer, and the specialized cultures of the pygmy and the Eskimo were, until very recently, all that could survive there. By the same token the Melanesians were even more fortunate, because they not only occupied lands of limited value, but by a political accident dwelt in one of the last well-populated areas of the world to be explored. There were several reasons for this oversight: Melanesia was isolated; navigation in its coral waters was hazardous; the terrain was difficult to penetrate; and there was very little to lure an explorer inland. Above all, Melanesia was a political confusion. On one side Holland was more interested in developing Java and the Spice Islands; Great Britain had Australia and New Zealand as more attractive areas for colonial energy; and France was dazzled by her more glamorous Pacific islands. The result was that most of Melanesia was left untouched until the crest of colonial ebullience was spent, and the foreign powers were taking a more cautious approach to overseas exploitation. But here, too, there is still a warning. Melanesia is no more difficult to develop than the interior of Brazil, and it continues to retain much of its native culture largely because development has not been attempted on a Brazilian scale.

More subtle were the psychological defenses that several of the successful primitive societies were able to erect against the alien invader. These

Catering to the amusement of visitors, a jovial Lapp youth totes clubs as a caddie at a resort hotel golf course in northwestern Sweden.

His traditional life style altered by industrial technology, an Eskimo in Canada's Northwest Territories hunts seals with a motorized tractor.

defenses were well camouflaged and are still difficult to identify and assess, but there is little doubt that they helped the indigenous cultures to fight off collapse. The Eskimos and the pygmies, for example, shared the healthy attitude that they should not take the invading culture too seriously. The early travelers' accounts make it clear that the Eskimos and pygmies found much to mock in the white man's civilization and at the same time lacked a rigid and ornate psychological framework of their own. They were essentially simple and uncomplicated peoples who placed little value on their own or any other cultural pretensions, and they therefore adapted quickly and easily to the new situation. Conversely, primitive societies that had highly developed metaphysical frameworks took the impact badly. Their worlds were too brittle, and they were buried in the wreckage when their gods and societies were overthrown in the cultural collision. For their part, the Cunas found that the answer was to take a positively virulent line. Broadly speaking, the island Cunas have survived because they thoroughly rejected the white man's civilization. By keeping on the move, changing their territory from the coastal plains to the central mountains, and then evacuating to the offshore islands of Panama, they deliberately avoided close contact with the white man. Furthermore, they were prepared to back up this policy with effective force, raising their own rebellion to declare independence from Panama and refusing to give outsiders permission to stay in their villages. Thus Cuna society, which was initially broken by the conquistadors, was able to regroup and change down to a simpler, sturdier level that shared the resilience of the well-balanced Eskimos and the pygmies.

The Maori of New Zealand succeeded in quite a different way. Instead of rejecting the newcomers' methods, they embraced them avidly and then turned them against the invader. Maori armies, equipped with firearms, became extraordinarily difficult to defeat; and Maori politicians quickly learned to negotiate with the white man on his own terms. The result was that the Maori literally fought their way into the invader's respect and then earned his admiration by showing that they could manipulate his techniques and skills. Yet the Maori, it should be added, were also lucky that official policy toward them was comparatively enlightened from an early date, and that no serious attempt was made either to exterminate or deport them. Also, it should be stressed that the Maori did not copy the white man with the wholehearted enthusiasm of their distant relatives on Hawaii or Tahiti, who made the mistake of adopting the ways of the new-comers so successfully that the indigenous culture was totally submerged.

Finally, there are the Lapps, one of the first primitive societies to be brought into contact with industrial man and therefore the society that has survived the longest. Here again, the Lapps seem to have owed much to their uncomplicated social and intellectual framework, which was ready to adapt to and refused to be overawed by the intruders. To a certain extent, also, the Lapps shared the benefits of a homeland that was inhospitable to settlement. But their real advantage was time. Cultural contact with the Lapps took place over several centuries and allowed ample time for both sides to come to terms with one another. It was not so much a cultural impact as a cultural abrasion, the gradual wearing away of Lapp culture to its

Aborigine Boy Scouts combine sounds of the Stone-Age "didjeridu" with those of the modern guitar at a songfest in Maningrida, Australia.

present condition, which both sides have resolved to preserve if possible.

The ingredients, therefore, of cultural survival are not far to seek. If the world's surviving primitive societies are to go on existing, they must be given these considerations: firstly, time to adjust to the new situation; secondly, a genuine physical security in the possession of their lands; thirdly, the very best medical protection available; and finally, a sense of cultural pride fostered by the continuation of their language, art, music, and society. Without this esprit de corps, there would be no point to survival and no real chance of its taking place. Also, if primitive man is to have a hope of living through another generation, it is crucial that the outside world appreciate and value his way of life. And just as essential, as A. P. Elkin has pointed out in a perceptive study of the modern condition of the Australian Aborigines, is that primitive man should understand us, the outsiders. Primitive societies must no longer be frightened, demoralized, or numbed by the industrial civilizations looming over their physical and intellectual frontiers. They must learn to live with this new creature, not by acculturation, which means being swallowed up in the maw of the new civilization, but by what Professor Elkin describes as "intelligent assimilation," a cultural adaptation that would allow primitive man to coexist with advanced societies.

This is why the Xingu National Park experiment is so important to the future of primitive societies all over the world: it embodies many of the features that could lead to their salvation—their own territory, dedicated medical help, and a slow introduction to the realities of the outside world so that they do not copy it but simply understand its ways. Among all the explorers and travelers who first brought the primitive societies to our attention, there was not one who claimed that native peoples would continue their lives unchanged. Sometimes the visitors lamented the inevitable alterations. Occasionally they judged the innocence and merit of the peoples they found. Nearly always they expressed the wish that somehow the best elements and singular qualities of these peoples could be retained. Today a scattering of philanthropic organizations like the World Council of Churches (now much less evangelistic in outlook) and the London-based Survival International are devoted to just this cause. They are striving to overcome the apathy of governments, to coordinate the ambitions of viable native minorities, and to extend a protective umbrella over the smaller helpless groups. The achievements vary greatly. In Brazil lesser-known tribes are still being snuffed out, but in Australia the Aborigines, so long neglected, are beginning to attract attention to their fight to have legal tenure over their lands and to repel the mineral prospecting companies that wish to encroach. Here and there one finds encouraging signs for the future. In Melanesia the colonial powers are taking firm but careful steps to educate the islanders into self-government. A few indigenous minorities like the Maori and the Lapps have already become adept at employing the opinion-making techniques of radio and newspapers, which they are using to keep alive their own cultural heritage as well as to present their external image to the outside world. But the majority of primitive societies are dishearteningly vulnerable. Their loss will mean that we will have quenched the last vestiges of harmless cultures, whose manifold and variegated patterns will never be seen again.

The Life of Primitive Man

Pressures and Changes

The Hopi and Mohawk traditional religious teachers above were photographed at the United Nations Conference on the Environment in Stockholm in 1972. With tribal peoples from Africa, Asia, and Oceania, they had journeyed to Sweden to appeal to the modern-day technological nations to regain a spiritual bond with all of creation, become one again with nature—as *they* still were—and care for the earth's resources before it was too late. Few listened to them, for the tide of "progress" in the world was running too strongly against the "primitive" societies. Losing their lands and lives, pressured increasingly to change, they everywhere faced a destiny symbolized by that of the Hopis themselves, whose ancient sacred shrines in Arizona were even then being obliterated by a coal strip mine.

Sri Lanka Veddas typif

Panama Cunas now face

UNITED PRESS INTERNATIONAL

Taiwan's Ahmis exemplify pockets of minority tribal societies that still survive in Asia.

Lapps see their crafts

groups from India to the East Indies.

loss of lands by the flooding of a dam.

displayed for sale to tourists in Norway.

Handing on an ancient skill, a Maori master carver instructs youths in New Zealand.

Living a Stone Age existence in Philippine rain forest caves, the Tasaday tribe of 27 persons was unbothered until 1966.

Then discoverers came upon them, and the balance, completeness, and security of their society and cosmos came to an end.

An international tennis star, Evonne Goolagong retains strong ties to her Australian Aborigine ancestry.

An instrument of enforced change: an armed and booted native polices Indians for Brazil's government.

Watched by former enemies on the hill, members of Papua-New Guinea villages throng to a mass election meeting in 1961.

In a first step toward the white man's system of self-rule, the people elected 6 natives to a 37-member legislative council.

In the subcontinent of India some 38 million people comprise 427 different minority tribes, regarded by the government as aborigines with varying languages, racial backgrounds, cultural traits, and levels of "primitiveness." The village guards at left are Nagas of northeastern India. At right, a full circle is reached: Australian Aborigines line up to enter a museum at Yuendumu in the Northern Territory, owned and managed by their elders to safeguard and preserve sacred tribal objects. The Eskimos below are seen holding a traditional drum dance in honor of a visit by the Canadian governor general to their village of Aklavik on the Mackenzie River.

Recommended Reading

Abbie, A. A. *The Original Australians.* New York: American Elsevier, 1970.

Anthropology Today. Del Mar, Calif.: CRM Books, 1971.

Berndt, Ronald M. *The World of the First Australians.* Sydney: Ure Smith, 1966.

Birket-Smith, Kaj. *The Eskimos.* New York: Crown, 1971 (reprint of 1936 ed.).

Bosi, Roberto. *The Lapps.* New York: Praeger Publishers, 1960.

Coates, Austin. *Western Pacific Islands.* London: Her Majesty's Stationery Office, 1970.

Collinder, Björn. *The Lapps.* Westport, Ct.: Greenwood, 1969 (reprint of 1949 ed.).

Coon, Carleton S. *The Living Races of Man.* New York: Alfred A. Knopf, 1965.

Elkin, Adolphus P. *The Australian Aborigines.* Garden City, N.Y.: Doubleday, 1964.

Freuchen, Peter. *Book of the Eskimos.* New York: Fawcett, 1969.

Gardner, Robert, and Heider, Karl G. *Gardens of War.* New York: Random House, 1969.

Goldman, Irving. *Ancient Polynesian Society.* Chicago: Univ. of Chicago Press, 1970.

Hilger, M. Inez. *Together with the Ainu.* Norman: Univ. of Oklahoma Press, 1971.

Howell, F. Clark. *Early Man.* Life Nature Library Series. New York: Time-Life Books, 1968.

Indians of Brazil in the Twentieth Century. Janice H. Hopper, ed. and trans. Washington, D.C.: Institute for Cross-Cultural Research, 1967.

Landor, Arnold H. S. *Alone with the Hairy Ainu.* New York: Johnson Reprint Corporation, 1970 (reprint of 1893 ed.).

Lévi-Strauss, Claude. *Tristes Tropiques; An Anthropological Study of Primitive Societies in Brazil.* New York, Atheneum, 1972.

Lothrop, Samuel K. *Coclé: An Archaeological Study of Central Panama.* Vols. 7 and 8, Memoirs of the Peabody Museum of Archaeology and Ethnology. Millwood, N.Y.: Kraus Reprint Co. (reprint of 1937–42 ed.).

Malinowski, Bronislaw. *Argonauts of the Western Pacific.* New York: E. P. Dutton, 1961.

Maybury-Lewis, David. *Akwe-Shavante Society.* London: Oxford Univ. Press, 1967.

Maybury-Lewis, David. *The Savage and the Innocent.* Boston: Beacon Press, 1968.

Mead, Margaret. *Growing Up in New Guinea.* New York: Apollo Editions, 1962.

Moore, Ruth E. *Man, Time and Fossils,* rev. ed. New York: Alfred A. Knopf, 1961.

Munro, Neil Gordon. *Ainu Creed and Cult.* New York: Columbia Univ. Press, 1963.

Oliver, Douglas L. *The Pacific Islands,* rev. ed. Cambridge, Mass.: Harvard Univ. Press, 1961.

Putnam, Anne Eisner. *Madami.* Englewood Cliffs, N. J.: Prentice-Hall, 1954 (pygmies).

Smith, Anthony. *Mato Grosso, the Last Virgin Land.* New York: E. P. Dutton, 1971.

Stefansson, Vilhjalmur. *My Life with the Eskimos.* New York: Macmillan, 1962.

Stout, David B. "The Cuna," in Julian Steward, ed., *Handbook of South American Indians,* Vol. 4. Washington, D.C.: Gov't. Printing Office, 1948.

Suggs, Robert C. *The Island Civilizations of Polynesia.* New York: New American Library, 1960.

Thomas, Elizabeth Marshall. *The Harmless People.* New York: Alfred A. Knopf, 1959.

Turnbull, Colin. *The Forest People.* New York: Simon & Schuster, 1968.

Turnbull, Colin. *Wayward Servants.* Garden City, N. Y.: Doubleday, 1965.

Van der Post, Laurens. *The Lost World of the Kalahari.* New York: William Morrow,.1970.

Vorren, Ørnulv, and Manker, Ernst. *Lapp Life and Customs.* London: Oxford Univ. Press, 1962.

Wauchope, Robert. *Handbook of Middle American Indians,* Vols. 1 and 4. Austin: Univ. of Texas Press, 1964–66.

Weiner, Joseph Sidney. *Natural History of Man.* New York: Universe Books, 1971.

Wendt, Herbert. *From Ape to Adam.* Indianapolis: Bobbs-Merrill, 1972.

Weyer, Edward. *Primitive Peoples Today.* Garden City, N. Y.: Doubleday, 1959.

Acknowledgments

The editors thank the following individuals and institutions for providing pictorial material and supplying information:

A. C. Cooper (Photographers) Ltd., London
American Museum of Natural History
 Josephine D'Orsi
 Helen B. Jones
Australian News and Information Bureau
Caroline Backlund, National Gallery of Art, Washington
Brooklyn Museum
 Arno Jakobson
 Michael Kam
Fernando de Mello Vianna
Department of Ethnography, British Museum
Krishna Dutt, New Delhi
Editions Hoa-Qui, Paris
Fundação Nacional do Indio, Rio de Janeiro
Robert Gardner, Harvard University
Anna Maria Gatti, Lugano, Switzerland
Richard A. Gould, University of Hawaii

Hamburgisches Museum für Völkerkunde und Vorgeschichte, Hamburg
James Houston, Escoheag, Rhode Island
George Hunter, Toronto
Information Service of South Africa
John Murray (Publishers) Ltd., London
Daniel W. Jones, New York
Elizabeth Katz, Cambridge, Massachusetts
Jerry Kearns, Library of Congress
Christopher Kirby, National Museums of Canada, Ottawa
Richard B. Lee, University of Toronto
Library of Parliament, Cape Town
Robert Liensol, Département Afrique Noire, Musée de l'Homme, Paris
Lorna Marshall, Cambridge, Massachusetts
Laurence K. Marshall, Cambridge, Massachusetts
David Maybury-Lewis, Harvard University
Museum of the American Indian
 Sanda Alexandride
 Frederick J. Dockstader
Museum of Primitive Art
 Allan D. Chapman
 Elizabeth Little

Museum für Völkerkunde und Schweizerisches Museum für Volkskunde, Basel
O Cruzeiro, Rio de Janeiro
Photothèque, Musée de l'Homme, Paris
Public Library, City of Johannesburg
The Rainbird Publishing Group Ltd., London
The Library of the Royal Anthropological Institute of Great Britain and Ireland
The Royal Geographical Society
The Royal Society
Vilma Chiara Schultz, Figeac, France
Norbert Sperling, Cambridge, Massachusetts
Sandy Steinhardt
Thames and Hudson, Publishers, London
S. Henry Wassén, Göteborg Etnografiska Museum, Göteborg, Sweden
Marvin Weill, United Nations
Witwatersrand University Press, Johannesburg

Maps by Cal Sacks
Index by Edmée Reit
Supplemental Copy Editing by Kaethe Ellis

Permissions

page 61 from *The Passing of the Aborigines,* by Daisy Bates. Copyright 1938. Reprinted by permission of John Murray (Publishers) Ltd., London, and Praeger Publishers, Inc., New York.

pages 70–71, 82, and 85–88 reprinted by permission of The World Publishing Company from *Tradition and Change in African Tribal Life,* by Colin M. Turnbull. Copyright © 1966 Colin M. Turnbull.

pages 78 and 80 from the book *Madami: My Eight Years of Adventure with the Congo Pygmies,* by Anne Eisner Putnam with Allan Keller. © 1954 by Anne Eisner Putnam and Allan Keller. Published by Prentice-Hall, Inc., Englewood Cliffs, New Jersey.

pages 88–89 by Colin M. Turnbull in *Journal of the Royal Anthropological Institute* (Vol. 89, 1959). Reprinted by permission.

pages 110–11 from *Coclé, an Archaeological Study of Central Panama,* by Samuel K. Lothrop. Copyright 1937. Reprinted by permission of The Peabody Museum of Archaeology and Ethnology, Cambridge, Massachusetts.

pages 118, 119–20, and 120 from *A New Voyage and Description of the Isthmus of America,* by Lionel Wafer, published by Cambridge University Press. Copyright 1934. Reprinted by permission of Cambridge University Press and the Hakluyt Society, London.

page 125 from *Unknown Tribes, Uncharted Seas,* by Lady Richmond Brown. Copyright 1924. Reprinted by permission of Gerald Duckworth & Co. Ltd., London.

page 129 from *French Explorers in the Pacific: Vol. I, The Eighteenth Century,* by John Dunmore. Copyright © 1965 Oxford University Press. Reprinted by permission of The Clarendon Press, Oxford.

pages 131 and 137–38 from *The Discovery of Tahiti* (The Journal of George Robertson), edited by Hugh Carrington, published by Cambridge University Press. Copyright 1948. Reprinted by permission of Cambridge University Press and the Hakluyt Society, London.

pages 146–47 from *The Journals of Captain Cook,* Vol. 1, edited by J. C. Beaglehole. Copyright 1955. Reprinted by permission of the Cambridge University Press.

page 154 from *Island of Love,* by Robert Langdon. Copyright © 1959. Published since 1968 and copyright by Pacific Publications (Australia) Pty. Ltd., Sydney, Australia. Reprinted by permission.

pages 207–10 from *Greenland by the Polar Sea,* by Knud Rasmussen. Copyright 1921. Reprinted by permission of William Heinemann Ltd., Publishers, London.

pages 210–11 from the book *The Eskimos,* by Kaj Birket-Smith. Published in the U.S.A. in 1936 by E. P. Dutton & Co., Inc., and used with their permission. Published in England by Eyre Methuen Ltd.

pages 212–13 from *Hunters of the Great North,* copyright, 1922, 1950, by Vilhjalmur Stefansson. Reprinted by permission of Harcourt Brace Jovanovich, Inc., New York, and George G. Harrap, Publishers, London.

pages 239 and 240 from *Ainu Life and Lore,* by John Batchelor. Copyright 1927. Reprinted by permission of Johnson Reprint Corporation.

page 266 from *Western Pacific Islands,* by Austin Coates. Copyright © 1970. Reprinted by permission of Her Majesty's Stationery Office, London.

pages 286–87 and 288 from *The Lapps,* by Björn Collinder, published by Princeton University Press. Copyright 1949. Reprinted by permission of the American-Scandinavian Foundation.

pages 304–5 from *Turi's Book of Lappland,* by Johan Turi, translated by Mrs. E. Gee Nash. Copyright 1931. Reprinted by permission of Jonathan Cape Ltd., London, and Harper & Row, Publishers, Inc., New York.

pages 330 and 332 from *The Savage and the Innocent,* by David Maybury-Lewis. Copyright © 1965 by David Maybury-Lewis. Reprinted by permission of Beacon Press, Boston, and Evans Brothers (Books) Limited, London.

Index   *Page numbers in boldface refer to captions.*